JUDAISM: THE FIRST PHASE

D1260762

Judaism: The First Phase

*The Place of Ezra and Nehemiah
in the Origins of Judaism*

JOSEPH BLENKINSOPP

WILLIAM B. EERDMANS PUBLISHING COMPANY
GRAND RAPIDS, MICHIGAN / CAMBRIDGE, U.K.

Published 2009 by
Wm. B. Eerdmans Publishing Co.
2140 Oak Industrial Drive N.E., Grand Rapids, Michigan 49505 /
P.O. Box 163, Cambridge CB3 9PU U.K.

Printed in the United States of America

14 13 12 11 10 09   7 6 5 4 3 2 1

ISBN 978-0-8028-6450-5

www.eerdmans.com

to my wife Jean
with love and gratitude

Contents

Contents

Acknowledgments

I wish to thank colleagues in the Society of Biblical Literature, the European Association of Biblical Studies, the (British) Society for Old Testament Study, and those who organized and participated in very productive conferences on the Neo-Babylonian and early Persian periods over the last several years in Tel Aviv (2001), Heidelberg (2003), Münster (2005), and Heidelberg (2008) and who have discussed with me different aspects of the present monograph. My thanks also go to past and present postgraduate students in the program of Christianity and Judaism in Antiquity at the University of Notre Dame who have sustained and stimulated my interest in the subject over the years, as well as other students encountered in my travels around the U.S., Europe, and the offshore islands. I am also happy to acknowledge a special debt of gratitude to the Andrew W. Mellon Foundation for the award of an emeritus research grant and for granting an extension of the tenure of the grant, thereby greatly facilitating the research and writing of the book. My dedicating the book to Jean, my wife, is one more acknowledgment of the great debt of gratitude I owe her.

Abbreviations

AB	Anchor Bible
ABD	*Anchor Bible Dictionary,* ed. David Noel Freedman. 6 vols. (New York: Doubleday, 1992)
ABRL	Anchor Bible Reference Library
AfO	*Archiv für Orientforschung*
AJSL	*American Journal of Semitic Languages and Literature*
AnBib	Analecta biblica
ANET	*Ancient Near Eastern Texts,* ed. James B. Pritchard. 3rd ed. (Princeton: Princeton University Press, 1969)
AP	Aramaic Papyri, in A. E. Cowley, *Aramaic Papyri of the Fifth Century* B.C. (1923; repr. Osnabrück: Otto Zeller, 1967)
APOT	The Apocrypha and Pseudepigrapha of the Old Testament, ed. R. H. Charles. 2 vols. (Oxford: Clarendon, 1913)
b.	Babylonian Talmud
BA	*Biblical Archaeologist*
BASOR	*Bulletin of the American Schools of Oriental Research*
BHT	Beiträge zur historischen Theologie
Bib	*Biblica*
BibLeb	*Bibel und Leben*
BJRL	*Bulletin of the John Rylands Library*
BN	*Biblische Notizen*
BRS	Biblical Resource Series
BWANT	Beiträge zur Wissenschaft vom Alten und Neuen Testament
BZ	*Biblische Zeitschrift*
BZAW	Beihefte zur Zeitschrift für die alttestamentliche Wissenschaft
CAH	*Cambridge Ancient History.*

CBC	Cambridge Bible Commentary
CBQ	*Catholic Biblical Quarterly*
CBQMS	Catholic Biblical Quarterly Monograph Series
CD	Cairo Geniza copy of the *Damascus Document*
CHJ	*Cambridge History of Judaism,* ed. W. D. Davies and Louis Finkelstein. 4 vols. (Cambridge: Cambridge University Press, 1984-2006)
CJ	*Classical Journal*
DDD	*Dictionary of Deities and Demons in the Bible,* ed. Karel van der Toorn, Bob Becking, and Pieter W. van der Horst. 2nd ed. (Leiden: Brill and Grand Rapids: Wm. B. Eerdmans, 1999)
DJD	Discoveries in the Judaean Desert
Ebib	Études bibliques
EDSS	*Encyclopedia of the Dead Sea Scrolls,* ed. Lawrence H. Schiffman and James C. VanderKam. 2 vols. (Oxford: Oxford University Press, 2000)
EvT	*Evangelische Theologie*
FAT	Forschungen zum Alten Testament
FB	Forschung zur Bibel
FGH	*Die Fragmente der griechischen Historiker,* ed. Felix Jacoby (Leiden: Brill, 1954-)
FO	*Folia orientalia*
FRLANT	Forschungen zur Religion und Literatur des Alten und Neuen Testaments
GGA	*Göttingischen Gelehrten Anzeigen*
HAT	Handbuch zum Alten Testament
HBM	Hebrew Bible Monographs
Hen	*Henoch*
HeyJ	*Heythrop Journal*
HKAT	Handkommentar zum Alten Testament
HSAT	*Die Heilige Schrift des Alten Testaments,* ed. Emil F. Kautzsch and Alfred Bertholet, 4th ed. (Tübingen: Mohr, 1923)
HSM	Harvard Semitic Monographs
HTR	*Harvard Theological Review*
HUCA	*Hebrew Union College Annual*
IB	*Interpreter's Bible,* ed. George A. Buttrick et al. 12 vols. (Nashville: Abingdon, 1951-57)
ICC	International Critical Commentary

IDBSup	*Interpreter's Dictionary of the Bible, Supplementary Volume*, ed. Keith Crim (Nashville: Abingdon, 1976)
IEJ	*Israel Exploration Journal*
Int	*Interpretation*
IOS	*Israel Oriental Studies*
JAOS	*Journal of the American Oriental Society*
JBL	*Journal of Biblical Literature*
JCS	*Journal of Cuneiform Studies*
JEA	*Journal of Egyptian Archaeology*
JJS	*Journal of Jewish Studies*
JNES	*Journal of Near Eastern Studies*
JNSL	*Journal of Northwest Semitic Languages*
JSJ	*Journal for the Study of Judaism in the Persian, Hellenistic, and Roman Periods*
JSJSup	Journal for the Study of Judaism in the Persian, Hellenistic, and Roman Periods: Supplement Series
JSOT	*Journal for the Study of the Old Testament*
JSOTSup	Journal for the Study of the Old Testament: Supplement Series
JSS	*Journal of Semitic Studies*
JTS	*Journal of Theological Studies*
KAT	Kommentar zum Alten Testament
KHC	Kurzer Hand-Commentar zum Alten Testament
LCL	Loeb Classical Library
LHB/OTS	Library of Hebrew Bible/Old Testament Studies
LXX	Septuagint
m.	Mishnah
MT	Masoretic Text
NCBC	New Century Bible Commentary
NEAEHL	*The New Encyclopedia of Archaeological Excavations in the Holy Land*, ed. Ephraim Stern. 4 vols. (Jerusalem: Israel Exploration Society and New York: Simon & Schuster, 1993)
NIB	*The New Interpreter's Bible*
NICOT	New International Commentary on the Old Testament
NTS	*New Testament Studies*
OBO	Orbis biblicus et orientalis
OCD	*Oxford Classical Dictionary*, ed. Simon Hornblower and Antony Spawforth. 3rd ed. (Oxford: Oxford University Press, 1996)
OLA	Orientalia lovaniensia analecta
Or	*Orientalia*

OTL	Old Testament Library
OTP	*The Old Testament Pseudepigrapha,* ed. James H. Charlesworth. 2 vols. (Garden City: Doubleday, 1983-85)
OtSt	Oudtestamentische Studiën
RB	*Revue biblique*
RevQ	*Revue de Qumran*
SBL	Society of Biblical Literature
SBLDS	Society of Biblical Literature Dissertation Series
SBLEJL	Society of Biblical Literature Early Judaism and Its Literature
SBLSCS	Society of Biblical Literature Septuagint and Cognate Series
SBLTT	Society of Biblical Literature Texts and Translations
SBLWAW	Society of Biblical Literature Writings from the Ancient World
SJLA	Studies in Judaism in Late Antiquity
SSN	Studia semitica neerlandica
STDJ	Studies on the Texts of the Desert of Judah
TADAE	*Textbook of Aramaic Documents from Ancient Egypt,* ed. Bezalel Porten and Ada Yardeni. 4 vols. (Jerusalem: Hebrew University, 1986-1999)
TB	Theologische Bücherei
TLOT	*Theological Lexicon of the Old Testament,* ed. Ernst Jenni and Claus Westermann. 3 vols. (Peabody: Hendrickson, 1997)
Transeu	*Transeuphratène*
TynBul	*Tyndale Bulletin*
VT	*Vetus Testamentum*
VTSup	Supplements to Vetus Testamentum
WBC	Word Biblical Commentary
WMANT	Wissenschaftliche Monographien zum Alten und Neuen Testament
YOS	Yale Oriental Series
ZAW	*Zeitschrift für die alttestamentliche Wissenschaft*
ZDMGSup	Zeitschrift der deutschen morgenländischen Gesellschaft: Supplementbände
ZRGG	*Zeitschrift für Religions- und Geistesgeschichte*
ZTK	*Zeitschrift für Theologie und Kirche*

Introduction

The origin of any religious movement often appears fairly straightforward on the surface, especially if a charismatic individual or shape-changing event is involved, but more and more complex as one digs below the surface. In the case of Jewish origins there is such an event, the Babylonian conquest of Judah in 586 B.C. But as we look further into it, we come up against the issue of continuity-discontinuity, whether in terms of the object of worship, adherence to narrative and legal traditions, religious institutions (priesthood, prophecy, etc.), social organization below the level of the ruling power, or even demographics. Since the early-modern period, discussion of this cluster of issues has been clouded by prejudicial theological and philosophical assumptions. Since the story has often been told, one or two examples will suffice. At one end of a broad spectrum of opinion are those biblical scholars and theologians during the nineteenth and the first half of the twentieth century, and residually thereafter, who brought to bear on their reading of the Old Testament theories of historical development prevalent in the intellectual milieu of the time. Many of these held university positions in Germany, the great heartland of theology and biblical studies, and the name which first comes to mind is that of Julius Wellhausen, whose *Prolegomena zur Geschichte Israels* (1883)[1] set the agenda for the study of the Old Testament for a century. Part romantic,

---

1. Translated into English by J. Sutherland Black and Allan Menzies under the title *Prolegomena to the History of Ancient Israel* (1957; repr. SBL Reprints and Translations. Atlanta: Scholars, 1994). This publication includes a reprint of Wellhausen's article on "Israel" in the *Encyclopedia Britannica.*

part rationalist, Wellhausen traced the process by which the naturalism of early Israelite religion and the ethical individualism of the prophets were stifled by the legalism and ritualism of a priestly hierocracy. For Wellhausen and those who accepted the hypothesis which he rounded out and refined, the law marked the beginning not of Israel but of Judaism.

According to Wellhausen, Ezra arrived in Judah from Babylon in the seventh year of Artaxerxes 1 (Ezra 7:8), bringing the law with him. For reasons unknown, he waited fourteen years to promulgate it, and did so in 444 B.C., a year after the arrival of Nehemiah in the province (Neh 1:1; 2:1). This law, which Wellhausen identified with the Pentateuch more or less as we have it, he described as the Magna Carta of Judaism.[2] But the Pentateuch, now including the Priestly ritual and cultic laws (P) as its principal component, was the product of a long period of gestation going back beyond the great divide of the fall of Jerusalem. An earlier defining moment, comparable to the public reading and exposition of the law recorded in Nehemiah 8, occurred in the eighteenth year of King Josiah, therefore 621 B.C., with the promulgation of the "book of the covenant". Together with most critical scholars at that time and since, Wellhausen identified this book with Deuteronomy. Deuteronomy, described by Wellhausen as "the connecting link between old and new, between Israel and Judaism",[3] marked the beginning of the end for prophecy, the purest and best expression of biblical religion, and the point where the law began to take over. Wellhausen did not see this as a positive development. The religion of legal and cultic observance supervised and maintained by the priesthood, with its typical expressions in P and Chronicles, stands in stark contrast to the nature religion of early Israel and even more so to prophecy. He compares the difference to that between dry wood and a green tree, between water in a cistern and water from a fountain, and between the letter and the spirit.[4] Leaving aside these prejudicial judgments, let us simply take it that for Wellhausen the transition from Israel to Judaism began in the last decades of the Judean monarchy and was essentially complete by the time of Ezra and Nehemiah.

A more ideologically explicit example of religious evolutionism is dis-

2. *Prolegomena*, 404-10.

3. *Prolegomena*, 362.

4. Further discussion in "Wellhausen and the Origins of Judaism" in my *Prophecy and Canon* (Notre Dame: University of Notre Dame Press, 1977) 17-23.

played in the *Biblische Theologie* of Wilhelm Vatke, which appeared in 1835, the year which saw the publication of the notorious *Das Leben Jesu* of David Strauss.[5] Though Wellhausen acknowledged having learned the best and the most from Vatke,[6] the latter's understanding of the transition from Israel to Judaism is quite different from that of Wellhausen. Vatke was much influenced by the dialectical philosophy of G. W. F. Hegel, whose lectures he had attended at the University of Berlin. At this point we enter the realm of almost mystical abstraction. Vatke took from Hegel the idea that Judaism marks the passage from the religion of nature to the absolute religion embodied in Christianity, and since the evolution always moves in a forward and upward direction, it must be possible in some way to view the postexilic period in a positive light. This is therefore the point at which Vatke parted company with such distinguished predecessors as J. G. Herder and W. M. L. de Wette and the point at which Wellhausen parted company with Vatke. Vatke even argued that the Persian period (sixth to fourth century B.C.), in which the emphasis fell on holiness, prayer, and the abolition of idolatry, marked the high point of Old Testament religion, though he spoiled it somewhat by adding that this was due in large part to Zoroastrian influence. Decline only set in with the emergence of the sects in the second century B.C.

A different type of historical evolutionism or developmentalism was emerging about the same time in the form of a theory of a continuous providential history which reaches its goal in Christ and the Christian church. First adumbrated in Eusebius's *Praeparatio Evangelica,* this approach was taken up by German Pietists in the eighteenth century and in the following century by conservative Lutheran theologians, one of the most prominent of whom was J. C. K. von Hofmann. Hofmann's christocentric theology was teleological rather than dictated by the kind of internal dynamic advocated by Vatke. The events recorded in biblical history can be understood only from their final goal, which, strictly speaking, implied that the Old Testament was intelligible only to the Christian reader.

---

5. *Die biblische Theologie wissenschaftlich dargestellt.* Vol. 1: *Die Religion des Alten Testamentes* (Berlin: Bethge, 1835). Vatke's work is summarized and discussed in Hans Joachim Kraus, *Geschichte der Historisch-Kritischen Erforschung des Alten Testaments* (Neukirchen: Verlag der Buchhandlung des Erziehungsvereins, 1956) 179-82, and John Rogerson, *Old Testament Criticism in the Nineteenth Century: England and Germany* (Philadelphia: Fortress, 1985) 69-78.

6. *Prolegomena*, 13.

Furthermore, the idea of an uninterrupted continuum of salvation history *(Heilsgeschichte)* leading to Christ made it difficult to know what to do with that part of the Old Testament which overlaps with the early history of Judaism. This was a problem which the adherents of *Heilsgeschichte* never succeeded in solving. Wellhausen may have had von Hofmann in mind when he observed, at the beginning of the *Prolegomena*, that "in dogmatic theology Judaism is a mere empty chasm over which one springs from the Old Testament to the New".[7]

An updated form of *Heilsgeschichte* appeared around the middle of the last century in the *Old Testament Theology* of Gerhard von Rad.[8] Von Rad organized his theology around the conviction that Israel was consti-tuted by God's action in salvation and judgment on the one hand and Is-rael's response or, more often than not, lack of response on the other. This model dictated the division of his *Theology* into two volumes dealing with Israel's historical and prophetic traditions, respectively. In the second vol-ume, von Rad expounded his basic thesis, which was that the prophets passed sentence of death on Israel and that the sentence was carried out through the instrumentality of the Assyrians in 722 and the Babylonians in 586 B.C. After the final disaster, when the law gradually became what he re-ferred to as an absolute entity *(eine absolute Grösse)* outside of time — pre-cisely the point at which Judaism entered history — this salvation history came to an end.[9] We can understand how von Rad, as a good Lutheran, might reject Torah religion as, in his view, life lived according to the works of the law, but this idea of a *Heilsgeschichte* that comes to an end at a par-ticular point in time, and then starts up again later, remains opaque. No doubt the difficulty of bringing the postexilic period, the period of Jewish origins, within a scheme of salvation history will help to explain why von Rad's biblical theology placed so much emphasis on the earliest, prestate traditions of the Hexateuch (the tribal league, early confessional state-ments, cultic festivals at prestate sanctuaries, etc.).

These, therefore, are examples of theologically or ideologically dense readings of the biblical texts which, while they seldom addressed the issue

7. *Prolegomena*, 1.

8. Vol. 1: *The Theology of Israel's Historical Traditions;* vol. 2: *The Theology of Israel's Pro-phetic Traditions* (New York: Harper & Row, 1962-65). Trans. of *Theologie des Alten Testa-ments*, 2 vols. (Munich: Kaiser, 1957-1960).

9. *Old Testament Theology*, 1:85-92 ("The Constituting of the Post-Exilic Cultic Com-munity"), esp. 91-92.

of Jewish origins head-on, locate them within either an evolutionary or a teleological understanding of biblical history. At the other end of the spectrum we find Yehezkel Kaufmann (1889-1963), a good part of whose scholarly agenda was dedicated to refuting the Wellhausenian synthesis.[10] In his *History of Israelite Religion* Kaufmann affirmed in straightforward fashion that the life of Israel as a nation came to an end and the history of Judaism as a religious community began with the fall of Jerusalem, yet at the same time contended that all the essentials were in place from the beginning: monotheism, complete freedom from magic and myth, and a law revealed to Moses. He accepted the four-source hypothesis for the Pentateuch (J, E, P, D), while affirming that all the sources were present from the beginning and were preserved unchanged down into the postexilic period, when they were compiled into one sacred text. He therefore rejected the possibility of constructing a history of Israelite religion based on the chronological sequencing of the sources, which was precisely the procedure followed by Wellhausen in his *Prolegomena*. There could therefore be no evolution from lower to higher forms of religious life. He was especially exercised to reject two of the main props of the Graf-Wellhausen hypothesis: the chronological priority of prophecy to law and the late, postexilic date for the Priestly material in the Pentateuch.

The results of Kaufmann's historical reconstructions are so much at variance with those of critical biblical scholarship in general that it is difficult to know how to go about evaluating them. His contention that right from the beginning Israel's religion was absolutely unique, and uniquely monotheistic, flies in the face of a massive amount of evidence to the contrary, both literary and artifactual. It is therefore hardly surprising that his views on the religious history of Israel have found few supporters. A particularly contentious issue still under discussion is the date of the Priestly material, both prescriptive and narrative, in the Pentateuch. Since for Wellhausen this material, together with Chronicles, expressed the essential features of the emergent Judaism of the postexilic period, it was of quite

---

10. Kaufmann's *magnum opus* was his *Toledot ha-'emuna ha-yisra'elit mime qedem 'ad sof bet sheni (The History of Israelite Religion from the Beginnings to the End of the Second Temple)*, 8 vols. (Tel Aviv: Bialik Institute-Devir, 1937-1956). An abridgement and translation of vols. 1-7 by Moshe Greenberg is available in *The Religion of Israel from Its Beginnings to the Babylonian Exile* (Chicago: University of Chicago Press, 1960), and parts of vol. 8 in a translation by C. W. Efroymson, *The Babylonian Captivity and Deutero-Isaiah* (New York: Union of American Hebrew Congregations, 1970).

fundamental importance for Kaufmann to establish a preexilic date by standing Wellhausen's arguments on their head. This therefore fills an important chapter of his *Toledot,* and his thesis still has its defenders.[11]

In the following chapters I aim to move beyond or behind these and similar heavily-weighted, ideologically-driven approaches even while writing about ancient ideologies. I would like to begin by asking myself and the reader questions of a more pragmatic nature. These will include the following: When does a distinctive social group identity begin to emerge in the aftermath of the liquidation of the Judean state and the deportations, and how is that identity constituted? When does it become proper to translate *yěhûdîm* as "Jews" rather than "Judeans"? How are we to assess the degree of continuity-discontinuity between ascriptive status (i.e., national identity) before the great divide and membership of several distinct groups competing for legitimacy after it? What historical realities lie behind the idea of a "return to Zion" *(šîvat ṣiyyôn)?* Restoration is routinely linked with exile, but neither the monarchy nor the apparatus of statehood was restored, and when the destroyed temple was eventually replaced by a smaller substitute, seven decades later, it served not as a national shrine but as an instrument of imperial control.[12]

I will argue that in attempting to answer these questions, and others generated by them, we are led to the first of the two centuries of Persian rule (539-332 B.C.) as the decisive period. The emergence of Judaism then falls into place as one small-scale aspect of a large-scale reshaping of the Middle East and the Eastern Mediterranean world. This period, after all, marked the end of the great Semitic empires which had dominated and shaped that world for millennia and which would reemerge only with the Islamic conquests of the seventh century A.D. The first of these two centuries witnessed the high point of Athenian culture in the Periclean age (461-429 B.C.) and the flowering of intellectual thought on the Greek mainland, Ionia, and southern Italy. The age of Ezra and Nehemiah was also the age of the itinerant Sophists, of Protagoras, Hippocrates, and Anaxagoras, mentor to Pericles. Parmenides arrived in Athens from Italy five years be-

---

11. Kaufmann, *The Religion of Israel,* 175-200. On the debate about the date of P, see my "An Assessment of the Alleged Pre-Exilic Date of the Priestly Material in the Pentateuch", *ZAW* 108 (1996) 495-518; Jacob Milgrom, "The Antiquity of the Priestly Source: A Reply to Joseph Blenkinsopp", *ZAW* 111 (1999) 10-22.

12. See the remarks of Rainer Albertz, "The Thwarted Restoration," in *Yahwism after the Exile,* ed. Albertz and Bob Becking (Assen: van Gorcum, 2003) 1-17.

fore Nehemiah arrived in Judah from Susa. Socrates was engaged in philosophical debate with his disciples at the same time that Nehemiah was rebuilding the city wall of Jerusalem. We might dramatize the contrast between the two cultures by imagining a theological conversation between Nehemiah and his contemporary Protagoras, author of the famous saying that "man is the measure of all things".

The remarkable contrast between Periclean Athens and the Jerusalem of Ezra and Nehemiah is to a considerable degree a matter of economics. As a later Jewish writer would point out, intellectual activity of the kind much in evidence in Athens at that time requires leisure, and leisure generally requires a degree of wealth (Sir 38:24–39:11). Both were in short supply in Nehemiah's Judah, and the situation would have been exacerbated by the fiscal policies of the Persian monarchs, a burden which the mainland Greek cities were spared.[13] From the Greek side, the tribute lists of the Delian League provide an indication of the wealth of Athens following on the defeat of Xerxes. In its constitution, moreover, Judah stood in stark contrast to Athens. It fit the pattern of temple-city-states under control of a Persian-appointed official, with its own domains,[14] and administered by a tax-exempt priesthood. A similar type of organization was common in Asia Minor, for example in Xanthus in Lycia, Comana in Cappadocia, and Zela in Pontus, and, on a much greater scale, in Mesopotamia. In Athens and other mainland Greek cities, on the other hand, the control of the state over cult and ritual had effectively nudged the development of Greek societies away from the temple-state type, making the *polis* the principal framework of religious activities.[15]

The first century of Persian rule also witnessed the formation of a strong national and ethnic identity in reaction to the Iranian overlord in Greek-speaking cities, Egypt, and no doubt also in the province of Judah in spite of its relative isolation. The change is reflected in different ways in the literature of the period, including the relevant biblical texts. We note, for example, the practice of citing sources, precisely transcribed, heavily edited, or invented as the case may be, and the appearance of personal

---

13. The economically-depressed situation is illustrated vividly in Nehemiah's memoir (Neh 5:1-19) and hinted at in prophetic texts from the Persian period (Hag 1:6, 9-11; Zech 8:10; Mal 2:13-16; Isa 58:3-4; 59:6, 9-15).

14. J. Blenkinsopp, "Did the second Jerusalemite temple possess land?", *Transeu* 21 (2001) 61-68.

15. See J. K. Davies, "Religion and the State," in *CAH*, 2nd ed., 4 (1988) 388.

memoirs of the kind attested in Herodotus, Ion of Chios, and of course Ezra and Nehemiah. There is also reason to think that interest in ethnic origins, which would be a hot topic in the Hellenistic period, was prepared for during the Persian centuries, for example in the final redaction of Genesis. We will return to this theme in the following chapter.

In a famous debate on this issue of origins between Eduard Meyer and Julius Wellhausen at the end of the nineteenth century, described in the following chapter, Meyer certainly exaggerated — as his adversary was not slow to point out — in claiming that "the origins of Judaism can be grasped only as resulting from the impact of the Persian empire".[16] He nevertheless opened up a broader political and cultural perspective on conclusions drawn previously exclusively or for the most part from the analysis of biblical texts of the Wellhausenian kind. This was a salutary move, one which would become an essential part of the study of early Second Temple Judaism.

Reading the relevant biblical texts in this broader political and cultural context, including the contemporary Greek-speaking regions, might also lead us to ask whether any comparable intellectual activity was going on in Jewish communities during this first Persian century. There can be no question that law *(tôrâ)* has always been constitutive of Judaism from its very beginnings. It is also the case, as we saw in our selective survey of opinion, that the place of law in Judaism has often been prejudicially assessed. However, it is also possible to think of this concentration on law as, at least potentially, a form of intellectualism comparable to what was happening in Greek-speaking lands. Beginning with Deuteronomy, the way *tôrâ* is referred to as the object of study and exposition is symptomatic of a unifying and synthesizing tendency, an intent to think of the law as a conceptual system comparable to and in some ways in competition with the philosophical systems of other peoples: "This is your wisdom and your (source of) understanding in the view of (other) peoples; when they hear these statutes they will think, 'this great nation must be a wise and discerning people'" (Deut 4:6). This conceptualization of Torah, furthered by identification with personified female wisdom *(ḥokmâ),* is a theme well documented and well discussed, and we may see it as the counterpart in Judah and the diaspora to what was happening in other parts of the Middle East and Levant.

---

16. Eduard Meyer, *Die Entstehung des Judentums* (1896; repr. Hildesheim: Olms, 1965) 71.

It may also remind us that the age of Ezra and Nehemiah was the age of the itinerant Sophists, and that, like the Stoics in the following century, the Sophists held that intellectual activity should be concerned in the first place with the morally good life, with "what is good for human beings to do under heaven for the brief span of their lives" (Eccl 2:3). The idea that philosophy should provide the impetus towards living the good life was, in fact, basic to Greek philosophy in general. It is not therefore so surprising that in some of the earliest contacts between Greeks and Jews the latter were recognized as belonging to a philosophical race.[17]

Having made that point, we must add that once it is established that Judaism first shows up on the screen of history during the two centuries of the Persian Empire, the focus must be on the canonical book Ezra-Nehemiah, our main source of information, supported by First Esdras (Esdras alpha) and Josephus, and on the profiles and activities of its two principal protagonists, Ezra and Nehemiah. In this part of our investigation, which occupies Chapters 2 and 3, Ezra and Nehemiah are considered less as objects of biographical interest and more as emblematic of ideological positions and agendas. Some long-standing problems will call for discussion, over and above the inconclusive debates about the formation of the book, the historical reliability of the memoirs and the documents cited, and the types of narrative it contains. In dealing with these issues I raise the possibility that Ezra arrived in the province, with or without imperial authorization, with the aim of imposing a policy of ritual ethnicity based on a rigorous, selective, and by no means self-evident interpretation of certain laws. I ask whether we should speak of this mission as a "return to Zion" or rather as a religious colonization with a strongly sectarian character, a distant analogy to the Pilgrim Fathers. I invite inquiry as to the legal basis for the unprecedented coercive dissolution of marriages with non-*golah* women. If it was to be carried out "according to the law", as Shecaniah insisted (Ezra 10:3), why were there no financial consequences

17. Theophrastus, head of the Lyceum after Aristotle retired, speaks of the Jews as a philosophical race *(philosophoi to genos ontes)*, while another Peripatetic, Clearchus of Soli, reports a discourse of the master in which he asserts that the Jews were descended from the Indian philosophers. Aristotle goes on to describe, in a somewhat patronizing manner, how he encountered a Jew who not only spoke Greek but had the soul of a Greek. Relevant texts in Menahem Stern, *Greek and Latin Authors on Jews and Judaism*, vol. 1: *From Herodotus to Plutarch* (Jerusalem: Israel Academy of Sciences and Humanities, 1976) 10, 46, 50. See also Martin Hengel, *Judaism and Hellenism* (Philadelphia: Fortress, 1974) 1:255-61.

of the kind documented, for example, in Aramaic marriage contracts from Elephantine? And what of the laws demanding concern and care for impoverished widows and orphans? In assessing what was at stake in Ezra's arrival in the province, it will be important to focus on the role of the *hărēdîm*, those who trembled at the word of Yahweh. Several scholars of the period are beginning to speak of these "tremblers" as embodying a kind of sectarianism present from the earliest period of Second Temple Judaism, and this too must claim our attention.

As for Nehemiah: Was his goal simply that of securing political autonomy for the province of Judah within the Persian imperial system, or is he represented as sharing the same agenda as Ezra, namely, the creation of a self-segregating, puritanical, theocratic state? And as patron and model for the Hasmoneans, was he ultimately responsible for the reterritorializing of Judaism, an issue which by no means disappeared with the incorporation of the Hasmonean kingdom into the Roman Empire?

Starting out from the canonical book, we move on to inquire into the roots of the ideology associated with Ezra and Nehemiah and to spell out how Ezra and Nehemiah were viewed as ideological points of reference in the later Second Temple period. These will occupy Chapters 4 and 5, respectively. I will argue that the ideology was incubated in the Babylonian diaspora during the century and a half separating the first deportations from the time of Ezra and Nehemiah, and that its prehistory takes in not only the Deuteronomic prohibitions concerning marriage outside the group (Deut 7:1-6; 23:2-9), the most frequently cited texts in Ezra-Nehemiah, but the so-called "law of the temple" in Ezekiel 40–48. The main prescriptions in this visionary program have to do with the exclusion of foreigners from the cult and therefore from the community; the distinction between altar priests (Zadokites) and temple priests (Levites); the role, much diminished and "theocratized", of the secular ruler; and the apportioning of land. I suggest that this program, put together over a period of time by the school of Ezekiel in the Babylonian diaspora, was taken over by the ultradevout Judeo-Babylonian group known in Ezra 9–10 as "those who tremble at the word of the God of Israel," whose mission was to make it the basis for a new theocratic polity in the province of Judah. An examination in the following chapter of the few references to Ezra and Nehemiah in later Second Temple texts will then enable us to form an estimate, partial and provisional as it must be, as to how the ideology fared and how lasting were the achievements of its two principal proponents. In the final chapter I return once again to the thesis of a sectarian element, which I believe was present in earliest Judaism as it was in earliest Christianity, in order to raise once again the possibility of continuity between that element and the overt sectarianism of the Hasmonean period.

The vast quantity of writing on early Judaism, how it related to the non-Jewish world at the level of religion, politics, or social contact and how it was perceived by others either negatively — what Peter Schäfer has called "Judeophobia"[18] — or positively has tended to start out from no earlier than the Hellenistic period. The position taken here is that in order to understand the situation at that time, and later, we must go further back in time to the aftermath of the liquidation of the Judean state, the consequent loss of the one center and focus of identity, and the struggle for a new identity in a fundamentally different kind of world. A further proposition is that the emergence, consolidation and persistence of this new identity was dictated by specifically religious issues rather than by political conflicts, among which the "persecution" of Antiochus IV has always been prominent. Part of an explanation for the neglect of developments in the pre-Hellenistic period, especially for those interested in perceptions of Judaism in the surrounding culture, is the complete absence of any relevant documentation at that time. No Greek author so much as mentions Jews or Judaism during the two centuries of Persian rule. I suspect that academic departmentalization may also play a part: the earlier period is abandoned to the biblical scholars, and the later one to the historians of antiquity and, for the last two centuries, those who specialize in the background of early Christianity. We must be humble, but we must also be prepared to cross these artificial boundaries if we are to see an issue such as this steadily and see it whole.

18. Peter Schäfer, *Judeophobia: Attitudes towards the Jews in the Ancient World* (Cambridge, MA: Harvard University Press, 1997).

Origins

Towards the Origins of Judaism

The question of the origins of any ethnic group and, by extension, any nation is rarely if ever susceptible of a straightforward answer. Once they have achieved a degree of collective identity most social groups, including nation-states, generate their own myths of origin which offer one kind of straightforward answer. Few imagine that such myths represent an accurate account of ethnic or national origins, but they nevertheless generate a will to believe reinforced by group solidarity and commemorative rituals, a situation abundantly illustrated in the Hebrew-Aramaic Bible. Even when, in rare cases, we can point to a defining, originating moment, like the Declaration of Independence on July 4, 1776 marking the birth of the American republic or the declaration establishing the State of Israel on May 15, 1948, such moments are far from providing an adequate account of origins. We could hardly begin to understand the United States of America or the State of Israel if we started out from these two points in time. In any case, such defining moments are not always present, leaving us with the task of balancing continuities against discontinuities in an attempt to determine at what point we have a phenomenon qualitatively different from its preparatory stages. Trawling back through the uncertainties of the past is therefore necessary, but it can lead into a morass of speculation and a quagmire of competing hypotheses. The task is — to change the metaphor — to find a way through this methodological minefield.

The problems facing us in attempting to say anything about Jewish origins will be apparent when we take into account the proliferation of movements, parties, and ideologies and the different ways of periodizing the past in recent scholarship on ancient Israel and Second Temple Judaism, a confusing situation exacerbated by the discovery and publication of the Qumran texts. One attempt at alleviating or circumventing the problem which has become quite popular in recent years is to postulate a plurality of Judaisms. According to Jacob Neusner, "there never has been a single, unitary and linear Judaism."[1] The preface to the *Dictionary of Judaism in the Biblical Period,* edited by Neusner and William Scott Green, uses the term "Judaisms" of the variety of Judaic religious systems in antiquity which eventually gave way to Rabbinic or Classical Judaism which has remained paramount to our own day.[2] More recently, Gabriele Boccaccini coined the term Middle Judaism for the five centuries from 300 B.C. to A.D. 200. This made it necessary to postulate an Ancient Judaism, which Boccaccini dates from the sixth to the fourth century B.C. The conclusion may seem reasonable enough, but we are given no clue as to how Middle Judaism emerged from Ancient Judaism. There is no Ezra, only one brief allusion to Nehemiah (p. 146), no Elephantine Jews, and no return from exile, an event of crucial significance in itself and for the sects of the Greco-Roman period as we shall see in due course. In his foreword to the book, James Charlesworth expressed justifiable concern about the lack of antecedents, and therefore about the lack of an adequate explanation, for Boccaccini's Middle Judaism, but pushed the chronological envelope back only as far as 350 B.C. His concern about Boccaccini's categorizing Christianity as one of several species of the genus Judaism has even more justification and could have been obviated if Boccaccini had put the early Christian movement more firmly and explicitly in the context of late Second Temple sectarianism.[3]

---

1. "Exile and Return as the History of Judaism" in *Exile: Old Testament, Jewish, and Christian Conceptions,* ed. James M. Scott. JSJSup 56 (Leiden: Brill, 1997) 223.

2. (New York: Macmillan Library Reference, 1996) 1:vii-viii. See also Neusner's essay on "Mishnah and Messiah," in *Judaisms and Their Messiahs at the Turn of the Christian Era,* ed. Neusner, William Scott Green, and Ernest S. Frerichs (Cambridge: Cambridge University Press, 1987) 278; also his article, "The Mishna in Philosophical Context and Out of Canonical Bounds," *JBL* 112 (1993) 291-304.

3. Gabriele Boccaccini, *Middle Judaism: Jewish Thought, 300 B.C.E. to 200 C.E.* (Minneapolis: Fortress, 1991). See also *Roots of Rabbinic Judaism: An Intellectual History from Ezekiel to Daniel* (Grand Rapids: Wm. B. Eerdmans, 2002), esp. 8-14: "From Judaism to Judaisms: Four Scholarly Models."

The unavoidable limitations of academic and scholarly specializations (Persian period, Hellenistic period, etc.) may have something to do with Charlesworth's justifiable concerns. The fact remains that if we wish to address issues about continuities and discontinuities in early Judaism we have to take the risk of crossing these artificial boundaries.

In a discussion of "One Judaism or Many?" Lawrence Schiffman takes the sensible view that the different approaches to the Jewish reality should be studied in dynamic and interactive relationship to each other and to what preceded and followed them.[4] All well and good, but a study of this kind would presumably also be interested in identifying the values, traditions, and practices shared by these different approaches. Such a study would aim to determine what is indispensably and irreducibly Jewish about them, to what extent they express the core values that can be called Judaic or Jewish, and what would suffice, in terms of beliefs or practices, to deny to any of them the right to be considered Jewish. This line of inquiry would sooner or later involve historical considerations and perhaps also the question of origins. But before proceeding any further one might feel constrained to ask: Why are beginnings important? Why does it matter at what point on the historical continuum we come down? The same questions could presumably be asked concerning any interpretation of the past, whether our own personal or family past or events of broad social and political scope. One obvious response would be that our understanding of the past always bears down on our understanding of the present and therefore necessarily becomes a factor in determining attitudes and orientation to action. There is the further consideration that in the course of our inquiry into origins we may allow the data to recalibrate the question, to lead to fuller and more satisfactory ways of formulating it, and to generate other questions about the phenomenon under consideration, in this instance about what are aboriginal and irreducible elements in Judaism as a social and intellectual system. The same could of course also be said, mutatis mutandis, for the study of Christian origins.

There are no doubt many different ways in which sociologists define what is distinctive about an ethnic group. There is, to begin with, the typically apodictic definition of Max Weber in his great work *Wirtschaft und Gesellschaft*:

---

4. Lawrence H. Schiffman, *From Text to Tradition: A History of Second Temple and Rabbinic Judaism* (Hoboken: Ktav, 1991) 4-5.

We shall call "ethnic groups" those human groups that entertain a subjective belief in their common descent because of similarities of physical type or of customs or both, or because of memories of colonization and migration; this belief must be important for the propagation of group formation; conversely, it does not matter whether or not an objective blood relationship exists.[5]

We see that for Weber the belief in descent from a common ancestor is no less effective for being subjective and artificial. According to a more recent publication, an ethnic group will exhibit, in different degrees and with different emphases, some or all of the following features: an expressive name, a myth of common ancestry, a shared history, elements of a shared culture which normally would include language and religion, a link with a homeland but not necessarily one actually occupied, and a sense of solidarity.[6] Not surprisingly, Judaism qualifies as an ethnic group with respect to most or all of these criteria, but more especially with the myth of common ancestry, that is, the assumption of a transgenerational, biological descent from a common ancestor. If any feature of ethnic consciousness is central and irreducible it will be this one. The historical unfolding of this myth is the great theme of the book of Genesis. Ethnic origins are traced back to creation and, more immediately, to the great deluge; to Noah and his three sons who repopulate the world; to Shem, first of the three; and, in the tenth generation, to Abraham, father of the people. The pattern, which is given cosmic resonance by borrowings from the ancient Mesopotamian *Atraḫasis* myth, also runs closely parallel with the Greek myth of Deucalion as recounted by the logographers Hecataeus of Miletus and Hellanicus of Lesbos. The three sons, or in another tradition grandsons, of Deucalion, the only survivor of the deluge, are the progenitors of the three branches of the Greek-speaking peoples, Dorians, Ionians, and Aeolians. In an alternative version, Deucalion's son or brother was Hellen, eponymous ancestor of the Hellenes. The ten generations before and after the deluge in Genesis chs. 5 and 11, however, follow the Mesopotamian pattern as reproduced in the *Babyloniaka* of Berossus, a Babylonian priest whose

---

5. *Economy and Society: An Outline of Interpretive Sociology* (Berkeley: University of California Press, 1978) 1:389; trans. of *Wirtschaft und Gesellschaft: Grundriss der verstehenden Soziologie*, 4th ed. (Tübingen: Mohr Siebeck, 1956).

6. John Hutchinson and Anthony D. Smith, eds., *Ethnicity*. Oxford Readers (Oxford: Oxford University Press, 1996) 6-7.

work, composed in the early third century B.C. during the reign of Antiochus I, was written to reaffirm the national identity of the Babylonians, at that time subject to Seleucid rule.[7] In one way or another, then, Genesis 1–11, shaped into a continuous account at a time of high interest in ethnic origins, can be read as an Israelite or early Jewish version of a historiographic-mythic pattern familiar throughout the Near East and Levant.

To judge by the fragments of historiographical writing which have survived from the Hellenistic Near East, ethnic origins was a hot topic during the Hellenistic period. Since great antiquity implied great authenticity, Jewish authors were anxious to compete with the claims advanced for their more powerful neighbors, the Egyptians, Babylonians, and Greeks. Moses is therefore represented by Eupolemus as the first of the sages (*prōtos sophos*), the first lawgiver, and the inventor of writing, which was then passed on to the Phoenicians and from them to the Greeks.[8] According to another Jewish writer, Artapanus, Moses was revered in Egypt as Hermes on account of his literary and interpretative skill. Earlier still, it was Abraham who taught the Egyptian Pharaoh astrology before returning to Syria.[9] A third Jewish historian, known as either Cleodemus or Malchus, applied the familiar topos of the three sons to the descendants of Abraham and Keturah, presenting them as the progenitors of Assyrians and Africans and allies of Heracles in his struggle with the Lybian Antaeus.[10] Josephus, on whom we depend for transmitting several of these fragments from a buried past, has his own elaborations on the biblical text, including the preeminence among other peoples of the first ancestors of Israel in the sciences, especially mathematics and astronomy (*Ant.* 1.69, 143-47, 166).

Though according to most scholars elaborated somewhat earlier, the biblical story of origins in Genesis 1–11 may be read as a more developed

7. For references, see the section "The Pentateuch as an Ancient Historiographical Work" in my *The Pentateuch: An Introduction to the First Five Books of the Bible.* ABRL (New York: Doubleday, 1992) 37-42. Also recommended is Frank Crüsemann, "Human Solidarity and Ethnic Identity: Israel's Self-Definition in the Genealogical System of Genesis" in *Ethnicity and the Bible,* ed. Mark G. Brett (Leiden: Brill, 1996) 57-76.

8. Emil Schürer, *The History of the Jewish People in the Age of Jesus Christ,* rev. ed. by Geza Vermes et al., 3/1 (Edinburgh: T. & T. Clark, 1986) 517-21; Carl R. Holladay, *Fragments from Hellenistic Jewish Authors,* vol. 1: *Historians.* SBLTT 39 (Chico: Scholars, 1983) 93-156.

9. Schürer, *The History of the Jewish People,* 3/1:521-25; Holladay, *Fragments,* 1:189-243.

10. Schürer, *The History of the Jewish People,* 3/1:526-28; Holladay, *Fragments.* 1:245-59.

and, in many ways, a more sober form of the same mythopoeic process; it also gives greater prominence to the unifying factor of the worship of Yahweh. It took some time for non-Jewish authors to notice and comment on the Jewish people and their origins, and therefore for the Jewish ethnos to achieve a degree of social visibility. No contemporary historian writing in Greek who covers the period of Achaemenid rule (sixth to fourth century B.C.) — principally Herodotus (to 479), Xenophon (to 362), Ctesias (to 382), and Thucydides (431-404) — so much as mentions Jews or Judaism. Herodotus refers twice to "Syrians of Palestine" (2.104; 7.89) who presumably would have included Jews, but in any case we learn nothing about them that we did not know already. Only from the time of the Macedonian conquest (332 B.C.) do we begin to have some reports about Jewish origins, of the kind mentioned earlier, most of them transmitted by later compilers — principally Diodorus Siculus, Josephus, and the ninth-century Byzantine polymath Photius.

Of these the most interesting for the question of origins is that of Hecataeus of Abdera, a contemporary of Alexander the Great and the first non-Jewish author writing in Greek to mention Jews. Hecataeus probably got his information from a Jewish source during a visit to Egypt. For the most part, his account of the Jewish myth of origins runs parallel to the biblical version. The pestilence which he says led to the expulsion of Israelites from Egypt may have been inspired by the ten plagues, and the different rites and sacrifices of the Jews in Egypt recall the request of the Israelite slaves to retire into the wilderness to sacrifice (Exod 5:1-3). Like the biblical Moses, the Moses of Hecataeus appointed priests and judges, set up the instruments of ritual, forbade the use of images in worship, gave people laws communicated to him by his God, and divided the people into twelve tribes.

So far so good, but at this point, where the Pentateuch comes to an end, the parallels disappear. Hecataeus states that Moses founded cities in Judah, among them Jerusalem, and even built the temple, perhaps misled by the account of the construction of the wilderness sanctuary in Exodus 25–31 and 35–40 or one similar to it. He also affirms that the Jews were ruled not by kings but priests, in the first place the high priest, which would seem to reflect the actual situation at the time of writing. This does not necessarily imply that the historical books were not available at that time because not yet written,[11] since that may have been all that his infor-

---

11. *Pace* Philip R. Davies, "Scenes from the Early History of Judaism," in *The Triumph of*

mant had the time or inclination to tell him or, more likely, because his interest was confined to ethnic origins. The account, not surprisingly, betrays a distinctly Hellenistic coloring. The attitude to Judaism is on the whole positive, though the author does refer to Moses establishing "an unsociable and xenophobic way of life."[12] In this connection we might also recall the opinion attributed to Aristotle by Clearchus of Soli, one of his disciples, that the Jews were descended from the Indian philosophers.[13]

Common ancestry is a belief, a dogma, a shared subjective apprehension not necessarily open to historical verification. It is well known that myths of origin, including myths of ancestral paternity, can also be invented. This may well be the case with the claim to be "children of Abraham," since the traditions about Abraham do not begin to take shape until the time of the exile.[14] We also need to bear in mind that the claim of shared descent from a common ancestor or ancestors serves the purpose of both integration and delimitation. In other words, it can serve as an instrument for reinforcing group identity and also for defining others out of the group. Origin traditions can be assigned to other peoples, often being simply invented to serve polemical purposes. The progressive exclusion of possible claimants to direct physical descent, and therefore to the land of Canaan, is a major theme in the stories about the ancestors in Genesis 12–50. Lot, nephew of Abraham, is easily persuaded to settle beyond the confines of the land, where the people are wicked (Gen 13:5-13). His sons, conceived incestuously, become the ancestors of the detested Moabites and Ammonites (Gen 19:30-38).[15] Ishmael, son of Hagar, Abraham's proxy wife, is sent away to live in the wilderness of Paran (Gen 16:1-16; 21:8-21).

Elohim: From Yahwisms to Judaisms, ed. Diana Vikander Edelman (Grand Rapids: Wm. B. Eerdmans, 1995) 163-68.

12. *apanthrōpon tina kai misoxenon bion eisēgēsato* (frg. 2, lines 25-26). For the text, see Menahem Stern, *Greek and Latin Authors on Jews and Judaism,* vol. 1: *From Herodotus to Plutarch* (Jerusalem: Israel Academy of Sciences and Humanities, 1976) 26-29. For the prejudicial accounts of Jewish Egyptian origins, see Peter Schäfer, *Judeophobia: Attitudes towards the Jews in the Ancient World* (Cambridge, MA: Harvard University Press, 1997) 15-33.

13. Stern, *Greek and Latin Authors,* 49-50. That the Jews were regarded as a philosophical race is also attested by Theophrastus and Megasthenes, contemporaries of Clearchus; see Stern, 10, 46.

14. See below, 138-39.

15. This will recall the absolute exclusion of Ammonites and Moabites from the Israelite assembly in Deut 23:3-8, following immediately on the clause excluding the *mamzēr,* traditionally understood to refer to those born of incestuous unions.

He will be the ancestor of Arab tribes, including the Kedarite Arabs who threatened Judah from the south and east during Nehemiah's governorship (Gen 25:13). The correspondence of these narratives with the situation in Achaemenid Judah will be evident. Among the more obvious parallels we mention the often-repeated promise of the land and efforts to make the promise good, the status of Abraham the immigrant as a resident alien (Gen 21:23; 23:4), the ideal boundaries of the land, corresponding in extent to the Transeuphrates satrapy (15:18), the list of indigenous peoples (15:19), the problematic relations with Edomites, Arabs (Geshem/Gashmu), and Ammonites (Tobiah), and negotiations for the purchase of real estate following Neo-Babylonian legal custom (23:1-20).

We conclude that the high level of interest in ethnic origins during the Hellenistic period is understandable only as a sequel to developments during the Achaemenid period immediately preceding. In the following section we want to look at this question of ethnic origins from a different direction, that of terminology.

Judeans or Jews?

One way of gaining a foothold on this slippery methodological slope would be to begin with the actual language used, specifically the designations or labels which the antecedents of modern Jews employed to identify themselves, or which were used by others to refer to them. In biblical usage the term "Hebrew" (*'ivrî*) denotes a social category, comparable to the *'apiru* of the Amarna letters and other second-millennium B.C. texts, whether *'ivrî* is understood to be linguistically related to *'apiru* or not. It assumes an ethnic connotation only at a later date, and that very rarely.[16] The designation "Israel," which made its first appearance on the famously controversial Merneptah (Meremptah) stele in the late thirteenth century B.C., is, together with the corresponding adjective "Israelite," far more common, but has been invested with a heavy theological surplus of mean-

---

16. Apart from Abraham the *'ivrî* (Gen 14:13), the term is used with reference to a social category exclusively by or in interaction with foreigners, specifically Egyptians and Philistines. Comparison between the slave law in Exod 21:2 and Deut 15:12 (also Jer 34:9, 14) illustrates the evolution of the term from a purely social to an ethnic connotation. Addressed by foreign sailors, Jonah identifies himself as a Hebrew (Jonah 1:9). As a personal name, *'ivrî* occurs only once (1 Chr 24:27).

ing. To anticipate: in Ezra-Nehemiah the terms "Israel," "Israelites," "the people of Israel" are used with exclusive reference to the *golah* group *(běnê haggôlâ)* in the Achaemenid province of Judah except where the allusion is purely historical.[17] "Israel" even occurs with this reference, quite implausibly, in the rescript of Artaxerxes mandating Ezra's mission (Ezra 7:15). A further extension of meaning, indicative of the increasing role of the temple and its officials, is the use of "Israel" to designate laity as distinct from priests, Levites, and other kinds of temple personnel.[18]

We may therefore focus on the gentilic *yěhûdîm*, understood to derive from *yěhûdâ*, "Judah," originally a topographical and tribal term which, according to immemorial custom, is also applied to the eponymous ancestor of the tribe. In due course, it came to designate the kingdom of Judah liquidated by the Babylonians in the early sixth century B.C. The biblical texts derive the term from the verbal stem *ydh*, "praise," assigning it the meaning "may Yahweh be praised" (Gen 29:35; 49:8), and some scholars have been prepared to accept this or a similar derivation.[19] In other biblical texts, however, "Judah" seems to refer in the first place to a topographical feature, as in "the hill country of Judah" (Josh 11:21, etc.), "the wilderness of Judah" (Judg 1:16), or "the Negev of Judah" (1 Sam 27:10). There is also reason to hold that Judah began its career as one of several interrelated proto-Arabian lineages, together with Kenites, Midianites, Jerahmeelites, and others. In that case, we would not expect a West Semitic (Canaanite-Hebrew) derivation, and in fact one scholar, Edouard Lipiński, has proposed an Arabic derivation from the verbal stem *whd (wahda)* with the meaning "gorge, ravine." Hence, according to Lipiński, the common expression *'ereṣ yěhûdâ*, usually translated "the land of Judah," would originally have referred to a region of deep valleys and gorges *(terre ravinée).*[20]

---

17. *yiśrā'ēl* (Ezra 2:59; 7:28; 10:2, 10; Neh 9:1; 13:3; *běnê yiśrā'ēl* (Ezra 3:1; 6:16, 21; 7:7); *'am yiśrā'ēl* (Ezra 2:2; Neh 7:7); *kol-yiśrā'ēl* (Ezra 2:70; 6:17; 8:25); *šivtê yiśrā'ēl* (Ezra 6:17); *zera' yiśrā'ēl* (Neh 9:2).

18. Ezra 2:2; 7:7; 8:29; 9:1; 10:1, 5, 25; Neh 10:39; 11:3, 20.

19. William F. Albright, "The Names 'Israel' and 'Juda' with an Excursus on the Etymology of *tôdâh* and *tôrâh*," *JBL* 46 (1927) 151-85 (a hypocoristic for *yěhûdě'ēl*, "May El be praised"); Alan R. Millard, "The Meaning of the Name Judah," *ZAW* 86 (1974) 216-20 (formed from the jussive Hophal of *ydh*).

20. E. Lipiński, "L'étymologie de Juda," *VT* 23 (1973) 380-1; see also Bob Becking, "Yehud," *DDD*, 925-26. On the North-West Arabian origins of Judah, see "The Midianite-Kenite Hypothesis Revisited and the Origins of Judah," *JSOT* 33 (2008) 131-53.

The term *yĕhûdîm*, therefore, began as a designation for a proto-Arabian lineage which came to inhabit the region called Judah and which took its name from that region. After the formation of the state, the public identity of the members of the lineage was defined by belonging to the kingdom of Judah as a political entity. At that time, therefore, the term was definitely ascriptive. In this historical context, the Hebrew expression should be translated "Judeans" or — less elegantly — "Judahites." Judeans are mentioned alongside Edomites and Syrians involved in military campaigns during the reign of Ahaz in the eighth century B.C. (2 Kgs 16:6), and shortly after the fall of Jerusalem *yĕhûdîm* and *kaśdîm* (Babylonians) were victims of Ishmael's murderous attack on the administrative center of the province in Mizpah.[21] The equivalent Akkadian term occurs in Assyrian inscriptions. Sennacherib's account of his punitive expedition in the year 701 B.C., for example, refers to the rebel king as "Hezekiah the Judean" *(ha-za-qi-a-ú ia-ú-da-ai).*[22]

So understood, Judeans were naturally not limited to those actually resident in Judah, no more than Englishmen resident in a foreign country cease to be English. So we hear of Judeans in Moab, Ammon, and Edom (Jer 40:11-12) and others in Egypt (Jer 43:9; 44:1). Tribal affiliation was, in the meantime, not forgotten after the formation of the state and may have experienced a revival during the Neo-Babylonian period, when the administration of the province passed from Jerusalem in Judah to Mizpah (Tell en-Naṣbeh) in Benjamin. Something of this can be detected already in the incident of the transfer of Jeremiah's deed of purchase of a parcel of land in Benjaminite territory to Baruch, a transfer witnessed by Judeans (Jer 32:12). The term "Judeans" belongs therefore to the same category as Edomites *('ădōmîm, bĕnê 'ĕdōm),* Syrians *('ărammîm),* and similar labels which identify individuals politically and, given the existence of national patron deities, also to some extent religiously.[23]

---

21. 2 Kgs 25:25; Jer 41:3. Judeans and Babylonians (Aram. *yĕhûdā'in, kaśdā'in*) are also mentioned together in Dan 3:8-12.

22. *ANET,* 287-88. A. Leo Oppenheim translated, incorrectly I believe, "Hezekiah, the Jew."

23. Continuity with the preexilic period is emphasized by Marc Zvi Brettler to the point of arguing in favor of extending use of the terms "Jew" and "Judaism" backwards to the beginnings; see his article "Judaism in the Hebrew Bible? The Transition from Ancient Israelite Religion to Judaism," *CBQ* 61 (1999) 429-47. A major concern of Brettler is the perpetuation of the Wellhausian periodization of the history, implying a negative evaluation of reli-

The same term occurs once in the singular, as a personal name. It belongs to a certain Yehudi, a high Judean official charged with the invidious task of reading Jeremiah's scroll to the presumably illiterate Jehoiakim, who promptly tore it up and threw it in the fire (Jer 36:20-23). Perhaps the name (meaning "the Judean") was acquired in a foreign country. The feminine equivalent *yĕhûdît* is the name of one of Esau's wives (Gen 26:34) and also, of course, the name of the heroine of the homonymous book *Judith*. Since this book was composed no earlier than the Hasmonean period, we may certainly take it to be named for "the Jewess," presumably as an idealized embodiment of Jewish womanhood. In addition to the patriarch, four other individuals bear the name "Judah," all four from a time when it was becoming common to take patriarchal names as personal names.[24]

The liquidation of the nation-state and the beginning of the homeland-diaspora polarity created a new situation which problematized the status of those who had, up until then, defined themselves with reference to the kingdom of Judah. The new situation is reflected in our principal internal sources for the Persian period, Ezra-Nehemiah and Chronicles, to which we shall return. The concentration of Chronicles on temple and cult will explain its use of predominantly traditional religious terminology, principally "Israel" and "Israelites," and why this text never uses the designation *yĕhûdîm*.[25] The only other distinctive ethnic allusion in Chronicles is to "Judah and Benjamin."[26] This formulation arose out of the situation following on the Babylonian conquest when, as we have just seen, the administrative center of the province moved from Jerusalem in Judah to Mizpah in Benjamin and, consequently, the social and political center of gravity in the region moved from Judean to Benjaminite territory. Tension and, probably, open conflict between Judeans and Benjaminites was a fac-

---

gious developments after the Babylonian exile, precisely the time of the emergence of Judaism. The concern is understandable, but it is rare to find examples of this *dépassé* attitude in critical scholarship today. I documented its rise and decline in "Old Testament Theology and the Jewish-Christian Connection," *JSOT* 28 (1984) 3-15 and, in a revised and expanded form, in *Treasures Old and New: Essays in the Theology of the Pentateuch* (Grand Rapids: Wm. B. Eerdmans, 2004) 18-35.

24. E.g., Judah, Neh 11:9; 12:8, 34, 36; Benjamin, Neh 12:34; Joseph, Ezra 10:42; Neh 12:14.

25. The Davidic genealogy dealing with the related Calebite and Kenizzite lineages mentions a Judean wife of a certain Mered (1 Chr 4:18). In this instance the reference is to a Judean clan comparable to Calebites and Kenizzites.

26. 2 Chr 11:3, 10, 12; 15:2, 9; 25:5; 31:1; 34:9.

tor in the political life of the province during the Neo-Babylonian and early Persian period and has left its mark on the historical traditions recorded in the Old Testament, especially those dealing with the rise and downfall of King Saul the Benjaminite.[27]

Coming now to Ezra: from the point of view of language, one of the most striking features of the Ezra narrative is the distinctive terminology for the people in the Aramaic section of the narrative (Ezra 4:8–6:18). In the Hebrew-language part we find either traditional nomenclature ("Israel," "Israelites," "people of Israel"); or "Judah and Benjamin," reflecting the influence of Chronicles (Ezra 1:5; 4:1; 10:9); or *haggôlâ, běnê haggôlâ,* "the diaspora or *golah* group," reflecting the Babylonian origins of the dominant elite in the province.[28] In the Aramaic section, however, the people as a whole are *yĕhûdayē'* (4:12, 23; 5:1), and their elders (5:5; 6:8, 14) and governor (6:7) are similarly identified. We may translate this Aramaic term either "Judeans" or "Jews" as we see fit, but it would be well to bear in mind similar usage in the roughly contemporary Aramaic papyri from Elephantine (second half of the fifth century B.C.). The Jewish settlers on the island of Jeb or Elephantine, near Aswan, below the first cataract of the Nile, refer to themselves and are referred to with the same term as in Ezra and are known collectively as *ḥêlā' yĕhûdayē',* "the Jewish garrison."[29] This is a significant point since none of these people, to the best of our knowledge, had ever set foot in Judah. The papyri also intimate that the cultural and religious links of the settlers were with the former northern kingdom of Israel rather than with Judah, most clearly in the respect (and dues) paid to the female deity Anath-bethel alongside of YHW (Yahu?), namely Yahweh, and the oaths sworn in the name of the male deity Herem-bethel.[30] The papyri never refer to the colonists as "Israel" or "Israelites."

27. See my "Benjamin Traditions Read in the Early Persian Period," in *Judah and the Judeans in the Persian Period,* ed. Oded Lipschits and Manfred Oeming (Winona Lake: Eisenbrauns, 2006) 629-45.

28. Ezra 1:11; 6:19; 8:35; 10:16.

29. See the index to A. E. Cowley, *Aramaic Papyri of the Fifth Century B.C.* (1923; repr. Osnabrück: Zeller, 1967).

30. From contributions to the fund of the Jewish temple at Elephantine, 12 kerashin and 8 shekels (128 shekels) were allotted for the cult of YHW, 12 kerashin (120 shekels) for that of 'Anath-bethel, and 7 kerashin (70 shekels) for Eshem-bethel (AP 22, lines 120-25; Cowley, *Aramaic Papyri of the Fifth Century B.C.,* 70, 72). On the deity Bêtēl, see Sergio Ribichini, "Baetyl," *DDD,* 157-59, and on 'Anath, see Peggy L. Day, "Anat," *DDD,* 36-43.

The Nehemiah narrative, exclusively in Hebrew, uses the designation *yĕhûdîm* in a fairly straightforward, primarily geographical sense with reference to the province of *yĕhûd* (Yehud). It is the equivalent of "Judeans" (*bĕnê yĕhûdâ*, Neh 13:16), "the house of Judah" (*bêt yĕhûdâ*, 4:10), or "Judah" *tout court* (*yĕhûdâ*, 4:4; 13:12). The story begins with Nehemiah's inquiry about the condition of the *yĕhûdîm* back in the old country (1:2), which might suggest that this designation was more likely to be used from a perspective external to the province of Judah. But the same term can refer to those living outside the province (Neh 4:12[MT 4:6]), and Sanballat, though himself a worshipper of Yahweh,[31] uses the same terminology, though with disparaging undertones, to refer to Nehemiah and his coworkers engaged in the fortification of Jerusalem: "What do these wretched Judeans think they are doing?" (4:1-2[MT 3:33-34]; cf. 6:6). Elsewhere in the Nehemiah narrative the expression has a more specialized connotation. In his memoir, Nehemiah notes that he had not told the *yĕhûdîm*, the priests, the hereditary nobles *(ḥōrîm)*, the administrative officers *(sĕgānîm)*, and the rest of the people of his plans for rebuilding the wall (2:16). Later, he reports a complaint about serious social and economic abuses of the common people and their wives against "their brothers the *yĕhûdîm*" (5:1). The common geographical-ethnic connotation does not fit either of these instances. The context suggests rather a reference to the economically dominant Judeo-Babylonian element in the province, those known elsewhere as the *golah*.[32] The same connotation is probable but less clear in the account of Nehemiah's provincial court, which included *yĕhûdîm* in addition to officials and foreigners (Persians?) (5:17). Finally, a more explicitly ethnic and religious tone can be heard when Nehemiah reacts intemperately to an encounter with *yĕhûdîm* who had married Ashdodite women and whose children could no longer speak the language of Judah *(yĕhûdît)*, namely, Hebrew (13:23-24) — a good indication, incidentally, of the importance of a common language in the maintenance of ethnic identity.

It seems, therefore, that usage during the Persian period was becoming more fluid and less restricted to the geographical-national connotation in

---

31. The Samarians who offered to cooperate in building the temple assured the Judean leadership that they worshipped and sacrificed to the same god as they (Ezra 4:2). A later Sanballat had two sons, Delaiah and Shelemiah, bearing good Yahwistic names. They were the recipients of a letter from the Elephantine leaders in 408 b.c. (AP 30:29 = TADAE 1: A4.7, pp. 68-71).

32. See my *Ezra-Nehemiah*. OTL (Philadelphia: Westminster, 1988) 224-25, 256, 259.

use before the destruction of the Judean state. The same conclusion is explicit in Josephus. Taking his cue from the mention in Ezra-Nehemah of Jews working on the city wall (Neh 4:1-2), Josephus adds the following clarification:

> This name (i.e., *ioudaioi*) by which they have been called from the time when they went up from Babylon is derived from the tribe of Judah; as this tribe was the first to come to those parts, both the people themselves and the country have taken their name from it. (*Ant.* 11.173)

Josephus would certainly have admitted the existence of continuities with the traditions of the predisaster age which he had recorded and paraphrased in the previous ten books of his *Antiquities*. But he seems to be saying here that, following on the return from exile, a new situation obtained which called for a new name. This is precisely the impression we get reading Ezra-Nehemiah. On the subject of nomenclature, Josephus records, at a later point, how the Samaritans, in petitioning Alexander for the privilege of tax exemption, made an unfortunate tactical error. In reply to Alexander's enquiry, they informed him that they were *hebraioi* and denied being *ioudaioi*, whereupon Alexander informed them that he had already awarded the privilege to the *ioudaioi* (*Ant.* 11.342-44). What they probably meant to say was that they considered themselves Jews but were not under the jurisdiction of the Jerusalem temple-state. The tactic was understandable but costly.

The attempt to trace a development in the use of terminology, and more specifically to determine when the term in question begins to carry an ethnic-religious rather than purely ethnic-geographical denotation, is complicated by the uncertain dating and chronological order of the relevant biblical texts. One of these is a remarkable saying which serves as a finale to Zechariah 1–8:

> In those days, from each of the nations with their own languages ten men will take hold of the hem (of the garment) of a Jewish man (*'îš yĕhûdî*), saying, "Let us go with you, for we have heard that God is with you." (Zech 8:23)

The form in which the saying is cast might be taken to imply a calculation that the Jewish population is destined to increase tenfold — which may not be far off the mark for the demographic increase of the Jewish ethnos from the Persian to the Roman period. Alternatively, the ten would represent the nations to which they belong, in which case the anonymous seer is expressing the Isaianic prospect of all the nations of the world embracing the Jewish faith: "Turn to me and accept salvation, all the ends of the earth!" (Isa 45:22). The wording of the request is also Isaianic, most clearly so where we hear foreigners exclaiming, "Surely God is with you, there is no other, there is no God but he" (Isa 45:14), perhaps with a lower-register echo of the Emmanuel saying (Isa 7:14). In another passage, we hear non-Jews encouraging each other in a similar way to go in pilgrimage to Yahweh's temple in Jerusalem:

> Let us by all means go to entreat the favor of Yahweh and to seek Yahweh of the hosts; I too am going. (Zech 8:21),

reminiscent of a text in Isaiah:

> It will come to pass in days to come
> that the mountain, Yahweh's house, shall be established
> at the top of the mountains,
> raised high over the hills.
> Then all nations shall stream towards it,
> many peoples shall come and say,
> "Up, let us go to Yahweh's mountain,
> to the house of Jacob's God,
> that he may instruct us in his ways,
> that we may walk in his paths. (Isa 2:2-3)

The time of composition of Zech 8:23 is uncertain. It has been appended to the saying immediately preceding (8:20-22), which is itself a later attachment to the basic prophecy (Zech 1:1–8:19) dated explicitly to the years 520-518 B.C. (1:1, 7; 7:1). At any rate, it comes from a time when Judaism was accepting proselytes. Even if the hem of the garment is not an allusion to the ṣîṣiyyôt ("tassels") prescribed in Num 15:38, the sense is clearly religious: the ten want to go with the Jew because "God is with you" ('ĕlōhîm 'immākem, in the plural). The addendum comes, then, from a time when the term yĕhûdîm had left the topographical-ethnic sense well behind.

The same conclusion holds even more clearly for Esther. Here, too, dating the text is a something of a problem. We know that the expanded Greek version of the book, the final edition, comes from the late second or early first century B.C. The date of the Hebrew text is less secure, but the language and the generally positive attitude to Persian rule support an earlier rather than later date, let us say the late fourth or early third century B.C.[33] The story tells how the Jewish people fared in Susa and elsewhere in the Achaemenid Empire during the reign of Xerxes. It is for the most part a narrative about official benignity and popular hostility. The Jewish people are referred to exclusively as *yĕhûdîm*, Mordechai is almost always referred to as "Mordechai the *yĕhûdî*," and Haman as "Haman, enemy of the *yĕhûdîm*." Neither Israel nor the God of Israel is mentioned, but these Jews observe their own laws (Esth 3:8), which we may suppose were based on religious premises. The religious substratum of the narrative comes to particularly clear expression in the notice that many of the inhabitants of the country "professed the Jewish faith" (Esth 8:17). The meaning of this verbal form *(mityahădîm)* could be that they converted to Judaism and were accepted, but the theme of the verb, the Hitpael, can also imply simulation, pretence. This may well be the meaning here since the reason given is fear of the Jews, the *furor iudaicus*. If this is the correct interpretation, it is none the less clear that the verb presupposes the possibility and the actual practice of becoming Jewish, namely, of proselytism.

This review of the incidence of the designation *yĕhûdîm* makes it difficult to accept the thesis of Shaye Cohen that the geographical-ethnic connotation gave way to the religious-cultural understanding of the term only in the Hasmonean period, the mid- or late-second century B.C., and that it was only at that time that Judaism began to accept proselytes.[34] It may be possible to interpret some texts of an earlier date which seem to speak about proselytes as optative or eschatological rather than reflecting current practice. Zech 2:11(MT 2:15), for example, states that "many nations shall attach themselves to Yahweh on that day," and the final "on that day" could be interpreted to imply that it was not happening at that time. But there are other sayings which cannot easily be so understood. Isa 14:1, for example, refers to *gērîm* who attach themselves to Israel and are incorporated into the household of Jacob, and the context makes it clear that in this instance the *gērîm* are proselytes, not resident aliens. Isa 14:1 is admit-

33. E.g., Carey A. Moore, *Esther.* AB 7B (Garden City: Doubleday, 1971) lvii-ix; Sidnie White Crawford, "The Book of Esther," *NIB* 3 (1999) 855-56.

34. Shaye J. D. Cohen, *The Beginnings of Jewishness* (Berkeley: University of California Press, 1999) 3-10, 69-174.

tedly part of a postexilic addendum, but not as late as the second century B.C. Isa 56:1-8, the initial prophetic statement in the third section of Isaiah, is addressed to foreigners and the sexually mutilated who are already members of the Jewish ethnos but whose good standing in the group is under threat, probably on the basis of exclusions listed in Deut 23:1-8(MT 2-9) or Ezek 44:4-9 or both. The final verse, Isa 56:8, is particularly interesting since it takes off from Isa 11:12, which refers to the repatriation of diaspora Jews but then adds, "I will gather yet more to him than those already gathered." Here, too, the context suggests the practice of accepting proselytes, a conclusion drawn from this text much earlier by Ibn Ezra. The way the term *yĕhûdîm (yĕhûdayē')* is used in the Elephantine papyri, Zech 8:23, and Esther, reviewed above, would also create problems for Cohen's thesis.

We therefore conclude that the two centuries from the fall of Babylon in 539 to the conquests of Alexander in 332 form the transitional period during which Judaism emerged from the rubble of the destroyed city and temple and the subsequent deportations. Our principal source for this period, Ezra-Nehemiah, describes situations and events somewhere near the halfway mark of this time span, in the mid-fifth century B.C. Interrogating this text should help to clarify the issue under discussion, even if the answers to the questions we put to it are not always entirely to our satisfaction.

A Clash of Titans: Eduard Meyer vs. Julius Wellhausen

This conclusion, that Judaism emerged during the two centuries of Achaemenid rule, has long been acknowledged in the scholarly tradition. Over a century ago it provided the occasion for a bruising debate between the two most outstanding scholars of the ancient Near East, inclusive of the history of Israel, of the later nineteenth century. In 1896 Eduard Meyer published his *Die Entstehung des Judentums (The Origins of Judaism)*, the central thesis of which was that Judaism was essentially a creation of the Persian Empire. After a detailed analysis of the Persian documents cited in Ezra 4–7, he concluded as follows:

> Just as the formation of pre-exilic Yahwism and the emergence of the prophets, their ideas and their activity, can be understood only against the background of the great events of world history which were being

played out in the Near East, in the same way the origins of Judaism can be grasped only as resulting from the impact of the Persian empire.[35]

His conviction that the emergence of Judaism was not only facilitated by but came about as the direct outcome of Persian imperial intervention entailed the further conviction of the essential authenticity of the correspondence between satrapal officials and the imperial court in Ezra 4–5, the decrees of Cyrus and Darius in Ezra 6 and that of Artaxerxes in Ezra 7. These measures — the permission to rebuild the temple under Cyrus and Darius and the establishment of Judaism based on the law under Artaxerxes I — he took to be in line with Persian imperial policy with respect to other subject peoples.[36] Meyer felt strongly about the essential authenticity of these texts. Those who rejected them, he maintained, did so out of a fundamental misunderstanding of the historical reality of Judaism. His basic premiss once established, he went on to trace the history in detail from the exile to Nehemiah, concluding with a chapter on Ezra's law book comprising the Priestly legislation in the Pentateuch.[37]

In the following year Wellhausen's review of *Die Entstehung des Judentums* appeared in the scholarly journal of the University of Göttingen (*Göttingischen Gelehrten Anzeigen*).[38] In tones of elaborate sarcasm Wellhausen pointed out that we did not need Meyer to tell us that without Cyrus the restoration and without Artaxerxes the reformation of Judaism would not have happened; we knew this already from the Old Testament. Nor did we need his help to discover the etymology of words in the official documents which anyone could look up in the available reference works. Meyer, he went on, was in the habit of proclaiming *ex cathedra* things he had just learned himself. Wellhausen took Meyer's insistence on the decisive role of the Persian Empire in the emergence of Judaism as a direct repudiation of his (Wellhausen's) own reconstruction of the religious history of Israel on the basis of his analysis of sources in the Pentateuch. The

---

35. Eduard Meyer, *Die Entstehung des Judentums* (1896; repr. Hildesheim: Olms, 1965) 71.

36. Meyer, *Die Entstehung des Judentums,* 70.

37. Meyer, *Die Entstehung des Judentums,* 94-243.

38. *GGA* 159 (1897) 89-97. For my account of the review, which I was unable to obtain, I am endebted to Reinhard Gregor Kratz, *Das Judentum im Zeitalter des Zweiten Tempels.* FAT 42 (Tübingen: Mohr Siebeck, 2004) 6-22, in addition to citations from it and references to it in Meyer's "Erwiderung" (see note 41 below).

principal results of this reconstruction, set out in his *Prolegomena zur Geschichte Israels*,[39] are well known: the law came after the prophets and marked the origins not of Israel but of Judaism; the final stage of this process was the Priestly Code (P), which was the literary expression of what Wellhausen called "the Mosaic theocracy"; Ezra's law, promulgated in 444 B.C., was the entire Pentateuch, in which the Priestly Code constituted the standard legislative element;[40] foreign domination was a concomitant of this final stage but was in no way responsible for it.

The review also attacked Meyer's reading of the official documents in Ezra-Nehemiah, about which Wellhausen had entertained doubts in several previous publications. The Cyrus decree which allegedly surfaced in Ecbatana (Ezra 6:1-5) Wellhausen regarded as historically worthless, fit only for the wastepaper basket. In general, he omitted no opportunity to point out what he considered absurdities in Meyer's study, such as Nehemiah the layman's supposedly deferential attitude to Ezra the priest. He also hinted darkly at plagiarism of his own work and concluded with some uncomplimentary remarks on Meyer's literary output as a whole.

Meyer was not slow to reply and, after disclaiming at some length any interest in personal polemics, went on to reply with animus equal to that of his opponent. When the editorial board of the Göttingen journal declined to publish his rebuttal, he wrote a more extensive response in 1897 which was included in later printings of *Die Entstehung* as an appendix.[41] Against Wellhausen's objections, he reiterated the case for the authenticity of the official documents cited in Ezra 4–7. The presence of Persian loanwords, many of them unfamiliar to the Greek translator, makes it less likely that the texts in which they occur were later inventions. The Aramaic into which the four documents in Ezra 4–6 were translated betrays evidence of the Old Persian original, thereby testifying to their authenticity. The practice of issuing rescripts dealing with specific cultic issues is illustrated by the inscription sent by Darius I to Gadatas, Persian ruler in Lydia. There is

---

39. (Berlin: Reimer, 1927, 6th ed.; first published 1883); trans. *Prolegomena to the History of Ancient Israel*, 1957; repr. SBL Reprints and Translations (Atlanta: Scholars, 1994). The English edition includes Wellhausen's article "Israel" from the *Encyclopedia Britannica*.

40. Wellhausen held that Ezra arrived in Jerusalem in 458 B.C. but waited fourteen years to promulgate the law, a year after the arrival of Nehemiah; *Prolegomena to the History of Ancient Israel*, 404-10.

41. Eduard Meyer, "Julius Wellhausen und meine Schrift Die Entstehung des Judentums: Eine Erwiderung," *Die Entstehung des Judentums* (Halle: Niemeyer, 1897) 249-72.

no reason to doubt that correspondence addressed to the great king would also have been made public, ending up eventually in the temple archives. The query as to how Zerubbabel managed to get his hands on the letter sent from the governor of the Trans-Euphrates satrapy to the great king and reproduced in Ezra 5:6-17 is not unanswerable; bribing a member of the chancellory staff would be one way of doing it.

It will not be necessary to comment on Meyer's point-by-point rebuttal of Wellhausen's many other objections. He concludes with the complaint that he is in a no-win situation. If he contradicts his opponent he is guilty of *lèse-majesté;* if he agrees with him he is a plagiarist. And as for Wellhausen's final shaft that he would be well advised to stop writing on Near Eastern matters, Meyer assures his opponent that "I will continue in the future writing on Oriental and even Old Testament matters as often as I think fit, let him think what he will. He doesn't have to read any of it."[42]

While it may seem that the debate generated more heat than light, it did raise issues which, after more than a century, are still important and still in several respects debatable. The exchange was also part of a larger debate, since both Meyer and Wellhausen were reacting against more negative assessments of the historical character of the documents in Ezra 1–7 published by such leading figures as Bernhard Stade, Theodor Nöldeke, and, somewhat later, the Dutch scholar W. H. Kosters. With regard to Wellhausen, we would have to take into account his negative attitude to Israel's cultic institutions and their literary expression in the Priestly source (P). His identification of Ezra's law with the Pentateuch, promulgated as the Magna Carta of Judaism in 444 B.C., and the identification of the founders of the canon with the signatories of Nehemiah's covenant, would be endorsed by few scholars today.[43] The unnecessarily spiteful and sarcastic tone of his review may, one suspects, be due to his uneasy consciousness of his own lack of attention to the impact of external forces on the course of Israel's religious history, and therefore on the destiny of Jewish communities during the first century of Achaemenid rule.

Meyer, on the other hand, tended to exaggerate in the opposite direction. On the authenticity of the official documents in Ezra 1–7, still a matter of debate, we would have to conclude that he was overoptimistic. It is unlikely that the correspondence in Ezra 4–5 was conducted in Old Persian

---

42. Meyer, "Erwiderung," 266.
43. *Prolegomena to the History of Ancient Israel,* 405-10.

and then translated into Aramaic, and the use of Persian loanwords in it does not provide reliable support for that proposal. As Wellhausen put it in typical fashion, if that were the case we would have to conclude that a good part of the book of Daniel was written in Old Persian. In order to establish that the Persian court issued rescripts on religious affairs in the provinces it was not necessary to introduce the Gadatas inscription, the authenticity of which, in any case, is in doubt.[44] The suggestion that the Artaxerxes rescript was composed by Jews and submitted to the authorities for approval resolves some problems, but such a procedure is otherwise unattested. Several other claims advanced confidently by Meyer — for example, the identification of Sheshbazzar with the Shenazzar scion of the Davidic royal house (1 Chr 3:18) — would be accepted by few today. Some progress has been made since the Meyer-Wellhausen exchange of views, but many of the issues over which they fought still remain without a clear and unequivocal solution.

From Monocentrism to Pluricentrism: A New Situation[45]

As long as the kingdom of Judah lasted, the identity of those who belonged to it was unproblematic. If you were not a resident alien *(gēr)* or a slave, you were by birth and parentage a Judean, in the same way that denizens of neighboring Edom were Edomites. Officially at least, you would also be a devotee of Yahweh since Yahweh was from of old the national deity of Judah, resident in the Jerusalem temple, which was a national, dynastic shrine.[46] This would naturally not have prevented recourse to other

44. Arguing the case against authenticity are Michael van den Hout, "Studies in Early Greek Letter-Writing," *Mnemosyne* 2 (1949) 19-41, 138-53; O. Hanson, "The Purported Letter of Darius to Gadates," *Rheinisches Museum* 129 (1986) 95-96; and most recently, Pierre Briant, "Histoire et archéologie d'un texte: La Lettre de Darius à Gadatas entre Perses, Grecs et Romains," in *Licia e Lidia prima dell'Ellenizzazione: Atti del Convegno Internazionale, Roma 11–12 Ottobre 1999,* ed. Mauro Giorgieri et al. Monografie scientifiche, Serie Scienze Umane e Sociali (Rome: Consiglio nazionale delle ricerche, 2003) 107-44.

45. The terminology is borrowed from Shemaryahu Talmon, "The Emergence of Jewish Sectarianism in the Early Second Temple Period," in *King, Cult and Calendar in Ancient Israel* (Jerusalem: Magnes, 1986) 165-201.

46. During the last decades of Judah's existence, and maybe earlier, the official Jerusalem cult also included a female deity, Asherah, either Yahweh's paredros or a prominent member of the pantheon. See 2 Kgs 23:4, 6; Ezek 8:3; Jer 44:17-19.

sources of spiritual comfort and sustenance, especially the veneration of ancestors, closer at hand and closer to the everyday life and concerns of a predominantly agrarian, peasant society as it was. In this debate about continuities and discontinuities it is always good to bear in mind that for such a society continuity is the norm. When we talk about "the religion of Israel" we need to be clear as to whether we are talking about what people were actually doing and how they were thinking in the religious sphere of their lives or what certain religious elites thought they ought to be doing and thinking. The biblical texts on which our conclusions are necessarily based deal for the most part with intellectual constructs or systems elaborated by priestly, prophetic, or scribal schools and individuals constituting a statistically small proportion of the population. It remains to be seen to what extent these ideas actually impinged on the life of the majority and brought about change at the level of social realities.

There is much in Ezra-Nehemiah to suggest continuity. The confessional prayer of Ezra (Ezra 9:6-15) and the matching lament in Neh 9:6-37, the latter, in the context, spoken by Levites but in LXX attributed to Ezra, appeal to the ancestors, the Abrahamic covenant, and the traditions about exodus, wilderness, and occupation of the land. Even though its function, as existing by leave of and under the aegis of the Persian king, was quite different from that of Solomon's temple, the temple of Zerubbabel was built on the site of the former edifice (Ezra 6:7),[47] and the sacred vessels in use in Solomon's temple were restored for use in that of Zerubbabel.[48] Another example of this concern for continuity is the emphasis on genealogies in Chronicles and Ezra-Nehemiah. These betray deep anxiety about ethnic identity in the postdisaster age, especially with respect to the priests and the Davidic line which span the great divide of the disasters of the early sixth century B.C.[49] The census list in Ezra 2 = Nehemiah 7 assumes,

47. Cf. the request of the Elephantine leadership to Bigvai governor of Yehud that their temple, destroyed in a pogrom, might be rebuilt "as it was built before" (AP 30:25 = TADAE 1: A4.7). This was a common practice which would later apply to synagogues.

48. Ezra 1:7-11; 7:19; 8:25-30, 33-34. According to the Historian of the Kingdoms, the gold and silver vessels used in the temple were broken up for bullion in both Babylonian campaigns against Jerusalem (2 Kgs 24:13; 25:13-15), though according to 2 Chr 36:10, 18, all the temple vessels were taken to Babylon at the time of the first deportation. See Peter R. Ackroyd, "The Temple Vessels: A Continuity Theme," *VTSup* 23 (1972) 166-81; repr. in *Studies in the Religious Tradition of the Old Testament* (London: SCM, 1987) 46-60.

49. 1 Chr 3:1-24; 6:1-53(MT 5:27–6:38). The tribal genealogies in 1 Chronicles 1-8, includ-

problematically, that the same people who were deported — in some cases about sixty years earlier — or their immediate descendants returned and settled in their original locations (Ezra 2:1). This assumption cannot be taken for granted. It is, for example, at odds with the fact that, of the seventeen lay agnatic units listed in Ezra 2:3-19 as among the first to arrive in Judah from Babylon, only two or three bear names attested in preexilic texts[50] and one, Bigvai, the third largest, is Persian. The same census list also contains statistics on priests officially registered as descendants of preexilic priests (Ezra 2:36-39) and stipulates that only those on the list were authorized to take part in temple liturgies (2:62).

In Ezra-Nehemiah the traditional terminology of "Israel," "the people of Israel," "Israelites," "all Israel" continues in use, but the situation is different in one fundamental respect: *it is no longer unproblematically clear to whom this language applies.* This is a crucial point on which the question of origins pivots. The "Israel" to which both Ezra and Nehemiah belong, and which they address in their autobiographical memoirs, is referred to as "the diaspora/*golah* group" *(běnê haggôlâ)* or "those back from captivity" *(haššāvîm min-haššěvî* or *habbā'îm mēhaššěvî).*[51] They form their own assembly *(qāhāl),* the members of which are listed in the census (Ezra 2:64 = Neh 7:66) and in other lists. The assembly has its plenary gatherings to solve outstanding problems and hear the law read and interpreted (Ezra 10:14; Neh 8:2). It also exercises the right to excommunicate members for failing to participate and no doubt for other offenses (Ezra 10:8).[52] It is a distinctive group composed, at least theoretically, of those who had returned from the eastern diaspora with their faith intact and who therefore are known as *běnê haggôlâ*[53] or, in the Aramaic section, *běnê gālûtā* (Ezra

---

ing the Davidic line and the temple personnel, are said to have been recorded in a document entitled "The Book of the Kings of Israel" (1 Chr 9:1). They eventuate in the list of lay and clerical settlers in Judah after the return from exile (1 Chronicles 9).

50. Shephatiah in Ezra 2:4 = Neh 7:9; cf. 2 Sam 3:4; Bani and Zakkai, perhaps hypocoristic for Benaiah and Zechariah, respectively. See further below, 81-84.

51. Ezra 8:35; Neh 8:17; cf. Ezra 2:1; 6:21.

52. It is worth noting that Ezra-Nehemiah uses the Deuteronomic term *qāhāl* ("assembly") rather than the more Priestly expression *'ēdâ* usually translated "congregation." The assembly justified the exclusion of members of mixed descent by appeal to the Deuteronomic law of the assembly in Deut 23:1, 3(MT 2, 4), which excluded certain ethnic categories and the sexually mutilated (Neh 13:1). In Chronicles, *qāhāl* occurs 32 times and *'ēdâ* only once (2 Chr 5:6).

53. Ezra 1:11; 6:19-20; 9:4; 10:6, 7, 16.

6:16). It most definitely did not include all inhabitants of the province of Judah (Yehud). The book Ezra-Nehemiah emanates from the *golah* or its successors in the Hellenistic period, and it is hardly surprising that it provides no information on the arguments of the many outsiders who also claimed continuity with the Israel of the traditions, the predisaster Israel, perhaps with as good reason.

This *golah* or diasporic section of the population of the province is at great pains to dissociate itself from the natives, those who had remained in Judah during the Babylonian conquest, or who had settled there in the meantime, who are referred to as "the people of the land."[54] These are definitely considered outsiders vis-à-vis the *golah* group. At the same time, it was possible for outsiders to join in the celebration of the festivals and therefore to become, with whatever qualifications, insiders. The Passover concluding the dedication of the altar was celebrated by the *golah* but also by "those who had joined them, separating themselves from the uncleanness of the nations of the land to seek Yahweh God of Israel" (Ezra 6:21). These are not foreigners, though there may have been foreigners among them. They would have seen themselves as belonging to the same ethnic stock as the *golah,* and their inclusion suggests that the latter were open in principle to outsiders, subject of course to certain nonnegotiable conditions. By the same token, as noted a moment ago, the *golah* exercized the right to expel as well as to admit members, and it is clearly stated that expulsion from their assembly had serious economic consequences for those expelled (Ezra 10:8).

The way in which the *golah* community in Ezra-Nehemiah identifies itself comes to expression in other significant self-descriptions. According to the report of the community leaders to Ezra, marriage with the local inhabitants resulted in contamination of the "holy seed" (*zeraʿ haqqodeš,* Ezra 9:2; cf. *zeraʿ yiśrāʾēl,* Neh 9:2). The only other place where this expression occurs is at the conclusion of the throne room vision in Isa 6:1-13. The vision ends with the dire prediction that both the land and its inhabitants will be left "like the oak or the terebinth which, when felled, will have only a stump remaining." To this a glossator, no doubt reflecting the experience of disaster after the fall of Jerusalem and the deportations, has added "Its stump is the holy seed *(zeraʿ qodeš)*." The point of this intertextual link will

---

54. *ʿam hāʾāreṣ* (Ezra 4:4), more commonly in the plural *ʿammê hāʾāreṣ* (Ezra 10:11; Neh 10:31-32) or *ʿammê hāʾărāṣôt* (Ezra 3:3; 9:1, 2; Neh 9:30; 10:29), and once *gôy hāʾāreṣ* (Ezra 6:21).

be seen more clearly if we go on to note the kind of language used in the confessional prayer of Ezra which follows, and which has clearly been composed for this occasion and for this place in the narrative. The prayer concludes as follows:

> After all that has happened to us on account of our evil deeds and our great guilt . . . shall we once again transgress your commandments, intermarrying with the peoples who practice these abominations? Would you not be angry with us to the point where there would be no surviving remnant at all? O Yahweh God of Israel, you are righteous, for we the survivors are still here today. We are here in your presence, guilty as we are, for none can stand in your presence because of this guilt. (Ezra 9:13-15)

The group on whose behalf the prayer is being recited is "the surviving remnant." In prophetic writings "the remnant" is the traditional way of referring to those who survive a catastrophic disaster.[55] Biblical texts allude, often with undisguised *Schadenfreude,* to the remnant of Babylon (e.g., Isa 14:22) or of neighboring, which is to say hostile, countries.[56] But the concept, if not the term itself,[57] is also applied with equal emphasis to the kingdom of Samaria in the prophecies of Amos, though it is not clear that it signifies the possibility of a *meaningful* future. The remnant of Israel will be like what is left after a lion has fed on a sheep (Amos 3:12), or after the destruction of nine-tenths of an army (5:3), or after a devastating earthquake (6:9-10). In Isaiah, whose debt to Amos is apparent at many points, the idea of the remnant is encapsulated in the symbolic name of the prophet's son Shear-Yashub (Isa 7:3). The name, literally, "a remnant will return," links the idea of survival with that of return, meaning return from exile. This was a key issue for the self-understanding of those sectarian or quasi-sectarian movements of the Greco-Roman period which saw themselves as the successors of the first to return from exile in Babylon. It pres-

55. On the terminology of the remnant, see Gerhard F. Hasel, *IDBSup*, 735-36; Hans Wildberger, *TLOT* 3:1284-92; Lester V. Meyer, *ABD* 5:669-71; Werner E. Müller and Horst Dietrich Preuss, *Die Vorstellung vom Rest im Alten Testament,* 2nd ed. (Neukirchen-Vluyn: Neukirchener, 1973).

56. Edom (Amos 9:12), Moab (Isa 15:9; 16:14), Syria (Isa 17:3), Philistia (Amos 1:8; Isa 14:30; Jer 25:20).

57. Amos refers once to "the remnant of Joseph," that is, the tribes of Ephraim and Manasseh, the core of the kingdom of Samaria (5:15).

ages both destruction and restoration, an end and a new beginning. And since the verb *šûv* ("return") also means "repent," the name can connote more than a physical return. Those who returned from exile were also the penitents of Israel. The ambivalence will be exploited often in the Qumran sectarian texts, especially in the Damascus Document (CD IV 2-3; VI 3-7).

Taking all this together, the terminology in Ezra-Nehemiah for the group in whose name and on whose behalf the book was composed implies a collective self-understanding without precedent. The claim to be the Israel which inherits the promises, commitments, and privileges to which the traditions testify was now limited to members of the *golah* who subscribed to its theology, its interpretation of the laws, and its religious practices. All other claims, including those of the inhabitants of Samaria, the Judeans who had never left the land, and presumably those elsewhere in the diaspora whose religious beliefs and practices differed from those of the *golah* leadership, were excluded.[58]

One implication of this situation which we will need to consider is that any inquiry into the origins of Judaism entails inquiry into the origins of the *golah* group and its distinctive ideology. In pursuing this line of investigation we will need to exercise caution in using such common terms as "restoration" or "return to Zion"[59], expressions which assume a degree of continuity which a critical reading of the sources does not warrant.

Who Are the Children of Abraham?

While the expression "the children of Israel" *(běnê yiśrā'ēl)* became the standard designation for residents of both kingdoms, the alternative expression, "descendants of Abraham," always had the potential for a broader and more inclusive application, until the point was reached where one could refer without comment to "the three Abrahamic faiths."[60] Here, too,

58. This may explain why the request for permission to rebuild their temple, addressed in 408 B.C.E. by the Elephantine Jews to Johanan the high priest and his priestly colleagues in Jerusalem, went unanswered; see Cowley, *Aramaic Papyri of the Fifth Century B.C.*, 111-13.

59. The expression *šîvat ṣiyyôn* ("return to Zion"), in frequent use, is taken from Ps 126:1, where MT *šîvat* is often emended to *šěvût/šěvît* ("captivity").

60. While the expression "children (lit., 'sons') of Abraham" *(běnê 'avrāhām)* occurs only once in biblical texts (1 Chr 1:28), "descendants (lit., 'seed') of Abraham" *(zera' 'avrāhām)* is fairly frequent (Isa 41:8; Jer 33:26; Ps 105:6; 2 Chr 20:7).

the implications of usage take us back to the early Persian period. Two conclusions about the figure of Abraham are now widely accepted in critical biblical scholarship. The first is that, with the exception of the triad "Abraham, Isaac, and Jacob," Abraham is not clearly and unambiguously attested earlier than the Babylonian exile. The second is that Abraham came to serve as a model for those who returned from Babylon to make a new beginning in Judah in the early years of Persian rule. As for the first: his name does not appear in prophetic writings before the Neo-Babylonian period. The first of four occurrences in Isaiah, alluding to the redemption of Abraham (Isa 29:22), is part of a postexilic addendum to an earlier woe saying (29:17-24),[61] and the remaining three (41:8; 51:2; 63:16) are in Deutero- or Trito-Isaiah. The Davidic-restorationist saying in Jer 33:23-26 which mentions the offspring of Abraham, Isaac, and Jacob comes from a time when the monarchy was no longer in existence,[62] and the allusion to Yahweh's loyalty to Abraham in Mic 7:20 concludes a passage which speaks of rebuilding the walls of Jerusalem (7:11)[63] and foreign nations licking the dust before Israel (7:16-17), an unpleasant fantasy which also appears in Deutero-Isaiah (Isa 49:23). The only other reference to Abraham in a prophetic text is Ezek 33:23-26, where the survivors of the catastrophe of 586 B.C., those who remained in Judah, lay claim to the land, identifying themselves as the numerous progeny promised to Abraham (e.g., Gen 12:2; 13:16), perhaps inspired by the Isaianic exhortation to "look to Abraham your father and to Sarah who gave you birth; when I called him he was but one, but I blessed him and made him many" (Isa 51:2). Like practically all the psalms, the two in which Abraham is mentioned in passing (Pss 47 and 105) cannot be dated; they belong to the hymnal of the Second Temple and were probably composed by Levitical liturgical musicians sometime during that long period. Deuteronomy refers often to Abraham, Isaac, and Jacob, generally in connection with the *conditional* promise of land,[64] but otherwise is silent on the person and activities of Abraham.

With respect to the extraordinarily rich narrative about Abraham in

61. See the note in my *Isaiah 1–39*. AB 19 (New York: Doubleday, 2000) 410.

62. Robert P. Carroll, *Jeremiah*. OTL (Philadelphia: Westminster, 1986) 634-39; William McKane, *A Critical and Exegetical Commentary on Jeremiah*, vol. 2: *Commentary on Jeremiah XXVI-LII*. ICC (Edinburgh: T. & T. Clark, 1996) 860-65.

63. Mic 7:11 uses the same relatively rare word for wall, *gādēr*, as occurs in Ezra's prayer (Ezra 9:9).

64. Deut 1:8; 6:10; 9:5, 27; 29:13(MT 12); 30:20; 34:4.

Genesis 11–25, we have witnessed a growing consensus over the last four or five decades that we owe it not to oral tradition handed down from before the formation of the state, much less from the Middle Bronze period, but to literary circles of the exilic and postexilic period, whether lay, Priestly, or Deuteronomic.[65] Some oral traditions about Abraham may have been in circulation earlier, similar to those about Jacob,[66] but if so they have not survived in written form. The point is that the narrative about Abraham in Genesis mirrors to a remarkable degree the situation in Jewish communities in the Neo-Babylonian and early Persian period. The most obviously paradigmatic incident is Abraham's call from God to leave Mesopotamia and depart for the land of Canaan (Palestine, Judah, Yehud), parallel with the first return in the early Persian period, which, according to Ezra 1:1, was also inspired by Yahweh. Yahweh "stirred up" *(hēʿîr)* Cyrus to issue his edict, which, though of pagan origin, then became an inspired text, fulfilling an earlier inspired text. The text in question is attributed to Jeremiah and is presumed to refer to the prediction of seventy more years of Babylonian supremacy (Jer 29:10-14; cf. 25:11-14), but it is closer to those Deutero-Isaianic texts which speak of Yahweh "stirring up" Cyrus (Isa 41:2,25; 45:13). Perhaps both sets of texts were conflated in the writer's memory. The first stage in the journey, from Ur of the Chaldeans in the south to Harran in the north, brings to mind the close ties between Babylon (Chaldea) and Harran during the reign of Nabonidus, last ruler of the Neo-Babylonian Empire and a devotee of the god Sin, the center of whose worship was in Harran.[67] We should add that use of the term "Chaldeans" *(kaśdîm,* Gen 11:28, 31) provides another clue to the origin of the tradition since it is not attested in biblical usage before the Neo-Babylonian period.[68] On arrival

---

65. Among the earliest to argue systematically along these lines were Thomas L. Thompson, *The Historicity of the Patriarchal Narratives.* BZAW 133 (Berlin: de Gruyter, 1974), and John Van Seters, *Abraham in History and Tradition* (New Haven: Yale University Press, 1975). In German and Anglophone scholarship Erhard Blum's treatment of the overall Deuteronomistic and Priestly sources in *Die Komposition der Vätergeschichte.* WMANT 57 (Neukirchen-Vluyn: Neukirchener, 1983) has been very influential. For a summary of these developments to the time of writing, see my *The Pentateuch,* 19-28, 99-102, 111-30.

66. Hos 12:2-6, 12-14(MT 3-7, 13-15). Amos is also familiar with Isaac (Am 7:9, 16) and Jeremiah with Rachel (Jer 31:15).

67. Paul-Alain Beaulieu, *The Reign of Nabonidus, King of Babylon, 556-539 B.C.* (New Haven: Yale University Press, 1989) 43-65.

68. 2 Kgs 25:4, 13, 25; Jer 21:4, 9; 32:5, 29; Hab 1:6; Ezek 11:24 (the land of exile); Isa 43:14; 48:14, 20.

in the land, Abraham appropriated for his god the religious centers through which he passed, beginning with Shechem (Samaria) and Bethel, the latter destined to play an important role in the religious life of the province after the destruction of the temple in Jerusalem. His first act, building an altar to Yahweh (Gen 12:7), set an example for the first arrivals from Babylon in the early Persian period (Ezra 3:1-3; cf. 1 Chr 21:28–22:1) with the purpose of warding off danger from "the people of the land."

The promise of land to Abraham and his descendants, first announced at Shechem after the initial stage of the journey (Gen 12:7), served to legitimate both the goal of the Judeo-Babylonian settlers to recover their real estate confiscated after the Babylonian conquest and the claim to inherit the land as a whole, a claim naturally disputed by those who had never left the land (Ezek 11:15; 33:24). It is interesting to observe that the ideal boundaries of the land in the Abraham story (Gen 15:18-19) correspond to the extent of the Trans-Euphrates section of the Babylon-Trans-Euphrates satrapy *(Babirush-Ebernari)* before the conquest of Egypt by Cambyses in 525 B.C.[69] The parallels extend to Abraham's dealings with the indigenous peoples. His close relations with the neighboring Arab tribes of Ishmaelites and Midianites, through marriage with Hagar and Keturah, respectively, are also consistent with the political history of the sixth and fifth centuries B.C. Kedar is a "son" of Ishmael, Abraham's firstborn (Gen 25:13), and by the Neo-Babylonian period the Kedarite Arabs had displaced the Edomites from much of their territory and had settled a broad swathe of land from the Transjordanian plateau to the Nile Delta. We recall that the sheik Geshem (Gashmu), head of the Kedarite tribal confederation, was one of Nehemiah's foreign opponents (Neh 2:19; 6:1-2, 6). Relations with Edom are more clearly delineated in the Jacob-Esau story, but the same wary approach and concern with clearly demarcated boundaries can be seen in Abraham's relations with Lot (Gen 13:5-18), a point noted earlier, and with local "kings" in the Negev (Gen 20:1-18; 21:22-34).

In his dealings with the indigenous peoples Abraham seems to have served for the Judeo-Babylonian immigrants as representative of a "soft" ideology in contrast to the "hard" ideology represented by the tradition of conquest and ethnic cleansing mandated by Deuteronomy and imple-

---

69. See also Deut 1:7; 11:24; Josh 1:4; 2 Sam 8:3; 1 Kgs 4:21 all of which name the Euphrates as the eastern boundary of the land.

mented in the book of Joshua.[70] The land through which he wandered as a stranger and alien (*gēr-větôšāv*, Gen 23:4) was sparsely populated, and apparently under no central authority. We hear nothing about the "abominations" of the indigenous peoples; in fact, Abraham does not comment at all on their moral character.[71] He negotiates with them (Gen 13:8-9; 26:15-33), and purchases a parcel of land rather than trying to obtain it by force (Genesis 23).[72] His choice of a Mesopotamian bride for his son is motivated by a normal preference in that kind of society for cross-cousin marriage rather than by the kind of ritually-based ideological considerations apparent in the Priestly version of the Jacob-Esau story (Gen 26:34-35; 27:46–28:2) and, much more explicitly and aggressively, in Ezra-Nehemiah.

Sarah, mother of the race, is mentioned only once outside of Genesis, in a postexilic Isaianic passage (Isa 51:2). Her initial infertility (Gen 11:30) and eventual miraculous maternity (Gen 17:15-19; 18:9-15) are mirrored in the destiny of the mother-city Zion, initially infertile but whose numerous children will settle the ruined towns of Judah (Isa 54:1-3).

In the situation of conflicting claims put forward in the aftermath of the Babylonian conquest, the issue of the legitimate descendants of Abraham, who were to inherit the Abrahamic promise, took on new urgency. Within a year of the fall of Jerusalem the survivors who were left in Judah were claiming to be the descendants of Abraham, thereby justifying their occupation of estates vacated by the deportees and their claim to the land as a whole: "Abraham was only one yet he took possession of the land; we are many, so the land is given to us as an inheritance" (Ezek 33:24). The argument is not particularly cogent, but in any case was refuted from the side

---

70. The language ("ideologia morbida, dura") draws on Mario Liverani, *Oltre la Bibbia: Storia antica di Israele*, 2nd ed. (Bari: Editori Laterza, 2004) 283-87.

71. Allusion to "the iniquity of the Amorites" (Gen 15:16) occurs in an incident edited or, more likely, composed by a Deuteronomic writer. See my *The Pentateuch*, 122-24 and the references on p. 132, n. 21. The etiological narrative about the incestuous origins of Moabites and Ammonites (Gen 19:30-38) served to disqualify them from participation in the Israelite assembly as *mamzērîm* (Deut 23:2-3[MT 3-4]; cf. Ezra 9:1; Neh 13:1-3, 23), but this disedifying narrative was not originally part of the Abraham cycle. In his dealings with Abimelech in the Negev, Abraham's misgivings about the moral character of the locals proved to be unfounded (Gen 20:11-18).

72. Several scholars have noted parallels between these negotiations and Neo-Babylonian land contracts. See Gene M. Tucker, "The Legal Background of Genesis 23," *JBL* 85 (1966) 77-84; Thompson, *The Historicity of the Patriarchal Narratives*, 295-96; Van Seters, *Abraham in History and Tradition*, 98-101.

of the deportees on the grounds that the promise was always conditional on observance of the moral and ritual law, a condition which they had not observed (Ezek 33:25-29). The Judeans who made the claim in the terms stated were not the only ones, and not the last, to overlook the conditional nature of the promise of land.

The Priestly (P) account of the covenant of circumcision offered to Abraham by Yahweh under the new name El Shaddai in Genesis 17 is clearly of prime importance in the contentious issue of the identity of the "children of Abraham." In the first address of El Shaddai (vv. 1-8), the covenant is made with Abraham and his descendants — *all* his descendants, including the twelve tribes descended from Ishmael. That Abraham will be the ancestor of peoples, not just one people, is stressed redundantly throughout the chapter, and to make the point even clearer we are told that Ishmael was circumcised and therefore received the sign of belonging to the covenant, that very day, well in advance of Isaac (vv. 23-27). But then the story takes a different turn when Abraham, who understandably finds the idea of having a child with a ninety-nine-year-old woman incredible, requests that Ishmael "live in your presence" (v. 18).[73] Yahweh's refusal of the request cannot mean that Ishmael is excluded from the covenant, which would make nonsense of what has been said to this point, but rather that he is not destined to be the *primary* bearer of the promises and commitments expressed in this covenant relationship. We will find a parallel situation with the next generation in which Esau, though firstborn and certainly within the Abrahamic covenant as a direct descendant, is destined to play a secondary role to Jacob (Gen 25:19-26). This interpretation of the passage is in keeping with the remarkably irenic tone of the P History.

With the increasing polarisation of parties, politics, and religious polemics in Judah under, successively, Persian, Ptolemaic, and Seleucid rule, the promise itself became problematic and subject to revision in the terms in which it had been traditionally understood. One example may be cited, a remarkable passage from a late redactional strand in Isaiah which expounds what its author takes to be the real — that is, the eschatological —

---

73. "Living in the presence of God," lit., "before the face of God," has cultic connotations, as occasionally in Psalms (Ps 22:27[MT 28]; 27:8-9; 89:15[16]). Thus Cain's banishment from the presence of Yahweh has undertones of no longer belonging to the Yahweh cult community. Perhaps then Ishmael, though still within the covenant, is no longer within the same cult community as the descent line which passes through Isaac and Jacob. I owe this point to an as yet unpublished paper of Dr. Konrad Schmid of the University of Zürich.

meaning of the name of the prophet's son Shear-Yashub ("a remnant will return"):

> On that day the remnant of Israel and the survivors of the household of Jacob will no longer rely on the one who struck them, but they will rely in truth on Yahweh the Holy One of Israel. A remnant will return, the remnant of Jacob to the God of Might. For even if your people Israel were as numerous as the sand of the sea, only a remnant of them will return. Destruction is decreed, with vindication abounding, for the Sovereign Lord, Yahweh of the hosts, will bring about the destruction that is decreed in the midst of the earth. (Isa 10:20-23)

The few who survived the judgment of exile with their faith intact, the prophetic remnant of Israel, now take the place of the people as numerous as the sands of the sea, a clear echo of the Abrahamic promise (Gen 22:17; 32:12[MT 13]). They also serve as an anticipation of the final convulsive judgment "in the midst of the earth" which only the few, the eschatological remnant, will survive. Implied is a radical reinterpretation of the Abrahamic promise not far removed from the drastic revisionism of early Christian polemics and of John the Baptist, who reminds his listeners that "God is able from these stones to raise up children to Abraham" (Matt 3:9 = Luke 3:8).[74]

---

74. I do not find much in the published Qumran material on the Abrahamic promise apart from the passages from Jubilees and Pseudo-Jubilees. There is the occasional allusion to the covenant with Abraham (CD XII 11, 4Q388a, 4Q389), circumcision (CD XII 6), and the blessing (4Q252 III 7), and in a Communal Confession (4Q393) there is a prayer for the group to which the pray-er belongs to be raised up as the remnant *(šĕʾērît)* of the forefathers in order to obtain the things established for them, the land in the first place. Paul's exegetical arguments in favor of the most inclusive interpretation of the promise (Rom 4:1-25; 9:6-7; Gal 3:6-14) go beyond the scope of our inquiry.

· 2 ·

Ezra

Putting Ezra-Nehemiah in Perspective

The fact that Ezra-Nehemiah is by far the most important historiographical source for our knowledge of Judaism during the Achaemenid
period can easily lead to a distorted and, to that extent, false view of what
was happening in the province of Judah during those two centuries. It is
therefore important to keep in mind other perspectives and the point of
view of other groups and individuals in the background of this text as we
look more closely at the profiles and careers of Ezra and Nehemiah and the
ideology which they embody. Getting a sense of proportion is all the more
important given the dominant prejudice in the biblical texts in favor of
those deported to Babylon, "the good figs" of Jeremiah contrasted with
"the rotten figs," those who remained in the land" (Jer 24:1-10). It will be
apparent that partiality towards the Judeo-Babylonian element is a basic
feature of the way events are related in Ezra-Nehemiah.

One aspect of this ideology inscribed in the texts has to do with the
demographics of the Neo-Babylonian and Persian period province of Judah, what has come to be known as "the myth of the empty land."[1] The
Historian of the Kingdoms concludes his account of Judah under the
monarchy with the lapidary phrase "Judah went into exile out of its land"

1. See Robert P. Carroll, "The Myth of the Empty Land," in *Ideological Criticism of Bibli-
cal Texts,* ed. David Jobling and Tina Pippin. Semeia 59 (Atlanta: Scholars, 1992) 79-93;
Hans M. Barstad, *The Myth of the Empty Land* (Oslo: Scandinavian University Press, 1996);
Joseph Blenkinsopp, "The Bible, Archaeology and Politics; or The Empty Land Revisited,"
JSOT 27 (2002) 169-87.

(2 Kgs 25:21 = Jer 52:27). This finale replicates the conclusion to the history of the kingdom of Samaria after the Assyrian conquest: "So Israel was exiled from their land to Assyria until the present time" (2 Kgs 17:23). The implication of a total or near-total emptying of the land is stated more explicitly in Jer 13:19: "Judah is exiled, totally taken into exile." This totalizing tendency may have been adopted from Assyrian inscriptions which record wholesale deportations. In the eighth century B.C., for example, Tiglath-pileser III claimed to have deported all the men *(puḫur nišešu)* of the house of Omri, namely, the kingdom of Samaria.[2] The author of Chronicles adds a new twist to this claim by introducing the idea that the time of exile was the sabbatical rest of the land (2 Chr 36:20-21), an idea taken over from the conclusion to the so-called Holiness Code (Lev 26:34-35):

> Then the land will enjoy its Sabbaths for as long as it remains desolate; the land will rest and enjoy its Sabbaths for as long as you are in the land of your enemies. For as long as it remains desolate it will make up for the rest it did not have on your Sabbaths when you resided in it.

The resulting inevitable conflict between ideology and reality, theory and facts on the ground, is reflected in the first section of Ezra-Nehemiah, which gives a confusing account of the earliest arrivals from Babylon, the first stage in the re-establishment of the Jerusalem cult, and the various obstacles the immigrants had to overcome (Ezra 1–6). In these chapters we are told that, on arrival, the immigrants all dispersed without let or hindrance to their towns (Ezra 2:70), while at the same time they were living in fear of the local inhabitants (3:3). The idea of a land depopulated as a result of the Babylonian conquest of 589-586 B.C. nevertheless flies in the face of political and social realities. It is generally accepted that the figures given in Jer 52:28-30 for the three deportations (in 597, 586 and 582 B.C.) provide a more reliable guide than the incomplete and much higher statistics in the History (2 Kgs 24:14-16; 25:11-12). Even if it represents only adult males, the Jeremian total of 4,600 for all three deportations must surely represent no more than 10 percent of the population of the province, and perhaps quite a bit less, while the total of 18,000 provided by the Historian of the Kingdoms (2 Kgs 24:14-16) for only the first of the three does not inspire confidence. This is especially so since the author informs us that only

---

2. On this and similar claims, see Bustenay Oded, *Mass Deportations and Deportees in the Neo-Assyrian Empire* (Wiesbaden: Reichert, 1979).

the poorest of the land *(dallat hā'āreṣ)* were left after both deportations (2 Kgs 24:14; 25:12). The Babylonian punitive campaign targeted Jerusalem, "the rebellious city harmful to kings and provinces" (Ezra 4:15). It was not in the interests of the conquerors to devastate the land and depopulate it. There were executions, certainly, and no doubt many died in the course of the campaign, but we should not underestimate the resilience of a population in such a situation to restore a semblance of normality. Many would have withdrawn to one or another of the inaccessible refuges with which the country is liberally supplied to reemerge when the dust had settled, as their descendants would do during later invasions of Macedonians, Ptolemies, Seleucids, and Romans. In fact, we are told that many of those who had gone to ground returned after the appointment of Gedaliah as governor (Jer 40:7; cf. 2 Kgs 25:23), some from the Transjordanian region (Jer 40:11-12), others from as far away as Egypt. The net result is that the first immigrants from Babylonia in the early Persian period, and the later group which accompanied Ezra in the seventh year of Artaxerxes I, entered a land with a more substantial and varied population than the canonical book Ezra-Nehemiah and the parallel version in 1 Esdras would give us to understand. We can therefore appreciate the difficulty of extracting information from our sources about these other Judeans, the almost silent majority, their religious views and their cultural and intellectual activity in general.

The Ezra Story

Ezra-Nehemiah, the book, is therefore the crucial text for understanding Jewish origins, but one which poses more problems for the alert reader than any other canonical composition. It should be obvious, in the first place, that it is not a book as we understand books. Like most biblical books, it was expanded and edited over a considerable period of time. In some cases the existence of earlier and later components is obvious. It names Levites active "in the days of Nehemiah the governor and Ezra the priest and scribe" (Neh 12:26), implying that this lay some considerable time in the past. It lists the high-priestly succession down to Jaddua, contemporary of Darius III and Alexander, more than a century after the time of Nehemiah in the mid-fifth century (Neh 12:11; *Ant.* 11.302-47). Other instances are less transparent. Several commentators have argued that

Nehemiah's covenant (Nehemiah 10) is considerably later than the time of Nehemiah, perhaps the outcome of a movement of renewal inspired by Levites in the early Hellenistic period. This hypothesis is based on a close scrutiny of Nehemiah's reforming activity documented in the last chapter of the book, to which the stipulations of the covenant closely correspond. We shall return to it at a later point of our inquiry. Other commentators maintain that the account of the first return and settlement under the early Achaemenids (Cyrus to Darius I) recorded in Ezra 1–6 derives from the author of Chronicles or the school of the Chronicler and is later than the account of the activity of Ezra and Nehemiah which was already in place. Convinced that the traditions about Ezra and Nehemiah developed independently of each other, others again have made out a case that the Nehemiah narrative was a later addition to the Ezra material. And this is not to inventory the many essays in literary analysis which divide up the text into several chronologically sequential layers.[3] All of this is hypothetical to a greater or lesser extent, but what is certain is that throughout this process emphasis would have been on the two principal protagonists, but less as objects of biographical interest than as emblematic and expressive of specific ideological agendas. This perspective will dictate the direction our investigation will take, and it is undertaken in the belief that to understand what Ezra and Nehemiah stand for is to understand something important about the origins of Judaism.

Our focus in what follows will therefore be exclusively on the profiles, agendas, and programs of the principals, Ezra and Nehemiah.[4]

About Ezra, the biblical book (and, at a secondary level, 1 Esdras and Josephus, *Ant.* 11.120-58) contains the following:

(1) An autobiographical account of his arrival in Jerusalem from Babylon during the reign of the Persian ruler Artaxerxes (most probably Arta-

---

3. Recent examples of redactional maximalism: Reinhard G. Kratz, *The Composition of the Narrative Books of the Old Testament* (London: T. & T. Clark, 2005) 49-86 (trans. of *Die Komposition der erzählenden Bücher des Alten Testaments* [Göttingen: Vandenhoeck & Ruprecht, 2000]); Juha Pakkala, *Ezra the Scribe: The Development of Ezra 7–10 and Nehemiah 8.* BZAW 347 (Berlin: de Gruyter, 2004).

4. The order in which the principals are treated is the order in the canonical book, but also assumes the chronological priority of Ezra to Nehemiah, that is, that Ezra arrived in Jerusalem in the seventh year of Artaxerxes I and Nehemiah in the twentieth year of the same monarch, therefore 458 and 445 B.C., respectively. For the defense of this order, see my *Ezra-Nehemiah.* OTL (Philadelphia: Westminster, 1988) 139-44.

xerxes I, 465-424 B.C.). His mission is authorized by an imperial rescript, and he is at the head of a company of immigrants bearing votive offerings for the temple (Ezra 7:11–8:34). This section has an introduction (7:1-10) and a conclusion (8:35-36), both in third person narrative form.

(2) An account in narrative form of Ezra's participation in the public reading and interpretation of the law leading to preparations for celebrating the festival of Sukkoth (Neh 7:73[MT 72]–8:18). The celebration of Sukkoth, or at least the preparation for the festival, is included since it contains the last mention of Ezra (Neh 8:13). On the second day of the seventh month (Tishri), in the course of a kind of seminar led by Ezra, those present come across the regulations governing the celebration of the festival and proceed to implement them. The inclusion of this passage is also suggested by the sequence of dates, from the first day of the seventh month when Israelites settled in their towns (Neh 7:73[72]; 8:2), to the second day of the same month when the people assembled around Ezra to hear the law explained to them (8:13), then to the twenty-fourth day of the same month when they celebrated a penitential liturgy (9:1).[5]

(3) An account, part first person, part third person, of a crisis caused by marriages contracted with native Judean women by men from the Babylonian diaspora, those already in the province and no doubt some of the new arrivals (Ezra 9–10). Ezra and his supporters adopt extreme measures to rectify the situation.

We will take a closer look at these three episodes in sequence.

(1) Ezra's Mission (Ezra 7:1–8:34)

Assuming that the monarch in the seventh year of whose reign Ezra arrived is Artaxerxes I (Ezra 7:7), the year would have been 458 B.C., leaving a gap of fifty-seven years counting from the last date mentioned in Ezra 1–6, that is, the fourteenth of the first month of 515 B.C. (6:19; cf. 6:15).[6] Apart from the complaints about Jewish immigrants addressed to the central au-

---

5. See further my *Ezra-Nehemiah*, 282-97.

6. For those who still argue for Artaxerxes II, the gap would be 117 years, that is, 515 to 398 B.C. It is interesting to note that 70 years — give or take a few months to allow for uncertainty about the beginning of the reign of Darius I — elapsed between the fall of Jerusalem and the completion of the second temple, and another 70 between the completion of the temple and Nehemiah's arrival in the province and completion of the wall of Jerusalem.

thorities during the reigns of Xerxes and Artaxerxes I (4:6-24), the record is silent about what happened during a gap covering most of the reign of Darius I, the entire reign of Xerxes, and the early years of Artaxerxes I. Ezra 7–10 therefore represents an independent block of narrative material, yet at the same time it seems to have been put together with the preceding block (Ezra 1–6) in mind. In other words, the account of the mission and activity of Ezra replicates in outline and in many points of detail the account of the first settlement, and does so in such a way as to suggest that the arrival of Ezra represents either a new beginning after a dark period or an alternative version of origins. The primordiality of Ezra, explicit in Second Ezra, where he is resident in Babylon thirty years after the fall of Jerusalem (2 Esd 3:1), is insinuated right at the beginning in the genealogy which represents him, in defiance of chronology, as the son and successor to the last preexilic high priest (7:1-5). The terms in which his mission is authorized in the imperial rescript confirm this impression of laying the foundations for a new beginning for the Jewish ethnos in Judah, indeed in the Trans-Euphrates satrapy as a whole.

The structural and thematic parallels between Ezra 1–6 and Ezra 7–10 are impressive. In both sections the action is set in motion by imperial decrees which manifest an amazing level of generosity towards the Jewish people (1:4; 6:1-12; 7:11-26). These decrees co-opt the resources and energies of the local imperial authorities on behalf of the Jerusalem temple (6:13; 7:21-24) and threaten punishment for noncompliance (6:11; 7:26). To this munificence are added generous subventions and votive offerings for the temple and "the God of heaven" from those who did not accompany the immigrants (1:4, 6; 7:16). On both occasions the sacred vessels for use in temple liturgy, originally broken up for bullion by the Babylonians (2 Kgs 24:13; 25:15), are returned (Ezra 1:7-11; 7:19; 8:27-30).[7] Both narratives provide a list of immigrants (2:1-67; 8:1-14), and on both occasions the primary aim is the restoration of worship, especially sacrificial worship (2:68–3:3; 6:17; 8:32-35). Both stress the important role of Levites (1:5; 3:8-11). They are appointed to their tasks after the first arrival (3:8), and their absence from the ranks of the immigrant group had to be made good before the second caravan could leave (8:15-20). Both groups celebrate Sukkoth in

---

7. Peter R. Ackroyd, "The Temple Vessels: A Continuity Theme," in *Studies in the Religion of Ancient Israel.* VTSup 23 (1972) 166-81; repr. in *Studies in the Religious Tradition of the Old Testament* (London: SCM, 1987) 46-60.

the seventh month (3:4; Neh 8:13-18), and it appears that, as the first chapter ends with Passover, so the second begins with the celebration of the same festival. Ezra fixed the date of departure from Babylon on the first of Nisan (Ezra 7:9; cf. Exod 12:2), and they set off on the twelfth of the same month (Ezra 8:31), which implies that they would have celebrated Passover en route like their ancestors coming out of Egypt. The significance of Passover as marking the inauguration of a new epoch is more clearly apparent in 1 Esdras, in which the first phase of the history begins with Josiah's Passover and concludes with the celebration of the same festival during the reign of Darius (1 Esd 1:1–7:15). Both groups, finally, experience opposition, the first from outside their ranks (4:1-5), the second from within (9–10).

It looks, in short, as if Ezra 7–10 was intended to promote the primordiality of Ezra's achievement, perhaps based on the premiss that earlier attempts had been flawed and incomplete. Judgment on the earlier generation of immigrants is suggested by the emotional reaction of Ezra on hearing the news of the marriages and his complaints about the infidelity *(ma'al)* of the *golah* group (Ezra 9:2, 4; 10:6). A negative judgment on the earlier generation of immigrants would also be consistent with the unexplained disappearance from the record of Zerubbabel and Joshua the high priest sometime during the reign of Darius and their substitution by the elders and the governor in negotiations with the satrapal authorities (5:3-17; 6:6-15). If Malachi is dated during the gap between the sixth year of Darius I and the seventh year of Artaxerxes I, a distinct possibility, his excoriation of the temple priesthood would fit the pattern of a bad period calling for a radical solution (Mal 1:6–2:9). Further corroboration of this reading of the narrative structure would be the chronologically impossible presentation of Ezra as direct successor to Seraiah, last Jerusalemite high priest executed by the Babylonians (Ezra 7:1-5; 2 Kgs 25:18-21), an anticipation of the backdating of Ezra to the immediate aftermath of the Babylonian conquest in the Ezra Apocalypse (4 Ezra).

There are other questions arising from the autobiographical sections of the Ezra story, which for convenience we will refer to as the Ezra memoir, which would call for discussion in a commentary but are not directly relevant to our present agenda and may therefore be simply mentioned without extensive comment. These questions would include the following: Are these first person passages excerpts from a longer memoir? Were they written by Ezra, or is the first person mode a literary device, perhaps (as some suppose) with a view to matching and competing with the Nehemiah memoir? How does the first person part relate to the juxtaposed narrative in the third person? These are interesting questions which can be left aside for the time being. There is, however, one point about the extent of the memoir which should be made. When Ezra thanks God for having made the Persian monarch well-disposed towards him, referring to the imperial firman, he mentions only the measures of Artaxerxes with respect to the temple and says nothing about law enforcement, though the decree deals with both (7:27-28). This would seem to imply that the decree immediately preceding (7:11-26), whatever its origin, was considered in the logical structure of the book as a whole as part of the memoir.

The Artaxerxes decree itself raises a host of issues on which an immense amount has been written. While aware that no proposal on the historical character of the rescript will go unchallenged, I will argue for one approach, leaving the reader to consult the commentaries for alternative interpretations, of which there are many. Briefly, then, I would maintain, first, that it is not in itself historically implausible that such a decree was issued. The central government did send individuals on specific missions to different parts of the empire, and the so-called Passover Papyrus from Elephantine is one of several indications that the authorities were not averse in specific situations to micromanaging affairs, including religious affairs, through their local representatives in the provinces.[8] Certain features of the rescript — the use of Aramaic, the diplomatic *lingua franca* of the Achaemenid Empire, and the occasional Persian loanword — are meant to enhance the impression that this was in fact a transcript of an authentic document.[9]

The Jewish character of the text is, notwithstanding, abundantly in evidence. The language of "volunteering" to go to Judah and to make offer-

---

8. For the text, see A. E. Cowley, *Aramaic Papyri of the Fifth Century B.C.* (1923; repr. Osnabrück: Zeller, 1967) 60-65. For other examples, see Elias J. Bickerman, "The Babylonian Captivity," *CHJ* 1 (1984) 357; Muhammad A. Dandamaev and Vladimir G. Lukonin, *The Culture and Social Institutions of Ancient Iran* (Cambridge: Cambridge University Press, 1989) 360-66; Joseph Blenkinsopp, "Temple and Society in Achaemenid Judah," in *Second Temple Studies*, vol. 1: *The Persian Period*, ed. Philip R. Davies, JSOTSup 117 (Sheffield: JSOT, 1991) 24-26.

9. It begins with the introductory formula which employs technical terms from Old Persian: "This is a copy of the memorandum" *(vězeh paršegen hanništěvān . . .)*. Adding local color, as with the allusion to the seven royal counsellors (cf. Herodotus 3.3, 31, 71, 83-84; Xenophon *Anab.* 1.6 4-5; Esth 1:14), would not have been difficult as we may see from the book of Esther.

ings for the temple (Ezra 7:13, 15-16), used also in the Cyrus decree (1:4), is characteristic of the books of Chronicles,[10] as is the expression "Judah and Jerusalem," which occurs some twenty-five times in 1 and 2 Chronicles and rarely elsewhere. "Israel," with the technical connotation of laity as opposed to priests and other cult personnel, is also late Judean usage and is completely out of place in an official imperial edict.[11] The list of sacrificial offerings (steers, rams, and lambs), identical with those mentioned in the decree of Darius (6:9), is also standard in Chronicles,[12] and a particularly telling instance is the allusion in the decree to these sacrificial animals and *their* corresponding cereal and drink offerings, a detailed point of Judean and early Jewish liturgical praxis with which the imperial court could hardly be expected to be familiar (7:17; cf. Num 15:1-16). The offerings and subventions for the temple, in amounts beyond dreams of avarice, not only replicate those mentioned in the decrees of Cyrus and Darius (Ezra 1:4; 6:17) but also recall offerings made at the dedication of Solomon's temple in the Chronicler's version of the event (1 Chr 29:6-9).[13]

It seems unnecessary to hold that the rescript within the rescript, enjoining on the authorities in the Trans-Euphrates satrapy to provide whatever Ezra requests (7:21-24), reproduces a distinct document, perhaps based on an original from the Seleucid period.[14] On the contrary, it is as thoroughly Jewish as the rest of the Artaxerxes rescript and parallels the decree of Darius previously recorded (6:9-10). The beneficiary of this lavish imperial generosity is referred to as "Ezra priest (and) scribe" (*'ezrā' kāhănâ sāfar),* no

---

10. *hitnāddēv,* 1 Chr 29:5, 6, 9, 14, 17; 2 Chr 17:16; also Ezra 1:6; 2:68; 3:5; Neh 11:2.

11. 1 Chr 9:2; 2 Chr 7:6; 19:8; 35:18; Ezra 9:1; 10:5, 25; Neh 11:3.

12. 1 Chr 29:21; 2 Chr 29:21, 32; cf. Ezra 8:35.

13. One illustration of the range of opinion is the article of Ulrich Kellermann, "Erwägungen zum Problem der Esradatierung," *ZAW* 80 (1968) 55-87, who argued that only the rescript and the list of precious metals and vessels in Ezra 8:26-27 represented authentic historical material and the rest of the Ezra story consisted in midrash composed by the author of Chronicles. Similar in that respect is the conclusion of Reinhard Kratz, *The Composition of the Narrative Books of the Old Testament,* 76-77, that the only historically credible part of the rescript is the rescript within the rescript addressed to the Trans-Euphratene treasurers (Ezra 7:21-22). There is then the problem that this paragraph contains the command to hand over to Ezra 100 talents of silver (about three and a quarter tons); cf. the total of 350 silver talents annual tribute from the entire Trans-Euphratene satrapy including the Phoenician cities, Syria, and Cyprus (Herodotus 3.91).

14. As proposed by W. Th. In der Smitten, *Esra: Quellen, Überlieferung und Geschichte.* SSN 15 (Assen: Van Gorcum, 1973) 19.

different from the rest of the edict (7:12), and those exempt from taxation are "priests, Levites, liturgical musicians, gatekeepers and temple servants" (7:24), the same categories and in the same order as in the introduction to Ezra's mission (7:7) and in the census list of Ezra 2. The reason given why measures to be taken on behalf of the temple and its personnel are required, namely, "lest (divine) wrath *(qeṣef)* come on the kingdom, the king, and his descendants" (7:23), reproduces a common theme in Chronicles, using in Hebrew much the same language as the Aramaic of the decree.[15]

The Deuteronomistic-Chronistic echoes continue to be heard loud and clear in the final section of the edict in which Ezra is directed to enforce observance of the law and appoint magistrates and judges (7:25-26). An expression such as "the wisdom of your God with which you are entrusted," parallel with "the law of your God with which you are entrusted" (v. 14), corresponds to a familiar Deuteronomic trope, namely, the law as the form of wisdom peculiar to Israel (Deut 4:6). It has no place in an Achaemenid royal document. The appointment of magistrates and judges also corresponds to the injunction to set up judges and officials in Deut 16:18, an injunction faithfully carried out as part of King Jehoshaphat's reforms according to Chronicles (2 Chr 19:4-11). A final parallel: "the law of your God and the law of the king" — two branches of law rather than one and the same law sponsored by both God and the king[16] — is reminiscent of measures undertaken by Jehoshaphat, one of the few good Judean kings according to the Historian, in setting up a final court of judicial appeal under the chief priest responsible for "the matter of Yahweh" and the governor charged with responsibility for "the matter of the king" (2 Chr 19:11; cf. 1 Chr 26:32). In this instance sacral and civil law called for two distinct jurisdictions, but in view of his dual office of priest and scribe Ezra could assume responsibility for both.[17]

A problem of a different kind is that of reconciling Ezra's mission as set out in the rescript with the jurisdiction of the satrap of the Trans-Euphrates region who is not even mentioned in the royal decree. There

---

15. This especially when dealing with neglect of temple worship as bringing down divine wrath on the people (2 Chr 19:2, 10; 24:18; 29:8).

16. As argued by Rolf Rendtorff, "Esra und das Gesetz," *ZAW* 96 (1984) 165-84.

17. The repetition of *dātā* ("the law") before "your God" and "the king" renders less likely the alternative reference to one and the same law, in the sense that the king endows the Jewish Torah with his own authority; *pace* Wilhelm Rudolph, *Esra und Nehemia samt 3. Esra* (Tübingen: Mohr, 1949) 75; Raymond A. Bowman, "Ezra and Nehemiah," *IB* 3 (1954) 630, et al.

may be an explanation for this extraordinary omission, perhaps in the disturbances in *Ebir-nāri* connected with the Egyptian revolt which lasted for most of the first decade of the reign.[18] But the broad judicial authority covering the entire satrapy given to Ezra, including remitting taxation, a matter over which the central authority was particularly anxious to maintain control, equals and even exceeds the normal range of satrapal authority. No less remarkable is the account of Ezra's group delivering the king's instructions to the satraps (sic) and governors of *Ebir-nāri* (Ezra 8:36).

It is not surprising, therefore, that the historical character of the rescript and of the other documents in Ezra-Nehemiah deemed to have been promulgated by Achaemenid rulers (Cyrus in Ezra 1:2-4 and 6:2-5, Darius in Ezra 6:6-12, Artaxerxes in Ezra 4:17-22 and 7:11-26) — and indeed the historical character of the Ezra story as a whole — has been endlessly debated and the debate will certainly continue.[19] In the early modern period Ezra-Nehemiah was regarded by most critical scholars as the continuation of 1-2 Chronicles. Those who defended or simply assumed this position, and there are scholars who still do so, had to take up the broader issue of the reliability of the information provided in 1-2 Chronicles.[20] Various assessments were made as to the respective roles of Ezra and Nehemiah and their chronological sequence, but there was little discussion about the historical character of Ezra until 1889, when two French scholars, Charles Bellangé and Maurice Vernes, came out with the radical idea that the traditions about Ezra were historically unreliable and Ezra himself largely a legendary figure. Four years later a more famous radical, Ernest Renan, argued that the Ezra figure was created by priests with a view to countering the prestige of the layman Nehemiah, a view perhaps influenced by the author's experience as a seminarian at Saint Sulpice.[21]

18. Such a situation may be hinted at in the correspondence between officialdom in Samaria and Artaxerxes recorded in Ezra 4:7-23.

19. The historicity issue is discussed by Lester L. Grabbe, "Reconstructing History from the Book of Ezra," in Davies, *Second Temple Studies*, 1:98-106; "What Was Ezra's Mission?" in *Second Temple Studies*, vol. 2: *Temple and Community in the Persian Period*, ed. Tamara C. Eskenazi and Kent H. Richards. JSOTSup 175 (Sheffield: JSOT, 1994) 286-99.

20. For a relatively benign judgment on this issue see Sara Japhet, "The Historical Reliability of Chronicles: The History of the Problem and Its Place in Biblical Research," *JSOT* 33 (1985) 83-107; repr. *From the Rivers of Babylon to the Highlands of Judah* (Winona Lake, Indiana: Eisenbrauns, 2006) 117-36.

21. *Histoire du Peuple d'Israël*, 4 (Paris: Calmann-Levy, 1893) 96-106.

None of these early essays proved as influential as the writings on the subject of Charles Cutler Torrey published over a period of more than half a century beginning in 1896. Some of the more important of these are available in his *Ezra Studies*, with a useful Prolegomenon by his former student William F. Stinespring.[22] Torrey carried the already well-established idea of the Chronicler as author of the Ezra narrative a step further by arguing that the entire Ezra story including the rescript, whether in Hebrew or Aramaic, whether in the first or the third person, is a fiction of the Chronicler created without benefit of sources. With Nehemiah the situation is different, since Torrey accepted the basic authenticity of the memoir in Nehemiah 1–2 and 4:1(MT 3:33)–6:19. Torrey wrote with wit and grace but took no prisoners; here is his judgment on the Chronicler as author of the Ezra story:

> It is evident that the Chronicler became an editor more from necessity than from choice. By taste and gift he was a novelist. He would doubtless have preferred to give freer rein to his imagination in composing the story of the Jews and their antecedents. But he was now writing not to interest but with an apologetic purpose. (*Ezra Studies*, 250-51)

At first widely rejected and even scorned, Torrey's conclusions came to exert an influence which can be seen, for example, in the commentary of Gustav Hölscher.[23] Sigmund Mowinckel mitigated Torrey's negative evaluation somewhat by arguing that the Chronicler had access to a source for the Ezra story but one which can no longer be recovered. A variation on this admittedly not very helpful suggestion was adopted by his successor in the chair at the University of Oslo, Arvid Kapelrud.[24] As noted earlier, Ulrich Kellermann accepted only the rescript as authentic — which is strange, since the indications of Chronistic influence (not authorship) are more clearly in evidence there than elsewhere. He argued, less confidently, for the authenticity of the list of bullion and vessels brought by Ezra for the temple in Ezra 8:26-27 — which is even stranger since the amounts are impossibly high. Kellermann proposed that the rest of the Ezra material

---

22. Charles C. Torrey, *Ezra Studies* (1910; repr. New York: Ktav, 1970).

23. *Die Bücher Esra und Nehemia*, 4th ed. HSAT 2 (Tübingen: Mohr, 1923).

24. Sigmund Mowinckel, *Studien zu dem Buche Ezra-Nehemia*, vol. 3: *Die Ezrageschichte und das Gesetz Moses* (Oslo: Universitetsforlaget, 1965); Arvid S. Kapelrud, *The Question of Authorship in the Ezra-Narrative: A Lexical Investigation* (Oslo: Dybwad, 1944).

was worked up as a kind of midrash on the rescript, later expanded by a *listenfreudig* scribe of the Hasmonaean period.[25] The midrash idea was taken up a few years later by W. Th. In der Smitten[26] but has not enjoyed much vogue among scholars in recent years.

A more elaborate approach to historicity was that of J. C. H. Lebram, according to whom the Ezra *Gestalt,* created as a mirror image and counter to Nehemiah, was generated out of the conflicts and controversies of the Hasmonaean period and was probably modeled on a founder of a dissident group at that time.[27] It is easy to accept a connection between personalities and issues in Ezra-Nehemiah and the emergence of sects in the Hasmonaean period, a point to which we shall return, but the decision about priority (Ezra traditions generated out of those about Nehemiah or the reverse) is more difficult to decide, and the historical character of Ezra as a powerful figure from the Persian period cannot so easily be reduced to a fictional retrojection. In Giovanni Garbini's *History and Ideology in Ancient Israel,* the biblical Ezra is nevertheless put to the sword in summary fashion and then resurrected in the person of the high priest Alcimus around the middle of the second century B.C.[28] The most recent contribution to the debate at the time of writing is that of Juha Pakkala. Pakkala is a redactional maximalist who claims to identify an extremely exiguous narrative core about Ezra, amplified successively by the itinerary narrative in ch. 8, the prayer in ch. 9, an expansion of the rescript in ch. 7, diverse contributions from *golah*-editors and Levitical editors, and various bits and pieces.[29]

In spite of the prevailing uncertainty, I believe there exists broad agreement among critical scholars that, if Artaxerxes did issue a rescript authorizing Ezra's mission, it has been heavily edited by a Jewish scribe, whether during the reign of Artaxerxes or later, whether employed at the court in Susa or resident elsewhere. The question to be decided then is whether the indications of contributions from a Jewish scribe, or Jewish scribes, are so prevalent and obtrusive as to suggest a Jewish literary creation rather than a heavily edited Jewish version of a Persian rescript. The position adopted

25. Kellermann, *ZAW* 80 (1968) 55-87.

26. In der Smitten, *Esra.*

27. J. C. H. Lebram, "Die Traditionsgeschichte der Esragestalt und die Frage nach dem historischen Esra," in *Sources, Structures and Synthesis,* ed. Heleen Sancisi-Weerdenburg. Achaemenid History 1 (Leiden: Nederlands Instituut voor het Nabije Oosten, 1987) 103-38.

28. (New York: Crossroad, 1988) 151-69.

29. Pakkala, *Ezra the Scribe.* See the chart summarizing his redactional stages, p. 301.

here is that the indications of dependence on Deuteronomy and Chronicles are clearly and abundantly in evidence to such an extent as to suggest that, whatever the historical and documentary basis on which it may have been constructed, the edict is, *in effect,* a Jewish literary creation. One possibility is that the rescript has conflated the profile of Ezra as restorer of the temple cult (Ezra 8) with that of Ezra as enforcer of the law (Ezra 9–10). There is no question that a Jewish author, writing during the late Persian or early Hellenistic period, could compose such a text in passable Aramaic. Allusions in Esther to edicts recorded by secretaries and dispatched into the provinces (Esth 3:12-15; 8:9-10), one aspect of the rich Persian coloring of that narrative, betray easy familiarity with the protocol and procedures of the Achaemenid court. That the rescript is the creation of a Jewish scribe does not, however, necessarily and of itself compromise the essential historicity of Ezra. All it implies is that attempts to extract a core of authenticity from the decree have not been successful and that therefore the imperial decree of authorization, if it ever existed, is no longer available to us.

If the decree is, in effect, a Jewish creation, it would in all probability have originated among the supporters of Ezra — of whom more will be said later — and as essentially their creation it would have served as a post-factum legitimation for control of the temple and its resources by the Ezra faction. It would also have supplied the authoritative basis for enforcing the law (in reality a particular and by no means obvious interpretation of a law) in the Trans-Euphrates satrapy, or at least in Judah, in the matter of marriage with local women (Ezra 9–10). When viewed from this ideological perspective, therefore, the narrative in Ezra 7–10, inclusive of the rescript, constitutes a well-integrated whole.

There is also some uncertainty concerning the tasks assigned to Ezra. While the rescript addresses him as charged with the dual assignments of restoring the Jerusalem cult and enforcing observance of the laws, in his prayerful reaction to it Ezra refers only to the first of these tasks:

> Blessed be Yahweh God of our ancestors who has so disposed the mind of the king to beautify the house of Yahweh which is in Jerusalem, and has made the king, his councillors and all his powerful officials well disposed towards me. (Ezra 7:27-28)

The profile of Ezra as leader of a caravan of immigrants with a strong interest in the Jerusalem temple, a later counterpart to Sheshbazzar, Zerubbabel, and Jeshua, is in itself quite credible and is confirmed by hints in the text that work on the temple continued beyond the reign of Darius I into that of Artaxerxes I. This is a hypothesis worth entertaining. We are told that the building of the temple was completed in accordance with decrees from Cyrus, Darius, and Artaxerxes (Ezra 6:14), on the face of it inconsistent with the notice in the following verse that the temple was completed in the sixth year of Darius — unless the monarch referred to is Darius II (423-405 B.C.), which seems unlikely. In his prayer, Ezra speaks of the raising up of the house of their God and repair of its ruins as brought about with the benevolent assistance of the Persian kings, which, in the context, would naturally include the Artaxerxes rescript (Ezra 9:9).[30] But it would be difficult, perhaps impossible, to reconcile this role with the profile of Ezra as representative and emissary of the Great King. This charge would have been essentially a one-person task, and the chosen individual would have had to be a person of high rank to be charged with a mandate to enforce "the law of your God and the law of the king" in the Jewish population of the entire Trans-Euphrates satrapy. The parallels for this role which come to mind are the Egyptian notable Udjahorresnet and the Milesian Histiaeus, both in the service of Darius I. The former, whose autobiographical account was written on his basalt statue now in the Vatican Museum, was sent from Susa back to Egypt in the third year of the reign of Darius I in order to reform the cult at the great sanctuary in Sais and reestablish the "Houses of Life," centers for the study of ritual and cultic matters and scribal activity in general.[31] The Milesian aristocrat Histiaeus, Darius's Ionian expert, requested and obtained permission to return to his own city Miletus in order to pacify Ionia (Herodotus 5.106-8; 6.1-5). Less reliable, and also less sycophantic, than his Egyptian counterpart, Histiaeus got himself into trouble with both Ionians and Persians and came to a bad end. While neither of these accounts is free from ideological bias — blatant self-interest in the case of the Udjahorresnet inscription, blatant hostility in Herodotus's account of Histiaeus — their respective

---

30. If work on the temple continued into the reign of Artaxerxes I it would help to explain the surprising notice in 2 Macc 1:18 that it was built by Nehemiah. Diana V. Edelman, *The Origins of the 'Second' Temple. Persian Imperial Policy and the Rebuilding of Jerusalem* (London/Oakville: Equinox, 2005) argues that the temple was built, not just completed, during the reign of Artaxerxes I. It is unfortunately impossible to address and critique the complex of arguments which she adduces in arriving at that conclusion.

31. On Udjahorresnet see below, 94-97.

profiles emerge clearly enough. This is not the case with Ezra since the biblical account, the product of a long process of editorial activity, oscillates between his priestly and scribal roles and attributes, between concern with law and with cult, and between the individual and the group.

Ezra's dual role — priest and scribe — comes to the fore in the narrative sequel to the rescript. The account of the return under Ezra's leadership focuses exclusively on the temple (8:1-36), while the following episode, dealing with the marriage crisis, is concerned exclusively with law and legal interpretation and says nothing of consequence about the temple (9–10).[32] There is therefore reason to wonder whether both roles were originally predicated of the one subject or whether one of the two was primary and the other added.

Ezra led the return to Jerusalem in his capacity as priest and restorer of the temple cult. The names and statistics in the list of those who accompanied him amount to 1,513 adult males (1,690 in 1 Esd 8:28-40), therefore four or five times that number of women and children are to be included. The list comprises two representatives of the emerging Aaronid priestly faction (Gershom and Daniel descendants of Phineas and Ithamar respectively), a descendant of the Judean royal house (Hattush ben Shecaniah), and members of twelve of the seventeen phratries in the caravan which is reported to have made the journey more than half a century earlier under the leadership of Zerubbabel and Jeshua (Ezra 2:1-67). Whatever the date and purpose of this earlier list of *golah* Jews,[33] it is quite credible that members of the same extended families or clans in Babylon might, at a later time, have decided to join their kinsfolk in that distant western province. In any case, whatever its origin and date of composition, the list of Judaeo-Babylonians who accompanied Ezra (8:1-14) provides a realistic and plausible glimpse into family groupings and relations between Judah and the eastern diaspora during the period in question. For the historian,

---

32. The one exception is the allusion to rebuilding and repairing the temple in the psalm of communal lamentation put into Ezra's mouth (9:9).

33. In *Ezra-Nehemiah*, 79-98, I presented the case, accepted by many commentators, for a date much later in the Achaemenid period. Hugh Williamson argued for the dependence of the Ezra 2 version of the list on Nehemiah 7 and for its authenticity as reproducing a list of "returnees" during the first twenty years or so of Achaemenid rule; see his *Ezra, Nehemiah*. WBC 16 (Waco: Word, 1985) 28-32; and "Judah and the Jews," in *Studies in Persian History: Essays in Memory of David M. Lewis,* ed. Maria Brosius and Amélie Kuhrt. Achaemenid History 11 (Leiden: Nederlands Instituut voor het Nabije Oosten, 1999) 149-51.

in fact, the lists in Ezra 2/Nehemiah 7 and Ezra 8 are among the least opaque source material in the book.

The checklist of "volunteers" who accompanied Ezra revealed that Levites, scant in numbers in the first migration (74 as against 4,289 priests) but required by the wording of Artaxerxes' rescript (7:13), were conspicuous by their absence. This deficit had to be made good, and it was made good by recruiting forty Levites, together with other cult personnel, from "Casiphia the place," an establishment under the direction of a certain Iddo (8:15-20). Iddo is a priestly name, and we may surely assume that the place in question was a place of worship of however modest proportions, since a clergy training center existing on its own somewhere in southern Mesopotamia seems highly unlikely.[34] The actual journey, described with undertones of the exodus and the trek through the wilderness traditions, took about four months (7:7-9; 8:31) and was completed without incident. On arrival in Jerusalem the votive offerings and precious vessels were delivered safely to the temple clergy (8:31-34).

The final paragraph (8:35-36), no longer in first person discourse, serves as the finale to this first episode. It concludes this part of the memoir as the third person passage in 7:1-10 introduces it.[35] It recounts the last stage of the relocation from Babylon: offering sacrifices, financed no doubt with donations mentioned in the rescript (8:35; 7:17), followed by delivery

34. As far as I know, Laurence E. Browne, "A Jewish Sanctuary in Babylonia," *JTS* 17 (1916) 400-1, was the first to propose that "Casiphia the place" was a Jewish temple. The peculiar designation brings to mind the Deuteronomistic use of "place" *(māqôm)* for the temple in Jerusalem (Deut 12:5; 1 Kgs 8:29; Jer 7:3, 6, 7). The possibility cannot be dismissed on account of the Deuteronomistic program of cult centralization since we do not know that it applied outside Judah. It certainly did not inhibit the Elephantine Jews from building a temple. See Rudolph, *Esra und Nehemia samt 3. Esra*, 83; Morton Smith, *Palestinian Parties and Politics That Shaped the Old Testament* (New York: Columbia University Press, 1971) 90-91. Smith thought it more likely that, following Zech 5:5-11 (the vision of the female figurine in a barrel being transported to Shinar where a temple was to be built for her), a syncretistic place of worship was built in Babylonia at the time the temple in Jerusalem was being rebuilt. The female in question, however, is more likely Asherah than Anath; her code name is "The Wickedness" *(hāriš'â*, suggestive of *'ăšērâ* by assonance).

35. The temporal phrase *bā'ēt hahî'* ("at that time") belongs at the beginning of v. 35 rather than at the end of v. 34; cf. the equally vague temporal indicator at the beginning of the introduction to the episode, *vě'aḥar haddĕvārîm ha'ēlleh* ("following on these events," 7:1). We would also expect Ezra to have delivered the royal commands to the satrapal authorities and to have told us that he did it, but the task was carried out by "the exiles who had come from the captivity."

of the king's instructions to the local Persian authorities (8:36). Emphasis is squarely on the group rather than on Ezra. They are described in full and solemn fashion as "the exiles back from the captivity" *(habbāʾîm mēhaššĕvî bĕnê-haggôlâ)*. The conviction that they are the ones who have inherited the ancient traditions and therefore embody the true Israel, the twelve-tribal Israel, is expressed in numerical symbolism in the twelvefold list of kinship groups (8:1-14), the twelve priests assigned the task of transporting the precious vessels (8:24), and the listing of sacrificial animals according to twelve and its multiples (96 and 72). What it means is that they, and they alone, are the true and authentic descendants of the twelve-tribal Israel of the exodus, wilderness, and conquest traditions.

(2) Reading and Interpreting the Law (Neh 7:73b[72b]–8:18)

At this point there is, in the opinion of most scholars, a major displacement in the order of events described.[36] It seems that the public reading of the law at which Ezra presided, and which in the present state of the text is folded into the account of Nehemiah's career (Neh 7:73b[MT 72b]–8:18), was originally situated after the account of the arrival in the province of Ezra and his caravan. That this was the original sequence is suggested in the first place by the dates: the immigrants arrive in the fifth month (Ezra 7:8-9), the public reading of the law takes place in the seventh month (Neh 7:73b; 8:2), and the assembly convoked to solve the marriage crisis is dated to the ninth month (Ezra 10:9).[37] Furthermore, the original location of the public reading of the law at this point, shortly after the rescript, fulfils the requirement of instructing the people in the law as mandated by Artaxerxes (Ezra 7:25), and the account of the marriage crisis which then follows provides an illustration of the punishments threatened in the rescript for failure to obey the law, in this instance confiscation of property (Ezra 7:26; 10:8). We recall that Shecaniah ben Jeiel, a layman, urges that the solution to the marriage crisis be "according to the law," and Ezra's inner support group are those who "tremble at the word of the God of Israel" (Ezra

36. A recent exception is Kratz, *The Composition of the Narrative Books of the Old Testament,* 69-70, who suggests that the public reading of the law may not have been transposed but inserted by another hand to synchronize the activity of the two protagonists.

37. In the sequence as it is in the book, the public reading in the seventh month follows the completion of the wall in Elul, the sixth month (Neh 6:15).

9:4; 10:3), which, in the context, must be taken to refer to the legal word. In general, the application of a particular point of law, or (as in this instance) a particular interpretation of a point of law, would more naturally follow than precede the public reading of the law and commitment to observe it. A parallel is available in Neh 9:2, which records how "those of Israelite stock" (lit., "the seed of Israel") separated themselves from foreigners *after* they had received public instruction in the law.

The question then arises why, in spite of this, the logical sequence of events — arrival in the province, endowment of the temple, public reading of and instruction in the law, regulation of marriage — was dislocated. The short answer would be that the public assembly had to take place in Jerusalem, and did in fact take place in the plaza at the Water Gate, which was possible only after Nehemiah had rebuilt the city wall, set up the gates, including the Water Gate, and secured Jerusalem. But short explanations are not always entirely adequate. The fact that Nehemiah the governor is said to be present and active in the proceedings alongside Ezra suggests a first attempt to synchronize the two leading figures and their activities. The Masoretic Text of Neh 8:9 may be translated literally as follows:

> Nehemiah — he was the governor — Ezra the priest, the scribe, and the Levites who instructed the people said to all the people, "This day is consecrated to Yahweh your God, do not mourn or weep."

The phrase "he was the governor" *(hû' hattiršātā')* has the appearance of an explanatory gloss, but several commentators, impressed by the fact that the verb is in the singular *(vayyō'mer)*, go further and eliminate "Nehemiah," or "Nehemiah and the Levites who instructed the people," from the verse. The one who goes on to address the people would then be Ezra alone, and Nehemiah's name, and probably also the reference to Levites, would have been introduced subsequently into the text. This makes good sense once the transposition is accepted. According to the rescript, it was Ezra's task to read and interpret the law (Ezra 7:25), which he does shortly afterwards (Neh 8:13). And it would be natural for an editor of the Nehemiah material to give Nehemiah precedence in his capacity as governor and as patron of the Levites by naming him first.

This text-critical conclusion is consistent with a close reading of the episode. That it does not unfold smoothly is at once apparent once we hear that Ezra reads from the book and then opens it (Neh 8:3, 5). As we proceed, we see other indications of either the expansion of an original brief account or a conflation of two versions. The versions do not come apart cleanly, but the composite nature of the account is easily detectable. On the one hand, it is Ezra who takes up his position on a dais, reads from the law, and presumably also expounds it since the session lasts from dawn to midday (v. 3); on the other hand, the Levites read from the book, rendering the meaning and expounding the recited text (vv. 7-8). In the one version Ezra is surrounded by thirteen laymen who flank him on either side; in the other, thirteen Levites take the lead while the people (i.e., the laity) stay in their place (vv. 4, 7).[38] We note that in both the marriage crisis and in this episode where Ezra is involved laymen take the initiative (cf. Ezra 10:2-4), whereas the special relationship between Nehemiah and Levites is apparent at several points in the Nehemiah memoir. Finally, the people are dismissed with words of good cheer by both Ezra (Neh 8:10) and the Levites (v. 11).

This is probably as far as we should conjecture, but if the *primary* connection of the public reading of the law is with Ezra, as seems to be the case, and yet the broader context is the story of Nehemiah told by himself, it seems fair to conclude that the original Ezra-laymen account was expanded at a later point in time by a Nehemiah-Levite version. If we wish to read into this a certain tension between Ezra the priest and Nehemiah the layman, and between the interests proper to both states, we may do so, but this should not lead us to forget that they are both represented as belonging to the same party and subscribing to the same basic agenda and ideology. The peculiarities of the literary phenomenon can probably be adequately explained in any case by the natural desire of an editor to synchronize the activities of the two principals.

(3) The Intermarriage Crisis (Ezra 9–10)

The third episode to be considered records the measures taken by Ezra and his supporters to deal with those members of the *golah* (the Judeo-Babylonian element resident in the province) who had contracted marital relations with native women (Ezra 9–10 = 1 Esd 8:68–9:36). It is important to

---

38. In MT *věhalěvîyyim* ("and the Levites") follows the list of names, but the copula is absent in 1 Esd 9:48, in LXX and Vulgate, and most of the names are characteristically Levitical.

stress at the outset that the women in question were not primarily, and certainly not exclusively, Gentiles.[39] It is clear that the complaint was about marriages with any women resident in the province, and perhaps also contiguous regions, who did not belong to the *golah*. There were no doubt foreigners among them, including the four ethnic groups excluded from the assembly of Israel (Deut 23:4-8),[40] but most would have been Judean descendants of those who had never left the land or Yahweh-worshippers from neighboring lands. The delegates from the north whose offer to assist in building the temple was rejected claimed to worship the same God as Zerubbabel and Jeshua and yet were considered as belonging to the *'am-hā'āreṣ* (Ezra 4:1-4). As his name shows, Tobiah belonged to a Yahweh-worshipping family and yet was rejected by Nehemiah as an outsider (Neh 6:17-19; 13:4-9).

Since the public confession of sin (Ezra 9:6-15), though probably added by a later hand,[41] is attributed to Ezra, the marriage crisis episode begins in first person discourse (9:1-15) but continues in third person narrative form (10:1-44). Ezra 9:1-5 reads as follows:

> When these matters had been settled, the leaders approached me and said, "The people of Israel, with the priests and Levites, have not kept themselves apart from the local population ('the peoples of the land') whose abominations resemble those of the Canaanites, Hittites, Perizzites, Jebusites, Ammonites, Moabites, Egyptians, and Edomites.[42] For they have taken wives from among their womenfolk for themselves and their sons, so that the holy race has mingled with the local population. Moreover, the leaders and officials have been to the fore in this un-

39. Contra Shaye J. D. Cohen, *The Beginnings of Jewishness* (Berkeley: University of California Press, 1999) 244.

40. Reading "Edomites" for MT "Amorites" with 1 Esd 8:69. In the standard lists of indigenous peoples, Amorites are listed third or higher. More significantly, the intent to conflate the standard Deuteronomic list with the four peoples excluded permanently (Ammonites, Moabites) or to the third generation (Egyptians, Edomites) in Deut 23:4-8 is apparent. On the exegetical blending of Deut 7:1-6 and 23:4-8, see Michael Fishbane, *Biblical Interpretation in Ancient Israel* (Oxford: Clarendon, 1985) 114-21.

41. Ezra's statement, "I knelt down and spread out my hands in prayer to Yahweh my God" (9:5), would have suggested the addition. Cf. the similar prayers at Neh 9:6-37 and Dan 9:4-19 and, less fully developed, 1 Macc 2:49-70 and 4Q504 = "Paroles des Lumières," in Maurice Baillet, *Qumrân Grotte 4.III (4Q482–4Q520)*. DJD 7 (Oxford: Clarendon, 1982) 137-68.

42. This sentence is a corrected version of my translation in *Ezra-Nehemiah*, 174, to take more adequate account of the prefixed preposition in *kĕtô'ăvōtêhem*.

faithful conduct." When I heard this report I tore my tunic and mantle, plucked hair from my head and beard, and remained seated in a stupor. Then there gathered around me all those who trembled at the word of the God of Israel on account of the infidelity of the exiles who had returned, while I remained seated in a stupor until the evening sacrifice. I rose from my fasting with my tunic and mantle torn; I knelt down and spread out my hands in prayer to Yahweh my God.

The use of theologically freighted language in this passage and in the prayer following, in keeping with the character of the Ezra memoir as a whole,[43] alerts us to the fact that this is not a stenographic report of what the leaders said and presages much more than the record of a one-time historical event. Why the change was made from the autobiographical to the narrative mode in a relatively brief passage is not clear. It is possible that 9:1-5, or, if we include the prayer, 9:1-15, was the only extract dealing with this issue from the Ezra memoir available to the editor. But it is also possible that use of first person discourse was part of the literary resources of an editor anxious to lend verisimilitude to his account of the episode, a device which is not unprecedented.

At any rate, the shift from first person to third person is not the only indication that the narrative is not of a piece.[44] For a while (9:1-5; 10:1-5), the story runs smoothly. Certain lay leaders (*śārîm*) inform Ezra of the widespread practice of intermarriage with the local population; the news triggers an extremely emotional reaction from Ezra, the more curious in view of the fact that four months had passed since their arrival in the province (7:8; 10:9).[45] Supported by "those who tremble at the word of the God of Israel," and after passing some time in a catatonic state, Ezra fasts and

43. *nivdĕlû* (*bdl*, Niphal), "separate oneself," a key term in discrimination between clean and unclean (also Ezra 6:21; 10:8, 11, 16; Neh 9:2; 10:29; 13:3); *bĕnê haggôlâ*, forming just one segment of the population of the province, is described as *hā'ām yiśrā'ēl*, "the people of Israel" and *zera' haqqodeš*, "the holy seed" (cf. Neh 9:2 and the gloss at Isa 6:13); *tô'ăvôt*, "abominations," a Deuteronomic term to describe unacceptable cult practices; a list of indigenous peoples which links the standard list in Deuteronomy and elsewhere (e.g. Deut 7:1; 20:17) with the four ethnic groups excluded from the Israelite assembly in Deut 23:4-8.

44. For a more detailed analysis, see my *Ezra-Nehemiah*, 187-91.

45. Josephus (*Ant.* 11.142) seems to suggest that there was an element of simulation or public relations in Ezra's extreme reaction: "Since he reasoned that, if he commanded them to put away their wives and the children born to them, he would not be listened to, he remained lying on the ground."

prays, the people rally to him, and a certain Shecaniah, a layman, proposes a covenant sealed with an oath to dismiss the women and their children. Ezra acquiesces in this plan, he administers the oath, and all the transgressors, clerical and lay, take the oath. This would seem to settle the matter, but then, in what we would be tempted to read as an alternative version (10:6-44), the whole episode begins again with Ezra praying, fasting, and mourning over the infidelity of his fellow diaspora Jews. A plenary meeting is summoned to resolve the issue, but when the assembly in the ninth month ends inconclusively, the matter is sent to committee and the offending parties are identified. A list of these is added (10:18-43), and this version concludes with a statement which in the Masoretic Text of 10:44 is unintelligible, but which may simply have reported that the women and children were sent away. [46] Only in this version is Ezra referred to as priest (10:16) and actually enters the temple (10:6).

Another puzzle concerns the role of Shecaniah. The story told in the first person begins with unnamed lay leaders taking the initiative, but in the third person narrative Shecaniah ben Jehiel, a member of the Elam phratry, is the dominant figure. He tells Ezra that the situation is bad but not hopeless. They must make a covenanted pledge to send away the indigenous women with their children. This is to be done according to the deliberations of Ezra[47] and the "tremblers," and it must be done legally, "according to the law." He then tells Ezra to get up off the ground and carry out his responsibilities in the matter (10:2-4). Shecaniah is a common enough name, but apart from the mention of his father as one of the transgressors in the marriage crisis (10:26) we hear no more about him. But he clearly had an important role in the episode, and we would like to know what it was. He may himself have been a leader of the *ḥărēdîm;* but in view of the composite nature of the narrative just referred to and the uncharacteristically passive role of Ezra, we might also entertain the possibility that a version of the incident featuring Shecaniah and his followers without Ezra has been incorporated into the Ezra story at this point.[48]

The marriages involved both fathers and sons (9:2), but there is no mention of *golah* women marrying local men, a possibility alluded to in

---

46. 1 Esd 9:36, *kai apelysan autas syn teknois* ("and they sent them away together with the children").

47. I am assuming that for MT *'ădōnāy* we should read *'ădōnî,* "my lord," with reference to Ezra (10:3). The Lord Yahweh does not advise; he commands.

48. A suggestion of Peter R. Ackroyd, "The Chronicler as Exegete," *JSOT* 1 (1976) 16.

Neh 13:25 in keeping with the wording of the admonition in Deut 7:3. Such marriages were less threatening since they would not have involved the possible alienation of the collective holdings of the *golah* group; they also avoided ritual pollution since the woman would no longer belong to the group. The womenfolk of "the peoples of the land," marriage with whom contaminated "the seed of Israel," would presumably have included indigenous Judeans and resident non-Judeans, including Ammonites, Moabites, Edomites, and women originating in Samaria and Philistia. Since many of these, including those originating outside of Judah, would have been worshippers of Yahweh, what is at issue is a theory of ritual ethnicity rather than simply what we would call religious affiliation. Since women could in certain circumstances inherit land (Num 27:1-11; 36:1-12), the prospect of loss of patrimonial domain would have served as a powerful additional motivation, just as the acquisition or reacquisition of land could have motivated those who intermarried with these taboo women in the first place. In Proverbs 1–9, "the son" addressed by the teacher is warned that sexual relations with "the outsider woman" *('iššâ zārâ/nokriyyâ)* can lead to loss of status in the assembly and loss of property.[49]

Another piece of information provided in the first version of the episode is the description of Ezra's support group as "those who tremble at the word of the God of Israel" (9:4) or "those who tremble at the commandment of our God" (10:3). Shecaniah urges that the covenant be made according to their decision together with that of Ezra, and that it be made "according to the law" (10:3). Since there is no law mandating coercive divorce and dismissal of children, what is at stake is a rigorist interpretation of the law or, more precisely, of the prescription in Deut 7:1-5 delivered in the course of a homily of Moses, forbidding marriage with the local peoples, a text quoted in Ezra's prayer (Ezra 9:12).

We should not fail to note how anomalous is the situation described in Ezra 9–10. What underlies the episode in the first place is a conflict of interpretations in which we have access to only one side of the debate. Josephus supports Ezra with the comment that the dissolved marriages constituted a violation of the constitution *(politeia)* and the ancestral laws *(Ant. 11.140).* But the collections of laws in the Pentateuch contain no law mandating the dissolution of marriage with a non-Israelite. The injunctions which Jose-

---

49. Prov 2:21-22; 5:7-14. See my "The Social Context of the 'Outsider Woman' in Proverbs 1–9," *Bib* 72 (1991) 457-73.

phus had in mind (Exod 34:11-16; Deut 7:1-6), and which he doubtless ascribed to Moses, occur in a homiletic, not strictly legal, context. The campaign of Ezra and his partisans to dissolve these marriages, with its inevitably disruptive and even tragic consequences, implemented a by no means self-evident interpretation of Exod 34:11-16 and Deut 7:1-6, perhaps conflated with Ezek 44:9. This was a minority opinion not shared by the population of the province as a whole, not to mention the other characters moving about in the background of the narrative. These included Samarians who also worshipped Yahweh (Ezra 4:1-2)[50] and Tobiah the Ammonite and his network of associates and relatives in Judah, they too Yahweh-worshipers (Neh 6:17-19; 13:4-5). It also went against the grain of traditional custom. In traditional societies endogamous marriage, marriage within the broader kinship network, often in the form of cross-cousin marriage, was generally considered the preferred option but without any overlay of ritual exclusivity. Nahor, Isaac, and Jacob married their nieces, respectively Milcah, Rebekah, and Rachel, a type of marriage which would be forbidden in the ritual laws of consanguinity and affinity (Lev 18:11-13). Samson's parents, who did not share the concerns characteristic of Ezra and his supporters, remonstrated with their son for taking a Philistine woman for a wife instead of one of his own kin (Judg 14:3). This was traditional practice which had nothing to do with ritual ethnicity, but it allowed for exceptions even among the great paradigmatic figures from the past. Abraham married two Arab women (Gen 16:15-16; 25:1-6), Moses married two Midianite (and therefore also Arab) women (Exod 2:21-22; Num 12:1),[51] and Joseph married the daughter of an Egyptian priest (Gen 41:45). Judah, ancestor of David, married a Canaanite woman (Gen 38:1-2), and his genealogy contains numerous instances of marriages with Ishmaelites, Calebites, Kenites, Egyptians, and partners from other neighboring peoples.[52] Only in the later retelling of the

---

50. A significant percentage of the names on contracts written up in Samaria in the mid- to late fourth century B.C. and recovered from the Abu Shinjeh cave in the Wâdi ed-Dāliyeh are Yahweh-theophoric, with the theophoric element either initial (Yehohanan, Yehonur, Yeho'ezer, etc.) or final (Mikayahu and the officials Hananiah and Delaiah, also known from AP 30 line 29, dated 408 B.C.). For the texts, see Douglas M. Gropp, *Wadi Daliyeh II: The Samaria Papyri from Wadi Daliyeh.* DJD 28 (Oxford: Clarendon, 2001) 33-116.

51. The Cushite woman (Num 12:1) was more probably from Cushan in Midian (cf. Hab 3:7) than Cush, the country to the south of Egypt.

52. Gary N. Knoppers, "Intermarriage, Social Complexity, and Ethnic Diversity in the Genealogy of Judah," *JBL* 120 (2001) 15-30.

ancestral history does Jacob leave for Mesopotamia in order to avoid following the bad example of Esau, who married local women.[53] At a later time, to take a final example, the Historian mentions without comment the mixed parentage of the Tyrian artisan Hiram: father Phoenician, mother Israelite of the tribe of Naphtali (1 Kgs 7:13-14).

An astonishing aspect of the account of the coercive dissolution of these marriages, but one easily overlooked, is that not only is nothing said about other possible and less drastic solutions to the problem, such as a ritual of purification or conversion, but nothing is said about the legal consequences of the action of Ezra and his faction. It is sometimes suggested that what was at issue was not divorce but a unique intervention of Ezra in pursuit of an all-important religious goal. But we recall how Shecaniah insisted that it be done according to the law, and in the eyes of the law what happened was in fact divorce, if coerced by a third party. In all law collections from the Near East and the Levant, marriage was a contractual arrangement, and the dissolution of the marriage, and therefore of the contract, always entailed serious economic consequences.[54] The biblical compilations are remarkable in having no laws dealing directly with divorce, who may initiate it, under what circumstances, and with what consequences. We can be sure nevertheless that marriage and the dissolution of marriage were at all times governed by contract, with significant material consequences for both parties. The biblical texts mention a *sēfer kĕrîtût*, generally translated "a bill of divorce,"[55] and in the allegory of Yahweh's relation with the woman Jerusalem he enters into a *bĕrît* with her (Ezek 16:8), as a result of which she becomes his "wife by covenant."[56] Some of the marriage contracts from the Jewish colony on the island of Elephantine, from the second half of the fifth century B.C., contain a detailed

53. Gen 26:34-35; 27:46; 28:1-5.

54. The Hammurapi collection states that "if a man marries a wife but does not draw up a formal contract for her she is not his wife" (par. 128). In the laws of Ur Nammu and Lipit Ishtar, divorce initiated by the husband involves a significant payment to the wife, up to 60 silver shekels, together with the return of the dowry. In the laws of Eshnunna, if children have been born to the couple, the husband who divorces loses the house and shared possessions (par. 59). Again in Hammurapi, divorce entails surrender by the man of half the shared property together with the dowry and, if there is no dowry, 60 shekels, depending on the status of the wife (par. 137-140). The texts are conveniently available in Martha T. Roth, *Law Collections from Mesopotamia and Asia Minor*. SBLWAW 6 (Atlanta: Scholars, 1995).

55. Deut 24:1; Jer 3:8; Isa 50:1.

56. Cf. the expression *'ēšet bĕrîtekâ*, "your covenanted wife," in Mal 2:14.

inventory of the goods which the woman brought into the marriage and which are to be returned to her in the event of divorce together with other significant disbursements. These contracts, especially the one from the archive of the thrice-married Miphtahiah, clearly a formidable lady, also show that marriage could be with an Aramean from nearby Syene or an Egyptian in addition to a Jewish member of the settlement, and that divorce could be initiated by the woman.[57] It is arguable, though unverifiable, that such practices were in line with conditions and practices prevailing in Israel and Judah during the time of the monarchy. All of this raises serious questions about the laconic ending to the episode in Ezra 9–10 — "So they sent them away, women and children alike" (10:44; 1 Esd 9:36).

The exclusion of unqualified members from the *golah* community is repeated, unexpectedly, in Neh 9:2 in preparation for celebrating a penitential service on the twenty-fourth of the seventh month. In this instance, however, those of Israelite stock (lit., "the seed of Israel") separated out all foreigners — that is, non-*golah* members, Jewish or non-Jewish — not just women. This incident, from which both Ezra and Nehemiah are absent, reads like an editorial construct based on the public reading and exposition of the law in Neh 7:73(MT 72)–8:12 combined with the account of the exclusion of non-*golah* women in Ezra 9–10. As in the later version of Neh 7:73(72)–8:12, in which Levites play a prominent part, the people are gathered together, the law is read and expounded for a specific period of time, the people stay in their place on their feet, and Levites conduct the service from a raised platform. As in Ezra 9–10, there are fasting, the traditional gestures of sorrow, and penitential prayer.

The pattern is repeated again in Neh 13:1-3, again with no overt connection with either Ezra or Nehemiah, in which the public reading of the law of the assembly (Deut 23:3-8) leads to the extrusion from the community of those of mixed descent, beginning with Ammonites and Moabites. Here, too, we seem to have an editorial construct, the purpose of which was to provide legal authority for Nehemiah's rough treatment of Jews who had married women from the Philistine city of Ashdod (Neh 13:23-

---

57. The most recent edition of the Elephantine papyri is that of Bezalel Porten and Ada Yardeni, *TADAE* 2: *Contracts* (1989); see esp. 30-33, 60-63, 78-83, 131-40. They are discussed by Edouard Lipiński, "Marriage and Divorce in the Judaism of the Persian Period," *Transeu* 4 (1991) 63-71; and John J. Collins, "Marriage, Divorce, and Family in Second Temple Judaism," in *Families in Ancient Israel*, ed. Leo G. Perdue et al. (Louisville: Westminster John Knox, 1997) 107-21.

27).[58] The roughing up was followed by the imposition of an oath based on Deut 7:3, the most quoted text in the book (Neh 13:25), which required them to avoid marriage with outsiders either for themselves or their children, male or female. They were, of course, already married; we are not told whether Nehemiah followed Ezra in obliging them to divorce their wives.

As for the consequences of these remarkable interventions, there can be no doubt that they enjoyed at most a temporary success. In fact, all the indications point to their predestined failure. The campaign was directed in the first place against members of the *golah* elite, both lay and clerical, who had taken the lead in intermarrying into local families (Ezra 9:2). Ezra-Nehemiah records a few examples: members of the Arah clan intermarrying with the Tobiads (Neh 6:17-18), the high priestly family making marriage alliances with the Sanballats (Neh 13:28), and there must have been many more. In connection with the much-discussed marriage of the Jerusalem priest Manasseh with Nikaso daughter of Sanballat, an event which Josephus dates to the time of Alexander, he records that "many priests and Israelites (i.e., laity) were involved in such marriages" (*Ant.* 11.312). These marriages served to consolidate the kind of integrated social elite favored by the Persians as a force for stability in the different satrapies and provinces. It is difficult to imagine that they would have taken kindly to a local official stirring up a hornet's nest by attempting to break up these alliances between leading families.

The Ezra Profile

The three episodes involving Ezra — his mission authorized by imperial decree, the public reading and interpretation of the law in accordance with his mandate in the decree, and the solution of a particularly urgent point of law — are prefaced by a passage introducing the first person Ezra narra-

---

58. Lack of the conjunction before "Ammonite and Moabite," together with the word order in the following verse, has persuaded most commentators that these two categories have been added, referring back to the action described in 13:1-3 following on the reading of the Deuteronomic law of the assembly. See Sigmund Mowinckel, *Studien zu dem Buche Ezra-Nehemia*, vol. 2: *Die Nehemia-Denkschrift* (Oslo: Universitetsforlaget, 1965) 41; Ulrich Kellermann, *Nehemia: Quellen, Überlieferung und Geschichte.* BZAW 102 (Berlin: Töpelmann, 1967) 53; Williamson, *Ezra, Nehemiah*, 397.

tive, or perhaps the Ezra material as a whole (Ezra 7:1-10). I have left discussion of this brief prefatory statement until now on account of its recapitulatory nature which makes it particularly suitable for raising some salient issues concerning ideology. Ezra 7:1-10 reads as follows, with what I take to be the original core of the passage in bold characters:

[Following on these events] **in the reign of Artaxerxes king of Persia, Ezra** [son of Seraiah, son of Azariah, son of Hilkiah, son of Shallum, son of Zadok, son of Ahitub, son of Amariah, son of Azariah, son of Meraioth, son of Zerahiah, son of Uzzi, son of Bukki, son of Abishua, son of Phineas, son of Eleazar, son of Aaron the chief priest.] [This Ezra] **went up from Babylon. He was a scribe skilled in the law of Moses which Yahweh God of Israel had given. Since he enjoyed the favor of Yahweh his God, the king granted his every request.**

[Some of the laity, priests, Levites, liturgical musicians, gatekeepers, and temple servants also went up to Jerusalem in the seventh year of King Artaxerxes.] **He arrived in Jerusalem in the fifth month** [that is, in the seventh year of the king], **for on the first day of the first month he fixed the date of departure from Babylon, arriving in Jerusalem on the first day of the fifth month, since he enjoyed the good favor of his God. For Ezra had set his mind on studying and observing the law of Yahweh, and on teaching statute and ordinance in Israel.**

The opening phrase, "following on these events," places the Ezra story in the context of the book as a whole and therefore in the broader context of new beginnings following on the events described in Ezra 1–6. The story is located in the reign of Artaxerxes (not Xerxes, as in Josephus, *Ant* 11.120) and, on the reasonable assumption that this is the same person as the Artaxerxes mentioned in Ezra 4:7-23 and 6:14, the ruler whom the author had in mind would be Artaxerxes I (465-424 B.C.). The gap between chs. 1–6 and 7–10 corresponds to the time span between the sixth year of Darius and the seventh of Artaxerxes,[59] therefore a gap of fifty-seven years. The arrival of Ezra represents a new beginning after a dark period, in which respect it fits a theological-historiographical pattern apparent in the work of the Chronicler: the pious Hezekiah follows the impious Ahaz, the good

---

59. We are told that the rebuilding of the temple was finished by the sixth year of Darius, meaning Darius I, therefore 516 (Ezra 6:15). Ezra arrived in Jerusalem in the seventh year of Artaxerxes I, therefore 458 B.C.

Josiah follows the not-so-good Manasseh,[60] Sheshbazzar, Zerubbabel, and Jeshua follow the deportations and exile. The period of more than half a century is passed over in silence with the exception of the brief allusion to complaints addressed to Ahasuerus (Xerxes) in Ezra 4:6 and emphasis on the infidelity of the first *golah* generation. 1 Esdras may be making the same point by taking Josiah's Passover as its point of departure followed by the dark period of the last four Judean kings. The idea was to present Ezra's mission as a new beginning, as truly originative.

The core narrative content of this introduction presents Ezra as a Judeo-Babylonian scribe with special competence in the Jewish law. The precise meaning of the expression *sōfēr māhîr* ("a skilful scribe") is disputed. In an influential work published in 1930, the Iranologist H. H. Schaeder argued that it stood for a high-level functionary at the Persian court, a kind of High Commissioner for Jewish Affairs, with responsibility for implementing and administering the law in operation among the Jewish ethnos in the Trans-Euphrates satrapy.[61] The hypothesis cannot be discusssed in detail here, but its principal weakness derives from Schaeder's optimistic view of the authenticity of the Artaxerxes rescript. The designation *sōfēr māhîr* is in any case an indigenous expression (see Ps 45:2[Eng. 1]), though it is also used to describe the ubiquitous sage Ahiqar as being wise and skillful *(sāfar ḥakkîm ûmāhîr)*.[62] But the function of law scribe here assigned to Ezra has no clearly defined precedent for the time of the Judean monarchy, nor does it occur in the Chronicler's history.[63] In the history of the monarchy, the *sōfēr* is a court official (e.g., Shebnah, 2 Kgs 18:18; Shaphan, 2 Kgs 22:3, 8-9), or a private secretary (Baruch, Jer 36:26), or a mere scrivener with his writing case and stylus (Ezek 9:2-3).

In biblical texts bearing on the situation during the monarchy, the only connection between the scribal office and the laws — meaning the drafting and interpreting of laws — occurs in Jeremiah's denunciation of

---

60. In the History of the Kingdoms (2 Kgs 21:1-18) Manasseh is downright bad, but according to the author of Chronicles (2 Chr 33:1-20) he made a bad start but military disaster led him to repent. He ended his reign in exemplary fashion as a restorer of true religion.

61. Hans Heinrich Schaeder, *Esra der Schreiber*. BHT 5 (Tübingen: Mohr, 1930).

62. First column of "The Words of Ahiqar," Cowley, *Aramaic Papyri of the Fifth Century B.C.*, 212.

63. There are indications in Chronicles that Levites were beginning to assume scribal responsibilities: the scribe Shemaiah is a Levite (1 Chr 24:6), and under Josiah some Levites were scribes (2 Chr 34:13), but without reference to legal matters.

the false pen of the scribes who have turned the law into a lie (Jer 8:8), the same class referred to elsewhere with the pejorative expression "handlers of the law" (*tōfĕsê hattôrâ*, Jer 2:8). These polemical statements raise the much-discussed issue of the relation between Jeremiah and the Deuteronomic law, a first draft of which some scholars believe was roughly contemporary with Jeremiah. Deuteronomy, however, does not refer to law scribes, but makes it clear that the law, and the statutory public reading of the law, are the responsibility of the priesthood.[64] If, then, Ezra is described in the final edited form of this introductory paragraph as both "scribe skilled in the law of Moses" and priest, one explanation would be that this dual function corresponds to an office which developed in the eastern diaspora after the deportations. Ezekiel, deported after the first Babylonian attack on Jerusalem in 597 B.C.E., for example, is a priest who exhibits distinctive scribal characteristics. In the core narrative content of the passage as I have identified it, however, Ezra is presented as a scribe but not a priest. In the account of the public reading of the law he is referred to more often than not as scribe (Neh 8:1, 4, 13), in the marriage crisis narrative as priest (Ezra 10:10, 16), and in the rescript as priest and scribe (Ezra 7:11, 12, 21). Whatever the precise role of a putatively historical Ezra may have been, on which we can only speculate, Deuteronomic theory, so influential throughout the book, would have required Ezra to be priest as well as scribe. Likewise for the author of Chronicles, instruction in and administration of the laws is the province of priest and Levite.[65] The expanded version of Ezra 7:1-10 has gone further by elevating Ezra to the high priesthood as direct successor of the last predisaster high priest. This enhanced status then became part of the received tradition about Ezra. He is described as such by the author of 1 Esdras (9:40, 49), and Josephus introduces him as *prōtos hiereus* ("first priest"), though in the same paragraph he identifies Joachim as *archiereus* ("chief priest," *Ant.* 11.121). A rabbinic *obiter dictum* will add that God told Ezra to stay in Babylon as long as the high priest Jeshua was alive since he was to succeed him (not Seraiah!) after his (Jeshua's) death (*Midr. Cant* 5:5). This is all very interesting, but there is no evidence that Ezra was high priest. His name occurs in none of

---

64. Deut 17:18; 31:9-13, 24-26. In Deut 31:9-13 Moses enjoins the solemn public reading of the law every seven years at Sukkoth to the entire community, men, women, and children. This injunction is clearly behind the account of the public reading by Ezra in Nehemiah 8.

65. 2 Chr 15:3; 17:7-9; 19:8-11; 31:4.

the lists in 1 Chronicles 6 and Nehemiah 12, and nowhere else in Ezra-Nehemiah is he referred to as such.[66]

However incongruous it appears in the literary context, which locates Ezra in the reign of a Persian monarch who ruled a century after the time of Cyrus, the backdating of Ezra to the period immediately after the fall of Jerusalem and deportations served to reinforce his role as founding father of the new commonwealth. The ideological motivation for this statement will be seen more clearly and precisely when we come to consider the similar backdating of the activity of Nehemiah as founding father in the festival letter in 2 Macc 1:19-36 and, later still, the locating of Ezra, also known as Salathiel, in Babylon thirty years after the fall of Jerusalem (2 Esd 3:1). The perversion of the Jerusalem priesthood during the Seleucid period, to the point where the high priesthood was awarded to the highest bidder, brought with it an increasing emphasis on the founding fathers, those who first returned from the diaspora with their faith intact and were therefore untarnished by the later corruption. A link with these first *šāvîm* (those who returned, and returned as penitents) will be a crucial aspect of the self-understanding of the sects of the Greco-Roman period, to the point of simply ignoring the later course of the history up to the emergence of the sect in question. These considerations, together with the parallels between the account of the first settlers in Ezra 1–6 and Ezra's mission in 7–10 mentioned earlier, justify the suspicion that Ezra's mission is being presented either as an account of origins alternative to that of Ezra 1-6 or a new beginning after the failure of the efforts of the first wave of immigrants.

A further and final point about this introductory paragraph: the list which it contains of those who accompanied Ezra from Babylon to Judah includes Levites (Ezra 7:7 = 1 Esd 8:5) and is therefore incompatible with the list in Ezra 8:1-14, from which Levites are absent. This Levitical deficit would call for immediate action (8:15-20). The list of six categories of cult personnel is, however, identical with and in the same order as the census of the first return in Ezra 2. This correspondence may be seen as another way of insinuating the primordiality of Ezra and his mission, but it also raises a query which will inevitably occur to the alert reader of the Ezra story: Was Ezra,

---

66. Klaus Koch, "Ezra and the Origins of Judaism," *JSS* 19 (1974) 190-91, claimed that "Ezra came as the real high priest," after deposing Meremoth, the high priest in office, an assertion for which there is no evidence whatsoever. See also on Ezra's alleged high priesthood, Ackroyd, *JSOT* 1 (1976) 18-19.

historically, the inspirer and leader of a return to the Judean homeland, comparable therefore to his predecessors Sheshbazzar, Zerubbabel, and Jeshua — the impression given by the first episode of the Ezra story (7:27–8:36) — or was his mission basically a personal charge, either to reform the temple cult or administer the law or both — as we might conclude from episodes dealing with the marriage crisis and the public reading of the law?

My own answers to these questions, very tentative as in the nature of the case they must be, are as follows. Since 1 Esdras is, in all probability, a second-order source with no significant information additional to the biblical book, and since Josephus (*Ant.* 11:120-58) is dependent on 1 Esdras and therefore at a further remove from the principal source, conclusions about the historical character of Ezra and his person and role will rest on our assessment of this complicated and largely uncooperative text. The vast range of opinion on these issues, which I have not attempted to document in detail, suggests the conclusion that certainty is, and will remain, unattainable. We can speak of *plausibility* in the framework of what is known about the policy of Achaemenid rulers, and Artaxerxes I in particular, towards subject provinces, and about the state of the empire around the mid-fifth century B.C. Hence, it is plausible that a group of Babylonian Jews, some of whose relatives had already relocated to Judah, should have followed in their footsteps during the reign of Artaxerxes I under the leadership of someone called Ezra. It is also plausible that they did so with due authorization, since relocating a significant number of people from one part of the empire to another would have required official consent. But it is also plausible that the same monarch would have sent an individual on an investigative mission to his Jewish subjects in the Trans-Euphrates satrapy at a critical period, in a manner similar to Udjahorresnet and Histiaeus during the reign of Darius I mentioned earlier.[67] But a plausible reconstruction is not history *wie es eigentlich gewesen ist,* and there is room to discuss whether the profile of a prominent diasporic figure leading his fellow Jews to Judah is compatible

---

67. Ezra's arrival in Judah during the early years of the reign of Artaxerxes I came at a time when the Egyptian revolt under the Lybian Inaros, supported by Athens, was at its height. The Persian forces sent to suppress the revolt had been defeated, Achaemenes, satrap of Egypt, had been killed, and it looked as if Egypt and neighboring provinces might be lost to the empire. To judge by Ezra 4:7-24, there may also have been disturbances in Judah. For further detail, see Pierre Briant, *Histoire de l'empire perse de Cyrus à Alexandre,* Vol. 1 (Paris: Fayard, 1996) 586-605 = *From Cyrus to Alexander: A History of the Persian Empire* (Winona Lake: Eisenbrauns, 2002) 569-88.

with that of a notable commissioned for a specific task by the imperial court and, if not, which of the two profiles has the greater plausibility.

One of the devices used by the authors and editors of the Ezra narrative, and for that matter the larger narrative of which it is part, is the frequent insertion of lists and official documents which give the story an air of historical verisimilitude. Among those which are part of the Ezra narrative (Ezra 7:11-26; 8:1-14, 25-27; 10:18-44), the one which, it seems to me, carries the most weight is the roster of immigrants who accompanied Ezra, including some of the same families already in the province (8:1-14). This supports the profile of Ezra, as scribe or priest, or scribe and priest — but certainly not high priest — and leader of a major caravan of settlers in the mid-fifth century B.C. Such an event would fit the pattern of close relations between Judah and the eastern diaspora and frequent comings and goings between them. Ezra 1–6 gives a blurred picture of the period from Cyrus to Darius I, and the idea of more than 50,000 people pulling up roots in Babylon and taking off for an unknown land in response to the edict of Cyrus is simply incredible. We may suppose that some Babylonian Jews accompanied the armies of Cambyses (a Persian ruler not mentioned in Ezra-Nehemiah) in the build-up for the invasion of Egypt in 525 B.C. A few years later the prophet Zechariah exhorts his fellow Jews to leave Babylon at the time of the Babylonian revolts against Darius in which some diaspora Jews may have participated (Zech 2:6[MT 10]), and he records the visit of three wealthy Babylonian Jews during the same reign (6:9-14). The satrapal official Rehum is said to have complained to Artaxerxes about diaspora Jews who were engaged in fortifying Jerusalem (Ezra 4:12), about whom we have no further information. Josephus reports that the Israelites as a whole remained in Babylon after the departure of Ezra, no doubt because he knows of several later groups leaving Babylon for Judah (*Ant.* 11:133). Some would probably have accompanied Nehemiah, as a rabbinic dictum affirms, and as late as the Seleucid period Jews were being repatriated to Judah from Babylon (*Ant.* 12:138). Hence the account of Ezra's caravan seems to me to merit attention as a historical datum.

We may take this a step further. Perhaps Ezra came to Jerusalem together with his fellow *hărēdîm*, with or without imperial authorization, with the deliberate agenda of enforcing his own interpretation of the laws in the spirit of Ezekiel and his fellow Zadokites, and by so doing creating a ritually pure community. The title *běnê haggôlâ* which they assumed on arriving in Judah indicates their close attachment to the eastern diaspora on which they depended for leadership and ideological guidance.[68] They were, in effect, a diaspora in reverse, a colony intent on imposing its own ideology and way of life.[69] The analogy of the Puritan colonizers of the New World in the early seventeenth century, while obviously imperfect, may be helpful. Viewed in this way, Ezra may be considered the forerunner of those sects of the Greco-Roman period which, according to one scholarly opinion, originated in Babylon and saw themselves as the successors of the founding fathers (*hāri'šônîm*, CD IV 6, 8).[70] These were the ones who returned from captivity with their faith intact, who will be known in sectarian texts from the Hasmonaean period as "the penitents of Israel" (*šāvê yiśrā'ēl*).[71] In short: while the Ezra narrative could not have been put together in its present form before the late Persian or early Hellenistic period, while its composition involved a considerable amount of creativity, and while the original portrayal of the protagonist has been obscured in the process of transmission, from this angle we can still discern the profile of a figure that is historically plausible, less so perhaps than that of Nehemiah, but more so than other biblical characters portrayed against a Persian period backdrop, characters like Daniel, Mordechai, or Esther. And the dominant image is that of a leader of a group (certainly a small minority; dare we call it a sect?) committed to a rigorist interpretation of the laws, especially laws governing the constitution of a community ritually segregated from "the impurity of the peoples of the land" (Ezra 9:11).

Ezra and the *Golah*

The term *gôlâ* can refer either to the condition of those deported from their homeland, or the place in which they were resettled, or the deportees them-

---

68. On the close connection with the Babylonian-Elamite diaspora, see Peter R. Bedford, "Diaspora-Homeland Relations in Ezra-Nehemiah," *VT* 52 (2002) 147-65.

69. The terminology for colonies and colonization (*apoikia, apoikesia, apoikizein*), as for example in the colonizing activity of Athens (e.g., Herodotus *Ant.* I 146; V 124), is used in LXX with reference to the *gôlâ* (Jer 36:1; Ezra 6:19, etc.) and by Josephus with reference to the Jewish diaspora in Alexandria (*Ap.* 2.38). See Louis H. Feldman, "The Concept of Exile in Josephus," in *Exile: Old Testament, Jewish, and Christian Conceptions*, ed. James M. Scott, JSJSup 56 (Leiden: Brill, 1997) 144-48.

70. See below, pp. 214-22.

71. CD IV 2; VI 5; VIII 16. The expression is Isaianic (Isa 59:20; cf. 1:27).

selves as a collectivity. In this last sense it occurs frequently in texts from the Neo-Babylonian period and later.[72] As a means of subjugating refractory peoples in their empire, or even beyond it, the Assyrians practiced deportation on a massive scale. After the fall of Samaria in 722 B.C. Sargon II claimed to have deported 27,290, a significant number but no more than a small fraction of the populations displaced as long as the Neo-Assyrian Empire lasted. It has been calculated that over a period of three centuries the Assyrians displaced as many as four and a half million people.[73] The Judeans were fortunate that their Babylonian conquerors did not continue the Assyrian practice of cross-deportation, which would have made a resettlement in Judah in the Persian period difficult if not impossible. The former kingdom of Judah, in which some immigrants eventually did settle, was much reduced in size as a result of inroads from neighboring peoples, especially Edomites from the south and east, but the appointment of a Judean deputy ruler by the Babylonians ensured that the province would survive as a diminished and impoverished but still autonomous entity within the Neo-Babylonian Empire.

A major task for anyone wishing to use Ezra-Nehemiah as historical source material is to understand how the Judeo-Babylonian *golah* relates to the rest of the population of Achaemenid Judah. There is the idea mentioned earlier that they entered a depopulated land, in which case the problem would not have arisen. In keeping with this myth, Ezra-Nehemiah represents them, after they arrived loaded down with bullion and votive offerings for the temple, dispersing peacefully and without let or hindrance to their assigned locations, clergy in Jerusalem, laity throughout the province (Ezra 2:70), as if coming home after a vacation abroad. Yet at the same time, we are told that they were in fear of "the peoples of the lands," in other words, the local population (3:3). Later, some of the indigenous population were permitted to join them in celebrating Passover once they had dissociated themselves from the ritual uncleanness of the rest of the population (6:21). Later still, there took place the episode of intermarriage of *golah* men with local women. In the preface to the census

---

72. Jer 28:4; 29:1, 20, 31; Ezek 1:1; 3:11, 15, etc.; Zech 6:10-11; Ezra 1:11; 9:4; 10:6. In the Aramaic section of Ezra the diaspora group is referred to as *běnê gālûtā'* (6:16), but more frequently as *yěhûdāyē'* (4:12, 23; 5:1; 6:7, 14); cf. Neh 5:1, where the same term appears to refer to the Judaeo-Babylonian elite.

73. Oded, *Mass Deportations and Deportees*, 19-20. For the Sargon II inscription, see *ANET*, 284-85.

list, finally, the Judeo-Babylonians are described as "those inhabitants of the province who had come up from the captivity of the *golah*," implying that they constituted a distinctive element within a larger population group (Ezra 2:1 = Neh 7:6).

The hypothesis elaborated principally by Joel Weinberg, that the *golah* group, once settled in Judah, constituted itself as a *Bürger-Tempel Gemeinde* (civic-temple community), attached to the temple and initially distinct demographically and territorially from the province, no longer seems to be in favor.[74] Weinberg argued that the list of repatriates in Nehemiah 7, which he took to be the original version, represented about 20 percent of the total population of the province at that time, the mid-fifth century, and that as a result of Nehemiah's activity the percentage increased to the point where the province was completely assimilated to the civic-temple community. The hypothesis has proved to be stimulating, but is weakened by the difficulty of coming up with reliable demographic statistics. Weinberg's handling of the topographical data is also problematic, based as it is on the supposition that the civic-temple community gradually extended its own settlements independently of the provincial administration. As inspired initially by Soviet-era sociological theory, the hypothesis also tended to underestimate the significance of a specifically religious ideology driving the course of events.

The *Bürger-Tempel Gemeinde* hypothesis was at any rate certainly correct in recognizing the organizationally and ideologically distinct nature of the *golah*. They had their own assembly *(qāhāl)*, the names of whose members were entered in a genealogical record.[75] Attendance at sessions of the assembly was mandatory, and absenteeism was severely punished (Ezra 10:8-15). Issues of concern to all were addressed in plenary sessions in an open space in the city. Oaths were administered, commitments made, and the names of the participants in the covenant recorded in writing.[76] The basic organizational unit was the large kinship group *(bêt 'āvôt)* united by descent, real or fictitious, from a named eponym and governed by tribal heads or elders *(rā'šîm, zĕqēnîm)*. Essential prerequisites for its survival and eventual dominance were acquisition of land and control of the cult.

74. For a summary with relevant bibliography, see my "Temple and Society in Achaemenid Judah," 22-53.

75. The census in Ezra 2 = Nehemiah 7 is a list of the *qāhāl* members entered into a *sēfer hayyaḥaś* ("genealogical record") which Nehemiah claims to have found (Neh 7:5).

76. Ezra 10:5, 9-44; Neh 5:1-13; 9:38–10:39(MT 10:1-40); 13:23-27.

These goals were closely connected since membership in the *golah* assembly was restricted to property owners and those who supported and participated in the common cult. In this respect, therefore, Weinberg was right to emphasize the importance of the temple as a central point of reference in the social arrangements and the economic life of the province. In this and other respects the Judeo-Babylonian colonists reproduced in their new environment elements of their social life as an ethnic minority in southern Mesopotamia.

The social and political organization we are describing was quite different in almost every respect from the situation under the monarchy. In place of a dynastic monarchy and the state apparatus that went with it, the semi-autonomous province of Yehud was under a governor, though, surprisingly, no governor is mentioned in connection with Ezra's activity. As was the case elsewhere in the Achaemenid Empire, the temple was under the patronage of the court in Susa, its status as such indicated by tax relief for temple personnel and the requirement that prayers for the royal family be incorporated into the temple liturgy (Ezra 6:10). To repeat: the basic kinship unit in the postmonarchic period, the *bêt 'āvôt* (cf. the Babylonian *bit abim*), was much larger than and of a quite different nature from the preexilic *bêt 'āv* ("patrilineal household"). On the basis of the numbers given for the seventeen lay agnatic units in Ezra 2 = Nehemiah 7, Weinberg calculated the average population of these Persian-period patrilineal groups to be between 800 and 1,000, somewhat larger than the contemporary average Iranian phratry, and greatly in excess of the size of the typical preexilic unit.[77] Important matters were discussed in plenary assemblies of the members of the *qāhāl*, another practice imported from Mesopotamia and unknown during the time of the kingdoms.

This issue of continuity-discontinuity can also be approached via the more hazardous route of a survey of the personal names in the lists in Ezra-Nehemiah. Onomastics is admittedly a fallible guide to social and political realities, personal names are not always clearly indicative of religious affiliation, names can change over time, and the same person can have more than one name — for example, a nickname or a *nom de guerre*. Yet the very low incidence of names in Ezra-Nehemiah known from preexilic texts, low even

---

77. Joel Weinberg, "Das *Bēit Ābōt* im 6.-4. Jh. v.u.Z.," *VT* 23 (1973) 400-14. The average size of the seventeen kinship units in Ezra 2 identified by their patronymics is in fact approximately 912 members, but the range is from 2,812 (Pahath-moab) to 98 (Ater).

when compared with Jewish names in cuneiform texts from the Neo-Babylonian and Achaemenid periods, would seem to call for an explanation. The problem is particularly in evidence in the list of settlers in Ezra 2, repeated in Nehemiah 7. The original purpose and date of this list have been much discussed. For the present purpose it will be enough to restate the commonly-held view that it comes from a time much later in the Persian period than the reign of Cyrus and that it is probably composite. It is certainly not a list of a huge transfer of population (about 50,000) in response to an edict of Cyrus issued shortly after the fall of Babylon in 539 B.C.[78] At the head of the list are the names of twelve leaders[79] of "those inhabitants of the province who came up from the captivity of the diaspora . . . and returned to Jerusalem and Judah, each to his own town" (Ezra 2:1 = Neh 7:6). This part of the list appears to have been assembled from the names of leading figures occurring throughout the book, five of them signatories to Nehemiah's covenant, and is therefore for the present purpose less significant. At least three of the names are Babylonian (Zerubbabel, Mordecai, Bilshan), the name Nehemiah occurs in one of the Samarian papyri attached to a slave,[80] Reelaiah and Mispar are unattested elsewhere, and Bigvai (Bagoas, Bagohi) is the name of the Persian governor of Judah in the last decade of the fifth century (AP 30:1; 32:1), leaving three names attested from the preexilic period (Jeshua/Joshua, Baanah, and Seraiah, this last the high priest executed by the Babylonians after the fall of Jerusalem) (Ezra 7:1-5).[81]

More to the point are the seventeen lay agnatic units listed under the name of their respective patronymics (Ezra 2:3-19). These names keep on reappearing throughout the book. Eleven of the seventeen take part in Ezra's caravan (Ezra 8:1-14), and thirteen are represented among the signatories to Nehemiah's covenant (Neh 10:1-27[MT 2-28]). Descendants of ten

---

78. Consult Rudolph, *Esra und Nehemia samt 3. Esra*, 7-28; Jacob M. Myers, *Ezra-Nehemiah*. AB 14 (Garden City: Doubleday, 1965) 10-22; Williamson, *Ezra, Nehemiah*, 21-39; Blenkinsopp, *Ezra-Nehemiah*, 79-93.

79. In Ezra 2:2 the sixth, Nahamani, is supplied from Neh 7:7. The following variants occur in the Nehemiah list: Azariah for Seraiah, Raamiah for Reelaiah, Misperet for Mispar, Nehum for Rehum. For the 1 Esdras names, see Ralph W. Klein, "Old Readings in I Esdras: The List of Returnees from Babylon (Ezra 2//Nehemiah 7)," *HTR* 62 (1969) 99-107.

80. Frank M. Cross, "The Discovery of the Samaria Papyri," *BA* 26 (1963) 111-12; Gropp, *Wadi Daliyeh II*, 65.

81. Interestingly, Azariah in Neh 7:7 for Seraiah in Ezra 2:2 is an alternative form of Ezra, who then follows Zerubbabel, Joshua, and Nehemiah.

of them agree to divorce their wives at Ezra's insistence (Ezra 10:18-44), and four (Parosh, Pahath-moab, Bani, and Zakkay/MT Zabbai) provide labor for Nehemiah's repair of the city wall (Neh 3:1-32). The names convey a strong impression of authenticity. Of the seventeen, only Shephatiah, Zakkai (if hypocoristic for Zechariah), and Bani (if hypocoristic for Benaiah) belong to individuals mentioned in preexilic texts, and if Adonikam is a variant of Adonijah (Neh 10:16[MT 17]) only one other is Yahweh-theophoric. While etymologizing about personal names is a hazardous business, a few may be nicknames, though it is well known that what were originally nicknames may end up as normal personal names.[82] Several others appear to be foreign (Zattu, Azgad, Ater[83]) or indicative of a diasporic situation (Pahath-moab,[84] Elam), and the one clearly Persian name, Bigvai (Bagohi), belongs to the third-largest phratry. Of the four priestly houses listed (Ezra 2:36-39), the first and the fourth, Jedaiah and Harim, occur only in texts from the Persian period or later, while Immer and Pashhur appear to go back to the last decades of the Judaean kingdom (Jer 20:1-6). None of the numerous priests whose names occur in Ezra-Nehemiah is identified as either Aaronite or Zadokite, and the same is the case with the priests at Elephantine.

The list of names in Ezra 2 therefore provides more information than the author or editor of the list intended to convey. To repeat the cautionary note made earlier, onomastics is not always a sure guide to social realities and political or religious affiliation, but this brief survey of the personal names of laymen and priests alerts us to the possibility that not all, and perhaps not many, of those who left Babylonia for Judah in the Persian period were descendants of the deportees of more than a century earlier, that not all were Jewish by birth, and that the links between the *golah* and the national past were more the product of ideology than either descent from common ancestors or cultural continuity. All of this notwithstanding, the immigrant community represented itself as the inheritors of the ancestral

---

82. For these names, see the relevant entries in Martin Noth, *Die israelitischen Personennamen im Rahmen der gemeinsemitischen Namengebung.* BWANT 10 (1928; repr. Hildesheim: Olms, 1980); and Ran Zadok, *The Pre-Hellenistic Israelite Anthroponymy and Prosopography.* OLA 28 (Leuven: Peeters, 1988).

83. However, Ater ('*āṭēr*, Ezra 2:16) is mentioned in one of the Samaria contracts as a son of the city prefect Delaiah; see Gropp, *Wadi Daliyeh II,* 58.

84. Pahath-moab is clearly a *nomen officii,* "Governor of Moab"; cf. Akkadian *paḥātu,* Hebrew *peḥâ.*

Israelite traditions and the heirs of the old Israel to the exclusion of all other potential or actual claimants. They referred to themselves as "Israel" (Ezra 9:1; Neh 7:7), "Israelites" (*běnê yiśrā'ēl*, Ezra 3:1), "all-Israel" (*kol-yiśrā'ēl*, Ezra 2:70; 6:17), "the seed of Israel" (*zera' yiśrā'ēl*, Neh 9:2) or "the holy seed" (*zera' haqqodeš*, Ezra 9:2), and other terms expressive of a strong link of continuity with the national and ethnic past.

In the account of the marriage crisis instigated by members of the *golah,* we hear that all who trembled at the words of the God of Israel on account of the infidelity of those who had married outside the group gathered around Ezra and took part in a demonstration that lasted until the evening (Ezra 9:4). The atmosphere was one of mourning, fasting, penitential prayer, and demonstrative signs of distress, not unlike the milieu described in Daniel (e.g., Dan 9:3-4). A layman of the Elam phratry, one Shecaniah, proposed a covenant to be carried out according to the counsel of Ezra and the "tremblers" *(ḥărēdîm),* and that it be done "according to the law" (Ezra 10:3). Since there is no law mandating coercive divorce and dismissal of children, it was a question of a rigorist interpretation of a law or, more precisely, of the injunction in Deut 7:1-6 delivered in the course of a homily of Moses, the same text quoted in Ezra's prayer (Ezra 9:12).

Apart from Ezra 9:4 and 10:3, *ḥārēd, ḥărēdîm* occurs as a designation only in Isa 66:1-5, where those who tremble at God's word are listed with the poor and afflicted in spirit and are addressed as a group excommunicated by the religious authorities, namely, the leading temple clergy. The ostensible reason appears to be the eschatological beliefs of the group addressed by the anonymous seer:

> Hear the word of Yahweh, you who tremble at his word!
> Your brethren who hate you,
> who cast you out for my name's sake have said,
> "May Yahweh reveal his glory, that we may witness your joy!"
> But it is they who will be put to shame. (Isa 66:5)

We cannot date this passage with assurance, but it is arguable that Ezra 9–10 and Isa 66:1-5 are referring to one and the same group viewed from different perspectives and at different stages of development. The possibility cannot be excluded on the grounds that the "tremblers" of Ezra 9–10 espoused a rigorist interpretation of law while those addressed by the anonymous seer in Isa 66:5 were a prophetic-eschatological group. The example

of the Qumran sects will suffice to make the point that legal rigor and prophetic eschatology are not mutually exclusive. Nor can the possibility be
dismissed on the grounds that the Isaianic group was shunned,
marginalized, and deprived while Ezra's support group was at the time referred to as in control. Deprivation is not the lot of all sectarian movements; witness the example of the Puritans in the New England colonies,[85]
and the point has been made that the success of Ezra and his party was
probably short-lived.[86]

It is well known that the *ḥărēdîm* are still with us, constituting a ritually self-segregating party which rejects the legimimacy of the State of Israel, the Jewish identity of non-Orthodox Jews, and the legitimacy of marriage with a non-*ḥărēdî* partner. They therefore have features in common
with the group which, at the beginnings of Judaism, constituted Ezra's
main support and to which he himself in all probability belonged.

We should be under no illusion that the inadequate and uncooperative literary data at our disposal can open the way for us into the promised
land of clear and certain knowledge of this crucial historical juncture. But
what we may be glimpsing behind the ideological scaffolding of Ezra-
Nehemiah and the comforting myth of the "return to Zion" *(šivat ṣiyyôn)*
is a process which, for most of those involved in it, would have been a settlement rather than a resettlement, an arrival in an adopted homeland
rather than a return. We might think of it as a process of colonization originating in the eastern diaspora, probably sanctioned by the imperial authorities, a process which I have called a diaspora in reverse. The religious
core of this enterprise was a group of enthusiasts dedicated to a rigorist interpretation of the law in the spirit of Deuteronomy and Ezekiel 40–48, a
group ritually segregated from the world outside, Jewish and, a fortiori,
Gentile, and perhaps also motivated by some form of eschatological belief.[87] This characterization will call for further elaboration in the chapters
following.

---

85. For a good discussion of deprivation theory, see Stephen L. Cook, *Prophecy and
Apocalypticism: The Postexilic Social Setting* (Minneapolis: Fortress, 1995) 35-46. The sectarian character of Ezra's *ḥărēdîm* will be argued from the point of view of an exclusionary relationship to the parent body.

86. On the *ḥărēdîm* of Ezra 9–10 and Isaiah 66, see my "A Jewish Sect of the Persian Period," *CBQ* 52 (1990) 5-20; *Isaiah 56–66*. AB 19B (New York: Doubleday, 2003) 51-54, 299-300.

87. Some prophetic and eschatological aspects of the Ezra profile are sketched by Koch,
JSS 19 (1974) 173-97.

· 3 ·

Nehemiah

The Nehemiah Story

In spite of the title at Neh 1:1, Ezra-Nehemiah is one book in both the Hebrew text and the Septuagint (LXX). One indication is that the Masoretic
sign marking the midpoint of the book *(ḥăṣî hassēfer)* is located at Neh
3:32, and the Masoretes provide only one verse total (685) situated at the
end of Nehemiah. In early Jewish and early Christian tradition the book
was known simply as Ezra and was no doubt attributed to him. According
to a rather odd rabbinic tradition, however, Nehemiah was the real author
but was forbidden to claim authorship on account of his bad habit of disparaging his predecessors.[1] Eventually, and inevitably, the two protagonists
were paired, somewhat like Aaron and Moses, the priest and the layman,
even though their names occur together in the biblical book only on three
occasions, all the result of late editorial activity. The first is the public reading of the law, where it is generally agreed that one of the two names has
been inserted (Neh 8:9). Then, at the dedication of the city wall, Ezra the
scribe led the southbound procession round the perimeter in a role clearly
inferior to that of Nehemiah as master of ceremonies. Here Ezra's name
has in all probability been inserted (Neh 12:36). Finally, at the conclusion
of a list of temple personnel, we are told that these priests and Levites offi-
ciated "in the days of Nehemiah the governor and Ezra, priest and scribe"
(Neh 12:26), the implication being that this was some considerable time in
the past. These instances aside, the two protagonists are quite distinct.

---

1. R. Jeremiah ben Abba in *b. Sanh.* 93b, with reference to Neh 5:15.

There is no linkage and no cross-referencing between them, even though, according to the chronological indications in the book, their high-profile activities are separated by no more than thirteen years. We shall see that this circumstance is consistent with and perhaps confirmatory of the hypothesis that the Nehemiah material was originally distinct and only secondarily brought into relation with the Ezra narrative.

Also to be considered is that 1 Esdras, which I take to be a Greek translation of one section of an alternative version of Chronicles-Ezra-Nehemiah, probably composed in the second century B.C., omits the Nehemiah material entirely, passing directly from the resolution of the marriage issue to the public reading of the law. As in the canonical book, the name appears in 1 Esdras among the leaders of the first immigrants (1 Esd 5:8; cf. Ezra 2:2 = Neh 7:7), which probably persuaded the author to add Nehemiah's name to that of Attharias in issuing the order which excluded certain claimants from the ranks of the altar priesthood (1 Esd 5:40). The name Attharias resulted from a misunderstanding of the Persian loanword *hattiršātāʾ* ("governor"), used elsewhere with reference to Nehemiah (Neh 10:2[Eng. 1]). For the same reason we find a certain Attharates presiding over the assembly in the square in front of the temple rather than Nehemiah, as in the biblical book (1 Esd 9:49; Neh 8:9). The two names therefore represent alternative attempts to deal with a word with which the author was unfamiliar.

If Ezra-Nehemiah is one book, it is at least clear it could not have been composed by Ezra, Nehemiah, or anyone else at one time. We might think of it rather as a work in progress over a considerable period of time extending well into the Hellenistic period. Some or all of the lists in the latter part of the book are among the most likely addenda: these include the signatories to Nehemiah's covenant (Neh 10:1-27[MT 2-28]), families resident in Jerusalem (11:1-24), settlements throughout Judah and beyond (11:25-36), temple personnel (12:1-26), and participants in the dedication of the wall ceremony (12:27-43). The names of Mattaniah the liturgical musician and precentor and his great-grandson Uzzi, in charge of the Levites and therefore presumably of a certain age, occur together as contemporary residents of Jerusalem in the same list (11:17, 22), while another great-grandson of Mattaniah, Zechariah, took part in the ceremony of dedication of the city wall during the lifetime of Nehemiah (12:35). A four-generation spread like this, beginning during Nehemiah's lifetime, is perhaps not impossible but more likely indicative of a later date for the list.

Another indication is the list of temple personnel in which the high-priestly dynasty is continued down to Jaddua, a contemporary of Darius III and Alexander, almost a century and a half after the time of Nehemiah,[2] and the same list concludes with Levitical leaders who served "in the days of Nehemiah the governor and Ezra, priest and scribe" (12:22-26). Elsewhere we are told that the entire people contributed to the upkeep of the liturgical musicians and gatekeepers "at the time of Nehemiah and Zerubbabel" (12:47). Pairing Nehemiah with Zerubbabel is, incidentally, reminiscent of Sir 49:11-13, which moves directly from Zerubbabel and Jeshua to Nehemiah, omitting Ezra.

The names of those who were resettled in Jerusalem following Nehemiah's repopulation of Jerusalem (Neh 11:1-24) are arranged according to the same categories and in the same order as the list of early settlers in Jerusalem in 1 Chr 9:2-17, and many of the names are the same. While it is theoretically possible that the author of Chronicles used Nehemiah as a source in this instance, it makes better sense to hold that a later scribal hand has drawn on the Chronicler's list to fill a gap in the record.[3] As for the settlement list in Neh 11:25-36, the fact that eleven out of the seventeen Judaean locations named were under Edomite control at the time of Nehemiah, and came under Jewish control only after the Maccabee conquests (1 Macc 5:65; 11:34), provides a strong argument for a considerably later addition to the book, though alternative explanations have been offered. A particularly transparent addendum occurs apropos of the Levitical responsibility for collecting the tithe. In both instances where this sensitive issue is raised (Neh 10:39 and 12:47), a codicil is appended mandating the handing over of the "tithe of the tithe," a kind of 10 percent handling fee, to the Aaronite priests who now supervise the entire operation. Nowhere else in Ezra-Nehemiah are the numerous priests named or referred to designated "sons of Aaron."[4]

Practically all commentators agree that Nehemiah's covenant (Neh 9:38–10:39[MT 10:1-40]) must be later than the time of Nehemiah himself, either in its entirety or in some of its particulars. We will come back to this important text later, but for the moment let us note that the insertion of

2. Neh 12:10-11; *Ant.* 11.325-29, 346-47.

3. The list is discussed in my *Ezra-Nehemiah*. OTL (Philadelphia: Westminster, 1988) 320-27.

4. With the exception of the priestly genealogy of Ezra in Ezra 7:1-5, copied from the succession of the high priesthood in 1 Chr 6:1-15(MT 5:27-41).

the list of signatories (10:1-27[2-28]) breaks the syntactic connection between 9:38[10:1] and 10:28[29] and was therefore almost certainly spliced in. Furthermore, the names themselves appear to have been assembled from lists elsewhere in the book, including the census list (7:5b-73a[MT 72a]), the work gangs engaged in rebuilding the wall (3:1-32), and the lists of priests (12:1-7, 12-22). There is also broad agreement that the stipulations of the covenant concerning marriage, Sabbath observance, and support of the temple are based on measures taken by Nehemiah as recorded in the final chapter.[5] Morton Smith made the more specific suggestion that Nehemiah's "firm commitment" *('ămānâ)* derived from Levites in the early Hellenistic period who, as opponents of the then dominant assimilationist party, attributed it to their hero Nehemiah. As such, he concluded, it may be described as "the first example of Jewish sectarianism."[6]

A date for Nehemiah's pact in the early Hellenistic period would not be out of line with indications elsewhere in the book of literary affinity with Chronicles composed in the late fourth or early third century, either shortly before or after the Macedonian conquest.[7] It will not be necessary to pursue this issue in detail at this point, except to repeat that this relationship is most clearly in evidence in Ezra 1–6, the first section of the book.[8] It is also detectable, if less abundantly, at several points thereafter, especially in the Ezra first person narrative inclusive of the rescript of Artaxerxes. In summary, it is probably safe to think of Ezra-Nehemiah

---

5. Sigmund Mowinckel, *Studien zu dem Buche Ezra-Nehemia*, vol. 1: *Die nachchronistische Redaktion des Buches: Die Listen* (Oslo: Universitetsforlaget, 1964) 135-45; Wilhelm Rudolph, *Esra und Nehemia samt 3. Esra* (Tübingen: Mohr, 1949) 172-81 (note that Rudolph held that Ezra-Nehemiah formed *der Schlussteil* of Chronicles, which he dated in the fourth century); Adolf Jepsen, "Nehemia 10," *ZAW* 66 (1954) 87-106; Hugh G. M. Williamson, *Ezra, Nehemiah.* WBC 16 (Waco: Word, 1985) 320-40.

6. Morton Smith, "The Dead Sea Sect in Relation to Ancient Judaism," *NTS* 7 (1960-61) 347-60; *Palestinian Parties and Politics That Shaped the Old Testament* (New York: Columbia University Press, 1971) 173-74.

7. Loring W. Batten, *A Critical and Exegetical Commentary on the Books of Ezra and Nehemiah.* ICC (Edinburgh: T. & T. Clark, 1913) 2-3, claimed that "it is quite impossible to place the work (i.e. Chronicles-Ezra-Nehemiah) earlier than 300 B.C." More soberly, Rudolph, *Esra und Nehemia samt 3. Esra,* xxiv-xxv, opted for the early fourth century, and that is the *opinio communis.*

8. H. G. M. Williamson, "The Composition of Ezra i–vi," *JTS N.S.* 34 (1983) 1-30, argued that this first section was composed after the Ezra narrative was combined with that of Nehemiah, therefore after the composition of Chronicles. See also my *Ezra-Nehemiah,* 47-54.

as a work in progress from the mid-fifth century down into the Hasmonaean period.

The core of Nehemiah 1–13 is a first person narrative, generally referred to as the Nehemiah memoir (German *Denkschrift*). It will be admitted that the profile of Nehemiah emerges from this memoir with much cleaner lines than that of Ezra. The memoir is also more extensive, more detailed, and more descriptively precise than that of Ezra. It is generally taken to include all or most of 1:1–7:5 and 13:4-31, but, not surprisingly, we must allow for a wide range of opinion beyond this generalization. We can do no more than present one or two examples from a thick dossier. Charles Cutler Torrey, who here as elsewhere goes his own way, extends the memoir only as far as 6:15-19, ending with Nehemiah's complaint about Tobiah and his faction. This is, for Torrey, the story of a truly religious man told by himself, but one who had no interest in the temple and what went on in it. To this memoir the author of Chronicles, none other than Ezra himself, added the census list (7:5b-73a[72a]), the narrative in the last three chapters (11-13), and the lists of Jerusalem residents and temple personnel (11 and 12).[9] To the two segments of the memoir Wilhelm Rudolph added the core narratives about the repopulation of Jerusalem (11:1-24) and the dedication of the wall (12:27-43) and argued that the list of workers on the wall (3:1-32) and the census list (7:6-72a) were inserted into the memoir.[10] A recent study by Titus Reinmuth distinguishes the part of the first person narrative dealing with the wall (1–4; 6:1–7:5; 12:27-43) from a *Denkschrift* dealing with social and legal reforms (5:1-19; 13:4-31), both then conflated and edited by a Torah-redactor who added other material including the prayer (1:5-11) and the covenant stipulations (10:30-39[MT 31-40]).[11] An even more recent study is that of Jacob L. Wright, who believes it possible to identify within the Nehemiah narrative as a whole seven strata, corresponding to stages in the reception of the book. These begin with the repair of the wall and end with supplements reflecting friction between temple and law.[12]

9. Charles C. Torrey, *The Composition and Historical Value of Ezra-Nehemiah*, BZAW 2 (Giessen: Ricker, 1896) 39-49; *Ezra Studies* (1910; repr. New York: Ktav, 1970) 248-51.

10. Rudolph, *Esra und Nehemia samt 3. Esra*, 211-13.

11. Titus Reinmuth, *Der Bericht Nehemias: Zur literarischen Eigenart, traditionsgeschichtlichen Prägung und innerbiblischen Rezeption des Ich-Berichts Nehemias.* OBO 183 (Freiburg: Universitätsverlag, 2002).

12. Jacob L. Wright, *Rebuilding Identity: The Nehemiah-Memoir and Its Earliest Readers.* BZAW 348 (Berlin: de Gruyter, 2004). Not yet published at this writing, the essay

A more radical approach to this issue is that of Joachim Becker, who argues that the first person narrative in Nehemiah 1–13 is pseudepigraphal fiction composed by the author of Chronicles according to specifically Chronistic theological perspectives and exhibiting typically Chronistic language and themes. He takes what he calls first person narratives in Chronicles to be comparable to the Nehemiah memoir, but in fact the examples he offers — e.g., King Abijah's speech before battle in 2 Chr 13:4-12 — do no more than exemplify the common practice among ancient historians (e.g., Thucydides) of putting dialogue and speeches into the mouths of their characters. On any showing, a memoir is something quite different.[13] Reinhard Kratz also highlights the contribution of the Chronicler and the influence of Chronistic language and themes, but concludes by reducing the original core of the memoir to the building and dedication of the wall; everything else is redactional elaboration.[14] In this connection mention should be made of the hypothesis put forward by Hugh Williamson according to which the core of the memoir was a report in Aramaic submitted to Artaxerxes after Nehemiah had been in office two years at the most. The writing of this report may have been inspired by the need to answer complaints submitted to the central authorities by his opponents about his actions and intentions, complaints to the effect that the fortification of Jerusalem was the first stage in a plan to restore the Judaean monarchy in his own person (Neh 6:5-7). Since Nehemiah had no shortage of enemies, this explanation cannot be summarily excluded. Noticing that the "remember me" *(zokrâ-lî)* motif is limited almost entirely to the later phase of his activities (5:19 and 13:14, 22, 31), and struck by its absence in connection with his main achievement, namely, the repair of the city wall, Williamson argued that the report to Artaxerxes must have been limited to his mandate to rebuild the city wall[15] — minus the prayers (1:4-11; 4:4-

---

of Mark J. Boda, "Redaction in the Book of Nehemiah: A Fresh Proposal," in *Unity and Disunity in Ezra-Nehemiah,* ed. Boda and Paul L. Redditt. HBM 17 (Sheffield: Sheffield Phoenix, forthcoming), deals with the difficult question of where the memoir takes up again after Neh 7:5, and therefore with the complicated issues raised by chs. 8-11. I thank Professor Boda for letting me see this essay in proof.

13. Joachim Becker, *Der Ich-Bericht des Nehemiabuches als chronistische Gestaltung.* FB 87 (Würzburg: Echter, 1998).

14. Reinhard G. Kratz, *The Composition of the Narrative Books of the Old Testament* (London: T. & T. Clark, 2005) 62-68.

15. Actually, his mandate was to rebuild the city, of which the restoration of the wall

5[MT 3:36-37]; 6:14) — and that later in his tenure of office he expanded it to include the achievements referred to in chs. 5 and 13.[16]

Williamson is certainly right in pointing to the disjunction between the two segments of the memoir of unequal length, and something will be said about this later. Reports were also no doubt required of provincial officials, including the kind exemplified by those referred to in Ezra 4:6-24 (1 Esd 2:16-24). But we may wonder whether either the wording or the content of the wall-building narrative is what we would expect in a report to the authorities in Susa. In the first place, the detailed account of the building (Neh 3:1-32) is not in first person narrative and is more than any busy bureaucrat would spend time poring over. Something to the effect that we built the wall up to half its height, we had good workers, and we finished it in fifty-two days (4:6[MT 3:38]; 6:15) would have been more to the point. The same misgivings are in order with respect to the night ride, the secrecy, problems encountered in the course of the work, and other details. Nehemiah's repeated complaints about opposition from within and without, some certainly real, others no doubt imaginary, could well have been counterproductive. They could have led Artaxerxes to follow the example of Darius and order a search in the archives, and the search could have come up with his earlier rescript forbidding the rebuilding of the rebellious city which had slipped his memory (Ezra 4:17-22).

Common to many redactional studies of the Nehemiah memoir, especially those which break it down into successive strata on the basis of content, is a tendency to ignore comparative material and, specifically, the literary and historical context of this autobiographical composition in which Nehemiah is presented as speaking to us from the mid-fifth century B.C., after the Achaemenid Empire had been in existence for a little over a century. It may therefore be helpful to look at the memoir from this perspective before proceeding further with our inquiry.[17]

---

would have been only the first stage (2:5). This raises another problem, since Artaxerxes had issued a firman some time earlier expressly forbidding the rebuilding of this city "harmful to kings and provinces" (Ezra 4:15, 17-24).

16. Williamson, *Ezra, Nehemiah*, xxiv-xxviii.

17. For what follows, see my "The Nehemiah Autobiographical Memoir," in *Language, Theology and the Bible: Essays in Honour of James Barr*, ed. Samuel E. Balentine and John Barton (Oxford: Clarendon, 1994) 199-212.

The Nehemiah Memoir in Its Contemporary Setting

First person narratives from early times are, for the most part, propagandistic and apologetic, and only occasionally anecdotal. The best-known examples are Mesopotamian royal inscriptions in the first person dealing with military campaigns, the building and dedicating of temples, and the like. With Herodotus and the gossipy Ctesias, we see the rudiments of the anecdotal type involving quite a bit of invention.[18] Characteristic of all of these, including the memoirs in Ezra-Nehemiah and, much later, the overtly apologetic *Bios* of Josephus, is an almost total lack of the qualities of subjectivity and self-awareness which first appear clearly in Augustine's *Confessions* and which are so prized in modern examples of the genre.[19] Arnaldo Momigliano remarked on the striking fact that, in Greek-speaking regions, biography and historiography originated about the same time, namely, in the fifth century B.C. during the heyday of Persian imperial rule.[20] While there are few if any direct contacts between Greeks and Jews during this period, as we saw earlier, it is fair to assume that both peoples were influenced by critical reaction to Persian imperialism. Ezra-Nehemiah and Esther evince a readiness to accommodate to Persian rule, even a positive attitude towards it. The mainland Greeks, on the other hand, were increasingly opposed to it, especially after the Ionian revolt under Darius I.[21] It is worth noting that in both Judah and Athens ethnic and national identity became a major concern about the same time.[22] As for the literary expression of this process of

18. Examples in Arnaldo Momigliano, "Fattori Orientali della Storiografia Ebraica Post-Esilica e della Storiografia Greca," *Quaderni 76* (Rome: Accademia Nazionale dei Lincei, 1966) 137-46.

19. Still in many respects unsurpassed is Georg Misch, *A History of Autobiography in Antiquity* (London: Routledge & Paul, 1950); trans. of *Geschichte der Autobiographie*, vol. 1: *Das Altertum*, 3rd ed. (Frankfurt-am-Main: Schulte-Bulmke, 1949; first published 1907).

20. Arnaldo Momigliano, *The Development of Greek Biography*, 2nd ed. (Cambridge, MA: Harvard University Press, 1993) 12.

21. The same can be said about Egyptians; see, e.g., Didier Devauchelle, "Le sentiment anti-perse chez les anciens Égyptiens," *Transeu 9* (1995) 67-80.

22. About the time of Nehemiah the Periclean law was enacted restricting Athenian citizenship to claimants both of whose parents were Athenian. See Fritz M. Heichlheim, "Ezra's Palestine and Periclean Athens," *ZRGG* 3 (1951) 251-53; J. K. Davies, "Athenian Citizenship: The Descent Group and the Alternatives," *CJ* 73 (1977-78) 105-21. On decrees of disenfranchisement *(atimia)* compared with exclusion from the *golah qāhāl* (Ezra 10:8) and the rab-

self-definition: it is hardly surprising if the international situation at that time generated new literary forms; if, for example, Greek political biography was stimulated by Persian biographical writings; or if Jewish historians began to incorporate archival documents cited verbatim; or if both began to show partiality for novelistic elements. In this respect it is interesting to observe that the lively biographical sketches in Herodotus and Xenophon are more often Eastern, and specifically Persian, than Greek in origin and character.

Nehemiah was also a contemporary of Ion of Chios, who wrote personal accounts of visits *(epidēmiai)* with notables of the stature of Pericles, Aeschylus, and Sophocles. Several of these contain autobiographical notes. Like so much else from that century, his work has survived only in fragments.[23] How much else of interest to our present investigation has not survived we of course do not know, but what there is suggests that Momigliano was correct in concluding that "autobiography was in the air in the Persian empire of the early fifth century, and both Jews and Greeks may have been stimulated by Persian and other oriental models to create something of their own."[24]

The Memoir Compared with Egyptian Commemorative Inscriptions

Parallels between Egyptian commemorative inscriptions and the Nehemiah memoir have been noted since the beginning of the last century,[25] but the first attempt at a systematic comparison was that of Gerhard von Rad in an article published in 1964.[26] Von Rad noted that the Egyptian texts address the reader and the deity directly, catalogue the speaker's achievements on behalf of the state, especially the care of temples and restoration of a disturbed public order, emphasize religious motivation, and feature the *Gedächtnismotiv,* the appeal to be remembered "for good." Von Rad also found a special point of contact in such expressions as "God

---

binic practice of *niddui,* see Gerald J. Blidstein, "ATIMIA: A Greek Parallel to Ezra X 8 and to Post-Biblical Exclusion from the Community," *VT* 24 (1974) 357-60.

23. *FGH*, 3B:276-83. See also the brief but informative article in *OCD*, 763-64.

24. *The Development of Greek Biography*, 37.

25. Alfred Bertholet, *Die Bücher Esra und Nehemia.* KHC (Tübingen: Mohr, 1902) 91.

26. Gerhard von Rad, "Die Nehemia-Denkschrift," *ZAW* 76 (1964) 176-87.

prompted me" and "God put it into my heart" (Neh 2:12; 7:5), which he took to be borrowings from the Egyptian prototypes.

The Egyptian texts preserve the same format from the Twenty-second Dynasty (945-715 B.C.) to the tomb text of Petosiris, late fourth or early third century B.C. The closest parallel, however, is the inscription written on the naophorous statue of the physician Udjahorresnet in the Vatican Museum, composed during the reign of Darius I.[27] It comes close to the Nehemiah text in its overtly, indeed obtrusively, apologetic intent, and like the Nehemiah memoir it records the author's role in resolving a critical situation. Its apologetic character is understandable given the author's compromised position as a Persian collaborator both during and after the conquest of Egypt by Cambyses. Nehemiah is apologetic in a different way, but he too was in basic sympathy with the imperial authorities while exploiting their benevolence for his own ends. Both came back to their own countries at a time of crisis, restored a disturbed social order, reformed the cult, ejected foreigners from the principal sanctuary (Jerusalem and Sais respectively), and provided for its upkeep.

There are, of course, differences. While the Egyptian inscription consists of forty-seven lines of hieroglyphic text, the Nehemiah *Denkschrift* is considerably longer, even in its excerpted form. It was probably written on papyrus and deposited in the temple archives — since it is addressed to the deity — whereas the Egyptian text had to fit on the open spaces of a basalt statue only 70 cm. high. Ulrich Kellermann also points out that the Nehemiah text deals primarily with one event while the Egyptian inscription contains a substantial catalogue of good deeds to the credit of the author.[28]

The Udjahorresnet inscription opens with a list of royal offerings made on behalf of the *ka* of the author, followed by a brief prayer to Osiris, lord of eternity (lines 1-6). There follow eight sections of unequal length, each beginning with the speaker's titulary followed by first person narrative. The sequence of events is in rough chronological order: activity under Cambyses, followed by the author's return to Egypt by order of Darius,

27. What follows is an abbreviated version of what I wrote in "The Mission of Udjahorresnet and Those of Ezra and Nehemiah," *JBL* 106 (1987) 409-21; and "The Nehemiah Autobiographical Memoir," 199-212.

28. Ulrich Kellermann, *Nehemia: Quellen, Überlieferung und Geschichte*. BZAW 102 (Berlin: Töpelmann, 1967) 80-82. This would be the case only for those who limit the memoir to the building of the wall, leaving aside the possibility that an editor has preserved only excerpts from the memoir.

and ending with a summary. The events in question are: (1) the author's appointment as chief physician and master of protocol after the conquest (lines 7-15); (2) cleansing of the Sais sanctuary of foreign elements, restoration of its cult and cult personnel and their endowments (16-23); (3) Cambyses' visit to Sais with gifts for the sanctuary, for which the author takes the credit (24-27); (4) Cambyses offers libations and ex-votos for the sanctuary, again at the urging of the author (28-30); (5) the author himself endows the sanctuary and tells how he saved the people during the invasion, protecting the weak against the strong (31-36); (6) he advances the cause of his family, especially his brothers (37-42); (7) he is sent back to Egypt by Darius to restore the House of Life, whose activities include the study of theology, medicine, temple administration, and ritual (43-45); (8) he details the honors bestowed on him by Cambyses and Darius; (9) the catalogue is rounded off with the remembrance prayer:

> O great gods who are in Sais! Remember all the benefactions done by the chief physician Udjahorresnet. May you do for him all benefactions! May you make his good name endure in this land for ever! (47)

The similarity with the Nehemiah text in both form and content is striking. Nehemiah also claims to have been sent to his homeland by another Persian ruler, to have restored and endowed the cult of the principal sanctuary, purged it of foreign elements, protected the weak against the strong, and furthered the careers of family members (Neh 5:14; 7:2). These parallels are not to be explained by direct borrowing, for which there is no evidence. It is rather the case that the formal features of the Near Eastern commemorative inscriptions continued to be reproduced, with local variations, throughout the Achaemenid Empire.

The most striking formal feature shared by these two texts is no doubt the prayer for remembrance, the *Gedächtnismotiv* with which, as I have suggested, the Nehemiah memoir probably ended: "Remember for my good, O my God, all that I have done for this people" (5:19). This is one of seven such invocations scattered unequally throughout the text,[29] all but two of which (4:4-5[MT 3:36-37]; 6:14) begin with the "remember me" formula. Three of the seven are directed against enemies and are therefore really imprecations (4:4-5[3:36-37]; 6:14; 13:29). This means that those in

---

29. Neh 4:4-5(MT 3:36-37); 5:19; 6:14; 13:14, 22, 29, 31.

which Nehemiah prays that God may remember him are restricted to the conclusion of the memoir, the final chapter, in which he claims to have reformed the cult (13:4-14), enforced observance of the Sabbath (13:15-22), and taken action to ensure the ritual purity of the community (13:23-31).

Having said all this, we would have to add that in several respects, and not only in length, the Nehemiah memoir is quite different from the Egyptian text. There is nothing in the latter comparable to the brief but vivid description of particular incidents — the night ride around the city wall (2:12-16), Shemaiah's plot and its undoing (6:10-14), the confrontation with Tobiah (13:4-9), the angry encounter with foreign women (13:23-27). The Nehemiah text also makes use of dialogue and even allows the protagonist to express emotion, including sadness and anger, especially anger, in reaction to certain situations. Some aspects of this portraiture can be explained in terms of traditional native sources; the Deuteronomic "biography" of Moses and the "autobiography" of Jeremiah come to mind. Be that as it may, it seems that in taking over the genre of the commemorative inscription the author of the Nehemiah memoir came up with a new Judaean way of writing history, and for this too he deserves to be remembered.

Genre and Literary Character of the Memoir

The two segments of the memoir (1:1–7:5 and 13:4-31) represent a very uneven coverage of an administration which lasted from the twentieth year of Artaxerxes I, therefore 445 B.C., to sometime after the thirty-second year of the same ruler (13:6), therefore not before 432 B.C. The longer excerpt (1:1–7:5) covers only the fifty-two days it took to rebuild the wall (6:15), while the shorter one records events in the final, possibly quite brief period of Nehemiah's term of office. The salient feature of the first segment is the pattern of opposition from the evil trio of Sanballat, Tobiah, and Geshem (Gashmu) and the spirited reaction of Nehemiah. Beginning with Nehemiah's arrival in Judah (2:9-10), the pattern unfolds as follows: a first stage in the work of reconstruction takes place; it attracts hostile attention from opponents ("When Sanballat *et alii* heard . . ."); which in its turn generates hostile reaction to Nehemiah's activity (anger, ridicule, threats, intimidation); which, finally, is followed by Nehemiah's countermeasures (rebuttal, prayer, vigorous action). This pattern is replicated through seven stages: Nehemiah's arrival on the scene (2:9-10); his decision to repair the wall (2:17-20); the work gets underway (4:1-5[MT 3:33-37]); the wall is half finished (4:6-9[3:38–4:3]); hostile plots are thwarted (4:17[11]); the work is completed apart from the gates (6:1-9); the work is finally completed (6:15-16). The patterning device seems to be deliberate, with the notice that the wall was half finished appropriately at the center of the septenary sequence. One would therefore think that the first person narrative was put together with more care than might at first appear.

Another patterning device in this first segment draws on the traditional language of the "holy war." Our attention is drawn to it at the point where Nehemiah assures his followers that their God will fight for them (4:20[MT 14]). The sequence is somewhat as follows: enemies conspire together; the righteous, whose numbers and resources are limited, call on their God for help; they form battle lines according to tribes; they are told they are not to fear since their God is on their side; the evil plans of the enemy are frustrated through divine intervention, and they are obliged to acknowledge the hand of God in what has transpired. This last item — "It seemed to them (the enemy) a truly astonishing achievement, and they realized that this work was our God's doing" (6:16) — can be compared with the exclamation of the psalmist: "This is Yahweh's doing, and it is marvellous in our eyes" (Ps 118:23).

The title *divrê nĕḥemyâ* ("the chronicles of Nehemiah," Neh 1:1) does not provide much guidance on the issue of genre. Where this title (*dĕvārîm, divrê X*) occurs as a superscript to prophetic (Jer 1:1; Amos 1:1) or didactic collections (Prov 30:1; Eccl 1:1), the reference is to sayings. This meaning is clearly inappropriate for Nehemiah 1–13, which is narrative rather than aphoristic and is neither prophetic nor sapiential. A better guide can be found in Chronicles, where *dĕvārîm* can refer either to the work of the putative author or the deeds of the subject which he recounts. Since Neh 1:1 introduces the Nehemiah story as a whole, not just the autobiographical parts, it should be understood as a chronicle about Nehemiah which incorporates first person narrative.

If we take the first person Nehemiah narrative as it is, together with its frequent prayers, invocations, and imprecations, and add to these the expressions of emotion, mostly anger, which are no less frequent, we would be inclined to read it as addressed to God rather than to the Persian emperor. This would be in keeping with one approach to genre which takes its cue from a common pattern in Psalms according to which a wronged party pleads its cause with God. Among recent and not-so-recent commentators, Kellermann has developed this approach the furthest. He argued that this *Gebet des Angeklagten* ("prayer of the accused"), which occurs in Jeremiah and Job in addition to canonical psalms, provides the closest parallel to the form in which the Nehemiah memoir is cast.[30] Taking over earlier studies on this *Gattung*,[31] Kellermann concluded that this kind of discourse is rooted in forensic procedures current in Judah. Kellermann's approach is suggestive, and there may be echoes here and there of forensic situations, especially in the "remember me" prayer to God for a hearing. We would have to add, however, that there is much in the first person narrative which cannot be construed in this way. In fact, there is nothing in the Israelite literary corpus quite like the Nehemiah memoir, with the obvious exception of the Ezra first person narrative, which in fact some investigators think was written as a counter to that of Nehemiah.

Another approach to the genre issue starts out from Mesopotamian inscriptions commemorating the accomplishments, mostly architectural and military, of the rulers of cities and states.[32] These inscriptions are in the first person, the speaker generally identifies himself in the opening sentence, the favor of the deity is invoked, and the piety, devotion, and assiduity of the royal speaker or writer are emphasized. Deeds are recorded, not necessarily in chronological order, opponents are denounced as impious and recommended for severe treatment by the deity, and the speaker's predecessors are often disparaged. Since the purpose was to keep the speaker's memory alive with both the deity and posterity, an inscription of this kind would have been set up in a public place, probably a temple, thus assuring a lasting memorial.[33] Some of these texts also contain the prayer

---

30. Kellermann, *Nehemia*, 84-88. The thesis is critiqued in a review by J. A. Emerton, *JTS* 23 (1972) 171-85; Willy Schottroff, *"Gedenken" im Alten Orient und im Alten Testament.* 2nd ed. WMANT 15 (Neukirchen-Vluyn: Neukirchener, 1967) 392-93.

31. Hans Schmidt, *Das Gebet des Angeklagten im Alten Testament.* BZAW 49 (Giessen: Töpelmann, 1928); Hans Jochen Boecker, *Redeformen des Rechtslebens im Alten Testament.* WMANT 14 (Neukirchen-Vluyn: Neukirchener, 1964).

32. The most thorough investigation along these lines was that of Sigmund Mowinckel, who returned to it several times over a period of about half a century. See esp. his "Die vorderasiatischen Königs- und Fürsteninschriften," in *Eucharistērion: Hermann Gunkel zum 60. Geburtstag,* ed. Hans Schmidt. FRLANT N.S. 19 (Göttingen: Vandenhoeck & Ruprecht, 1923) 1:278-322; and *Studien zu dem Buche Esra-Nehemia,* vol. 2: *Die Nehemia-Denkschrift* (Oslo: Universitetsforlaget, 1965).

33. Cf. Isa 56:5 and 1 Macc 14:48-49. A good example is the inscription of Idrimi of Alalakh which was discovered in a temple in that city; for the text, see *ANET,* 557-58; and Sid-

to a deity to bear in mind *(zakāru)* the good deeds of the speaker or the evil deeds of his opponents. Nebuchadnezzar II, for example, prays as follows to the Babylonian imperial patron-deity: "O Marduk, my lord, remember my deeds favorably for good; may these my good deeds be always before your mind."[34]

The prayer to be remembered "for good" came to serve as a model for commemorative inscriptions of different kinds throughout the Near East during and well beyond the two centuries of Achaemenid rule. It can be found, for example, in Aramaic synagogue inscriptions (דכיר לטב) as late as the Byzantine period.[35] The commemorative intent is the same whether the petitioner is the ruler of an empire or a pious Jew who has put up the money for a pillar or a mosaic in the local synagogue.

The Nehemiah Memoir in the Context of the Book (Nehemiah 1–13)

The Nehemiah story combines first and third person discourse. It is basically a narrative about Nehemiah which incorporates autobiographical material. Rather than inviting an elaborate theory of redactional stratification, the uneven distribution of the autobiographical parts (roughly chs. 1–7 and ch. 13) suggests that an editor has excerpted passages from a more complete first person account no longer extant. The same conclusion follows from the abrupt beginning — after the title — where we would expect the author of the memoir to introduce himself. As we read on, it soon becomes clear that the first person narrative is not a straightforward transcription from an original source. In the first section, the prayer uttered by Nehemiah on hearing the bad news from Judah (1:5-11a) has probably been inserted by an editor, a common procedure. It uses familiar Deuteronomic and Chronistic language, speaks of prayer offered by day and night which

---

ney Smith, *The Statue of Idri-mi* (London: British Institute of Archaeology in Ankara, 1945). Further discussion of these inscriptions can be found in John Van Seters, *In Search of History: Historiography in the Ancient World and the Origins of Biblical History* (New Haven: Yale University Press, 1983) 60-68; Tremper Longman III, *Fictional Akkadian Autobiography* (Winona Lake: Eisenbrauns, 1991) 60-77, 216-18.

34. *ANET*, 307; see also *ANET* 316, 317, 562-63. On these and similar formulations, see the study of Schottroff, *"Gedenken" im Alten Orient und im Alten Testament*.

35. Schottroff, *"Gedenken" im Alten Orient und im Alten Testament*, 86-89.

does not fit the context, does not refer to the occasion which elicited it, and anticipates the request for a leave of absence. More significant are two major dislocations in the sequence of events recorded. The pattern reproduced in the first part of the memoir — work on the wall, opposition from different quarters, neutralization of opposition by prayer and vigorous countermeasures — is interrupted by Nehemiah's account of his removal of social abuses concluding with his personal *apologia* (5:1-19). The record of these social reforms calls to mind Solon's first person account of his social and political reforms carried out a century and a half earlier and reported in Aristotle's *Constitution of Athens.*[36] It also resembles the restoration of social order as a standard topos in Egyptian biographical and autobiographical inscriptions, for example, those of Djed-khons-ef-ankh (Twenty-second Dynasty) and Udjahorresnet. This part of Nehemiah's *apologia* would fit much better at the end of the memoir than in its present position. It recapitulates twelve years in office and concludes with the "remember me" formula addressed to the deity *(zokrâ-lî)*, elsewhere restricted to the last chapter of the book. It would therefore make a more fitting conclusion to the memoir than the inconsequential allusion to the wood offering with which the memoir now ends (13:31).

Another structural problem is the location of the service of dedication of the city wall (12:27-43). We would expect the ceremony to follow soon after the work was finished and the city repopulated, but it has been moved forward to serve as the finale to a series of episodes beginning and ending with lists (7:5b–12:26). The account of the dedication ceremony introduces first person discourse here and there (12:31, 38, 40), but the narrative is on the whole in the third person, with no first person plural where we would most expect it. The presence of Ezra as leader of the liturgical musicians (12:36) cannot very well be part of the Nehemiah memoir, as we have seen, and lists of names, like those of the lay and clerical participants in the circumambulation of the wall, are generally subject to updating with the passage of time and changing situations.[37] Torrey solved the problem

---

36. See Edwin M. Yamauchi, "Two Reformers Compared: Solon of Athens and Nehemiah of Jerusalem," in *The Bible World: Essays in Honor of Cyrus H. Gordon,* ed. Gary Rendsburg et al. (New York: Ktav, 1980) 269-92. The text of Aristotle can be found, with H. Rackham's translation, in *LCL* 285 (Cambridge, MA: Harvard University Press, 1935): *Athenian Constitution,* v-ix.

37. The list of Levitical participants features a certain Zechariah (12:35), whose genealogy, if correct, makes him the great-grandson of the Mattaniah settled in Jerusalem by

more drastically by arguing that the entire episode is a pure invention of the Chronicler.[38] We might suggest more cautiously that it is the work of an editor writing long after the time of Nehemiah, one obviously familiar with Chronicles, who understandably attempted to reproduce the style of the memoir.

The first long segment of the memoir ends with the completion of the wall, the securing of Jerusalem under the command of Nehemiah's brother Hanani, and plans for a synoecism, a transfer of population into the city (7:1-5a). The long census list which follows (7:5b-73a[MT 72a]) is introduced in the first person (7:5b), and in its present context is meant to provide a demographic basis for the repopulation of the city. It nevertheless does not serve that purpose and does not belong to the memoir. The list of those relocated in Jerusalem by a process of decimation, and perhaps not on such a voluntary basis as the narrator wishes us to think, follows somewhat later (11:1-24) and is of a completely different nature from the census list in Nehemiah 7, especially with respect to the lay component. I suggest that in such a succinct narrative as is Nehemiah 1–13 the reproduction of the Ezra 2:1-67 list of "those who had come up in the beginning," or "those who had come up from the captivity of the diaspora," calls for an explanation which goes beyond the scope of the memoir. Its location at this point, the conclusion of Nehemiah's epic task, creates an *inclusio* with the other version of the list in Ezra 2:1-67. It not only links Nehemiah's achievement with the beginnings, the first return and work on the temple as recounted in Ezra 1–6, but signifies the end of a phase and the fulfillment of a preordained plan. Like the "register of the house of Israel" in Ezekiel (Ezek 13:9), it can be read as symbolic of the saved community, the creation of a community out of those who had survived the exile with their faith intact, even as embodying a kind of realized eschatology. In this sense it can be read as anticipating the list of the founders *(hāri'šônîm)* referred to but not reproduced in the Damascus Document (CD IV 2-12) and, more distantly, the 144,000 sealed out of every tribe of Israel in the Christian apocalypse (Rev 7:1-8).

The second and shorter segment of the memoir in the last chapter of the book consists in three sections of unequal length, each beginning with a vague temporal phrase ("now before this," "in those days," "also in those

---

Nehemiah (11:17; cf. 1 Chr 9:15). In that case his *floruit* would have been about the middle of the fourth century B.C.

38. Torrey, *Ezra Studies*, 248-49.

days") and concluding with the traditional remembrance formula *zokrâ-lî* ("remember me") addressed to God. These sections deal sequentially with reform of temple management (13:4-14), Sabbath observance (13:15-22), and exogamous marriage (13:23-31). I add to this the suggestion made earlier that Nehemiah's *apologia* in 5:14-19 (or 5:1-19) probably followed these measures, thus bringing the memoir to a more fitting conclusion.

Though clearly quite separate in origin, the census list (7:5b-73a[MT 72a]) is incorporated into the memoir by the prefatory statement that Nehemiah found it (where, he doesn't say; 7:5b). In the context, it seems to have been intended to serve as a basis for the synoecism, though the actual notice about this important event and the list of those to be transferred to Jerusalem comes only later (11:1-24). We saw that the public reading and exposition of the law that follows is basically Ezra material which has been expanded with a a parallel version featuring Nehemiah the governor and Levites (7:73b[72b]–8:12). Still involving Ezra in his scribal capacity (8:13), the reading of the law follows, which leads in its turn to the celebration of Sukkoth, no doubt with reference to Deut 16:13-15 and 31:9-13. At this point (Neh 8:13-18), we are told that the Israelites had not celebrated this festival since the time of Joshua bin-Nun (v. 17). This is transparently a literary trope characteristic of Chronicles (cf. 2 Chr 30:25-26; 35:18), serving here as another way of aligning current events with ancient traditions. Since, however, MT has the unusual spelling Jeshua *(yēšûaʿ)*, the retrospective allusion may originally have been to the celebration of Sukkoth by the first immigrants in which Jeshua the priest played the leading role (Ezra 3:1-6).[39] The brief account of a penitential service which follows (Neh 9:1-5), while modelled on the public reading of the law in 7:73b[72b]–8:12, serves to introduce the confession of sin recited by Levites and Nehemiah's covenant by excluding from participation all those not of "the seed of Israel," in other words, all those of foreign stock.

It is noticeable how in the preparation for the covenant,[40] as in the covenant itself, Levites play a dominant role. It is they who read and ex-

---

39. On that reading of the sense of the text, *bin-nûn* would have been added to bring it into closer conformity with the similar expressions in Chronicles which look back to the time of Solomon (2 Chr 30:25-26) and Samuel (2 Chr 35:18).

40. Instead of *běrît*, the Hebrew terms used are *ʾămānâ* ("firm commitment," only here at 10:1[Eng. 9:38] and 11:23), *ʾālâ* ("curse"), and *šěvûʿâ* ("oath," 10:30[29]). Since oath-taking implied a self-imposed curse, these two terms should be read as hendiadys, similar to "the covenant and oath," less literally, "the sworn covenant," of Deut 29:12(MT 11).

pound the law (8:7-12) and conduct the penitential service (9:1-5), which ends with their intonation of a psalm:

> From age to age
> May they bless your glorious name
> Exalted beyond every blessing and praise!

which then merges with the long public confession of sin following.[41] They are named before priests in the introduction to the signed and sealed agreement (9:38[MT 10:1]) and, allowing for some variant forms, most of the Levites involved in the penitential service (9:4-5), and many of those named in the public reading of the law (8:7-12), appear as signatories to the covenant (10:9-13[MT 10-14]). In the text itself Nehemiah the governor heads the list of signatories which, exceptionally, precedes rather than follows the stipulations, and from which Ezra is conspicuously absent.

Nehemiah 10 is significantly different from the standard Deuteronomic *běrît*, a bilateral agreement involving the people of Israel as a whole by means of which they commit themselves to the observance of the law in general terms.[42] Nehemiah's "firm commitment," on the contrary, is undertaken by a specific segment of the population, lay and clerical. It is a written and sealed document to which the signatories attach their names and by which they oblige themselves unilaterally under oath to fulfil certain specific obligations. It is also a new and one-time agreement, not a

---

41. According to LXX, Ezra recites the prayer. The communal confession of sin was added by a redactor whose theology, according to Hugh Williamson, does not conform to that of Nehemiah; see his essay, "The Belief System of the Book of Nehemiah," in *The Crisis of Israelite Religion,* ed. Bob Becking and Marjo C. A. Korpel. OtSt 42 (Leiden: Brill, 1999) 276-87. On this confessional prayer, see the references in my *Ezra-Nehemiah,* 297; and, more recently, Rolf Rendtorff, "Nehemiah 9: An Important Witness of Theological Reflection," in *Tehillah le-Moshe: Biblical and Judaic Studies in Honor of Moshe Greenberg,* ed. Mordechai Cogan, Barry L. Eichler, and Jeffrey H. Tigay (Winona Lake: Eisenbrauns, 1997) 111-17; Mark J. Boda, *Praying the Tradition: The Origin and Use of Tradition in Nehemiah 9.* BZAW 277 (Berlin: de Gruyter, 1999). Volker Pröbstl, *Nehemia 9, Psalm 106 und Psalm 136 und die Rezeption des Pentateuchs* (Göttingen: Cuvillier, 1997), tries to demonstrate that Nehemiah 9 proves that the Pentateuch was fixed and authoritative at the time of composition.

42. In addition to the commentaries on Nehemiah 10, see Klaus Baltzer, *The Covenant Formulary in Old Testament, Jewish, and Early Christian Writings* (Philadelphia: Fortress, 1971) 43-47; the remarks of Dennis J. McCarthy, "Covenant and Law in Chronicles-Nehemiah," *CBQ* 44 (1982) 25-44; David S. Sperling, "Rethinking Covenant in Late Biblical Books," *Bib* 70 (1989) 50-73.

covenant renewal.[43] This type of "sworn covenant" seems to have been part of a strategy characteristic of the dominant *golah* group. At one point of the first person narrative we hear about a similar commitment imposed by Nehemiah on the wealthy nobility, lay and priestly, with the obligation to return confiscated land and houses to an impoverished peasantry and discontinue the practice of making loans at interest and selling into indentured service. This, too, was confirmed by an oath dramatically mimicked by Nehemiah (5:11-13). In the second, briefer segment of the memoir, those Judaeans who had married women from Ashdod, and whose children no longer spoke Hebrew, were obliged by Nehemiah, after a show of violence, to swear an oath to observe the law as stated in Deut 7:3 to avoid such marriages. Since they had already contracted these marriages, we do not know whether Nehemiah followed the example of Ezra and coerced them into divorcing their wives and sending away the children or whether the oath was administered to others contemplating such marriages (13:25-27).

The pattern is much the same with the agreement imposed by Ezra in his campaign against marriage with women outside of the *golah*. It is confirmed by an oath, and therefore a self-imposed curse (Ezra 10:5); it is limited to specific signatories, i.e., members of the *golah* whose names are recorded in writing (10:18-43); and it deals with one specific issue. We might compare it with the Chronicler's account of a covenant made during the reign of the Judaean king Asa (2 Chronicles 15). This covenant involved a plenary gathering, attendance at which was mandatory and enforced with penalties. Whereas absentees at Ezra's assembly only forfeited their membership in the *golah* assembly together with their immovable property (Ezra 10:8) — no small penalty — those who absented themselves from Asa's assembly were threatened with the death penalty (2 Chr 15:12-15). This type of pact may be seen as transitional between the standard Deuteronomic form of the covenant in which the entire people is involved and the kind of sectarian covenant exemplified in the Qumran texts, especially the Damascus Document (CD).[44] I referred earlier to the proposal of Mor-

---

43. I do not see how the reading of the law, Sukkoth, the penitential service and confessional prayer leading to the covenant can be construed as forming a coherent covenant renewal ceremony, as argued by Michael W. Duggan, *The Covenant Renewal in Ezra-Nehemiah (Neh 7:72b-10:40): An Exegetical, Literary, and Theological Study.* SBLDS 164 (Atlanta: SBL, 2001).

44. See Baltzer, *The Covenant Formulary*, 99-122; James C. VanderKam, "Covenant," *EDSS* (2000) 1:152-54.

ton Smith according to which Nehemiah 10 reflects a covenant made by a Levitical sect and attributed to Nehemiah in the early Hellenistic period, an anticipation of the covenant in the land of Damascus.[45]

The form in which the ceremony is laid out is unusual in several respects. It is unusual, in the first place, for the list of signatories to precede the stipulations of the agreement. Participants in and witnesses to an agreement are commonly listed after the statement of terms, as in the Elephantine papyri (e.g., AP 28, witnesses to an assignment of slaves). The heading also lists the parties to the agreement in a different order from that of the list, and the lay leaders are designated differently, *śārîm* ("princes" or "leading dignitaries") in the heading as against *rā'šîm* ("heads," "leaders") in the list (10:15[Eng. 14]). Most commentators have concluded that the list of names, which breaks the natural syntactic nexus between 9:38(MT 10:1) and 10:28(29), has been added, and this conclusion is strengthened by the obviously artificial nature of the record itself. The list of twenty-two priests has drawn heavily on the archival lists in 12:1-7 and 12:12-21, and most of the forty-four names of laity are taken from the census in Ezra 2/Nehemiah 7 and the list of workers on Nehemiah's wall-building project (Neh 3:1-32).

The list of signatories would therefore predispose us to regard the covenant, in its final formulation, as considerably later than the time of Nehemiah. An even clearer indication of a later date is the correspondence between the stipulations of the sworn agreement and the reforming activity of Nehemiah during his second tour of duty recorded in 13:4-31. The only exception is the commitment to observe the seventh fallow year (Exod 23:10-11; Lev 25:1-7) and the quite distinct law of *šĕmiṭṭâ*, the remission of debts in the seventh year and restitution of persons or property taken in pledge (Deut 15:1-18). If, however, the passage in which Nehemiah coerced the upper-class laity and clergy to make full restitution to their debtors (Neh 5:1-19) stood originally at the end of the memoir, as I proposed earlier, the correspondence would be complete. From this literary fact we may draw the historical conclusion that the pact described in Nehemiah 10 reflects a movement in the late Persian or early Hellenistic period to implement the agenda of Nehemiah and therefore testifies to the enduring effect of his reforming activity.

The first and probably the most important item was the prohibition of

45. Smith, *NTS* 7 (1960-61) 355-59.

intermarriage with "the peoples of the land," a prohibition essential for implementing Nehemiah's policy of ritual ethnicity, and now no longer restricted to marriage with indigenous women (Neh 10:30[MT 31]; 13:25). Sabbath observance as a distinctive marker of ritual identity is expanded to cover buying as well as selling and is to apply in addition to festivals (10:31a[32a]; 13:15-22). These two stipulations therefore provide good examples of expansive legal interpretation. Enforcement of *šĕmiṭṭâ* (remission of debts) served as a powerful tool for curbing the power of the aristocracy, lay and clerical, which was one of the primary aims of Nehemiah as governor (10:31b[32b]; 5:1-13). The last three stipulations aim to assure the maintenance of the Jerusalem cult: the temple tax of a third of a shekel (10:32[33]; 13:10);[46] the wood offering (10:34[35]; 13:31a), required for the fire of the morning and evening sacrifices (Lev 6:9, 12-13[MT 2, 5-6]) but not specifically mandated in the Pentateuch; and firstfruits and tithes (10:35-39[36-40]; 13:12-13, 31b). The commitment to tithing had special significance in view of Nehemiah's close association with Levites in his struggle to control the temple, its personnel and resources. The stipulation added to the tithe article (10:37b-38[38b-39]), that it was to be collected by Levites, reflects Nehemiah's vigorous action in support of the Levites neglected during his absence at the imperial court (13:10-12). The codicil added to this stipulation, that it was to be collected under the supervision of the Aaronite priesthood to whom was to be ceded 10 percent of the tithe (therefore a tithe of the tithe), reflects a later attempt to control the Levites on the part of the temple priesthood. In the meantime, Nehemiah's appointment of a panel to control collection and distribution of the tithe, consisting in a priest, a Levite, a temple musician, and a scribe who no doubt represented his interests as governor (13:13), helped to assure a good measure of civic control over this important resource.[47] It is Nehemiah's support of the Levitical order which gives plausibility to Smith's suggestion, mentioned earlier, that the pact derives from Levites in the early Hellenistic period as a means of perpetuating the work of their hero Nehe-

---

46. Given the inexorable tendency of taxation to increase, the half-shekel tax of Pentateuchal law (Exod 30:11-16; 38:25-26) would be later than the Nehemiah covenant. It remained at a half-shekel into the Roman period (Josephus, *Ant.* 18.312; *War* 7.216-18; Matt 17:24-27). Cf. the two shekel tax payable for the Elephantine temple and the cult of Ya'u, Ishumbethel, and Anathbethel in AP 22.

47. See Joachim Schaper, "The Temple Treasury Committee in the Times of Nehemiah and Ezra," *VT* 47 (1997) 200-6.

miah and that it was directed against the then dominant assimilationist party headquartered in the Jerusalem temple.[48]

The Nehemiah Profile

Almost all scholars who have given close and critical attention to Ezra-Nehemiah agree that Nehemiah emerges as a much more solid and credible historical figure than Ezra. His autobiographical record is more clearly defined within its editorially-arranged narrative framework than that of Ezra. One linguistic indication of its literary integrity is the terminology used to describe Judaean society: only in the first long section of the memoir do we find the threefold formulation *ḥōrîm, sĕgānîm, hā'ām* (or *yeter hā'ām*), namely, hereditary nobles, administrative officials, ordinary people, or the rest of the people. In the nonmemoir parts of Nehemiah 1–13 other terms are used for the socially prominent, including *śārîm* (princes, chiefs), *rā'šîm* (heads, leaders), *'addîrîm* (noblemen).[49] In general, the Nehemiah autobiographical passages are more credible and, in the context of contemporary political and literary history, more plausible than those purporting to come from Ezra. The memoir is, of course, heavily propagandistic, hence the need to distinguish between the generally credible historical situations and events which it records and the interpretative "spin" placed on them by the writer.

The author and subject of the memoir was a member of an old Jerusalemite family (Neh 2:2-5). He was not a descendant of the Judaean royal house,[50] nor was he a eunuch, as some commentators have supposed he

48. For a more detailed discussion of the stipulations of "the sworn covenant" as a form of halakic development, see, in addition to the commentaries, David J. A. Clines, "Nehemiah 10 as an Example of Early Jewish Biblical Exegesis," *JSOT* 21 (1981) 111-17; Michael Fishbane, *Biblical Interpretation in Ancient Israel* (Oxford: Clarendon, 1985) 129-34, 165-66, 213-16. Fishbane observes appositely that "the laws in Neh. 10 are not meant for all Israel, but rather for a small sectarian group which wished to be separate from the 'peoples of the land' (and other Israelites)" (165). On the structure of the covenant, see David A. Glatt-Gilad, "Reflections on the Structure and Significance of the 'amānāh (Neh 10.29-40), *ZAW* 112 (2000) 386-95.

49. For the threefold formulation in the memoir, see Neh 2:16; 4:14; 19[8, 13]; 5:7; 7:5. It is worth noting that these terms do not occur at all in Chronicles.

50. As maintained by Kellermann, 156-57, on which see the review by Emerton, *JTS* 23 (1972) 177.

must have been as cupbearer to Artaxerxes at the court in Susa. Some royal cupbearers or stewards were eunuchs and some were not. If Nehemiah had been a eunuch, one or another of his many enemies would have used it against him, especially since the sexually mutilated were excluded from the Israelite assembly and therefore from entering the temple (Deut 23:1[MT 2]).[51] The royal wine steward was a post of no mean status and honor, but also no mean danger. Herodotus tells of a certain royal official called Prexaspes whose son was cupbearer to Xerxes and who, in an excess of candor, told the king that he (Xerxes) had a reputation as a heavy drinker. In a fit of rage Xerxes took his bow and shot the son of Prexaspes, his faithful cupbearer, through the heart (3.34-35). The historians also provide rather more routine examples of what this office entailed. We are told, for example, that the goblet is to be offered to the king with three fingers, but not before some of the wine is poured into the left hand and sipped, poison being the method of choice for disposing of opponents in the numerous intrigues at the Persian court.[52]

Like the court physician Democedes (Herodotus 3.125, 129-37), and perhaps also the Egyptian notable Udjahorresnet, Nehemiah used his position to obtain a leave of absence, in his case in order to repair the sepulchres of his ancestors and to rebuild the ruined city. Nehemiah was one of several Jews serving in an administrative position in the vast Persian imperial bureaucracy. Apart from those who are assigned such a role in fictional narratives (e.g., Ahiqar, Tobit, Mordecai, Daniel alias Belteshazzar), we have the Hananiah whose name crops up in the Elephantine papyri as a link between the satrap Arsham — and ultimately Darius II — and the colony. Several scholars have been tempted to identify him with Nehemiah's relative Hanani, who seems to have led a delegation from Judah to Susa to solicit Nehemiah's assistance (Neh 1:2) and who later was appointed military commander of Jerusalem (7:2). Bezalel Porten even made the interesting but unverifiable further suggestion that he, rather than Bigvai (or Bagohi, AP 30:1), may have succeeded Nehemiah as governor of the province.[53] We gather from the papyri that Hananiah's arrival in the province, and his passing on to the leadership of the colony a message

51. *eunouchos* in LXXB and LXXS is an understandable scribal slip for *oinochoos* ("wine steward"), as in LXXA.

52. Xenophon, *Cyr.* i.3.8-10.

53. Bezalel Porten, *Archives from Elephantine: The Life of an Ancient Jewish Military Colony* (Berkeley: University of California Press, 1968) 130-33, 279-82.

from the satrapal court about when to celebrate Passover–Unleavened Bread, may have coincided with, and perhaps have precipitated, the hostility on the part of the priests of the god Khnum which led to the destruction of the Jewish temple.[54]

After his appointment as governor of the province, Nehemiah set about the task of fortifying and repopulating Jerusalem. How much further his ambitions extended we are not told, except through the prejudiced but perhaps not entirely uninformed voice of his opponents. Rumors emanating from Sanballat of Samaria and the Kedarite Arab sheik Gashmu alleged that repair of the city wall was intended as the prelude to rebellion and the proclamation of an independent state under Nehemiah as king (Neh 6:6-7). Some commentators are prepared to accept these allegations as plausible, but it is difficult to believe that Nehemiah could have entertained such unrealistic, not to say suicidal, ambitions. At any rate, the memoir relates how he set about achieving the goals explicitly stated in his commission.

Nehemiah was apparently appointed governor (*peḥâ*, 5:14; 12:26; *tiršātāʾ*, 8:9; 10:1[2]) in the same year, 445 B.C., in which he obtained his leave of absence from the court (5:14).[55] The biblical record testifies that he was not the first to fill this office[56] and that therefore the hypothesis of Albrecht Alt, that Judah was previously under the jurisdiction of Samaria and that Nehemiah's principal achievement as its first governor was to establish its relative autonomy within the Achaemenid Empire, cannot be sustained, a conclusion now widely accepted.[57] Three decades ago Naḥman

---

54. AP 21; dated to the fifth year of Darius II, therefore 419 B.C.

55. Robert North's arguments for Nehemiah as a "charismatic building contractor" rather than governor are ingenious rather than persuasive, and based in part on speculative textual emendation. Nehemiah's delivery of letters from Artaxerxes to provincial governors in the Transeuphrates satrapy implies no more than that he was appointed after his arrival in Judah. See Robert North, "Civil Authority in Ezra," in *Studi in Onore di Edoardo Volterra*, 6 (Milan: Giuffrè, 1971) 377-404.

56. Sheshbazzar (Ezra 5:14; cf. 1 Esd 2:12 *prostatēs*), Zerubbabel (Hag 1:1, 14; 2:2, 21). Mal 1:8 refers to but does not name a governor of the province, and Nehemiah himself refers to his predecessors in the office of governor (Neh 5:15).

57. Albrecht Alt, "Die Rolle Samarias bei der Entstehung des Judentums," *Festschrift Otto Procksch zum 60. Geburtstag* (Leipzig: Deichert & Hinrichs, 1934) 5-28 = *Kleine Schriften zur Geschichte des Volkes Israel*, 2 (Munich: Beck, 1953) 316-37. One of the few defenders of this theory in recent decades is Sean E. McEvenue, "The Political Structure in Judah from Cyrus to Nehemiah," *CBQ* 43 (1981) 353-64.

Avigad published two inscribed seals and some seventy seal impressions (bullae), with the help of which he reconstructed a sequence of eight governors of the province. While it is important to bear in mind that most of these finds are unprovenanced, the sequence of governors put together by Avigad is credible. The list is as follows:

Sheshbazzar (Ezra 5:14)
Zerubbabel (Hag 1:1, 14)
Nehemiah (Neh 5:14; 12:26)
Bagohi (Bigvai) (AP 30:1)
Yehezqiyah (coins from Beth-zur and Tell Jemme)
Elnathan (bullae)
Yeho'ezer (jar impression from Ramat Rachel)
Ahzai (jar impression from Ramat Rachel; Neh 11:13?)[58]

Whatever conclusions we reach about the government of Judah after Nehemiah — that is, during the second century of Achaemenid rule — it seems certain that he had predecessors in the office of governor, at least the first two listed by Avigad. It is against these that he levels the fairly standard accusation of fleecing the common people while maintaining their own extravagant lifestyle.

As governor, Nehemiah would have had a court of however modest dimensions. If Jerusalem was undefended and seriously underpopulated in the early years of his tenure, as we are led to believe, the administrative center of the province may still have been at Mizpah (tell en-Naṣbeh, about eight miles north of Jerusalem) — a situation perhaps implied in the cryptic reference to Mizpah as "belonging to the jurisdiction (lit., 'throne') of the governor of Trans-Euphrates."[59] There is much that we do not know

---

58. Naḥman Avigad, *Bullae and Seals from a Post-Exilic Judean Archive.* Qedem 4 (Jerusalem: Hebrew University Institute of Archaeology, 1976). See also Frank Moore Cross, "Aspects of Samaritan and Jewish History in Late Persian and Hellenistic Times," *HTR* 59 (1966) 201-11; "Samaria and Jerusalem in the Era of the Restoration," in *From Epic to Canon: History and Literature in Ancient Israel* (Baltimore: Johns Hopkins University Press, 1998) 173-202; John W. Betlyon, "The Provincial Government of Persian Period Judea and the Yehud Coins," *JBL* 105 (1986) 633-42; H. G. M. Williamson, "The Governors of Judah under the Persians," *TynBul* 39 (1988) 59-82.

59. If the reference is to the residence of the satrap on his visits to the province, as I suggested in my commentary (*Ezra-Nehemiah*, 235), this would increase the likelihood that it

about the history of the province in the mid-fifth century B.C., to say the obvious, and what conclusions have been drawn from the archaeological data do not always inspire confidence.[60] Nehemiah alludes at several points of the memoir to his retainers *(nĕʿārîm)*, who no doubt included a bodyguard (4:16, 23[MT 10, 17]; 5:10, 16; 13:19). These are occasionally mentioned in association with family members who lived at his expense (4:23[17]; 5:10, 14), including his brother Hanani and other brothers referred to but not named (1:2). Surrounded by enemies on every side — both real and, we suspect, imaginary — it was natural that Nehemiah should rely heavily on relatives, and we may assume that Hanani, appointed commander of the Jerusalem garrison (7:2), was not the only family member assigned a prominent position in Nehemiah's administration. The court also included *yĕhûdîm*, probably referring to members of distinguished Judeo-Babylonian families,[61] administration officials, foreigners including no doubt Persians, and the inevitable hangers-on and freeloaders. For a small, impoverished province, a retinue of a hundred and fifty looks like a quite impressive set-up.

The Nehemiah memoir gives the impression of enemies on every side. As the story develops it becomes clear that the principal external opponents, the Sanballat dynasty in Samaria and the Tobiah dynasty in Ammon, were closely connected to the Judaean nobility, both lay and priestly. Connections were cemented by marriage alliances among these "sworn associates."[62] Tobiah married into the distinguished Judean Arah family (Neh 6:18; cf. 7:10 = Ezra 2:5), while his son Jehohanan married the daughter of Meshullam, descendant of another prominent family (Neh 6:18). Tobiah's contacts in Judah enabled him to win lucrative commercial concessions in the temple economy during Nehemiah's temporary absence in Susa (13:4-9). These did not survive Nehemiah's return, and for the later

---

was still the administrative center of the province, as it had been since the Babylonian conquest (2 Kgs 25:23, 25; Jer 40–41).

60. E.g., was Bethel destroyed in the late Neo-Babylonian or early Persian period, as William F. Albright, *Archaeology and the Religion of Israel*, 5th ed. (Garden City: Doubleday, 1968) 166; and James Leon Kelso, "Bethel," *NEAEHL* (1993) 1:194, claim; or as late as the mid-fifth century, as George Ernest Wright and Paul W. Lapp, in Ephraim Stern, *The Material Culture of the Land of the Bible in the Persian Period, 538-332 B.C.* (Warminster: Aris & Phillips, 1982) 31, 254, 280 n. 71, maintain?

61. On the meaning of this term, see my *Ezra-Nehemiah*, 223.

62. *baʿălê šĕvûʿâ*, lit., "masters of the oath" (Neh 6:18); cf. Akkadian *bēl adē*.

history of the Tobiad dynasty we have other sources of information. The family of Sanballat, governor of Samaria, had also married into the Jerusalemite high-priestly family, no doubt with the idea of sharing in, and perhaps eventually taking over, control of the temple and its considerable assets (13:28). Josephus's account of the marriage of Manasseh, brother of the high priest Jaddua, to Nikaso, daughter of Sanballat of Samaria (*Ant.* 11.302-45), is in all likelihood a version of the marriage of the grandson of the high priest Eliashib to the daughter of Sanballat the Horonite in Neh 13:28.[63] At any rate, these alliances were not the only source of tension between Nehemiah and the Judean *ḥōrîm*. We hear complaints about their economic exploitation of the peasantry by indentured service, enclosure of patrimonial domain, and distraining property for nonpayment of debts, for which they incurred Nehemiah's wrath (Neh 5:1-13). Sanballat, Tobiah, and their ally, the Kedarite Arab sheik Geshem (Gashmu), also attempted to undermine Nehemiah's standing vis-à-vis the imperial administration by spreading the rumor, with the help of prophets male and female, that repairing the defenses of the city was the first stage in Nehemiah's plan to seize power and declare himself ruler of an independent Judah (6:5-7). Nehemiah, of course, denied the allegation, but his actions since arriving in the province at least justify comparison with those of contemporary *tyrannoi* in Greek-speaking regions.[64]

The brief account in the memoir of Nehemiah's social reforms (5:1-13) reveals a scene of acute economic distress among the peasantry and small landowner class, in which respect the situation apparently had not changed from the previous century.[65] The principal complaint arose out of the inability of the small landowner living at a subsistence level from one harvest to the next to produce a surplus and thus be in a position to purchase seed for the next planting and feed for the animals. Failure to pay debts contracted (for example) as the result of a period of drought or infestation by locusts (e.g., Joel 1-2) led to handing over children or other dependents into indentured service or even, in extreme circumstances, the mortgaging or confiscation of the plot of land on which the survival of the

63. See my *Ezra-Nehemiah*, 365; Lester L. Grabbe, *A History of the Jews and Judaism in the Second Temple Period*, vol. 1: *Yehud: A History of the Persian Province of Judah* (London: T. & T. Clark, 2004) 155-59.

64. See Morton Smith's presentation of Nehemiah as a typical *tyrannos* in *Palestinian Parties and Politics*, 103-9.

65. Hag 1:5-6, 10-11; 2:15-16; Zech 8:10; Isa 58:3-4.

household depended. The province also had to pay its contribution to the Transeuphratene tribute of 350 talents of silver (Herodotus 3.91). This additional burden was collected from the peasant population in the form of a land tax (cf. the Babylonian *ilku*), to which, of course, was added the collector's fee. In order to pay this tax most small landowners would have to borrow at a rate of interest which, for us today as much as we complain, would be considered confiscatory. We do not have the figures for Judah, but the rate levied by the Murašu banking house was about 40 percent, and in the Jewish colony on the island of Elephantine about 60 to 75 percent.[66]

It is not surprising that Nehemiah singled out the temple priests among those who shared responsibility for creating or exacerbating this situation of social and economic distress (5:12-13). Since we must assume that temple personnel were tax-exempt, as was the case elsewhere in the empire, the burden of taxation was correspondingly greater for the rest of the population. There was also the third-of-a-shekel temple tax (10:32[MT 33]), and the sacrificial system must have taken its toll on livestock. Like Solon in Athens a century and a half earlier, Nehemiah claimed to have pushed through radical social reforms by obliging the lay and priestly aristocracy to forgive debts, return property taken in pledge, and to implement the *šĕmiṭṭâ* provision of law (Deut 15:1-18) by releasing those already sold into indentured service. The obligation to return property taken in pledge was also one of the stipulations of Nehemiah's covenant (Neh 10:31b[32b]).

Reading between the lines of the memoir, and sometimes on the lines, we come across many indications of the presence in the province of Judah and in the diaspora of representatives of a Judaism very different from the kind which Ezra-Nehemiah was written to promote and which comes to expression in the beliefs and practices of the two principal protagonists. Sanballat, governor in Samaria, had close contacts with the high priestly family in Jerusalem (Neh 13:28) and was certainly himself a worshipper of Yahweh. Two sons of a later Sanballat, Delaiah and Shelemiah, bear good Yahwistic names,[67] the Samarians themselves protested to Zerubbabel and Joshua that they worshipped and offered sacrifice to the same God as their

66. For Murašu, see Robert P. Maloney, "Usury and Restrictions on Interest-Taking in the Ancient Near East," *CBQ* 36 (1974) 1-20; for Elephantine, Porten, *Archives from Elephantine*, 78-79.

67. They were recipients of a letter written by the leaders of the Elephantine settlement in 408 B.C. (AP 30:29 = 31:28).

Judean neighbors (Ezra 4:1-4), and there is the onomastic evidence from the Samarian papyri discussed earlier. Tobiah, head of the powerful Transjordanian family based at 'Araq el-Emir, also had close associations with the staff of the Jerusalem temple (Neh 13:4-9) and with many well-connected Judean aristocrats (6:18). He had married into the Arahite family (6:17-19; Ezra 2:5 = Neh 7:10), and his father-in-law, Shecaniah, was of Davidic descent (1 Chr 3:21-22; cf. Ezra 8:3). In addition, his son Jehohanan was married to a daughter of Meshullam ben Berechiah, a family which may also have had Davidic connections (1 Chr 3:20).[68]

It bears repeating that this kind of situation and these kinds of connections were the norm and not the exception in Jewish life in the province. The priests and laymen, lowly born and aristocrats, goldsmiths, apothecaries, and merchants who worked, voluntarily or otherwise, on repairing the wall (Neh 3:1-32), the common people and their wives who complained about their desperate economic condition (5:1-5), the Jews whose children couldn't speak Hebrew (13:23-24) — not so different from the Jews on the island of Elephantine who had their own temple but traded and intermarried with their non-Jewish neighbors — remind the reader that the majority of Jewish people in the province at that time had very different ideas from those of Ezra and Nehemiah about what was or was not essentially implied in being Jewish.

Nehemiah is presented not only as a member of the upper-class *golah* segment of the population but also as an exponent of the rigorist legalism which characterized Ezra and his associates. This quasi-sectarian orientation, with its roots in the eastern diaspora and its orientation heavily dependent on Deuteronomistic theology and the teaching of Ezekiel and his school, was a significant factor in Nehemiah's conflictual relations with the lay and especially the priestly aristocracy in the province. His ejection of Tobiah from the temple precincts and ritual purification of the space he had occupied (13:4-9) is one pointer in this direction. As Morton Smith

---

68. In the list of work details employed in work on the city wall, the same Meshullam was assigned to the stretch opposite his own room (Neh 3:30). By an interesting coincidence, the rare term *niškâ* (here translated "room") occurs elsewhere only with reference to the temple storerooms (12:44) and the room in the temple which the priest Eliashib made available for Tobiah and from which he was unceremoniously ejected by Nehemiah (Neh 13:7). Siegfried Mittmann, "Tobia, Sanballat und die Persische Provinz Juda," *JNSL* 26 (2000) 1-50, is right to stress the authentic Jewishness of Tobiah and Sanballat, but it is evident from the relations between them and Nehemiah that they did not belong to the *golah*.

suggested, Nehemiah probably justified this overriding of priestly privilege by appeal to legal traditions either preserved or created ad hoc by the rigorist party to which he belonged.[69]

As a counter to the power and prestige of the priestly aristocracy, Nehemiah also fostered good relations with the lower order of temple clergy, the Levites, setting them up on a permanent basis in the temple and providing them with the necessary economic support (13:10-13). He also made use of them as, in effect, temple police (13:19, 22) and even as provincial administrators (3:17). The association between Nehemiah and Levites is also in evidence in the public reading of the law (8:7-12) and in the signed covenant (10:9-13[MT 10-14]), as we saw earlier. These and other aspects of Nehemiah's activity raise some basic questions which will continue to occupy us throughout our inquiry. Was Nehemiah's goal the creation of an "isolated, puritanical, theocratic state"?[70] Was Nehemiah, as leader of the "Yahweh alone party" (Morton Smith's well-known designation), the originator of the nationalistic and territorial aspect of Judaism which would emerge with the Hasmonaeans and remain a potent and problematic factor thereafter?

69. Smith, *Palestinian Parties and Politics*, 107-9.
70. Grabbe, *History of the Jews and Judaism*, 307.

4

Ezra-Nehemiah: The Roots of the Ideology

The Diaspora Situation

By the time of Ezra's arrival in Judah the Jewish diaspora in Babylon had been in existence for almost a century and a half. Beginning with the first Babylonian campaign against Jerusalem in 597 B.C., successive waves of deportees were settled in southern Mesopotamia. None of the Jewish settlements named in our sources has been identified,[1] but the principal sites were in the region of the city of Nippur southeast of Babylon. This region, which still suffered from the effects of Assyrian punitive campaigns under Sennacherib and Ashurbanipal, was marked out for redevelopment in the early Achaemenid period, and ethnic minorities were destined to play a significant role in this process. Conditions do not appear to have been unduly harsh. The exiled King Jehoiachin, his five sons, and retainers, though in effect prisoners at the imperial court, were maintained at the expense of the royal commissariat.[2] Apart from being employed in temples or by private individuals, slaves did not play a major role in the economy of the region. Most deportees were not enslaved, since it was more cost effective to

---

1. Tel Aviv (*tēl 'ābîb*, Ezek 3:15) near the river Chebar, the *nār kabāru* or "Grand Canal" mentioned in the Murašû archives from the Achaemenid period; *tēl melaḥ, tēl ḥaršā', kĕrûb, 'addān, 'immēr* (Ezra 2:59 = Neh 7:61); Casiphia (Ezra 8:17).

2. Ernest F. Weidner, "Jojachin, König von Juda, in babylonischen Keilschrifttexten," in *Mélanges Syriens offerts à Monsieur René Dussaud.* Bibliothèque archéologique et historique 30 (Paris: Guenther, 1939) 2:923-35; David B. Weisberg, *Texts from the Time of Nebuchadnezzar.* YOS 17 (New Haven: Yale University Press, 1980).

settle them as tenant farmers to produce food for an expanding population and contribute to the imperial tax base.

It was also fortunate that deportees from Judah and other territories conquered by the Babylonians were permitted to maintain their own distinct organization under imperial supervision, and we may suppose that this arrangement continued after the Persian conquest. Thousands of cuneiform tablets from sites in southern Mesopotamia (Uruk, Ur, Sippar, Nippur) provide a rich source of information on local conditions, among which the archive of the commercial house of Murašû discovered in Nippur in 1893, and consisting in more than 700 cuneiform tablets, is for our purpose the most productive. This archive, covering the second half of the fifth century, deals for the most part with contractual and administrative arrangements about real estate, but incidentally provides information directly or indirectly relevant to the situation of ethnic minorities in the region including Jews. Some of the tablets refer to a type of dependent, feudal association or collectivity called a *ḥatru*. The members of these collectivities were supported by the grant of a parcel of land and were supervised by an official *(šaknu)* whose principal function was to see to the prompt payment of dues and taxes into the imperial exchequer. Some of these collectivities were for military personnel, some for professional classes (e.g., boatmen, carpenters), and some for ethnic minorities included Iranians, Carians, Phrygians, Tyrians, Arabs, and Indians.[3] No Jewish *ḥatru* has come to light, though some Jewish individuals are mentioned who belonged to professional *ḥatrus*. In general, the Murašû archive provides rich testimony to the openness of the region to development by immigrants and the high level of interethnicity precisely in that part of Mesopotamia where the deportees from Judah were settled.

The principal and practically the only source of information on the Jewish ethnic minority in that region is the incidence of Jewish personal names, either Yahweh-theophoric names or names familiar from biblical texts. However, the use of this onomastic material calls for caution. There are instances of Persians giving their children Babylonian names, children with Jewish names whose parents' names are Babylonian, and parents with Jewish names whose children bore theophoric Babylonian

---

3. On the *ḥatru*, see Matthew W. Stolper, *Entrepreneurs and Empire: The Murašû Archive, the Murašû Firm, and Persian Rule in Babylonia* (Istanbul: Nederlands Historisch-Archaeologisch Instituut, 1985) 70-103.

names.[4] Michael D. Coogan lists twenty Yahwistic names with non-Yahwistic patronymics and six with patronymics bearing the name of a deity other than Yahweh.[5] The ethnic origin of a name is therefore an important clue rather than an infallible guide to the ethnicity or religion of the bearer of the name.[6] Persons bearing Jewish names fill a variety of social niches and discharge a range of functions including principals and witnesses in deeds about property, foremen, messengers, government agents, shepherds, and scribes. The impression we get is of a high level of integration of the Jewish ethnic minority into the social and economic life of the region by the mid- to late fifth century B.C. In that international and interethnic environment intermarriage must have been common. Many of the deportees would have taken Jeremiah's advice to seek the welfare of the place to which they had been sent, to build houses, plant gardens, take wives, and raise sons and daughters (Jer 29:5-7), and not all the wives would have been taken from among their own people.[7]

What can be known or reasonably surmised about the organization of

---

4. Elias J. Bickerman gives the examples of Nathaniah son of Beluballit and Igdaliah son of Nana-iddima; see "The Babylonian Captivity," *CHJ* 1 (1984) 356. A certain A-mu-še-e, probably Jewish, gave his sons theophoric-Babylonian names (Šamaš-iddina and Nabû-ittannu), and his daughter Kaššâ married Guzānu, a Babylonian; see Ran Zadok, *The Earliest Diaspora: Israelites and Judeans in Pre-Hellenistic Mesopotamia* (Tel Aviv: Tel Aviv University Diaspora Research Institute, 2002) 29, 58-59.

5. Michael D. Coogan, *West Semitic Personal Names in the Murašû Documents.* HSM 7 (Missoula: Scholars, 1976) 120-21.

6. Coogan, *West Semitic Personal Names in the Murašû Documents*, 49-53; Matthew W. Stolper, "A Note on Yahwistic Personal Names in the Murašû Texts," *BASOR* 222 (1976) 25-28; Ran Zadok, *The Pre-Hellenistic Israelite Anthroponymy and Prosopography.* OLA 28 (Leuven: Peeters, 1988) 305-12; *The Earliest Diaspora: Israelites and Judeans in Pre-Hellenistic Mesopotamia.* On the texts from Našar and āl-Yāhūdu ("Judahville") containing a significant number of Yahweh-theophoric names, see Francis Joannès and André Lemaire, "Trois tablettes cunéiformes à onomastique ouest-sémitique," *Transeu* 17 (1999) 17-34; Laurie E. Pearce, "New Evidence for Judeans in Babylonia," in *Judah and the Judeans in the Persian Period*, ed. Oded Lipschits and Manfred Oeming (Winona Lake: Eisenbrauns, 2006) 399-411. Final judgment on this last batch of data must await scientific publication of the texts.

7. On the situation of the Jewish settlers in Babylonia in general, see E. Eph'al, "The Western Minorities in Babylonia in the 6th-5th Centuries B.C.: Maintenance and Cohesion," *Or* 47 (1978) 74-90; "On the Political and Social Organization of the Jews in Babylonian Exile," in *XXI Deutscher Orientalistentag Vorträge*, ed. Fritz Steppat. ZDMGSup 5 (Wiesbaden: Steiner, 1983) 106-12; Muhammad A. Dandamaev, "Babylonia in the Persian Age," *CHJ* 1 (1984) 326-42; Bickerman, "The Babylonian Captivity," 342-58.

the Jewish ethnic minority, one of many in that part of Achaemenid Babylonia? We are fortunate to have an interesting analogue in the Jewish settlement on the island of Elephantine at the first cataract of the Nile contemporary with the Murašû archive. Like the latter, the Aramaic papyri and ostraca from Elephantine have the advantage over the biblical texts that they are contemporary with the events and situations they describe. The origins of the colony are unknown, but it came under Persian control after the conquest of Egypt by Cambyses and served as a military garrison guarding the southern frontier of the country linked with the Aramaean garrison at Syene (Aswān) on the mainland. The settlers refer to themselves as Jews *(yĕhûdāyē')* and the garrison as "the Jewish force" *(ḥēlā' yĕhûdāyē')*. The garrison commander *(rav ḥēlā')* was Jewish; he worked in tandem with the chief priests but answered to a Persian overseer *(frataraka)*, who was himself answerable to the satrap of Egypt. The settlers lived side-by-side with Egyptians, several took Egyptian names, and some married Egyptians.

"The force" had its own temple dedicated to the national god Yahu (Yaʿu?) but felt comfortable accommodating other deities whom the settlers brought with them from Palestine. In one of the papyri the list of contributors to the temple fund concludes by assigning the largest portion to Yahu/Yaʿu (Yahweh), a portion only slightly smaller to the female deity Anathbethel, and a much smaller amount to Eshem-bethel (AP 22 column 7). The temple, built before the Persian takeover of the country, was destined to be destroyed in a pogrom in 411 B.C. Permission to rebuild it was eventually obtained three or four years later from Bigvai (or Bagohi), governor of Judah, but whether it actually was rebuilt we do not know. It is clear that providing support for the temple (as in the papyrus detailing contributions) and participating in its cult, especially its sacrificial cult, were important *civic* duties. Membership in the assembly of the *golah* in Judah *(qĕhal haggôlâ)* entailed similar obligations with respect to "the God who is in Jerusalem" and his temple. As described in Ezra-Nehemiah, this situation appears to reproduce significant aspects of the social organization of the deportees in the Babylonian diaspora. The internal affairs of self-governing collectivities formed by ethnic minorities in the Nippur region appear to have been regulated by an assembly *(puḥru)*, always of course under the watchful eyes of the imperial authorities, to which the *qĕhal haggôlâ* would be roughly parallel. The parallel between Jews in Egypt and Jews in Mesopotamia would be even closer if we could accept that the Babylonian Jews built their own temple, perhaps at "the place Casiphia" mentioned in the account of the lead-up to Ezra's mission (Ezra 8:17).[8] Attached to such a center of worship would have been something analogous to the Egyptian "house of life" in which ritual and theological studies were carried on, though of course on a much smaller scale than the Egyptian type.[9] Alternatively, or additionally, the gatherings of Judean elders in Ezekiel's house (Ezek 8:1; 14:1; 20:1) suggest that community organization entailed a rudimentary synagoguelike network, as *Tg. Ezek* 11:16 affirms.[10]

Priests would have played a leading role in the Babylonian diaspora as they did at Elephantine. Elders *(zĕqēnîm)* were also active in the social life of diaspora communities (Ezek 8:1; 14:1; 20:1), as later in Judah during the rebuilding of the temple (Ezra 5:3-17) and in the attempt to resolve the marriage crisis (10:8, 14). Levites and other temple personnel were being trained (8:15-20), and prophets were active, sometimes apparently too active for their own good.[11] Which of the biblical texts that most scholars assign to this period may have been written in Babylon continues to be debated. A few scholars locate some or all of the Jeremiah prose discourses and sermon material in the Babylonian diaspora,[12] and the long-standing issue of the original location of the Second Isaiah (chs. 40–55), whether composed in Judah, Babylon, Phoenicia, or Egypt, flares up from time to time.[13] The result in both cases is a stand-off. We cannot even be sure that Lamentations, often thought to have been written for pious visitors to the site of the ru-

---

8. The hypothesis was argued by Laurence E. Browne, "A Jewish Sanctuary in Babylonia," *JTS* 17 (1916) 400-401, and Abram Menes, "Tempel und Synagoge," *ZAW* 50 (1932) 268-76. Morton Smith, *Palestinian Parties and Politics That Shaped the Old Testament* (New York: Columbia University Press, 1971) 90-91, thought it more likely that a temple was built in Babylonia at the time of the rebuilding of the Jerusalem temple. See above (p. 60, n. 34); also my *Ezra-Nehemiah*. OTL (Philadelphia: Westminster, 1988) 163-66.

9. Alan H. Gardiner, "The House of Life," *JEA* 24 (1938) 157-79.

10. Commenting on *wā'ĕhî lāhem lĕmiqdāš mĕ'aṭ,* "I became for them a sanctuary for a little while" or "a sanctuary in small measure," the Targum reads, "I have given them synagogues second only to my holy temple, because they are few in number."

11. Jer 29:21-23: the prophets Ahab and Zedekiah, executed no doubt for seditious activity, perhaps during the suppression of the revolt in Babylon in 595-594 B.C.

12. See esp. Ernest W. Nicholson, *Preaching to the Exiles: A Study of the Prose Tradition in the Book of Jeremiah* (Oxford: Blackwell, 1970).

13. Hans M. Barstad is the most strenuous defender of a Palestinian origin for Isaiah 40–55; see his monograph *The Babylonian Captivity of the Book of Isaiah* (Oslo: Novus, 1997); and the statement in my *Isaiah 40–55.* AB 19A (New York: Doubleday, 2002) 102-4.

ined temple (rather like pious Jews praying at the *kōtel* today), was not composed by some homesick Jew somewhere in southern Mesopotamia.

Much uncertainty remains due to inadequate documentation, but it is arguable that the situation in Achaemenid Judah as described in Ezra-Nehemiah cannot be explained without reference to the situation in the Babylonian diaspora, and indeed represents an adaptation to the Judean context of the situation obtaining there. The *golah qāhāl* reproduces significant aspects of the Babylonian assembly *(puḫru)* which regulated the internal affairs of self-governing collectivities, including ethnic minorities. The *bêt 'āvôt* corresponds to the *bit abim*, the large kinship unit in Neo-Babylonian and Achaemenid Babylonia. In both Judah and Babylonia participation in the assembly was limited to property owners and senior cult personnel. In Judah, and apparently also in Elephantine, good standing in the assembly was contingent on support of and participation in the temple cult. In both Judah and Jeb (Elephantine) the temple was the indispensable focus of urban development, as it was of civic and religious life, and this too reflects a common Babylonian pattern of immemorial antiquity.

Projections of a Restored Past in Postdisaster Prophecy

A century and a half or, more precisely, the 139 years from the deportation of the eighteen-year-old Jehoiachin (597) to the arrival of Ezra in Judah (458) was time enough for the Jewish community in and around Nippur to have settled down and developed its own modus vivendi, institutions, traditions, and no doubt parties and factions. There was also time enough for the complex of theological ideas associated with Ezra and Nehemiah to emerge and incubate. During the first half of this long period, down to the early years of the Persian Empire, the situation and the mood of the expatriate communities remained less settled and stable. Political events would at times have seemed to justify hope for a change of fortunes for the deportees and their descendants. One such event would have been the internal rebellion which confronted Nebuchadnezzar in the tenth year of his reign (596/595).[14] The suppression of this rebellion was followed by another campaign against the western states which, encouraged by the acces-

14. D. J. Wiseman, *Chronicles of Chaldaean Kings* (London: British Museum, 1956) 36-37, 72-73.

sion of a new Pharaoh, Psammeticus II in 595, and incited by their prophets, planned to take part and perhaps did so.[15] Another occasion would
have been the death of Nebuchadnezzar and the accession of Amel-
marduk in 562. The Historian of the Kingdoms ends his narrative by recording that Amel-marduk released Jehoiachin from prison which, in the
light of the Weidner cuneiform tablets mentioned in note 2 above, we may
interpret as release from confinement to the imperial court in Babylon
(2 Kgs 25:27-30). This could have been interpreted as the first step towards
reinstating Jehoiachin as dependent ruler in Jerusalem, as Nebuchadnezzar
had done with Mattaniah (Zedekiah) and perhaps also with Gedaliah.[16]
But after reigning for less than two years Amel-marduk was assassinated
and nothing came of it.

Expectations would have risen even higher with the conquests of
Cyrus II culminating in the fall of Babylon to the Persians in 539, events
which form the background to the poems and sermons of the Second Isaiah, whether composed in Judah, Babylon, Phoenicia, or elsewhere. This
anonymous prophet and poet offered reassurance and comfort to the deportees with the prospect of an imminent return to Judah, the rebuilding
of Jerusalem and its temple, and the restoration of the ravaged economy of
the country — all this through the divinely inspired agency of Cyrus himself, who is named in the poems (Isa 44:28; 45:1).[17] These expectations were
not fulfilled, leading to the unsatisfactory situation depicted in the third
section of Isaiah (chs. 56–66). Two decades later, rebellions which broke
out in practically all parts of the empire against the usurper Darius I during the first two years of his reign (522-520) led a smaller number in Jewish
communities to dream about a restoration of the nation under the
Davidite Zerubbabel (Hag 2:20-23; Zech 6:9-14). The outcome was that

15. Jer 27:3, 9-10, 14-17. The activity of the prophets Ahab, Zedekiah, and Shemaiah in
Babylon and Hananiah in Judah fit this situation (Jer 28:1-17; 29:8-9, 15-23, 29-32).

16. For Mattaniah, see 2 Kgs 24:17. The absence of a title in the relevant biblical texts
about Gedaliah (2 Kgs 25:22-23; Jer 40:5, 7, 11; 41:2, 18), gratuitously supplied in some modern
versions (NRSV adds "governor"), may be due to embarrassment at his non-Davidic descent. The assassin Ishmael, who was of the royal line, is described as a chief officer of the
king (*rav hammelek*, Jer 41:1); if the king in question was Gedaliah this would have provided
him with a motive for his deed on which otherwise the texts are silent. Of possible relevance
is also the seal discovered during the excavation of Tell el-Naṣbeh belonging to a royal official called Jaazaniah *(ly'znyhw 'bd hmlk)*, the same name borne by a member of Gedaliah's
circle (2 Kgs 25:23).

17. For the historical background, see my *Isaiah 40–55*, 92-104.

one after the other the rebellions were suppressed, as recorded on the Bisitun rock inscription. Darius then undertook in effect a refoundation of the Persian Empire, bringing the dreams of independence to an end, at which point Zerubbabel disappeared from the scene.

The many anticipations and predictions in prophetic texts of a change of fortune come from the earlier section of this period, when Jewish communities in the Near East were still under Babylonian control. In biblical texts these expectations are frequently encapsulated in the expression *šûv šĕvût* (or, less often, *šûv šĕvît*[18]), which can be used in a general sense of a reversal of fortune, as when God restored the fortunes of Job at the end of the book (Job 42:10) or held out the possibility of reversing the dire situation of the kingdom of Samaria (Hos 6:11). By exploiting the similarity between the verbs *šûv* ("turn," "return") and *šāvāh* ("take captive"), however, the expression could be referred more specifically and pointedly to the anticipated reversal of the condition of exile, the end of the period of divine judgment.[19] The expression occurs with the greatest frequency in the so-called Book of Consolation in Jeremiah 30–31 and related sayings attached to this section,[20] to which we can add the prediction of seventy years of Babylonian rule (Jer 29:10-14). There is a long-standing debate as to how to position the predictions in these two chapters in relation to the book as a whole, Jeremiah's career, and the period in general. Since this issue cannot be adequately discussed here, the reader may be referred for the range of opinion to the recent critical commentaries.[21] It can be said, however, that the difficulties involved in reconciling these comforting predictions with Jeremiah's career and with those prophecies deemed by most scholars to be authentically Jeremian are formidable. When last we hear of Jeremiah he is in Egypt preaching the same message of judgment to the incipient Egyptian diaspora, for example predicting that Yahweh will be watching over the deportees for harm and not for good (Jer 44:1-14, 20-30). The predictions in chs. 30–31, on the other hand, predict the end of subjection to foreign rule, return from exile in the land of the north, the rebuilding and re-

18. Num 21:29; Ezek 16:53; Zeph 2:7; Ps 85:1[2]; 126:4.

19. John M. Bracke, "*šûb šebût*: A Reappraisal," *ZAW* 97 (1985) 233-44.

20. Jer 30:3, 18; 31:23; 32:44; 33:7, 11, 26.

21. For contrasting views the reader might consult Robert P. Carroll, *Jeremiah*. OTL (Philadelphia: Westminster, 1986) 568-70; and William McKane, *A Critical and Exegetical Commentary on Jeremiah*, vol. 2: *Commentary on Jeremiah XXVI-LII*. ICC (Edinburgh: T. & T. Clark, 1996) clvi-clxiv.

population of Jerusalem, the fertility of the land, and, inevitably, the reestablishment of the native dynasty. These predictions, similar to those in the Second Isaiah, remained unfulfilled.[22] It is difficult to accept that, in its present form, the Book of Consolation could be genuinely Jeremian.

The Prehistory of the Ideology in Ezra-Nehemiah

Both confessional prayers in Ezra-Nehemiah (Ezra 9:6-15; Neh 9:6-37) lament the condition of servitude which had long been the lot of the Jewish people, but there is no longer any prospect of a reversal of fortunes, a return to the past. The situation has changed. What we have seen so far of the ideology of Ezra-Nehemiah is one reaction to that changed situation. The question we want to ask now is whether the few texts datable to the exilic or early postexilic period give us any information on the prehistory of that ideology. Though the law book referred to on several occasions in Ezra-Nehemiah cannot be simply identified with Deuteronomy, the influence of Deuteronomy will be at once obvious, especially in legal matters. Not surprisingly, there is no consensus on the editorial history of Deuteronomy or the dates to be assigned to the successive stages in its formation. Since it refers quite specifically at times to deportation and exile, most commentators have allowed for a postexilic strand.[23] More speculatively, there are several features of the homiletic and legal material in the book which make better sense after than before the disasters of the early sixth century: Moses addresses a people poised to enter the land, and the requirement of cult centralization fits the much reduced dimensions of Neo-Babylonian or early Persian Yehud better than the kingdom of Judah. This said, the influence of Deuteronomic theology on Ezra-Nehemiah is pervasive. The prayers are Deuteronomic in language and theme, and the law which Ezra was commissioned to enforce was basically Deuteronomic. A

22. See Konrad Schmid and Odil Hannes Steck, "Restoration Expectations in the Prophetic Tradition of the Old Testament," in *Restoration: Old Testament, Jewish, & Christian Perspectives,* ed. James M. Scott. JSJSup 72 (Leiden: Brill, 2001) 41-81. On the ambiguities of the term "restoration," see Rainer Albertz, "The Thwarted Restoration" in *Yahwism after the Exile,* ed. Albertz and Bob Becking (Assen: van Gorcum, 2003) 1-17.

23. Deut 4:26-28; 28:36-37, 63-68; 29:27; 30:1-10; cf. similar allusions in the associated History (1 Kgs 8:46-53; 2 Kgs 17:19-20), the last paragraph of which (2 Kgs 25:27-30) must be later than 562 B.C.

first instance concerns what the immigrants were to do after arriving in the land:

> When Yahweh your God brings you to the land which you are about to enter to take possession of it, driving out many nations before you — Hittites, Girgashites, Amorites, Canaanites, Perizzites, Hivites, and Jebusites, seven nations greater and more powerful than you — and when Yahweh your God delivers them over to you and you defeat them, you must utterly destroy them. You must make no covenant with them and show them no mercy. You are not to intermarry with them, either giving your womenfolk in marriage to their men, or taking their womenfolk as brides for your men. For this would turn away your people from allegiance to me. They would offer cult to alien deities, with the result that Yahweh's wrath would be kindled against you and he would soon destroy you. (Deut 7:1-4)

This passage is referred to in Ezra's prayer (Ezra 9:6-15) and is cited by Nehemiah in the oath administered to the men who had married Ashdodite women (Neh 13:25). Its prohibition of intermarriage with the natives is also behind the first and principal stipulation of Nehemiah's covenant (Neh 10:30[MT 31]). Closely related is the absolute exclusion from the Israelite assembly of Ammonites and Moabites and the banning to the third generation of Edomites and Egyptians in Deut 23:3-8(MT 4-9). This stipulation was invoked by Nehemiah (Neh 13:1-2, 23) and insinuated into the account of Ezra's campaign against intermarriage (Ezra 9:1). It looks as if at some editorial stage Deut 23:1-8(MT 2-9) has been interpreted intertextually and given a broader application in the light of Deut 7:1-6. In Ezra's prayer (Ezra 9:1) the standard list of indigenous peoples destined for destruction has been modified to include the four excluded in Deut 23:1-8(2-9);[24] and in chastising the Jews who had married foreign women Nehemiah cites the bad example of Solomon as reported in 1 Kgs 11:1-2, where the four banned peoples also appear. But it is important to add that in the two Deuteronomic texts the motivation for exclusion is, respectively, the risk of adopting foreign cults and previous hostility towards Israel on the part of Ammonites and Moabites; neither text prohibits connubium on the grounds of ritual defilement. In Ezra-Nehemiah, however, the situation is different: Judah has become "a land defiled with the defilement of

24. Reading *věhāʾădōmî* for MT *věhāʾěmōrî*.

the peoples of the lands" and "filled from one end to the other with their ritual impurities" (Ezra 9:11). The prevalence of specifically ritual language in Ezra-Nehemiah, especially in describing intermarriage as "contamination of the holy seed" (Ezra 9:2), would therefore lead us to look beyond Deuteronomy in our effort to grasp what is central to the ideology or theology of the *golah*.[25]

The prophetic text which is equally but less overtly decisive, and for which a Babylonian location is reasonably secure, is Ezekiel.[26] While evidence is lacking for direct and demonstrable dependence of Ezra-Nehemiah on Ezekiel, similarity with respect to ideology, theme, and agenda is close enough to justify further inquiry. In the first place, the parallels between the individual profiles is impressive. Ezekiel and Ezra are both presumed to be Zadokite priests (see Ezra 7:1-5), and priests who manifest prophetic traits. Both speak in the autobiographical mode, and both address the exclusivist *golah* community, Ezekiel in Babylon, Ezra in Judah.[27] Ezra's concern with law and legal interpretation is obvious, but Ezekiel also uses declarative formulae of a forensic nature and other kinds of legal language (e.g. 14:12-20; 18:5-24) and presents his teaching in the form of case histories (3:16-21; 33:1-6). He is much concerned with ritual law, beginning with his dismay at being told to eat food prepared in a ritually incorrect manner (4:14). In a more general sense, the "very high mountain" which he was shown in vision and on which he was set down (40:2), replicates Mount Sinai on which Moses received the blueprint[28] of the wilderness sanctuary and the laws governing its cult and cult personnel (Exod 24:15-18). So both Ezekiel and Ezra, each in his own way, replicates the role of Moses and the giving of the law.[29]

There are other points of contact. Ezra's reaction to the news about

25. Ritual language occurring in Ezra-Nehemiah — *niddâ* (Ezra 9:11), *tum'â* (Ezra 6:21; 9:11), *'ērev, hit'ārav* (Ezra 9:2; Neh 13:3) — is absent from Deuteronomy.

26. On minority views of the book as composed in Judah, or as a later pseudepigraphical work (Charles Cutler Torrey), see Walther Eichrodt, *Ezekiel.* OTL (Philadelphia: Westminster, 1970) 7-11; Walther Zimmerli, *Ezekiel 1.* Hermeneia (Philadelphia: Fortress, 1979) 3-8; Steven Shawn Tuell, *The Law of the Temple in Ezekiel 40–48.* HSM 49 (Atlanta: Scholars, 1992) 5-8.

27. Ezek 1:1; 3:11, 15; 11:24-25; 12:3, 4, 7, 11; 25:3; Ezra 8:35; 9:4; 10:6-8, 16.

28. *tavnît*, Exod 25:9; cf. *toknît*, Ezek 43:10. On this replication, see Jon D. Levenson, *Theology of the Program of Restoration of Ezekiel 40–48.* HSM 10 (Missoula: Scholars, 1976) 37-53.

29. For Ezra as a second Moses, see *b. Sanh.* 21b; *b. Sukka* 20a.

marriages with local women recalls the physical and emotional condition of Ezekiel following on his first vision, especially his sitting on the ground in a catatonic state, for which the same term is used of Ezra.[30] Both speak of the hand of Yahweh being on them, a metaphor for a special relationship, especially of a prophetic-ecstatic kind.[31] In Ezekiel's vision of the city and temple, dated to the autumn of 592 B.C. (Ezek 8:1–11:25), an angel-scribe is told to set aside by marking on the forehead with a *tāv* (the last letter of the Hebrew alphabet) those who sigh and groan over the abominations going on in Jerusalem shortly before its destruction (9:4). As with the mark of Cain, this sign identifies the individual in question as belonging to a group under the protection of a deity. Those who are mourning over Jerusalem constitute the remnant, the only survivors of the disaster about to fall on Jerusalem, and therefore in the nature of the case those who would be associated with Ezekiel in exile. They invite comparison with Ezra's support group, "those who trembled at the word of the God of Israel on account of the infidelity of the *golah*," a group which must have come into existence in the Babylonian diaspora.

The likelihood of associative links between Ezekiel and Ezra-Nehemiah can therefore be accepted. There is no question that the prophecies and visions of Ezekiel have been worked over and expanded by disciples and scribes, for whom the designation "school of Ezekiel" may be accepted. This Ezekiel school would have been active for an indefinite period following on the prophet's activity, which, according to the chronological indications in the book, covered the years from 593 to 571 B.C., the temple vision being dated to 573 B.C. The extent of this editorial activity is variously estimated, but signs of expansion and elaboration are especially in evidence in the account of the vision of the mobile chariot throne (1:4-28; 3:12-15; 10:1-22), the oracular discourses and poems directed at foreign peoples (chs. 25-32), Gog from the land of Magog (chs. 38-39), and the vision of the new temple, city, and land (chs. 40-48). This last, the "temple law" *(tôrat habbayit)*, will be our principal concern in what follows. Whatever date we assign to these nine chapters, it is antecedently probable that either the editor of the Ezra material or Ezra himself, assuming some degree of historical reality, would have been familiar with the work of the disciples and scholars responsible for its final form. I

---

30. Ezek 3:15, reading *mĕšômēm* for MT *mašmîm* as in Ezra 9:3.
31. Ezek 1:3; 3:14, 22; 8:1; 33:22; 37:1; 40:1; Ezra 7:6, 9, 28.

hope to show that the agenda or program of Ezra as presented in the biblical book has, in fact, much in common with, and in all probability owes a debt to this school of Ezekiel.

Temple and Divine Presence

Most of the deportees settled in southern Mesopotamia would have followed Jeremiah's advice to seek the welfare of their place of settlement — and their own welfare at the same time — and in fact Josephus observes that at the time of Ezra's mission the Israelite nation as a whole remained behind (*Ant.* 11.133). We need to bear in mind that by the time of the mission, the seventh year of Artaxerxes I (458 B.C.), the Babylonian diaspora had been in existence for almost a century and a half, long enough for the formation of parties and factions and the incubation of distinctive theologies or ideologies. We can hardly doubt that right from the beginning there were those Judeo-Babylonians, probably a minority, who were planning for the future and who cherished the hope that the Jerusalem temple would be rebuilt and its cult restored. Ezra-Nehemiah dates the attempt to realize that goal to the beginning of the reign of the first Achaemenid ruler Cyrus II (539-538), but the ground must have been prepared during the more than half a century that had elapsed since the first deportations.

This brings us to the first and the most important of the links with Ezekiel. It was portentous and crucial for future developments that the most radical plan for a new beginning was the inspiration of a Zadokite priest immersed in the symbolic universe of cult and ritual — one who, unlike the author of Isaiah 40-55, did not look to the world of international politics for salvation. In the first of Ezekiel's visions he is shown the mysterious chariot throne, the *merkava*, premier text for one of the most powerful strands in Jewish mysticism (Ezek 1:4-28). The throne is mobile, and in the course of the vision the prophet sees the divine effulgence, the "glory of Yahweh" *(kĕvôd-YHWH)*, move from its place, equipped for both aerial and ground transport by means of the four winged creatures and the wheels *('ôfannîm)*, respectively (3:12-13), as the God of Israel leaves his house (8:6). Its progress is duly reported as the visionary experiences accumulate. Movement begins when the seer hears the sound of the living creatures' wings and the wheels beginning to turn (3:12-13; cf. 10:15-17). In the second vision the chariot throne moves to the threshold of the temple (9:3;

10:3-5), thence to the east gate (10:15-19), and from there, finally, to the Mount of Olives east of the city (11:22-23). The movement is clearly in the direction of a destination in the eastern diaspora where the initial vision is reported as having taken place by the *nār kabāri*, the canal which looped around the city of Nippur in southern Iraq (1:3).

Locating the vision in a foreign land, the land of exile, gave assurance that the God of Israel could and would be present outside his own land and his own house, a point not as obvious then as it is now. The link between deity and territory, no less problematic in our day than it was in antiquity, is illustrated by the incident of David's flight to Philistine territory where he cursed those who had driven him out "to serve other gods" — those gods, in other words, whose writ ran in Philistia (1 Sam 26:19). There is also the case of the Syrian general Naaman, who, healed by the prophet Elisha but obliged to return to his own country, took two mule loads of Israelite soil back with him so he could continue to worship Yahweh in Damascus on Yahweh's own earth (2 Kgs 5:17-19). In the present instance, as in others, Ezekiel conforms to the tradition, of Priestly origin, according to which the original revelation of the divine name took place in Egypt, a land full of idols, not as in early traditions in the wilderness of Midian (Exod 6:28). The change indicates that this Priestly tradition, reflecting life outside of Judah, has moved beyond the idea of a territorial deity. Finally, in the vision of the new temple, the seer witnesses the Glory *(kāvôd)* returning from the east to the city and taking up residence once again in the newly-built temple. Like Virgil with Dante, Ezekiel's guide leads him until he takes his stand at the east gate of the visionary temple area. There he sees "the Glory of the God of Israel coming from the direction of the east" (Ezek 43:1-2).

The movement of the Glory from Jerusalem to the Babylonian *golah* and its anticipated return to take up residence in the Jerusalem temple, once it was built according to a prophetically-mandated blueprint, provided the theological template for those in the eastern diaspora who entertained the hope of an eventual religious and political restoration in Judah. Preeminent among these, according to Ezra-Nehemiah, were the Zadokite priests Joshua ben Jehozadak and Ezra.

The vision of the new temple in Ezekiel 40–48, which now follows the strange text about Gog from the land of Magog (38–39), may at one time have followed directly on ch. 37, which concludes with the prospect of a new sanctuary:

I will set my sanctuary in their midst for ever; my dwelling will be with them for ever; I will be their God and they will be my people. The nations will know that I, Yahweh, sanctify Israel when my sanctuary is in their midst for ever. (37:26-28)

At the same time, the vision (chs. 40–48) gives the impression of a self-contained and independent unit, but one which retains its connections with the other visionary experiences of Ezekiel through the theme of the exile and return of the Glory. It is generally acknowledged that these chapters contain expansions and elaborations of different kinds well beyond the date assigned to this section, 573 B.C., possibly even beyond the completion of the actual temple erected early in the reign of Darius I according to the biblical sources. Practically all critical scholars agree that the composition of these nine chapters extends well beyond the active lifetime of Ezekiel himself.[32] In his International Critical Commentary published in 1936, G. A. Cooke understood this section to contain the continuation of Ezekiel's experience, and even imagined the prophet poring over architectural blueprints between ecstatic visions. He found Ezekiel's own contribution in chs. 40–44, with some few addenda, and in 46:19–47:12 (the temple kitchens and the river flowing from the temple); the rest he took to be later expansion.[33] Walther Eichrodt also finds additions and elaborations from different hands in these chapters, and Walther Zimmerli reads them as the culmination of a lively process of growth and redaction.[34] Similar analyses are on offer from other commentators.[35]

---

32. Exceptions are Menahem Haran, "The Law-Code of Ezekiel XL–XLVIII and Its Relation to the Priestly School," *HUCA* 50 (1979) 45-71 (Ezekiel is dependent on P from the late preexilic period); and Moshe Greenberg, "The Design and Themes of Ezekiel's Program of Restoration," *Int* 38 (1984) 181-208; *Ezekiel 1–20.* AB 22 (Garden City: Doubleday, 1983) 15.

33. G. A. Cooke, *The Book of Ezekiel.* ICC 21 (Edinburgh: T. & T. Clark, 1936) 425-27.

34. Eichrodt, *Ezekiel,* 530-31; Walther Zimmerli, *Ezekiel 2.* Hermeneia (Philadelphia: Fortress, 1983) 327-28.

35. See esp. Hartmut Gese, *Der Verfassungsentwurf des Ezechiel (Kap.40-48) traditionsgeschicht untersucht* (Tübingen: Mohr Siebeck, 1957), who argued for a progressive expansion featuring a *nāśî'* strand, one dealing with the land, and a third with Zadokite privileges. Tuell, *The Law of the Temple in Ezekiel 40–48,* believes that the final version corresponds to the situation in Achaemenid Judah and was intended to serve as a realistic social and political blueprint. See bibliography to the time of writing in H. H. Rowley, "The Book of Ezekiel in Modern Study," *BJRL* 36 (1953/54) 146-90; and an update in Paul M. Joyce, "Temple and

One example of what appears to be an editorial addendum is the description of the temple in Ezek 41:15b-26. This temple has features in common with Solomon's temple, but the only similarity to Zerubbabel's temple is its curious two-dimensional external form (41:13-14; Ezra 6:3). Some of its other architectural features might conceivably suggest a realistic plan for a future construction, and the same can be said for the description of the altar (Ezek 43:13-27), which, according to Deuteronomic law, was to be set up on entering the land (Deut 27:6-7). The importance of this requirement was appreciated by the first immigrants who obeyed Deuteronomy in this respect, following the example of the Chronicler's David in setting up an altar to avert disaster before the temple was built.[36]

The vision of the new temple is dated to the twenty-fifth year of the exile, therefore 573 B.C. This date marks the halfway point to the Jubilee, the time for renewal, and therefore the time for a new beginning with a new temple (Ezek 40:1). We detect here a muted eschatological or at least a purposefully futuristic note, and we may well ask whether this deliberately symbolic date may have contributed to the high expectations inspired by the victorious campaigns of Cyrus twenty-five years later as reflected in Second Isaiah.[37]

A reading of Ezra-Nehemiah might suggest that the activity of Ezra represents the fulfillment of that essential part of the program of Ezekiel which had to do with the temple. The location of the Ezra narrative, after the account of the first return and the building of the temple under Zerubbabel, could however give the impression that in this respect Ezra played a minor, second-order role with regard to the temple. Yet the Aramaic account concludes by saying that the work was done "by command of the God of Israel and by command of Cyrus, Darius, and Artaxerxes king of Persia" (Ezra 6:14). In spite of the definitive statement in the following verse (6:15), which states that the building was completed by the sixth year of Darius — generally taken to be Darius I, therefore 516/515 B.C. — this seems to imply that the building activity continued beyond that point in time, an

---

Worship in Ezekiel 40–48," in *Temple and Worship in Biblical Israel*, ed. John Day. LHB/OTS 422 (London: T. & T. Clark, 2005) 145-63.

36. Ezra 3:1-3; cf. 1 Chr 21:28–22:1.

37. The passage of another Jubilee takes us to the accession of Darius I and the beginning of the convulsive events reflected in Haggai and Zechariah 1–8, when the question of the right time to build the temple was being discussed ("The time has not yet come to build Yahweh's house," Hag 1:2).

implication by no means implausible.[38] Other nagging questions remain. Why was it necessary for Ezra to bring with him such a large number of temple personnel of both high and low status when the temple had been functioning for about sixty years (Ezra 7:7; 8:1-2, 15-20)? Why were subventions on such a large scale required (7:15, 20-24)? Why do we get the impression that the sacrificial system had been discontinued (7:17; 8:35)? Why was another set of sacred vessels for temple use called for (7:19; 8:24-30, 33-34)? And when Ezra, in the prayer attributed to him, says that God had allowed them to build God's house and repair its ruins (9:9), was he speaking of events more than half a century in the past or was he not rather referring to what he and his associates had recently accomplished? We should not be misled by the reference to "beautifying" the temple (Ezra 7:27), as if it were only a question of refurbishing, renovating, and touching up. Applied to the temple, this expression, with the verbal stem *p'r,* is taken from a postexilic Isaianic poem which also refers to sacrificial animals and the use of precious timber in the construction of the temple, and therefore predates the actual construction (Isa 60:7, 13). With respect to the Jerusalem temple, therefore, it seems that, if Ezra's role was not primordial, it represented in effect a new beginning; and if he was not himself associated with the school of Ezekiel, his agenda replicated that of Ezekiel and his disciples.

These considerations permit us to draw two conclusions. First: Ezra's agenda corresponded closely to the theology of the school of Ezekiel and was probably influenced by it. Second: Whatever the historical situation may have been, Ezra's mission is presented in the canonical book as a new beginning, perhaps even an account of beginnings alternative to the version presented in Ezra 1–6.

Ezekiel's Law of the Temple *(tôrat habbayit)*

The seer's visionary experience begins when he is shown "a structure like a city" and is introduced to his guide (Ezek 40:1-4). The guide shows him the wall which separates the temple precincts from the rest of the city and protects its special sanctity, lingering over the east gate through which the

---

38. Cf. the statement in the letter of Judah Maccabee to Aristobulus that Nehemiah, active under Artaxerxes I, built (rebuilt?) the temple (2 Macc 1:18), consistent with his request for timber for the gates of the temple fortress in Neh 2:8.

Glory would soon be seen returning to the temple (40:5-16). There then follows the tour of the outer courtyard with its north and south gates, the towers and other architectural features, and the exterior appearance of the temple itself (40:17–41:15a). Of special interest are the separate sacristies for temple priests and altar priests (40:45-46a) which provided a pretext for a codicil, probably added by a later hand, that only the descendants of Zadok may serve at the altar and offer sacrifice (40:46b). Surprisingly little attention is paid to the interior of the temple. Its wood walls are panelled with cherub and palm decorations like Solomon's temple (1 Kgs 6:23-29, 32-35), but the only piece of furniture in it is the wooden altar (Ezek 41:15b-26). The guide then takes the seer on an inspection of the northern and southern sacristies, bringing him back to the east gate in time to see the entry of the Glory of the God of Israel, the return from its exile recounted in the first part of the book, symbolic of the restoration of the Jerusalem cult. In describing this moment in the vision (43:1-3) the seer conveys in a kind of stammer the impression of being overwhelmed:

> He led me to the gate, the gate which faces to the east, where the Glory of the God of Israel was coming from the east, with a sound like the sound of great waters, while the earth was lit up by the effulgence. The vision was like the vision that I saw, like the vision that I saw when he came to destroy the city; like the vision that I saw at the river Chebar; and I fell flat on my face.

The return of the Glory to the inner sanctuary of the temple is the climactic event towards which the prophet's long visionary tour has been leading and the necessary prelude to the giving of "the law of the temple" (Ezek 43:12) which the seer receives and writes down standing in the inner temple courtyard. The parallelism with Moses on Mount Sinai in the Priestly version of the event is striking. In the account of the event in Exodus 24–31, the Glory comes to rest on the mountain, Moses enters the cloud, and in a visionary experience receives instructions for the building of the wilderness sanctuary — also mobile — and the duties and privileges of the priests who will officiate in it. The revelation on Mount Sinai concludes with the Sabbath precept (Exod 31:12-18), thereby anticipating the importance of Sabbath celebration in Ezekiel's temple vision,[39] and in

---

39. Ezek 44:24; 45:17; 46:1-5, 12.

both visions the actual liturgy begins, like the beginning of a new creation, on the eighth day.[40]

The prescriptive part of the temple vision begins with the command to set up and ritually purify the altar in preparation for sacrifice to be carried out exclusively by Zadokite altar priests (Ezek 43:13-27). In Ezra-Nehemiah the first immigrants build the altar shortly after arriving in obedience to the law of Moses, a probable allusion to Deut 27:5-8. The only point at which the two accounts differ is that the seven-day consecration of the altar in Ezek 43:26 becomes the seven days of Sukkoth in Ezra 3:3-4. In Ezekiel there follows the rule that the east gate of the outer court must remain closed. Since the Glory returned to the temple through this gate, the implication is that the deity will no longer leave his residence (Ezek 44:1-3). The visionary is then told that the open spaces at both the outer and inner east gates of the temple are to serve for liturgies involving the civil ruler (*nāśî'*, 44:1-3; 46:1-11), to whose place in the visionary scheme of things the visionary, and we with him, will return.

Facing the temple, the seer is given instruction about "entrances and exits," meaning qualifications for entrance into the temple and participation in its liturgies, in addition to situations warranting exclusion from it (44:4-5).[41] Since these are also entrances into and exits from the group, this indicates a point of importance for the ideology of Ezra-Nehemiah. Recorded next are rules that deal with the following matters:

(1) the exclusion of foreigners from entrance into the temple and participation in its liturgies (44:4-9)
(2) the respective status and duties of temple priests (Levites) and altar priests (Zadokites) (44:10-31)
(3) the privileges and duties of the secular ruler (44:1-3; 45:7-17, 21-25; 46:1-18; 48:21-22)
(4) the distribution of territory surrounding the temple (45:1-6; 47:13–48:29).

These instructions and admonitions, essential elements in the community rule of the school of Ezekiel, were taken over by the the diaspora party to

---

40. Lev 8:33-35; 9:1; cf. Ezek 43:27.

41. We should probably read *limvô'ê habbayit*, "to the entrances of the house (temple)" (44:5), referring to admission and exclusion; cf. 43:11 which uses the same terms in speaking about the physical entrances and exits.

which Ezra, Nehemiah, and their associates belonged in Babylonia. They thus bore directly on the agenda which this party brought with them and attempted to implement in the province of Judah (Yehud). Beyond that, they bring us up against some of the core issues in the struggle of the emergent Judaism of the Persian period to define and consolidate its identity. We shall consider these four items in sequence.

(1) The Status of Foreigners

The law concerning foreigners (Ezek 44:4-9) is set out in the familiar pattern of prophetic discourse consisting in indictment followed by verdict, the latter introduced by the solemn asseveration formula "Thus says Yahweh (God)." In this instance, however, a legal ruling takes the place of the verdict, providing an example of the contamination of a prophetic with a legal formulation. The passage in question reads as follows (44:6-8):

> Say to the rebellious house of Israel: Thus says Yahweh: Put a stop to all your abominable practices, house of Israel, allowing foreigners, uncircumcised in heart and flesh, to enter my sanctuary, thus profaning my house whenever you offer me my food, the fat and the blood, thus violating my covenant with all your abominable practices. You have not performed your duty towards me with respect to my sacred offerings. You have appointed foreigners to take your place in the performance of your duty towards me in my sanctuary.

Israel, the "rebellious house," is therefore accused of allowing foreigners not only to desecrate the temple by their presence at the sacrificial liturgies but to officiate actively as temple personnel. The law itself then follows in apodictic form:

> No foreigner uncircumcised in heart and flesh may enter my sanctuary, none among all the foreigners who reside among the people of Israel. (44:9)

The qualification with which this legal decision concludes is important. While the terminology is not always exact, the expression used here, *běnê-nēkār*, refers to those of foreign descent who are living alongside Israelites. They are therefore to be distinguished from citizens of foreign nations *(zārîm)*, in other words, rank outsiders. These *běnê-nēkār,* "internal foreigners" we might call them, were perceived as constituting a temptation to religious infidelity, a potential fifth column, since *běnê-nēkār* tend to worship *'ělohê-nēkār,* foreign deities,[42] and are a source of contamination for the community.

In reading this categoric and rigorously exclusivist ordinance in Ezekiel it is important to bear in mind that it represents a position adopted by a particular faction, a minority group which is attempting to impose its own anti-assimilationist and potentially xenophobic ideology on the Jewish community as a whole, no doubt in the face of widespread opposition or indifference. It is by no means the only position on the insider/outsider issue represented in the biblical texts. In the legal material of Priestly origins in the Pentateuch it is stipulated that this kind of "internal foreigner" who is a member of an Israelite household must be circumcised (Gen 17:12, 27). The ordinances for Passover, also of Priestly origin, exclude foreigners (i.e., non-Jews) from participating on principle (Exod 12:43), but an exception is made for the resident alien, the *gēr,* a person of foreign origin residing with an Israelite household, who may share in the meal if circumcised and therefore integrated into the community (Exod 12:48-49).[43] We sense in this type of concession an anxious concern to eliminate grey areas, to be clear about boundaries, who is in and who is out, but foreigners, including internal foreigners, are not ipso facto a source of contamination.

A quite different position from that of Ezek 44:4-9 comes in a saying which serves as a prelude to the third section of Isaiah (Isa 56:6-7), perhaps from a century after the time of Ezekiel, though the date is uncertain:

> The foreigners who adhere to Yahweh,
> to minister to him, to love his name, to be his servants,
> all who observe Sabbath and do not profane it,

---

42. E.g., Gen 35:2, 4; Deut 31:16 ("the foreign gods in their midst"). The ruling in Ezek 44:6-9 overlaps with the Deuteronomic law which requires that the members of a household execute one of their own who secretly advocates worship of an alien deity and that all the inhabitants of a town who have taken up the worship of other deities must be put to death and the town totally destroyed (Deut 13:6-18).

43. In these prescriptions for participation in Passover, it seems that *ben-nēkār* (Exod 12:43) applies to foreigners in general, and *gēr* (12:48-49) is the equivalent of the *ben-nēkār* in the limited sense of a person of foreign descent attached to an Israelite household.

who hold fast to my covenant,
them will I bring to my holy mountain,
I will give them joy in my house of prayer;
their burnt offerings and sacrifices will be welcome on my altar.

These foreigners, who have "joined themselves to (the religion of) Yahweh" but are living in fearful anticipation of being expelled from the community, are assured of their good standing "in my house and within my walls" (Isa 56:5), that is, as participants in the temple cult (Yahweh's house) and in the civic life of the community (the walls, by metonymy the city). The assurance is also given, in defiance of the ritual law (Lev 22:25) and the ordinances in Ezekiel, that they may offer material for sacrifice and that their temple sacrifices will be accepted. In other words, they are members of the cult community in good standing. This amounts, in effect, to the abrogation *on prophetic authority* of three authoritative legal ordinances: Lev 22:25, which forbids accepting sacrificial material from foreigners; Deut 23:1-8(MT 2-9), which excludes specific ethnic categories from membership in the Israelite assembly and therefore from taking part in the cult; and Ezek 44:4-9, which forbids foreigners from entering the temple. This declaration set a precedent of potentially great importance while at the same time presaging a problem of authority and control throughout the history of Judaism and, for that matter, Christianity.

In this connection we should also mention the narrative and legal material in the Pentateuch attributed to the Priestly source (P), though the relation between this material and the Ezekiel *tôrâ* as appropriated in Ezra-Nehemiah raises questions which we cannot hope to follow up adequately at this point. To state it briefly: for P all humanity is created in the divine image.[44] In the damaged postdiluvial world, the world we inhabit, the first covenant, between God and "every living creature," took place long before Israel appeared on the scene of history (Gen 9:8-17). The same source represents Abraham entering the land as a *gēr-vĕtôšāv*, a resident alien (Gen 23:4). He deals courteously with the people living there, negotiates living space (13:8-12) rather than violently appropriating it, and purchases land from the indigenous Hittites rather than seizing it by force (23:1-20). Jacob also purchases a parcel of land (33:19-20) and, after his sons had wreaked vengeance on the Shechemites, complains that they had rendered him odi-

---

44. Gen 1:26-27; 5:1-32; 11:10-26.

ous to the inhabitants of the land (34:30). There is, of course, a concern about marrying outside the kinship network,[45] but on the whole P seems to be presenting a model for settlement in the land quite different from the type mandated by Deuteronomy and the Ezekiel temple law, and perhaps in direct opposition to it. Of special interest is the insistence in the P legal material that there is to be one law for the *'ezraḥ* and the *gēr,* for the native-born and the resident alien.[46] The native-born son of Israel is even told he must love the alien as himself (Lev 19:33-34). As Elias Bickerman observed, an Athenian contemporary of Ezra would be astonished to hear that he had to love the metics.[47] With Ezek 44:6-9 we are in a different world.

The question whether this ruling of Ezek 44:9 about "the foreigner in your midst" influenced the measures taken by Ezra and Nehemiah is worth asking, even though Ezra-Nehemiah makes no direct reference to the Ezekiel temple law. We can begin with Nehemiah since his activities are generally thought to reflect historically credible situations and events in a more perspicacious manner than the Ezra narrative. In its present form, Nehemiah's memoir concludes with his prayer to God to be remembered, among other things, on account of having purified the temple and its personnel from everything foreign (Neh 13:30). One of the actions to which he is referring is the expulsion of Tobiah from the temple precincts and the ritual purification of the space occupied by him during Nehemiah's absence at the Persian court (Neh 13:4-9). Tobiah, a wealthy entrepreneur, well connected to the clerical and lay Judean aristocracy (6:17-19), had used these connections to obtain commercial concessions in the temple economy. He was a Yahweh-worshipper, as his name demonstrates, but since he did not belong to the *golah* he was *ben-nēkār,* a foreigner. Following Ezekiel's temple law, therefore, his presence in the temple profaned it, hence the need for a ritual of purification. Another passage, not from the memoir, records how "those of Israelite stock (lit., 'the seed of Israel') segregated themselves from all foreigners" before taking part in a penitential service (Neh 9:2). Here, too, it is clear that "the seed of Israel" is limited to those who belong to the *golah* and subscribe to its ideology and agenda.

A similar measure followed a public reading of the law, a brief passage

45. Gen 26:34-35; 27:46; 28:1.

46. E.g., with respect to Passover (Exod 12:19, 48), atonement (Lev 16:29), laws of clean and unclean (Lev 17:15), and ritual in general (Num 15:29-30).

47. Elias Bickerman, *From Ezra to the Last of the Maccabees* (New York: Schocken, 1962) 19.

also not part of the memoir (Neh 13:1-3). This session seems to have been dedicated to reading, expounding, and applying the laws in Deuteronomy. At any rate, following on the reading of the Deuteronomic law excluding Ammonites and Moabites from entering the assembly of God (Deut 23:1-8[MT 2-9]), we are told that those present implemented Nehemiah's policy by ejecting from the community not only Ammonites and Moabites but "all those of mixed descent" (Neh 13:3). This action was the result of a more expansive interpretation of the law in question (Deut 23:1-8[2-9]). The Hebrew term corresponding to "those of mixed descent" ('ērev) indicates foreigners[48] but contains an additional nuance of a mingling, an adulteration by alien elements, a contamination by foreign bodies.[49] Here, too, exclusion from participation in the cult is implied since the decision occurred on the same day as the ceremony of the dedication of the wall (Neh 13:1). Since the *golah* was an entity both political and cultic, exclusion from the assembly in any case entailed exclusion from participation in the cult.

The legal stipulation in Deut 23:1-8(2-9), probably not part of the original draft of the Deuteronomic legislation, is more specifically exclusive than that of Ezek 44:6-9. It lists four categories excluded from membership in the assembly *(qāhāl):* the sexually mutilated, the *mamzēr,* usually translated "bastard" (NRSV "born of an illicit union"), Ammonites and Moabites *in perpetuum,* Edomites and Egyptians to the third generation. A question arises as to the meaning and scope of the prohibition of "entering into the assembly of Yahweh." According to one rabbinic opinion, the basic issue is about marriage:

> All who are forbidden to enter the assembly may intermarry among themselves. R. Judah, however, forbids it. R. Eliezer says, "They that are of assured descent may intermarry with others that are of assured descent, but they that are of assured descent may not intermarry with those of doubtful descent, nor they of doubtful descent with others of doubtful descent. The following are of doubtful descent: the *shetuki* (father unknown), the *asufi* (both parents unknown), and the Samaritan. (*m. Qidd.* 4:3)

48. Cf. Exod 12:38; Jer 25:20; 50:37.

49. Cf. Ezra 9:2, where intermarriage with local women is described as an adulteration or contamination of the "holy seed," using a verbal form corresponding to *'ērev* (*vĕhit'ārĕvû*).

Another rabbinic pronouncement gets neatly round the problem of Ruth, a Moabite woman who according to Deut 23:3(4) should not have married an Israelite but did:

> An Ammonite or a Moabite is forbidden, and forbidden for all time (to marry an Israelite), but their women are permitted to do so. An Egyptian or an Edomite, whether male or female, is forbidden only for three generations . . . *mamzērîm* and *nĕtînîm* (temple servants) are forbidden, and forbidden for all time, whether male or female." (*m. Yebam.* 8:3)

Deut 23:1-8(2-9) does in fact permit an allusion to marriage since the immediate context deals with sexual issues inclusive of marriage (22:13-30[MT 23:1]). However, the broader issue is membership in the assembly which, in the Ezra-Nehemiah context, means membership in the *golah*.[50]

The implications of the law in Ezek 44:9 excluding those of foreign descent from participating in temple worship in any capacity are not spelled out in this section of "the law of the temple" or anywhere else in the book. One special category of foreigners, resident aliens *(gērîm)*, is granted the same legal status as the native born in the allotment of land (47:22-23) and is not to be exploited (22:7, 29), but there is as yet no suggestion that the *gērîm* are integrated into the community in matters of religious observance. In the Priestly legislation the *gēr* is, under certain conditions, on the same footing as the native born *('ezrāḥ)* in the observance of festivals,[51] including Sabbath (Exod 20:10; 23:12), and in offering sacrifices (Lev 17:8-16; 22:17-20). The resident alien is also bound by the same obligations in respect to such matters as the laws of consanguinity and affinity (Lev 18:26).[52] The distinction between *gēr* and *'ezrāḥ* does not appear in Ezra-Nehemiah, but we are told that the Passover and the Feast of Unleavened Bread following the dedication of the rebuilt temple were celebrated by the diaspora community together with "all those who had joined them, after separating themselves from the impurity of the local population" (Ezra 6:19-22).[53] These people

50. In addition to the commentaries on Deut 23:1-8(2-9), see Shaye J. D. Cohen, *The Beginnings of Jewishness* (Berkeley: University of California Press, 1999) 248-52.

51. Exod 12:19, 48-49; Lev 16:29; Num 9:9-14.

52. See Christiana van Houten, *The Alien in Israelite Law.* JSOTSup 107 (Sheffield: JSOT, 1991) 109-57; Rolf Rendtorff, "The *Gēr* in the Priestly Laws of the Pentateuch," in *Ethnicity and the Bible*, ed. Mark G. Brett (Leiden: Brill, 2002) 77-87.

53. The language of "joining," i.e., associating with Israel (verbal stem *lvh* Niphal), oc-

who attached themselves to the *golah* group would be the equivalent of *gērîm*, but we are not told how their incorporation took place and what their new legal status entailed. Whether the author of the temple law in Ezek 44:9 contemplated the possibility of these internal foreigners joining the community of Israel we do not know. What we can say is that if they were included among those debarred from the temple they would also have been excluded from membership in the community.

(2) Marriage Policy and Ritual Ethnicity

The question of membership, who may belong and who may not, inevitably raises the issue of marriage, a subject on which the law of the temple unfortunately provides no guidance, not directly at any rate. In Ezekiel's allegory of Jerusalem as a wayward woman (Ezek 16:1-63) we are told that the father was an Amorite and the mother a Hittite, which hints at an explanation for her waywardness. We can compare this edifying chapter with the haggadic narrative in Lev 24:10-23 about the blasphemer born of a mixed marriage (father Egyptian, mother Israelite; v. 10) which carried the same implication. 2 Chr 24:26 provides a rather more opaque example in its account of the assassination of King Joash in which the author has altered his source (2 Kgs 12:21[MT 22]) with a view to assigning to the two assassins mothers originating, respectively, in Ammon and Moab.[54]

In Ezra-Nehemiah the issue of intermarriage is paramount. In his memoir, Nehemiah records an encounter with Judeans who had married women from the Philistine city of Ashdod whose children could no longer speak "Judahite" *(yĕhûdît)*, namely, Hebrew (Neh 13:23-27).[55] The empha-

---

curs in later prophetic texts (Isa 14:1; 56:3, 6; Zech 2:11[15]) and in Esther (Esth 9:27) and in the participial form would be the equivalent of *gēr*, but it would be misleading to speak of these without qualification as proselytes. It is worth noting that, unlike the Priestly legislation, the Ezra text does not mention circumcision.

54. The change can, however, be adequately explained with reference to Deut 23:2-9 rather than Ezra 9–10, as argued by M. Patrick Graham, "A Connection Proposed Between II Chr 24,26 and Ezra 9–10," *ZAW* 97 (1985) 256-58.

55. According to MT, the encounter was with Ashdodite, Moabite, and Ammonite women, but lack of the conjunction before the last two suggests an addition inspired by the exclusion from the assembly of these two peoples in Deut 23:3-6(MT 4-7), reflected also in Neh 13:1-3. See the textual note in my *Ezra-Nehemiah*, 362.

sis on language is interesting, since language has always been an important index of national identity, whether Gaelic in Ireland, or Welsh in Wales, or, for that matter, Hebrew during the rebellion of Simon bar Kokhba and in the modern Zionist movement. It therefore points up the political aspect of the agenda of Nehemiah, which can be described telegrammatically as ritual ethnicity. In this instance, Nehemiah made the transgressors take a solemn oath not to intermarry with the local population (though they had already done so), but we are not told that he followed the example of Ezra in forcing them to divorce their wives and send away the children. The oath imposed on the transgressors is in the form of a citation of Deut 7:3 adapted to the situation, and therefore parallel to Ezra 10:5, and is reinforced with the cautionary example of Solomon's addiction to foreign women (13:26-27; cf. 1 Kgs 11:1-2). In a slightly different form, the prohibition shows up among the stipulations of Nehemiah's covenant (Neh 10:30[MT 31]). Nehemiah also records, as accruing to his credit, how he banished from the province a member of the high priestly family who had married the daughter of Sanballat, governor of Samaria. He ends with an imprecation: "Remember them, my God, because they have defiled the priesthood" (13:28-29).[56]

To summarize: Nehemiah's specific contribution was in the application of ritual principles to politics. The goal of a ritually segregated, religiously homogeneous and autonomous polity dictated his actions from the beginning of his tenure of office, including his struggle against the priestly and lay aristocracy for control of the temple and its resources, spiritual and temporal. The most significant, and in many ways the most problematic outcome of his pursuit of this goal was its adoption by the Hasmoneans who looked to him as their model and inspiration. Their aim of translating the ideal into terms of territory and conquest had consequences which Nehemiah may have dreamed of but could hardly have anticipated.

Something has been said already about the account in Ezra 9–10 of Ezra's coercive dissolution of marriages between *golah* males and local women. It begins in first person (9:1-15) and continues in third person narrative (10:1-44), but after the oath is administered and the issue settled (9:1–10:5) it starts all over again with Ezra's praying, fasting, and mourning, followed by the assembly and the sending away of the women and

---

56. On the relation between this incident and the one recorded by Josephus in *Ant.* 11.302-12, see above, 113.

children (10:6-44). The language throughout is heavily theological and manifests few indications of concern to provide a straightforward and realistic record of a historical event. The civic leaders who bring the bad news to Ezra describe the transgressors not as Judeans but as "the people of Israel" and "the holy seed." They represent the local population, the cause of the problem, as the nations destined for extermination by Joshua.[57] Marriage with local women is described in terms borrowed from the ritual lexicon, the language of mixing, segregation, and abomination.[58] In Ezra's prayer, a scribal composition rather than the transcription of an actual prayer, the marriages with local women are placed in the context of a land rendered unclean by the pollutions and abominations of its inhabitants, exhibiting a particularly dense concentration of the same kind of language (Ezra 9:10-11).[59]

The law in Ezek 44:9, itself an innovation, simply states that those of foreign descent living in Judah may not enter the temple. The measures undertaken by Ezra and Nehemiah, which implement an ideology elaborated among Zadokite priests in the Babylonian diaspora and imported back into the province of Judah, spelled out what they took to be implicit in Ezek 44:9 in terms of a policy of ritual ethnicity. What was required, and what was attempted, was the thoroughgoing ritualization and segregation of the *golah*. Following their selective appeal to tradition, the line of reasoning based on the stipulation in Ezekiel's temple law could have run somewhat as follows: Since the political community is also, and essentially, a cult community, participation in the common cult is an essential condition for membership. But if those of foreign descent are forbidden entry to

---

57. The eight nations mentioned in Ezra 9:1 represent a conflation of the standard list of indigenous peoples (as in Deut 7:1-5) with the four whose inhabitants were excluded either in perpetuum (Ammon, Moab) or to the third generation (Egypt, Edom) from belonging to the Israelite assembly (Deut 23:1-8[2-9]).

58. "Mingling," *hit'ārēv* (Ezra 9:2); cf. Neh 13:3: "They separated from Israel all those of mixed descent *(kol-'ērev)*; "segregation": verbal stem *bdl* (Niphal and Hiphil); cf. Lev 10:10; 11:47; 20:24-26; Num 16:21; "abomination," *tô'ēvâ*: cf. the dietary restrictions of the Egyptians (Gen 43:32) and the violations of rules governing sexual relations (Lev 18:22, 26, 29-30; 20:13). Condemnations of such *tô'ēvôt* are especially frequent in Ezekiel, where the term occurs more than 40 times. On the term *ma'al*, referring to cultic transgressions and covenant violations, see Jacob Milgrom, "The Concept of *ma'al* in the Bible and the Ancient Near East," *JAOS* 96 (1976) 236-47.

59. *niddâ*, a metaphor with reference to menstruation; *tô'ēvôt*, "abominations"; *tum'â*, "ritual uncleanness."

the temple, they cannot participate in the cult and are thereby excluded from membership in the community. The political community must be composed exclusively of those ritually qualified for participation in the temple cult; hence, finally, the need to exclude ritual taint requires the dissolution of marriages contracted with nonmembers and the dismissal of both the women and their children.

Though the ideal embodied in Ezek 44:9 was never lost from sight, and continued to be recognized as a characteristic of Jewish belief and practice,[60] there are indications that the creation of a ritually self-segregating commonwealth, the goal pursued by both Ezra and Nehemiah, was not an unqualified success. If it had been, we would have expected a different conclusion to the Ezra story and, on the assumption that Nehemiah followed Ezra, it would not have remained to be done all over again a few years after Ezra's disappearance from the scene. Throughout the period of the Second Temple the ideal of ritual segregation, representing the agenda of a specific minority group, never went unchallenged. Prophetic sayings from that time and later express an attitude to outsiders, whether "internal foreigners" or foreigners in general, quite different from that of Ezra and Nehemiah.[61] If Ezra had been successful, Ruth the Moabitess would never have married Boaz, Achior the Ammonite (Judith 14:10) would never have been accepted into Judaism, and Jonah would have been saved a great deal of trouble and embarrassment. Taking in the broader picture, the remarkable demographic expansion of the Jewish people between the Achaemenids and the Romans would remain inexplicable if the goal pursued by Ezra and Nehemiah had remained the only available option.

(3) Temple Priests and Altar Priests

The superscript or preface to the book informs us that Ezekiel was a priest (Ezek 1:3). His denunciation of his fellow priests on the eve of the disaster

---

60. Needless to say, also as an indictment often directed at Judaism in late antiquity; e.g., Tacitus, *Histories* 5.5 (*apud ipsos fides obstinata, misericordia in promptu, sed adversus omnis alios hostile odium . . . alienarum concubitu abstinent*).

61. Esp. in Isaiah, e.g., 56:1-8; 66:18-21. One of the most remarkably irenic is the blessing pronounced over the two evil empires of Israel's historical experience: "Blessed be my people Egypt, Assyria the work of my hands, Israel my possession!" (Isa 19:25)

gives us, by way of contrast, a good idea of what, for him, the priesthood entailed. He indicts them in the following terms:

> The priests no longer instruct. (7:26)
> The priests of the land have done violence to my instruction, they have profaned my holy things, they have not maintained the distinction between the sacred and the profane, they have not taught the distinction between the unclean and the clean, and they have disregarded my Sabbaths, so that I am profaned among them. (22:26)

Instruction, especially instruction in ritual law and religious observance in general, is clearly a primary responsibility. Chapters 1–39 provide good examples of instruction in the form of casuistic or case law on such matters as personal moral responsibility (14:12-20), rejection of the traditional idea of intergenerational moral accountability (the sins of the fathers visited on the sons, 18:5-18), and the possibility and necessity of repentance (33:10-16). While the profile of Ezekiel in the discourses, sermons, and poems in these chapters is predominantly that of a prophet, he was also a priest and, as such, was closely involved in the study, interpretation, and implementation of sacred law. This association prepares the reader for the promulgation of the temple law in chs. 40–48. In general, however, chs. 1–39 present a straightforward and undifferentiated view of the priest's profile, function, and concerns. They are also silent on the subject of Levites as a distinct category of cult personnel.

When we move to the vision of the city and temple in chs. 40–48 we note some differences in the understanding and practice of the priestly role. In the first place, a distinction is made throughout the vision between altar priests and temple priests, corresponding to the distinction between priests who may "approach" and those who may not — in other words, between those who may sacrifice and those who may not.[62] Both categories are levitical, that is, "sons of Levi" or "levitical priests,"[63] but

---

62. Ezek 40:45-46; 44:8, 14-16; 48:11; cf. Num 3:28, 32; 18:3-5; 31:30, 47. The language of "approaching" *(qrv)* entails the idea of sacrificing, expressed by means of the causative theme of the same verb, the idea therefore of "bringing near" an offering (Ezek 43:22-24; 44:7, 15, 16, etc.). The sacrificial undertones can still be heard in the Pauline term *prosagōgē*, "access," "approach" (Rom 5:2).

63. *kōhănîm halĕviyyîm* (Ezek 43:19; 44:15-16); the designation is standard in Deuteronomy (Deut 17:9, 18; 18:1; 24:8; 27:9).

the only ones who may now sacrifice, and therefore qualify as altar priests, are the descendants of Zadok *(běnê ṣādôq)*. This important distinction comes up at intervals throughout chs. 40–48.[64] In the longest of these Zadokite passages, by many thought to be interpolations, the distinction between the two categories, and the consequent demotion of non-Zadokite priests to secondary status in the temple hierarchy, is justified on the grounds that Zadokites were the only priests who remained faithful while the people of Israel led by their priests "strayed," meaning presumably engaged in unacceptable forms of worship (44:5-16). Since Wellhausen this "time of straying" is generally taken to refer to the period preceding the Josian reform when the "high places," that is, cult centers in different parts of the country, were disestablished (2 Kgs 23:9). The transgressive priests would therefore be the former priests of the "high places," now unemployed as a result of Josiah's reforming zeal.[65] But the denunciations of contemporary priests by prophets during the last phase of the Judean monarchy suggest that the Jerusalem priests after the time of Josiah were capable of quite a bit of "straying" themselves. The priests demoted in Ezekiel 40–48 would therefore very likely have included those among the Jerusalem priests denounced by Ezekiel who survived the murder and mayhem that followed the fall of Jerusalem, and who were left behind during the deportations.

It would be naive, however, even assuming the basic historicity of 2 Kings 22–23, to suppose that Josiah succeeded in suppressing all cult centers apart from the temple in Jerusalem and exterminating all their clergy, and there are indications that such places and such people were still functioning after 586 B.C. in both Judah and the diaspora.[66] The author of the vision narrative, or interpolator, could therefore have had in mind non-Jerusalemite priests who continued to function in sanctuaries outside Jerusalem. According to one hypothesis of venerable antiquity, recently restated, the Bethel sanctuary, in close proximity to the administrative center

---

64. Ezek 40:45-46; 43:19; 48:11. In Ezek 40:46b the phrase beginning *hēmâ běnê ṣādôq* ("these are the descendants of Zadok") and in 43:19 *'ăšer hēm mizzera' ṣādôq* ("who are of the 'seed' of Zadok") have been inserted, as is generally recognized; see Eichrodt, *Ezekiel*, 545; Zimmerli, *Ezekiel 2*, 368, 433.

65. Julius Wellhausen, *Prolegomena to the History of Israel*. SBL Reprints and Translations (1885; Atlanta: Scholars, 1994) 179-81.

66. See the chapter on "The Survival of the Syncretic Cult of Yahweh" in Smith, *Palestinian Parties and Politics*, 62-74. See also the same author in *CHJ*, 1:233-40.

at Mizpah in Benjaminite territory, was reactivated after the Babylonian conquest to serve as the principal, imperially-mandated sanctuary in the province during the period prior to the restoration of Jerusalem in the early or middle Persian period. The close association between Bethel and the traditions about Aaron would then suggest that the Bethel sanctuary during the Neo-Babylonian and early Achaemenid periods gave the "sons of Aaron" a *pied-à-terre* in Judah, leading eventually to conflict between the Bethel Aaronites and Zadokites from the Babylonian diaspora. Conflict would have led at some point to compromise between these two priestly families reflected in the genealogies, especially the high priestly (Levitical-Aaronite) succession in 1 Chr 6:1-15(MT 5:27-41) in which Zadok occupies the central position.[67]

The origin of the Zadokites has proved to be no less elusive than those of the Aaronites. Zadok first appears on the scene as David's priest together with Abiathar (2 Sam 8:17; 20:25). His descent from Eli and the priestly house of Shiloh through Ahituv, Eli's grandson (2 Sam 8:17; 1 Sam 14:3), has been widely questioned, and several alternative hypotheses about his origin (Gibeonite, Jebusite, etc.) have been advanced over the last two centuries at least, but are not our present concern. Zadok played an active role in matters religious and political during the reigns of David and Solomon, but from then on down to the Zadokite passages in Ezekiel 40–48 the record is silent on both him and his descendants. Notwithstanding this huge gap, the scholarly tradition has continued to transmit the idea that the Zadokite priestly family descended from David's priest of that name maintained a monopoly of the high priestly office during the period of the Judean monarchy.[68] But the actual situation is that none of the priests mentioned during these four centuries is referred to as Zadokite (or, for that matter, as Aaronite) and that evidence for a hereditary high priestly office, as opposed to the practice of royal appointment of incumbents under the monarchy, is lacking.[69] What might appear to be an exception, the reference to Azariah son of Zadok as the priest under Solomon (1 Kgs 4:2), doubles with the mention two verses later of Zadok and Abiathar as priests, occurs in a textually corrupt passage, and *hakkōhēn* is missing from

---

67. See above, 74-75.

68. E.g., Aelred Cody, *A History of Old Testament Priesthood*. AnBib 35 (Rome: Pontifical Biblical Institute, 1969) 141-45; George W. Ramsey, "Zadok. 1," *ABD*, 4:1034-36.

69. This point is argued by John R. Bartlett, "Zadok and His Successors at Jerusalem," *JTS* n.s. 19 (1968) 1-18.

LXXB.[70] There is therefore no mention of Zadok or descendants of Zadok in biblical texts from the account of his activities under David and Solomon to Ezekiel's temple law.

This being the case, we are justified in looking for Zadokite origins in the period subsequent to the liquidation of the Judaean state and the Davidic monarchy. A possible clue pointing to an origin in the Babylonian diaspora is the patronymic of the high priest Joshua (Jeshua) ben Jehozadak.[71] According to the Chronicler's genealogical schemata, Jehozadak, son and successor of Seraiah executed by the Babylonians, was deported to Babylon (1 Chr 6:14-15[MT 5:40-41]). However, both Jehozadak's relationship with Seraiah and his deportation to Babylon follow from the author's use of the name as a bridge between the preexilic and postexilic high priesthood and should be treated with suspicion. At any rate, the Judeo-Babylonian origin of Joshua ben Jehozadak indicates that the Zadokite high priesthood, which remained in power from the time of the high priest Joshua to the deposition of the high priest Jason in 171 B.C., and which was named for David's chief priest, had its remote origins in the Babylonian diaspora during the period prior to the Persian conquest.

In Ezra-Nehemiah Zadok occurs as a Judeo-Babylonian name, but there is only one possible case of a priest of that name.[72] Ezra himself is given an Aaronite-Zadokite pedigree (Ezra 7:1-5), but it is agreed that his high-priestly credentials have been taken over from the master genealogy of the high priesthood in 1 Chr 6:1-15(MT 5:27-41). The genealogy was, however, correct to the extent that, as a diaspora priest, he was almost certainly Zadokite. Ezekiel and Ezra-Nehemiah share a strong insistence on a legitimate priesthood. Lists of temple personnel were compiled (Neh 12:22-23), priests had to be registered, and those who could not verify their status with reference to a written record were excluded from liturgical officiating and therefore from making a living (Ezra 2:61-63 = Neh

---

70. James A. Montgomery, *A Critical and Exegetical Commentary on the Books of Kings.* ICC (Edinburgh: T. & T. Clark, 1951) 113-14; John Gray, *I & II Kings.* OTL (Philadelphia: Westminster, 1963) 127.

71. Hag 1–2; Zech 6:9-14; Ezra 3:2, 8; 5:2; 10:18; Neh 12:26.

72. The patronymic of Zadok ben Immer, who worked on repairing the wall, is priestly, but the mention of priests collectively in the previous verse raises a question about his Zadokite status (Neh 3:29). Zadok ben Baana, engaged in the same task, is a layman (3:4), as are the Zadok who signed Nehemiah's covenant (10:21[MT 22]) and the scribe Zadok on the committee for supervising the tithe (13:13).

7:63-65). One of the three families of disqualified priests claimed descent from a priest who had married the daughter of a Gileadite and taken the name of his in-laws, thereby violating the levitical law requiring a priest to marry a virgin from his own kinship group (Lev 21:14-15). Ezekiel also refers to a register in which one must be enrolled to qualify for entry into the land of Israel, namely, the province of Judah (Ezek 13:9). Those threatened with disqualification in this instance were prophets, but the same would apply a fortiori to priests. The insistence on legitimacy, on identifying those qualified for membership and office in the community and those who were not, helps to explain the many lists of names in Ezra-Nehemiah.

On this issue of priestly families, an intriguing problem is the presence of Aaronite names in the *golah* community in Judah. Leading the list of those who accompanied Ezra from Babylon to Jerusalem were two priests, Gershom descendant of Phineas and Daniel descendant of Ithamar (Ezra 8:2), and on their arrival one of the priests awaiting them in Jerusalem was Eleazar son of Phineas (8:33). In the genealogies Phineas is son of Eleazar and grandson of Aaron, while Ithamar is Aaron's fourth son (Exod 6:25; 1 Chr 6:4[MT 5:30], etc.). These two names create a problem for the hypothesis associating Aaronite priests with Bethel. The hypothesis relies on the association between Jeroboam's cult establishment at Bethel (1 Kings 12) and the golden calf episode in which Aaron played a dubious role (Exodus 32). It is supported by the notice, in the account of the war of extermination against Benjamin in Judges 20-21, that Phineas ministered before the ark in Bethel (Judg 20:27-28). We would therefore not expect Aaronite priests immigrating from Babylon with Ezra. One solution to this problem might be along the following lines. The obscure nature of the fault — a cultic *faux pas* of some kind — which led to the instantaneous death of Aaron's two oldest sons, Nadab and Abihu (Lev 10:1-7),[73] suggests that their untimely death served some undisclosed purpose.[74] Perhaps the elimination of Nadab and Abihu and their replacement by Eleazar and Ithamar, these last two of diasporic origin and therefore not originally Aaronite (Ezra 8:2, 33), was one aspect of the compromise between Judaeo-

73. In addition to the commentaries, see Roland Gradwohl, "Das 'Fremde Feuer' von Nadab und Abihu," *ZAW* 75 (1963) 288-96.

74. The names Nadab and Abihu are practically identical with Nadab and Abijah, sons of Jeroboam, founder of the Bethel calf cult (1 Kgs 14:1, 20), and all four have in common a failure to live out the natural course of their lives (1 Kgs 14:17-18; 15:21-30).

Babylonian Zadokites and Bethel Aaronites, and it was effected by incorporating two prominent diasporic priestly houses into an already existing Aaronite line of descent. In the genealogies Eleazar and Ithamar now follow Nadab and Abihu as third and fourth sons, but in effect serve as progenitors of a family line which is both Aaronite and Zadokite.

The distinction between altar priests and temple priests, corresponding to the distinction in Ezek 44:10-16 between Zadokites and Levites, is not unambiguously attested before the law of the temple in Ezekiel. In Deuteronomy the standard term for priests functioning in the central sanctuary is *hakkōhănim halĕviyyîm* ("levitical priests"), who, in addition to their service at the altar, have judicial, didactic, and diagnostic functions. In terms of status and competence, there is no distinction between these and the levitical priests who served at the local shrines decommissioned by Josiah according to 2 Kgs 23:8-9. These could, in principle, be employed at the central sanctuary (Deut 18:6-7), though, predictably, the priests employed there were not about to let this happen (2 Kgs 23:9). Being therefore unemployed, these Levites became, together with widows and orphans, charter members of the disenfranchised class during the Judean monarchy (Deut 12:18-19; 14:27, 29; 27:9, etc.). In other words, Deuteronomy shows no distinction of status among priests.[75]

In Ezra-Nehemiah priests are never identified as either Aaronite or Zadokite,[76] but the distinction between altar priests and temple priests (i.e., Levites) is taken for granted, hence the routine allusion in Ezra-Nehemiah to "priests and Levites."[77] Several of the duties assigned to these Levites also correspond to Ezek 44:10-14. These include general supervision and maintenance of the temple fabric (Ezek 44:11, 14; 45:5; Neh 11:15-16), preparing the sacrificial material (Ezek 44:11; Ezra 6:20), and in general assisting the altar priests. The task of instruction in the law, on which Ezekiel is silent, is prominent in Ezra-Nehemiah (Neh 8:1-12), as it is in

75. The passage from a one-tier to two-tier priesthood (three-tier including the high priestly office) is traced by Joachim Schaper, *Priester und Leviten in achämenidischen Juda: Studien zur Kult- und Sozialgeschichte Israels in persischer Zeit*. FAT 31 (Tübingen: Mohr Siebeck, 2000).

76. Ezra's descent from Aaron (Ezra 7:1-5) is taken from 1 Chr 6:1-15(MT 5:27-41), and the allusion to the priestly "tithe of the tithe" (Neh 10:38[39]; 12:47) refers back to "the time of Zerubbabel and Nehemiah."

77. Ezra 1:5; 2:70; 3:12; 6:16; Neh 13:29, etc. Levites are priests; they slaughter the Passover sacrifice for their "brethren the priests" (Ezra 6:20).

Chronicles. We may take this to reflect the impact of the Deuteronomic movement and the importance of instruction in the law in the diaspora after the loss of the temple cult. Levitical functions were progressively broadened to include liturgical music and gatekeeping, neither of which specialization is mentioned in Ezekiel. These appear to be still distinct categories in Ezra-Nehemiah[78] but are clearly and explicitly designated levitical in Chronicles.[79] The minimum age for enrollment in the levitical ranks also seems to have been progressively raised from twenty (Ezra 3:8; 1 Chr 23:24-27), to twenty-five (Num 8:24), then to thirty (Num 4:3, 23, 30; 1 Chr 23:3), perhaps corresponding to the broadening scope of levitical activities. The status and prestige of the Levites would have been enhanced by Nehemiah's recruiting them in his struggle for control of the temple and its resources. He settled them in Jerusalem, financed them with the tithe, and employed them as temple police (Neh 13:10-13, 22).[80]

It is an understatement to say that there is much we do not know about priesthoods and cults in Israel of the biblical period. One of the most obscure sections of this history is the century and a half from the first deportations to the arrival of Nehemiah in the Persian province of Judah. What we learn from the temple law in Ezekiel near the beginning of this period and from scattered and often obscure references in Ezra-Nehemiah towards its end gives us the blurred image of a power struggle for control of the temple and its resources, both spiritual and temporal, with all that that entailed. At the clear and present risk of oversimplifying, we can say that on the one hand there were those who claimed descent from Zadok, of Babylonian, diasporic origin, and those who claimed descent from Aaron and who came into their own in the reactivated Bethel sanctuary after the destruction of the temple in Jerusalem. The ensuing compromise, apparent from the genealogies and the Chronicler's history, would set the stage for the dominant role played by the Jerusalem priesthood after the disappearance of Nehemiah from the scene.

---

78. Ezra 2:41-42 = Neh 7:44-45; also Ezra 2:70; 7:7; 10:24; Neh 10:28(MT 29); 11:19, etc.

79. 1 Chr 9:17-27; 15:16-24; 23:2-6, etc.

80. The enhancement of the status of Levites by Nehemiah does not justify the conclusion that the entire book was composed by Levites, as argued by Kyung-Jin Min, *The Levitical Authorship of Ezra-Nehemiah.* JSOTSup 409 (London: T. & T. Clark, 2004). There is also no indication elsewhere in the book that Levites enjoyed the same status as altar priests.

(4) The Privileges and Duties of the Secular Ruler

In Ezekiel's temple law, the term *nāśî'* is used exclusively for the secular ruler in preference to the normal term *melek,* "king." The only exception is the occasion when the seer hears a voice from the temple denouncing the kings of Israel for engaging in sexual rites ("whoring") and for setting up funerary stelae in close proximity to the temple;[81] and the only occasion where the term occurs in the plural is a denunciation of those kings of Judah who oppressed their people and expropriated their land (Ezek 45:8-9).[82] The usage is therefore quite different from that of early narrative strands, primarily in the Pentateuch, where the *nāśî'* is a tribal leader, a sheik. Such were the *nĕśî'îm* of the Ishmaelite Arabs (twelve, as in Israel; Gen 17:20; 25:16) or the Midianites (Num 25:18; Josh 13:21), and such was Abraham flatteringly described as "a great sheik" *(nĕśî' 'ĕlohîm)* by a Hittite anxious to get a good price for his land (Gen 23:6). This usage is updated in the Priestly narratives in which the tribal leaders function together with and subordinate to the priests within the congregation,[83] and much the same is characteristic of usage in Chronicles.

There can be no question that the author of the legal program in Ezekiel 40–48 is presenting a priestly or hierocratic ideal of the secular ruler, one even more idealistic and partisan than the constitutional monarchy ideal of Deuteronomy. According to the Deuteronomic law, the king must be native-born, must abjure the usual trappings of monarchs including a harem, and remain under the tutelage of the levitical priests learned in the law (Deut 17:14-20). In Ezekiel practically everything that is said about the duties and privileges of the ruler is connected in one way or another with the temple cult. He is assigned a special cultic area at the outer eastern gate of the temple, where he presides over the laity in the celebra-

---

81. Ezek 43:6-9, reading *pigrê malkêhem bāmôtām* ("funerary steles of their kings, their high places") at the end of v. 7. For this meaning of *peger,* see David Neiman, *"pgr:* A Canaanite Cult-object in the Old Testament," *JBL* 67 (1948) 55-60.

82. Cf. Ezek 19:1, the title to a lament over *nĕśî'ê yiśrā'ēl* referring, as the poem which follows indicates, to two of the last kings of Judah, Jehoahaz and either Jehoiachin or Zedekiah.

83. These *nĕśî'ê hā'ēdâ* (tribal leaders) took part in judicial decisions (e.g., Num 27:2), were responsible for contributing cult offerings (Num 7:3-88) and were involved in a predictably unsuccessful protest against the authority of Moses and Aaron (Num 16:2). See also Exod 16:22; 34:31; 35:27.

tion of Sabbath and new moon (44:1-3; 46:1-8). His territory marches with that of the temple land and lies between land assigned to Judah and to Benjamin (45:7-8a; 48:21-22). Mention of land provides the lawgiver with the occasion to prohibit enclosure of peasant land holdings, the formation of latifundia, and the falsification of weights and measures (45:8b-12), all abuses of which kings were accused by the prophets during the time of the kingdoms. His participation in the other festivals is mandated (46:9-10), and in all of this the lawgiver emphasizes the ruler's duty to provide material support for the operation of the temple cult (45:13-25; 46:11-15).

The temple law is, basically, a blueprint for a theocracy in which politics is subordinated to religion and the secular ruler to the highest religious authorities. A contemporary analogy (writing in early 2007) might be the situation of the president of Iran, Mahmoud Ahmadinejad, subject to the authority of the ayatollahs, in the first place the supreme authority, Ayatollah Ali Khamenei.

None of this seems at first sight to be relevant to the concerns expressed in Ezra-Nehemiah. The term in question appears in this book only once, with reference to Sheshbazzar designated *nāśî' lîhûdâ,* usually translated "prince of Judah" (Ezra 1:8). In this account of the enthusiastic response to the rescript of Cyrus, all we are told about Sheshbazzar is that his task was to convey the votive offering and sacred vessels to Jerusalem (1:6-11). According to the Aramaic source, however, he was also appointed governor *(peḥâ),* was authorized to rebuild the temple, and as a first step towards fulfilling this mandate laid its foundations (Ezra 5:14-16). Thus far, his profile corresponds to that of the *nāśî'* in Ezekiel 40–48. Some commentators have toyed with the idea that Sheshbazzar is to be identified with Zerubbabel.[84] Zerubbabel, who was indeed a prince of Judah since he was the grandson of the exiled Davidic scion Jehoiachin (1 Chr 3:19), was a leader of the first immigration (Ezra 2:2). He was also appointed governor (Hag 1:1) and worked on building the temple (Ezra 3:8-11). Moreover, Josephus also appears to identify him with Sheshbazzar (*Ant.* 11.11-14). The parallels are impressive, but can be adequately explained by the tendency of the writer or editor to telescope events during the earliest period and to backdate later events and personalities into prime time, the age of the

---

84. A recent example is A. Bartal, "Once more, who was Sheshbazzar?," *Beth Mikra* 24 (1979) 357-89. On the issue in general, see Sara Japhet, "Sheshbazzar and Zerubbabel," *ZAW* 94 (1982) 66-98.

founding fathers. In general, Ezra 1–6 is not the kind of text calculated to provide reliable information on the *historical* identity of the characters mentioned in it. Josephus can be discounted, since his knowledge of the Persian period is patchy at best. He also confuses Sheshbazzar with Shethar-bozenai, thereby making him not just a prince of Judah but eparch and governor of Syria and Palestine into the bargain.[85]

Nehemiah was certainly governor of Judah and therefore, to judge by the titles assigned to Sheshbazzar in Ezra 1–6, also merits the title *nāśî*. While we have no evidence that either the Nehemiah memoir or any other material dealing with Nehemiah was written with any part of Ezekiel in mind, in several respects his actions fit the profile of the *nāśî*, the ideal secular ruler, in Ezekiel 40–48. Once the city wall was finished, much of his attention was focused on the maintenance of the temple and the support of its personnel. These are major concerns in the rulings about the *nāśî* in the law of the temple,[86] as they are in Nehemiah's sworn covenant (Neh 10:32-39[MT 33-40]) reflecting policies pursued during his tenure as governor, especially it seems after his return from the imperial court (12:44-47; 13:4-9, 10-13). This second administration witnessed an intense effort to enforce Sabbath observance (13:15-22), also a matter of particular importance in Ezekiel 40–48 (45:17; 46:1-8). Moreover, Nehemiah's campaign to eliminate indentured service and the confiscation of land for nonpayment of debt (Neh 5:6-13; cf. vv. 15-19) parallels the responsibility of the *nāśî* in Ezek 45:8-9 for the maintenance of social justice.

Nehemiah was a layman, and therefore much of the legislation in Ezekiel 40–48 lay outside of his competence. But we observed earlier that the redefinition of civic leadership in Ezekiel 40–48 brings it within the confines of the cultic life of the community, and this is certainly verified in the Nehemiah story. To cite one further example: his role as master of ceremonies in the dedication of the wall (Neh 12:27-43) recalls the account of Ezekiel's *nāśî* leading the people in procession in the appointed festivals (Ezek 46:9-10).

In summary: at the political level, the law of the temple envisages the subordination of the secular authority to the priesthood, in effect a theocratic polity. At the level of political realities, however, the situation was rather more complex. The crisis throughout the Persian Empire during the

---

85. *Ant.* 11.93, 100; cf. Ezra 5:3; 6:6; 1 Esd 6:3.
86. Ezek 44:1-3; 45:7-17, 21-25; 46:1-18; 48:21-22.

first two years of the reign of Darius I led prophets to proclaim the governor Zerubbabel ruler of an independent Judean kingdom (Hag 2:20-23; Zech 3:8; 4:7). We do not know what came of this prophetic agitation, but in the event Darius prevailed and Zerubbabel disappeared. In the obscure passage Zech 6:9-14 the secular ruler, identified with the messianic code name ṣemaḥ, usually translated "Branch,"[87] is to rule with a priest by his side, and this situation is to represent a compromise agreement between the secular and religious authorities. During the administration of Nehemiah, who was clearly not content to occupy the same role, the balance was tipped in favor of the secular arm. Nehemiah's role and his *modus agendi* were closer to those of Greek tyrants like Pisistratus of Athens, Polycrates of Samos, and Histiaeus of Miletus a few generations earlier.[88] By soliciting popular support through programs of social reform (Neh 5:1-13), and by recruiting Levites as allies against the priests (13:10-13, 22), he succeeded in maintaining control of the temple and curbing the power of the priestly aristocracy. Theocracy would have to wait for a more propitious occasion.

(5) The Land

Once the possibility of a return to Judah could be contemplated, the appropriation of the real estate of the deportees by those who remained in the land promised to emerge as a major source of conflict. Disputes about title to individual estates were, moreover, inevitably linked with conflicting claims by those who remained and those who returned to inherit the land as a whole based on appeal to tradition. The Judeans who had never left the land argued pre-emptively that they were the true inheritors since the deportees had "gone far from Yahweh" (Ezek 11:14-15; 33:23-24). The logic of this argument seems to be that the deportees had been expelled from the cult community, no doubt on account of their sinful behavior, and had

---

87. Cf. Jer 23:5 and 33:15, referring to a ruler of the Davidic royal house, and Zech 3:8, announcing to the high priest and his associates the advent of 'avdî ṣemaḥ ("My servant Branch").

88. On Nehemiah as a typical *tyrannos*, see Smith, *Palestinian Parties and Politics*, 107-9. The rumors spread by Sanballat that Nehemiah was planning to set up an independent kingdom with himself as king (Neh 6:6-7) were almost certainly false but, given his actions, hardly implausible.

therefore lost title to their real estate and, at the same time, had forfeited the right to inherit the land promised to them by the ancestors.[89] The clinching argument was that they, the ones who had never left the land, were the true descendants of Abraham: "Abraham was only one man but he got possession of the land; we are many [i.e., the many descendants promised Abraham], the land is surely given to us to possess" (Ezek 33:23-24).

The diaspora Jews, represented by Ezekiel, refuted this argument by pointing, in time-honored fashion, to the many and various "abominations" of the native Judeans. We have seen that "abomination" is a favorite term with Ezekiel, with primary reference to addiction to non-Yahwistic cults associated with violence and sexual deviance. But since the land promise was conditional on religious fidelity, a point often overlooked,[90] whatever claim they might have had has been invalidated, and in any case Ezekiel's visions had shown that Yahweh was still present to the deportees in the land of their exile. It is this counterargument which underlies the rejectionist attitude towards the local inhabitants in evidence throughout Ezra-Nehemiah, nowhere more clearly than in Ezra's reaction to the marriages of *golah* Jews with native women (Ezra 9:1-15).

In the temple vision the land of Israel, divided evenly among the twelve tribes, is laid out around the land assigned in quadratic symbolism to the temple, the priests, Levites, and the secular ruler (Ezek 45:1-8; 47:13–48:29). The detailed logometrics need not concern us. The main point is that possession of the land is thereby shown to be a function of cult, just as membership in Israel and title to an individual plot of land were contingent on participation in and support of the common cult. This is quite simply a prescription for theocracy, the fulfilment of the ideal of "a kingdom of priests, a holy nation" (Exod 19:6).

In Ezra-Nehemiah, the practical concern of those among the immigrants who originated in Judah must have been to recover their real estate. This can be seen in the emphasis on family records and the listing of Judean places of origin in the census list (Ezra 2:20-29 = Neh 7:25-38). We may be sure that property was a factor behind marriage alliances between

---

89. Gen 12:7; 13:14-15; 15:17-21, etc. Foreigners would address the same reproach to the exiles: "These are Yahweh's people, and yet they had to leave his land" (Ezek 36:20).

90. The conditional nature of the occupation of the land is emphasized repeatedly in Deuteronomy (Deut 4:1, 25-28, 40; 5:33; 6:3, 15; 8:1, 19; 11:9, 17, 21) and related texts. In his final admonition, Joshua urged the people to avoid intermarriage with those left in the land, since this would lead to adopting their cults and hence expulsion from the land (Josh 23:6-16).

immigrants and native Judean women. The larger issue of the land promise was understandably muted by a realistic appreciation of political realities, though this did not prevent occasional accusations of seditious intent
from different quarters at different times during the two centuries of
Achaemenid rule. Such accusations were leveled against the immigrant
community during the reigns of Darius I (Ezra 5:3-10), Xerxes (Ezra 4:6),
and Artaxerxes I (Ezra 4:7-16; Neh 6:5-9). Nehemiah may have been recalled to the court at Susa as a result of such accusations (Neh 13:6), since it
does not seem that the priest Eliashib and his friend Tobiah expected him
back. But if accusations had been brought against him, Nehemiah must
have cleared himself with the king and his ministers, which was bad news
for Eliashib and Tobiah.

Subjection to foreign rule indefinitely postponed the realization of the
ideal polity, and was therefore basically unacceptable. The theme of Neh
9:6-37, a communal lament attached to a penitential ritual and pronounced by Levites (in LXX by Ezra), is the giving of the Abrahamic
promise of land and its rejection by the beneficiaries. The outcome is that
they have been delivered into the power of "the peoples of the lands" and
have been enslaved since the time of the Assyrians. The Ezra prayer is more
explicit as to why this has happened, namely, that by intermarrying with
the indigenous peoples and taking over their "abominations" they have
polluted the land. The first order of business, therefore, is to cleanse the
land of the people and the practices which pollute it and to start all over
again with a ritually pure people, preparing for the day when the promise
could be redeemed.

To summarize: The agenda which, in their different situations and according to their different functions, Ezra and Nehemiah strove to implement
was incubated in the Babylonian diaspora and was a product of its history
going back to the earliest deportations. Whenever and by whomsoever
drafted, Deuteronomic laws defining group membership and proscribing
intermarriage were of basic importance. In addition, the points of agreement between the agenda of Ezra and Nehemiah (irrespective of historicity) and the temple law in Ezekiel 40–48 are impressive enough to suggest a
relationship of dependence with special regard to community boundaries,
the operation of the cult, and the creation of a theocratic polity. It is reasonable to conclude that the teachings of Ezekiel were mediated through a
circle or school of disciples whose existence and activity can be deduced

from the redactional history of the book, especially in the law of the temple in chs. 40–48. This was very definitely a minority group, perhaps associated with those set aside by the *tāv* who sighed and moaned with Ezekiel over the infidelity of the many (Ezek 9:4) — not essentially different, therefore, from Ezra and his "tremblers" who mourned over the infidelity of the *golah* (Ezra 9:4).

5

Ezra and Nehemiah: History and Ideology

Ezra and Nehemiah as Ideological Points of Reference

The book Ezra-Nehemiah was put together to promote a particular understanding of Israel, the agenda of a particular party, and an ideology imported from the Babylonian diaspora which drew its inspiration primarily from certain aspects of Deuteronomic theology and the "law of the temple" *(tôrat habbayit)* in Ezekiel 40–48. The use of first person narrative for both Ezra and Nehemiah was an effective way of achieving this end and, at the same time, relegating those who did not belong to their party or subscribe to their ideas and practices to insignificance and their different ways of being Jewish to background noise. After assessing what the canonical book has to say about the two principals, it is time to ask what impact their activities and ideas had on Jewish communities during the remainder of the Second Temple period and what legacy they left to the Jewish people thereafter. Did the Ezra and Nehemiah of the book continue to function as ideological points of reference during the following centuries? What became of their program? To what extent was it successful? These are questions which can be asked, and should be asked, even by those who find little of historical reality in Ezra-Nehemiah or who regard the leading characters as literary creations rather than historical figures.

We speak of *their* program, but it would not be surprising if Ezra and Nehemiah came to represent, in some respects, contrasting points of view. Most obviously, Ezra was a priest and Nehemiah a layman. Ezra's concerns were therefore more directly to do with cult, ritual, and sacral law, Nehemiah's with the political sphere. The incident about intermarriage is an example of Ezra and his core group of supporters in action; Nehemiah's agenda was the application of ritual theory to the political arena with the purpose of creating a politically and religiously homogeneous polity. Nehemiah made no bones about exercising his authority as governor, so it is no surprise that where his name occurs in the book alongside that of Ezra he takes precedence. Moving the public reading of the law into the part of the book dealing with Nehemiah's career allowed him not only to take part but to preside assisted by his supporters, the Levites (Neh 8:9). Likewise, where the two are brought together in the ceremony dedicating the city wall Ezra plays a role subordinate to Nehemiah (Neh 12:36), and on the only other occasion where their names occur together Nehemiah, as governor, is named first (12:26).

But there are scholars, especially among those who doubt or deny outright the historical reality of Ezra, who argue that the Ezra narrative was created to counter Nehemiah's prestige and was placed before the Nehemiah narrative to make a point about precedence. This line of argument goes back to the early "radicals," conspicuously Ernest Renan, who read the memoir of Ezra the priest as a deliberate contrast to that of Nehemiah the layman.[1] In support of this perspective on the book it has been observed that Ezra is presented as enjoying the good will of the ruler in fuller measure than Nehemiah (Ezra 7:6), that unlike Nehemiah he meritoriously declined the protection of a military escort on the journey (Ezra 8:22; Neh 2:9), and that he had a more positive reception on arrival in Jerusalem than Nehemiah, who had to carry out his reconnaissance of the wall under cover of the dark (Ezra 8:31-36; Neh 2:11-20). There is also the common assumption that the authority of the priest is intrinsically greater and will always trump that of any layman, even a head of state or, in this case, the governor of a province. However one construes the relation between the two parts of the book, the fact that on the few occasions where their names appear in later Second Temple texts they never occur together is consistent with the hypothesis of a combination in the canonical book of two originally distinct accounts.[2]

---

1. *Histoire du Peuple d'Israël*, 4 (Paris: Calmann-Levy, 1893) 96-106. More recently, along the same lines, see J. C. H. Lebram, "Die Traditionsgeschichte der Esragestalt und die Frage nach dem historischen Esra," in *Sources, Structures and Synthesis*, ed. Heleen Sancisi-Weerdenburg. Achaemenid History 1 (Leiden: Nederlands Instituut voor het Nabije Oosten, 1987) 114, 120-21.

2. Josephus's account, to be considered shortly, deals with both Ezra and Nehemiah but

We shall see that these contrasting functions, and the relative importance attributed to one or the other, have a part to play in the partisan
struggles leading to the emergence of the sects of the Hasmonaean period,
but they should not distract our attention from the ideology to which both
Ezra and Nehemiah subscribed. Both were Jews from the eastern diaspora
who came to Judah with a definite agenda;[3] both are presented as advocat-
ing and implementing the regulation of membership in the *golah* by strict
enforcement of marriage law through coercive sworn agreements;[4] both
were concerned for the temple and the integrity of its personnel and endowments. Both, finally, were solicitous in promoting the observance of
the laws understood according to their own interpretation.[5] The question
we now go on to ask is whether Ezra and Nehemiah continued to function
as ideological points of reference throughout the remainder of the Second
Temple period, and whether the traditions about them converge or go in
separate directions. Ideally, we would trace a continuous interpretative trajectory originating in the book and extending throughout the subsequent
centuries, but lack of adequate documentation renders this task impossible. For most of that period, the last century of Achaemenid rule and the
Hellenistic period down to Antiochus IV (175-164 B.C.), about two and a
half centuries, we are traversing a bleak and mostly silent landscape as far
as the history of Judaism is concerned. There are few if any relevant biblical texts which can be dated with assurance. Josephus, our principal source
apart from the biblical texts, is not well informed on the later Persian period. After his lengthy paraphrase of Esther (*Ant.* 11.184-296) he ran out of
biblical source material, and where he seems to have some independent information, for example on the high priesthood, the historical contexts in
which he places incidents, as well as many of the details, are justifiably con-

---

without any cross-referencing or overlap. Since Josephus drew on 1 Esdras from which
Nehemiah is absent, he must have had access to an independent Nehemiah source, similar to
the account in the canonical book.

3. If both were active during the reign of Artaxerxes I, and Nehemiah arrived in Judah
thirteen years after Ezra, it is not impossible, though unverifiable, that Ezra knew Nehemiah
before his arrival. At the time of Nehemiah's mission, and perhaps for some time previous to
it, Nehemiah had an important post at the court in Susa, some 300 kilometers east of
Nippur. The visit of his brother Hanani and his party as described in Neh 1:1-4 sounds like a
delegation urging him to use his influence with the king on behalf of his people.

4. Ezra 10:3-5; Neh 10:28-30(MT 29-31); 13:25.

5. Ezra 10:3-5; Neh 7:72–8:12; 10:28(MT 29); 13:1-3.

sidered suspect. The situation is not promising, but we can at least make a start by reviewing the few texts in which either Ezra or Nehemiah is mentioned, or from which one or the other is conspicuously absent, in the hope of joining some of the dots on the line.

Closely Related Texts: Chronicles, First Esdras, Josephus

Since Ezra-Nehemiah was in the making for a considerable period of time — according to some scholars down to the Hasmonaean period — the successive stages by which the book reached its final form, to the limited extent that we can reconstruct them, should be considered as part of this interpretative trajectory. Examples of later compositional strata, noted earlier, include lists of temple personnel, Nehemiah's covenant, and the first section of the book (Ezra 1–6). This last, the account of the eventual reestablishment of the Jerusalem cult by the first immigrants from Babylonia, raises the disputed issue of shared authorship of part or all of the book with Chronicles. That Ezra was the author of both Chronicles and Ezra-Nehemiah, with Nehemiah playing a supplementary role, was the traditional view in Judaism (*b. B.Bat.* 15a), an updated version of which was defended by Charles Cutler Torrey and William Foxwell Albright.[6] In the early nineteenth century Leopold Zunz, one of the founders of *Judenwissenschaft*, maintained the essential unity of Chronicles and Ezra-Nehemiah but reversed the traditional opinion by making the Chronicler the author of Ezra-Nehemiah.[7] This quickly became and remained for a long time the *opinio communis*,[8] though in recent years it has come under

---

6. Charles C. Torrey, *Ezra Studies* (1910; repr. New York: Ktav, 1970) 208-51 ("There is not a garment in all Ezra's wardrobe that does not fit the Chronicler exactly," 243); W. F. Albright, "The Date and Personality of the Chronicler," *JBL* 40 (1921) 104-24. Jacob M. Myers, *I Chronicles.* AB 12 (Garden City: Doubleday, 1965) lxxxvi-lxxxvii, favors this view but admits it cannot be demonstrated.

7. *Die gottesdienstliche Vorträge der Juden historisch entwickelt* (Berlin: Asher, 1832) 13-36.

8. E.g., Wilhelm Rudolph, *Esra und Nehemia samt 3. Esra* (Tübingen: Mohr, 1949) xxii-xxiv (the theory of common authorship, he says, "leidet keinen Zweifel"); Antonius H. J. Gunneweg, "Zur Interpretation der Bücher Esra-Nehemia," *VTSup* 32 (1981) 146-61; Peter R. Ackroyd, "Chronicles — Ezra — Nehemiah: The Concept of Unity," *ZAW* 100 (1988 sup.) 189-201; K.-F. Pohlmann, "Zur Frage von Korrespondenzen und Divergenzen zwischen des Chronikbüchern und dem Esra/Nehemia-Buch," *VTSup* 43 (1991) 314-30.

attack, in the first place from Sara Japhet and Hugh Williamson, who rec-
ommend reading Ezra-Nehemiah as a work independent of Chronicles.[9]
An eventual solution, if there is ever to be one, may turn out to be more
nuanced than either of these polar opposites, especially if we understand
Chronistic authorship in the broad sense of a scribal school sharing the
same goals, language, and religious outlook on the past.

Chronicles is essentially a history of Israel from the first to the second temple. It begins, in effect, with the bringing up of the ark to Jerusalem by David (1 Chr 13:1-14), the first stage towards the creation of the
Jerusalemite cult, and ends with the mandate received by Cyrus to rebuild the temple in Jerusalem (2 Chr 36:23). Linked genealogies begin
with the creation of humanity and conclude with the list of the first immigrants to return from Babylon (1 Chr 9:1-44), a bold way of affirming
the significance and primordiality of the first immigrants who returned
to Zion to rebuild the temple. It would therefore be natural to follow on
by reading the account of the rebuilding of the temple and resumption
of the cult in Ezra 1–6 as the continuation and culmination of that history either by the same author or one of his school. It fits the pattern of
the last section of Chronicles in which religious and especially cultic renewal follows a dark period: Hezekiah after Ahaz, Josiah after Manasseh,
and now Zerubbabel and Joshua the high priest after the disaster of the
destruction of city and temple, all three ending with the celebration of
Passover (2 Chr 30:1-27; 35:1-19; Ezra 6:19-22). This continuity of structure, which induced the author of 1 Esdras or his *Vorlage* to begin his
narrative with Josiah's Passover, is matched by continuity in theme, motif, and language. It would be tedious to present the arguments one more
time, but the structural parallels between the building of the first and the
second temple should be mentioned. Preparations for temple-building
are similar,[10] the altar is set up before the temple is built in order to ward
off danger (Ezra 3:2; 1 Chr 21:18–22:1), and both temples are endowed by
the heads of households (Ezra 2:68; 1 Chr 26:26). Attention focuses in

---

9. Sara Japhet, "The Supposed Common Authorship of Chronicles and Ezra-
Nehemiah Investigated Anew," *VT* 18 (1968) 330-71; "The Relationship between Chronicles
and Ezra-Nehemiah," *VTSup* 43 (1991) 298-313; *I and II Chronicles*. OTL (Louisville: Westminster John Knox, 1993) 3-5; H. G. M. Williamson, *Israel in the Books of Chronicles* (Cambridge: Cambridge University Press, 1977) 5-70; "The Composition of Ezra i–vi," *JTS N.S.* 34
(1983) 1-30; *Ezra, Nehemiah*. WBC 16 (Waco: Word, 1985) xxii-xxiv.

10. Ezra 3:7; 1 Chr 22:2, 4, 15; 2 Chr 2:9, 15-16 (MT 8, 14-15).

both cases on the sacred vessels,[11] the order of sacrifices and enumeration of sacrificial material is identical, and there is great interest in the performance of liturgical music.[12]

In arguing against the thesis of common authorship of Chronicles and Ezra-Nehemiah, Japhet and Williamson make much of what seems to them to be a major focus on David in Chronicles and a lack of interest in him in Ezra-Nehemiah. The argument runs as follows: nineteen out of sixty-five chapters in Chronicles are devoted to David, while apart from topographical allusions to the city of David and the graves of David (Neh 3:15-16; 12:37) and the name of a descendant of David (Hattush, Ezra 8:2), he is largely invisible in Ezra-Nehemiah. The point is well taken, but the argument is pressed too far. Both books are interested in David primarily as founder of the cult, provider for the temple, and organizer of the temple musicians.[13] In both Chronicles and Ezra-Nehemiah the profile of David (rather than Moses) as founder of the Jerusalem cult offsets the role of Cyrus as the one who sanctioned and financed the second temple. This was a problem for some rabbis, as we see from the statement of R. Isaac in *Pesiqta Rabbati* (32:5): "Why did the Shekinah not dwell in the second temple which the *bĕnê haggôlâ* built? It was because it was (really) Cyrus who built it."

Another point at issue is the Chronicler's apparent lack of interest in the exodus and conquest traditions and their pervasive if not always explicit presence in Ezra-Nehemiah. If, however, we read Chronicles as a history from the first to the second temple, we would not expect these traditions to be treated at comparable length to the narratives in the Pentateuch. But if Ezra-Nehemiah is read as a later extension of the same history from the same authorial source, broadly understood, it would result that what is absent at the beginning of the work is present typologically at the end, most clearly in Ezra's exodus from Babylon and peril-

11. Ezra 1:7; also in the Ezra section: 7:19; 8:25-30, 33-34; cf. 1 Chr 28:13-18; 2 Chr 5:1. Chronicles omits the notice in 2 Kgs 24:13 that the vessels were broken up for bullion in anticipation of their restoration as recorded in Ezra 1:7-11.

12. More than a century ago, S. R. Driver, in *An Introduction to the Literature of the Old Testament* (1891; repr. Cleveland: Meridian, 1956) 535-40, drew up a detailed and extensive list of lexical, syntactic, and idiomatic features shared by Chronicles and Ezra-Nehemiah. On the thematic parallels, see my *Ezra-Nehemiah*. OTL (Philadelphia: Westminster, 1988) 51-54.

13. Ezra 3:10; 8:20; Neh 12:24, 36, 45-46.

ous journey through the wilderness into the land of promise.[14]Another argument against the hypothesis of common authorship of Chronicles and Ezra 1–6 contrasts the Chronicler's generally sympathetic attitude to the inhabitants of the former kingdom of Samaria with the hostility of the *běnê haggôlâ,* the exclusive embodiment of Israel, to the people of Samaria and their rulers. The author of Chronicles does indeed omit the denunciation of the Samarians as sinners and idolaters in his source (2 Kgs 17:7-18), and does refer to Judean rulers who reach out to those among their northern neighbors who were well-disposed (2 Chr 15:9; 30:1-12), but he nevertheless makes it quite clear that the future lies with Judah as a cult community gathered around its temple in Jerusalem. So, for example, in his address to Jeroboam and his army before engaging them in battle, Abijah boasts that God is on the side of the Judeans because they possess the one legitimate sanctuary and priests to serve it: "We keep the charge of Yahweh our God but you have abandoned him" (2 Chr 13:4-12). At a somewhat later time King Amaziah, on prophetic advice, rejects the offer of military assistance from the kingdom of Samaria since "Yahweh is not with Israel, with all these Ephraimites" (2 Chr 25:6-10). Hezekiah invites the same neighbors from the former kingdom of Samaria to share in his Passover (2 Chr 30:18, 25), but indigenous Judeans who had "separated themselves from the impurity of the nations of the land" were also invited to share in Passover together with the *golah* group after the completion of the second temple (Ezra 6:21).

A provisional conclusion would run somewhat as follows. Based on similarity of language, theme, and ideology, the balance of probability favors a reading of Ezra 1–6 as the continuation of the Chronicler's history. Whether the Ezra narrative (Ezra 7–10; Nehemiah 8) represents a further extension of the history from the same source is much less clear. There are indications of Chronistic language and themes in these chapters, but they can be adequately explained by influence from a putative Chronistic school with its distinctive vocabulary and topoi without postulating common authorship. The Nehemiah first person and third person narrative, finally, betrays relatively little evidence of Chronistic influ-

---

14. Since the journey began on the twelfth of the first month (Ezra 8:31), they would have replicated the first Passover by celebrating the festival as the long trek through the wilderness was getting underway. Note too the duodecimal symbolism: representatives of twelve lay kinship groups in addition to priests and a scion of the royal dynasty (8:3-14), twelve leading priests (8:24), twelve sacrificial animals (8:35).

ence. The absence of the Nehemiah story from 1 Esdras is one of several pointers to its separate origin and later attachment to the canonical book.

In addition to Chronicles and the Greek (LXX) translation of Ezra-Nehemiah (Esdras beta), 1 Esdras (Esdras alpha) also attests to continued interest in the career and ideas of Ezra well into the Hellenistic period. This version reproduces 2 Chr 35:1–36:21 (corresponding to 2 Kgs 23:21–25:30), beginning with Josiah's Passover and covering events to the end of the kingdom; most of Ezra 1–10, though in a somewhat different order;[15] and Neh 7:73–8:13a, the public reading and exposition of the law. A major addition is the story of the three bodyguards at the court of Darius (3:1–5:6), a variation of a popular tale type which has been adapted and expanded to promote the stature of Zerubbabel and provide a more interesting, if even less plausible, explanation for the generosity of the Persian monarch in permitting and financing the rebuilding of Jerusalem and its temple. 1 Esdras served Josephus as a major source for the period and therefore cannot be later than the late first century A.D. On linguistic grounds it is generally dated to the second century B.C.[16]

The problem of the relation of 1 Esdras to the canonical books has not proved easy to solve. Since it is agreed that it does not draw on the LXX of Ezra-Nehemiah (Esdras beta), its principal source must have been either 2 Chronicles 35–36 and Ezra-Nehemiah in the Masoretic form in which we now have them, either in the original Hebrew and Aramaic or Greek translation, or an alternative and perhaps earlier version in some respects different in content and in the order of events. If the former, then the addition of the court narrative, the omission of the Nehemiah story, and the different order in which the events are presented call for an explanation. Given the state of affairs in Judah at the time of writing, the author may have wished to demonstrate what the temple and its personnel ought to represent and how they ought to be serviced and provided for. Since the way the story is told makes it clear that the rebuilding of the Jerusalem temple was inspired and mandated by God (1 Esd 2:3-4) and the actual work providentially guided and protected, there could also be an implicit polemic against temples other

---

15. The sequence in 1 Esdras is Ezra 1; 4:7-24a; 2:1–4:5; 4:24b–6:22; 7-10.

16. The Greek of 1 Esdras, better than Esdras beta, is similar to that of Sirach, Esther, 1 Maccabees, and the LXX of Daniel.

than the one in Jerusalem, in particular the temple built by Onias IV in Heliopolis around 170 B.C.[17]

An argument has been made that the silence of 1 Esdras on the activity of Nehemiah is due to deliberate omission, either on account of antipathy towards what he stood for, or with a view to placing the achievements of Ezra in higher relief, or both. The omission of the Nehemiah narrative from 1 Esdras would inevitably enhance the status of Ezra, now explicitly presented as high priest (*archiereus*, 1 Esd 9:40, 49) as well as reader in the law of the Lord (*anagnōstēs tou nomou kuriou*, 8:8, 19; 9:39, 42), but it is far from clear that the omission was deliberate. The author knows about Nehemiah as governor of the province, and in spite of misunderstanding the Persian loanword *hattiršatā'* ("governor," 9:49), he mentions him alongside the phantom Attarates (or Attharias) as issuing decisive rulings in the early period of the settlement (5:40). The author may have had before him an earlier version of the Ezra story to which the Nehemiah narrative had not yet been attached; and it may be that it was subsequently attached in such a way as to drive a wedge between the two parts of the Ezra narrative (Ezra 7–10 and Neh 7:72b–8:12).[18] In view of the fact that the traditions about Ezra and Nehemiah developed separately and independently of each other throughout the Second Temple period, this would not be surprising. On the other hand, the tale of the three bodyguards at the court of Darius (1 Esdras 3–4) may have had the purpose of elevating the status of Zerubbabel at the expense of Nehemiah. It has been inserted, in defiance of chronology, immediately after the decree of Artaxerxes forbidding the rebuilding of Jerusalem, and it represents its hero extracting from Darius the fulfilment of his vow to rebuild the city, in other words, to do what another monarch commissioned Nehemiah to do (Neh 2:5). On that reading, the three founders of the new society in Persian-period Judah would be the high priest Joshua/Jeshua, the Davidic Zerubbabel, and Ezra priest and scribe.[19]

---

17. Josephus, *Ant.* 12.387-88; 13.62-73, 283-87.

18. Dieter Böhler, *Die heilige Stadt in Esdras α und Esra-Nehemia.* OBO 158 (Freiburg: Universitätsverlag, 1997) 304-6 and passim, argues that variations in the MT Ezra narrative vis-à-vis 1 Esdras, of earlier date, were necessitated by the insertion of the Nehemiah narrative during the Maccabean period.

19. See R. J. Coggins and M. A. Knibb, *The First and Second Books of Esdras.* CBC (Cambridge: Cambridge University Press, 1979) 4-5, 75; Jacob M. Myers, *I & II Esdras.* AB 42 (Garden City: Doubleday, 1982) 9-10. Hypotheses about the purpose of 1 Esdras are discussed in

1 Esdras provides some additional information, not in itself implausible, about Edomite encroachment on Judean territory and participation in the Babylonian campaign against Jerusalem, including the surprising claim, in the inserted story of the three bodyguards (1 Esd 4:45, 50), that the Edomites burned the Jerusalem temple. On the whole, however, it has little independent value as a historical source over and above Ezra-Nehemiah, and this is so even if it is taken to represent a version earlier than the canonical book.

It is clear from Josephus's history of the Jewish people during the Persian period, including his profile of the person and career of Ezra (*Ant.* 11.120-58), that his principal, perhaps his only, source was 1 Esdras.[20] Ezra is introduced as leading priest (*prōtos hiereus*) in the Babylonian diaspora (cf. 1 Esd 9:40, where he is *archiereus*, "high priest") and personal friend of Xerxes[21] during the high priesthood of Joiakim, successor of Jeshua/ Joshua in Jerusalem (cf. Neh 12:10). Having decided to go to Jerusalem, he secured a letter of support from the king, read it to the Jews in Babylon, and sent a copy to the Jewish community in Media. Many then packed up and left with him, though Josephus notes that "the Israelite nation as a whole remained in the country" (11.133). There follows an account of the journey, arrival in Jerusalem, and handing over of the sacred vessels. Josephus attributes the marriage crisis, which he describes in some detail with his own typical elaborations, to a violation of the constitution and the laws of the country without further explanation (11.140).

This incident is followed by the celebration of Sukkoth which is reported in the canonical book but absent from 1 Esdras; perhaps the author deduced a reference to this festival from the date, the seventh month, and the allusions to a joyful holy day, repeated three times in 1 Esd 9:49-55. The location of the assembly, in the forecourt of the temple, corresponds with 1 Esdras (9:38), as also the request addressed by the people to Ezra to bring along the book of the law of Moses (9:39). Josephus, however, omits the ac-

---

Emil Schürer, *The History of the Jewish People in the Age of Jesus Christ*, rev. ed. by Geza Vermes et al., 3/2 (Edinburgh: T. & T. Clark, 1987) 708-18.

20. On Ezra and his times in Josephus, see Louis H. Feldman, "Josephus's Portrait of Ezra," *VT* 43 (1993) 190-214; "Restoration in Josephus," in *Restoration: Old Testament, Jewish, & Christian Perspectives*, ed. James M. Scott. JSJSup 72 (Leiden: Brill, 2001) 223-61.

21. Josephus's substitution of Xerxes for Artaxerxes (11.121; cf. 1 Esd 8:1) was the result of a misguided attempt to correct the chronology of his source.

count of Ezra's public reading and interpretation of the law with the help of a panel of Levites (9:42-48).

Since Nehemiah is absent from 1 Esdras, Josephus must have had access to a separate version of the Nehemiah story (*Ant.* 11.159-83).[22] As is his wont, Josephus fills in the gaps in the narrative with novelistic embellishments. The situation in Judah and Jerusalem as reported to Nehemiah, cupbearer to Xerxes (11.159), was so bad that the streets were full of corpses after the country had been overrun by the surrounding nations. Nehemiah received the bad news as the result of a casual encounter with some Hebrew speakers who happened to be visiting Susa, and who detained him so long that he had to perform his cup-bearing duties unbathed. Josephus has little to add to his source, but a point of interest is his report that Nehemiah requested permission of Xerxes to both rebuild the city and complete the rebuilding of the temple (11.165, 169). This addition to the version in the canonical book (Neh 2:5-8) may be unhistorical but is not wildly implausible. Ezra 6:14 states that the building of the temple continued into the reign of Artaxerxes, and we shall see that the letter to Aristobulus in 2 Maccabees (2 Macc 1:18) flatly asserts that it was Nehemiah who built the temple.

According to Josephus, Nehemiah arrived in the twenty-fifth year of Xerxes, an impossibility since Xerxes reigned for only twenty years (485-465 B.C.). Far from concealing his intentions on arrival, as in the canonical book, he called a public meeting in the temple courtyard and made a speech (*Ant.* 11.168-171). His night ride around the perimeter took place after the building had begun and served to illustrate not his fear of opposition but his indifference to food and sleep (178). Josephus puts greater emphasis on the hardships and opposition Nehemiah had to endure, extending the time it took him to complete the city wall, which would remain as his perpetual monument (11.183), from fifty-two days (Neh 6:15) to two years and four months (11.179). At the end of it all, he too died at an advanced age, being of a kind and just nature and most anxious to serve his countrymen (*Ant.* 11.183).

Josephus's tendency to elaborate on and embellish his sources is well represented in his account of Ezra and Nehemiah. Names of rulers are changed to fit an improved chronology, lists are generally omitted as calculated to bore his urbane readers, and observations and events potentially damaging to the reputation of his subjects are omitted. As noted earlier,

22. Louis H. Feldman, "Josephus's Portrait of Nehemiah," *JJS* 43 (1992) 187-202.

there is in Josephus no overlap and no cross-referencing between Ezra and Nehemiah. Ezra arrived in Judah in the seventh year of Xerxes (135 B.C.) and Nehemiah in the twenty-fifth year of the same monarch (168), and together they satisfy Josephus's desire for chronological order by filling in the gap between Darius and Artaxerxes. In their aims and achievements the two complement each other. There is therefore in Josephus no indication of negative feeling against either protagonist and no attempt to elevate the one over the other.

In Praise of Nehemiah: Ben Sira and II Maccabees

We come across another example of the danger of arguing *e silentio* in the didactic treatise written by Jesus ben Sira and recommended to the public by his grandson, who translated it into Greek. It includes a review of the great personalities of the Jewish past in chs. 44-49, which can be read as a small-scale example of the classical Greek encomiastic biography *(epainos)* exemplified on a much larger scale in the writings of Isocrates (ca. 436-338 B.C.) and Xenophon (ca. 428-354). Ben Sira's encomium concludes with a paean of praise for the high priest Simon II, known as "the Righteous One" *(haṣṣāddîq)*, a contemporary of the rivals Ptolemy V and the Seleucid Antiochus III.[23] Together with the blessing pronounced on the high priest at an earlier point (Sir 45:26), this hymn of praise suggests that Simon was alive and functioning as high priest at the time of writing, which therefore places the composition of the work in the last years of the third or the early years of the second century B.C. There are other clues to the author's high esteem for the priesthood. The series begins and ends with Enoch, a priestly figure (44:16; 49:14), and Aaron is assigned a much longer and more detailed treatment than Moses, one which emphasizes his liturgical and educational functions (45:6-22). Following in the steps of the author of Chronicles, David's role as liturgical founder and reformer is also emphasized (47:8-10).

In the last part of the encomium Zerubbabel and Joshua are praised

---

23. Sir 50:1-21. Josephus (*Ant.* 12.43, 157), however, identifies Simon I, son of Onias I, founder of the Oniad dynasty, as "the Righteous One." His identification is vigorously defended by James C. VanderKam, *From Joshua to Caiaphas: High Priests after the Exile* (Minneapolis: Fortress, 2004) 138-57, though he does not rule out Simon II (p. 182).

for having rebuilt the temple (Sir 49:11-12). They are followed by Nehemiah, whose memory is destined to survive — an oblique allusion to the memoir — on account of his public works. At this point the Greek text reads as follows:[24]

> As for Nehemiah, his memory will long endure:
> he raised up for us the walls that had fallen,
> setting up gates and bars,
> and rebuilding our ruined houses. (49:13)

These achievements, stated in rather pedestrian fashion, find a parallel in the praise of the high priest Simon, who repaired and fortified the temple, laid the foundations for a defensive wall, and, in general, prepared the city to sustain a siege (50:1-4). The parallelism can be explained by taking account of the situation at the time of writing. Simon was the son of Onias II and descendant of Onias I, founder of the Oniad high-priestly dynasty. Serious problems for both Onias II and Simon were created by the activity of Joseph Tobias and his son Hyrcanus, wealthy entrepreneurs and tax collectors, whose activities during the second half of the third and the first quarter of the second century B.C. are well documented.[25] These Tobiads, who illustrate a way of being Jewish quite different from that of Ezra and Nehemiah, were descendants of "Tobiah, the servant/slave, the Ammonite" (Neh 2:10) whom we encountered as one of Nehemiah's most persistent and dangerous opponents. It appears that at both junctures in the history of the family, the Tobiads were attempting to get political and economic control of the Jerusalem temple. Joseph Tobias, related by marriage to Onias II, had a keen interest in the financial assets of the temple (*Ant.* 12.160), and his son Hyrcanus had a large sum on deposit in the temple treasury (2 Macc 3:11). Their ancestor, contemporary of Nehemiah, was likewise related by marriage to the high-priestly family and obtained a commercial concession in the temple at that time (Neh 13:4-9). These con-

---

24. For the fragmentary Hebrew text from the Cairo Genizah, see Benjamin G. Wright, *No Small Difference: Sirach's Relationship to Its Hebrew Parent Text.* SBLSCS 26 (Atlanta: Scholars, 1989) 38-40.

25. The principal sources are the so-called Tobiad Romance in *Ant.* 12.160-236 and the Zenon papyri. The history of the family was traced out, with the help of some speculation, by Benjamin Mazar, "The Tobiads," *IEJ* 7 (1957) 137-45, 229-38. For an update, see Lester L. Grabbe, *Judaism from Cyrus to Hadrian*, vol. 1: *The Persian and Greek Periods* (Minneapolis: Fortress, 1992) 192-98.

nections would help to explain the honorable mention accorded Nehemiah by Ben Sira and the linking of his achievements with those of the high priest.

A puzzling aspect of the encomium is that it passes over Ezra in silence. Since it is not at all likely that the author was ignorant of Ezra and his activities,[26] several scholars have assumed that the author must have disagreed with Ezra's policy of coercive divorce, especially in view of the fact that marriage between Jews and non-Jews was widely tolerated at the time of writing. Ben Sira did not have occasion to comment on the intermarriage crisis involving Ezra and his supporters, so we can only speculate as to what his opinion on the subject would have been. He certainly had no qualms about divorce. He advised the husband whose wife refused to obey him to divorce her (Sir 25:25-26), and as a fully certified misogynist and exponent of the "spare the rod spoil the child" educational philosophy, he would not have been concerned about the fate of the divorced women and their children.[27] More directly relevant is the high profile he assigns to Phineas grandson of Aaron, ranked "third in glory" after Moses and Aaron (45:23-25). Phineas was granted "a covenant of perpetual priesthood" on account of his religious zeal in the incident at Baal-peor recorded in Numbers 25, and the zealous act which won him this accolade was the assassination of the Israelite Zimri together with Cozbi, a noble Midianite lady. Since what provoked Phineas's zeal was the spectacle of Zimri presenting the woman to his Simeonite kin (*'aḥîm*) and to the entire assembly (*'ēdâ*),

---

26. J. C. H. Lebram held this opinion on the grounds that Ben Sira had at his disposal only Haggai, Zechariah 1–8, the Aramaic parts of Ezra-Nehemiah which mention Zerubbabel and Joshua, and the Nehemiah book before its incorporation into Ezra-Nehemiah; "Die Traditionsgeschichte der Esragestalt und die Frage nach dem historischen Esra," in *Sources, Structures and Synthesis*, ed. Heleen Sancisi-Weerdenburg. Achaemenid History 1 (Leiden: Nederlands Instituut voor het Nabije Oosten, 1987) 126-27. Both Sheshbazzar and Ezra are missing from the encomium because the narrative parts of Ezra-Nehemiah had not yet been written. This is not really an argument since it postulates what the author had available to him purely on the basis of what he actually mentions. Lester L. Grabbe, *Ezra-Nehemiah* (London: Routledge, 1998) 88, concludes that either Ben Sira did not know Ezra-Nehemiah or, if he did, he didn't consider it important. For those who, like C. C. Torrey and Giovanni Garbini, believe that Ezra is a fictional character a simpler explanation is at hand.

27. On Ben Sira's views on women, see Sir 9:1-9; 25:25-26; 26:1-9, 13-18. The nadir is his aphorism to the effect that "better is the wickedness of a man than a woman who does good" (42:14).

it was a matter not of a casual sexual liaison, as the writer would have us believe, but a marriage ceremony between a high status Israelite and an equally high status foreign woman. Such marriages were condemned on the same grounds on which Ezra condemned them, namely, that they led to the adoption of foreign cults, in this instance that of the Baal of Peor. Ben Sira's praise of Phineas is followed by a blessing on the descendants of Aaron (45:26) and a eulogy on those paradigms of religious zealotry, Joshua and Caleb (46:1-10).

Since therefore there seem to be no grounds for supposing that the author would have disapproved of Ezra's solution to the marriage crisis, an alternative explanation for the omission of Ezra may be suggested. Ben Sira's primary focus is on the high priesthood, as we have seen, and its legitimacy would have been for him a major concern. He would have been familiar with Simon's genealogy, and from it he would have known that, in spite of the claim of Aaronite lineage in Ezra 7:1-5, Ezra appears in none of the genealogical tables on which the legitimacy of the high priesthood rested. This would have been sufficient to drop him from the list of the illustrious ones, but a further consideration may have played a part. In the encomium, Simon the Righteous receives high praise for his building activities: he repaired and fortified the temple, laid the foundations for walls and attended to the water supply (Sir 50:1-4). This would at once suggest pairing him with Nehemiah, who is praised for rebuilding and fortifying the city. Perhaps, then, Ezra was excluded since he did not build anything.[28] One way or another, it would be imprudent to make too much of an ideological factor in the omission of Ezra from the encomium.

Nehemiah's Cromwellian combination of military prowess and ostentatious piety made him a natural choice as model and patron for the Maccabee family. The Maccabees traced their descent to the priest Joiarib, first in the list of the twenty-four divisions into which the Jerusalem priesthood was divided (1 Macc 2:1; 1 Chr 24:7), and it appears that the name of this priest was added subsequently to the list of priests and Levites who were the first to arrive from Babylon (Neh 12:6).[29] This would have had the advantage of connecting the Maccabees with the founding fathers

28. On this view of the matter, see the review by J. A. Emerton, *JTS N.S.* 23 (1972) 184-85. For other suggestions, see Peter Höffken, "Warum schwieg Jesus Sirach über Esra?" *ZAW* 87 (1975) 184-201.

29. Among the priests listed as contemporaries of Zerubbabel and Jeshua, his is the only name preceded by the conjunction, hence probably inserted.

of the new commonwealth, the "return to Zion" generation. The canonical book itself finds a place for Nehemiah among the leaders of the first immigration, alongside Zerubbabel and Jeshua (Ezra 2:2 = Neh 7:7), and he is likewise backdated to that seminal epoch in a letter, almost certainly a forgery,[30] from the council of elders in Jerusalem to the Jewish-Egyptian notable Aristobulus about the observance of the Feast of Sukkoth (2 Macc 1:10–2:18). The letter purports to have been written after the death of Antiochus IV Epiphanes and the liberation of the city and temple. It makes the surprising claim that it was Nehemiah rather than Zerubbabel and Jeshua who set up the first altar and built the temple (1:18). The temple sacrifices could be resumed only after Nehemiah, commissioned by an unnamed Persian king, supervised the relighting by miraculous means of the sacred fire concealed after the destruction of the temple. This new role for Nehemiah would have been consistent with the ideology of 2 Maccabees which claimed divine sanction for the second temple, reinforced by miracles (3:22-28).[31] The letter also refers to the temple archives established by Nehemiah containing "books about kings, prophets and the writings of David, and letters of kings about votive offerings." This notice reads like a stage in the formation of the canon, rivaling claims made later on behalf of Ezra in the Ezra Apocalypse. In this respect also Nehemiah anticipated Judah Maccabee, who collected books lost during the war of independence (2:13-14). The letter cites the source for its information as the records and memoirs of Nehemiah.[32] This would be a fair description of the canonical book, except for the problem that the latter contains none of the information about Nehemiah given here.

The Maccabean adoption of Nehemiah as patron and role model can readily be understood in light of his political and religious aims and achievements: defending the integrity of Judah from external enemies, re-

---

30. Martin Hengel, *Judaism and Hellenism* (Philadelphia: Fortress, 1974) 1:100 and n. 340; Grabbe, *Judaism from Cyrus to Hadrian*, 1:261. A rabbinic tradition identifies Nehemiah with Zerubbabel based on the fiction that Zerubbabel (meaning "born in Babylon") was his Babylonian name.

31. Robert Doran, *Temple Propaganda: The Purpose and Character of 2 Maccabees.* CBQMS 12 (Washington: Catholic Biblical Association, 1981). On the purpose and ideology of the letter, see Theodore A. Bergren, "Nehemiah in 2 Maccabees 1:10–2:18," *JSJ* 28 (1997) 249-70.

32. *en tais anagraphais kai en tois hypomnēmatismois tois kata ton Neemian* (2 Macc 2:13).

storing and preserving the purity of the temple and the legitimacy of the high priesthood, and nation-building in general. Nehemiah's opposition to Tobiah, whose descendants were among the principal exponents of a liberal, philhellenic approach to Jewish life and mores in the early Hellenistic period, would have been an additional factor. If, as was suggested earlier, the Nehemiah narrative was a later addition to the Ezra material, it may therefore have been attached to the book during or shortly after the Maccabee uprising, perhaps even later than the interpolated story of the three guardsmen in which, as we saw, Zerubbabel replicates the achievements of Nehemiah. It was therefore only after the interpolated passage was in place that 1 Esdras could be read as directed polemically against the reputation and legacy of Nehemiah.

Ezra Between the Canonical Book and Rabbinic Attestations

It is disconcerting that, apart from the parallel narrative in 1 Esdras and the brief notice about him in Josephus, which is dependent on 1 Esdras, Ezra is not mentioned, whether to praise or to blame, in any extant text from the Second Temple period. This is so even where we might expect to find him named. In his deathbed address Mattathias, father of the Maccabees, recommends to his sons the example of the great religious zealots of the past. The list includes "Phineas our father," Joshua, Caleb, the three young men in the fiery furnace of Daniel 3, but no Ezra.[33] The author of the festival letter in 2 Macc 1:10–2:18, who attributes the restoration of the Jerusalem cult and even the rebuilding of the temple to Nehemiah, might well have linked him with Ezra but either did not know about him or anticipated that his readers would not know about him, or did not care to mention him. Even acknowledging that only a fraction of the literary production of the later Second Temple has survived, this relative silence on Ezra has strengthened the hand of those scholars who argue that the Ezra of the canonical book is either entirely or in great part a literary creation rather than a historical figure.

The silence is all the more eloquent when contrasted with the high status accorded Ezra in rabbinic writings, much higher than Nehemiah. Nehemiah was given credit for enforcing the Sabbath law and was one of

33. 1 Macc 2:49-70; *3 Macc.* 6:1-15.

the "men of the Great Assembly" (*'anšê kĕnesset haggĕdôlâ*), but practically anyone who was anyone in the Second Temple period belonged to that august body (*b. Šabb.* 123b). He is identified with Zerubbabel, this being his Babylonian name (*b. Sanh.* 38a), in effect another way of backdating him to the beginning of the restoration. The rabbis accorded a much more enthusiastic reception to Ezra.[34] He was one of the five *ṣaddîqîm* together with Abraham, Moses, Aaron, and Hezekiah (*b. Meg.* 11a). As a Torah disciple of Baruch he benefited indirectly from the teaching of Jeremiah. Though authorized to return and rebuild the temple, he put off his departure as long as Baruch was alive, convinced as he was that Torah takes precedence over temple (*b. Meg.* 16b). In addition to performing the duties of high priest, Ezra founded the first yeshiva, presided over the Great Assembly, wrote the book of Judges, authored the Targum, and compiled the Mishnah. He prescribed the public reading of Torah on set occasions and introduced the square script in which it was to be copied. Above all, he was the one who restored Torah, so that if Moses had not preceded him he would have been worthy to receive it directly from God (*b. Sanh.* 21b; *b. Sukkah* 20a, etc.). He even divided Torah into its divisions (*pārāšôt*) for liturgical use (*b. Meg.* 31b) and enacted the "Ten Regulations" governing such important matters as the set times for studying Torah and such minutiae as when to do the laundry or eat garlic (*b. B. Qam.* 82a-b; *b. B. Bat.* 22a). According to a late tradition recorded by Benjamin of Tudela, he died in Persia, but Josephus says that he died at an advanced age in Jerusalem (*Ant.* 11.158).[35]

A position intermediary between the profile of Ezra in the canonical book and the Ezra of the rabbis is occupied by the pseudepigraphal text known as *4 Ezra*, in which Ezra is presented as a Moses figure. A Christian reworking of a Jewish apocalyptic composition, *4 Ezra* consists in seven visions vouchsafed, we are told in the opening verse, to the seer Salathiel, also known as Ezra (*4 Ezra* 3:1). Salathiel is the Greek rendering of Hebrew Shealtiel (1 Chr 3:19 LXX), and Shealtiel was the father of Zerubbabel[36] or, according to 1 Chr 3:17-19, his uncle. The identification of Ezra with this

---

34. On rabbinic views about Ezra, see Gary G. Porton, "Ezra in Rabbinic Literature," in Scott, *Restoration*, 305-33.

35. For other Ezra legends, see the index to Louis Ginzberg, *The Legends of the Jews*, 7 (Philadelphia: Jewish Publication Society of America), and for later Ezra texts, mostly Christian and derivatives of 1 Esdras, see *OTP*, 1:561-604.

36. Ezra 3:2; 5:2; Neh 12:1.

Salathiel-Shealtiel in *4 Ezra,* chronologically impossible, is still, in my opinion, best explained as the result of a combination in the book of several apocalyptic texts, including one featuring Salathiel and another featuring Ezra, by a compiler writing in the late first or early second century A.D. The objection that Shealtiel is otherwise unknown as the recipient of apocalyptic revelations is hardly decisive. He was, after all, the son of the exiled Judean king Jehoiachin and could be presumed to be alive thirty years after the fall of Jerusalem when the seer is said to have had the visions. His son Zerubbabel will feature in an apocalyptic work *(Sefer Zerubbavel)* several centuries later. The chronological issue should not be pressed either. Chronology did not prevent the identification of Ezra, active under Artaxerxes I, with the son and successor of Seraiah, last preexilic high priest (Ezra 7:1-5). It is, moreover, difficult to accept that an ancient author would have found the seer's skepticism about divine providence reprehensible enough to transfer imputability from the unimpeachable Ezra to an unknown surrogate.[37] One indication that a Salathiel apocalypse, together with several other apocalypses (principally the Eagle Vision in *4 Ezra* 11-12 and The Man from the Sea in ch. 13) has been reassigned editorially to Ezra is that, with the exception of the first verse, Ezra's name occurs only in the redactional links between the seven visions.[38] I therefore find the analysis of G. H. Box still the best working hypothesis.[39]

In any case, these disputes about the composition of the book are largely irrelevant for our present purpose since, apart from the opening verse, only in the last chapter, the seventh and final vision, is anything said about Ezra. This chapter recounts how Ezra, like Moses, hears a voice from a bush which informs him that God had revealed to Moses both the law to be published openly and esoteric matters to be kept secret. The end of the age is near, therefore Ezra is to bear in mind all the signs, dreams, and interpretations which had been revealed to him. Since the law book had been burned thirty years earlier at the fall of Jerusalem, he is, again like Moses, to sequester himself for forty days, then prepare writing materials, and as-

37. These arguments in favor of the unity of *4 Ezra* are advanced by John J. Collins, *The Apocalyptic Imagination,* 2nd ed. BRS (Grand Rapids: Wm. B. Eerdmans, 1998) 196-200. A similar position is taken by Myers, *I & II Esdras,* 119-21; and, much earlier, by Montague Rhodes James, "Ego Salathiel qui et Esdras," *JTS* 18 (1917) 167-69, who, unsurprisingly in view of his other claim to fame, described the Salathiel apocalypse as a "ghost book."

38. 4 Ezra 5:16-19; 6:10; 7:2, 25; 8:2; 12:12.

39. G. H. Box, *The Ezra Apocalypse* (London: Pitman, 1912); and in *APOT,* 2:549-53.

semble five scribes to take dictation. After addressing the people for the last time, Ezra is offered a cup from which he drinks a fiery liquid in the strength of which he dictates, over the course of the forty days, ninety-four books, twenty-four for all and sundry, the worthy and unworthy, and seventy reserved for "the wise among your people" (cf. Dan 11:33). For those who read and understand what they are reading these seventy secret texts will be of surpassing value since they contain "the spring of understanding, the fountain of wisdom, the river of knowledge" (*4 Ezra* 14:47).

Consider for a moment the implications of this remarkable claim. The author accepts the biblical canon of twenty-four books,[40] but claims a higher status for the seventy esoteric (i.e., apocalyptic) writings, including, we would suppose, his own work. In support of this claim he enlists the authoritative support of Ezra, whom he represents as an apocalyptic seer. He is, however, aware of Ezra's role as restorer of the law, a second Moses, whether he was familiar with the biblical book or not. This is apparent from the way he sets the scene with the voice from the bush and the forty-day sequestration, and the action is set in motion with the information that the law had been burned during the destruction of Jerusalem and must be restored (*4 Ezra* 14:21). But the author also represents Moses on Mount Sinai as receiving, in addition to the written law, not the oral law of standard rabbinic teaching, but esoteric information about the future course of history, information which is reserved to the few (14:6).[41] As the replica of *that* Moses, Ezra is to reproduce not only the Law and the Prophets but seventy esoteric texts, and it is important to note that he is to do this not on the authority of Moses but, having drunk the fiery liquid, by direct inspiration and unmediated authorization.

The Ezra of *4 Ezra* is therefore not the creator of the biblical canon in the Wellhausenian sense,[42] nor is his accomplishment presented here as a counter to Nehemiah as founder of a library of sacred writings (2 Macc 2:13) since there is no evidence that the author was familiar with that tradition. What is of interest is that he combines the role of restorer of the law

40. Twenty-two in Josephus, *C. Ap.* 1.37-41, corresponding to the twenty-two letters of the Hebrew alphabet.

41. The idea of Moses receiving esoteric knowledge concerning the future at Sinai and passing it on to a chosen intermediary is not peculiar to *4 Ezra*; see *Jub.* 1:26-29 and the *As./ T. Mos.* 1:15-18.

42. Julius Wellhausen, *Prolegomena to the History of Israel.* SBL Reprints and Translations (1885; Atlanta: Scholars, 1994) 409-10.

with that of prophet and apocalyptic sage. In this respect, the presentation of Ezra and his associates in *4 Ezra* can be seen as an extension of the profile of Ezra and his supporters, the *ḥărēdîm*, in the canonical book, who combined legal rigorism with prophetic emotionalism.

In summary: beginning with the way they are presented in the canonical book, Ezra and Nehemiah represent contrasting profiles in that Ezra was a priest and Nehemiah a layman, a mere "Israelite,"[43] even if governor of the province. In their respective spheres of operation they nevertheless were motivated by the same ideology and implemented the same agenda originating in the Babylonian diaspora. Nehemiah came into his own as the patron of the Hasmoneans, the model for their application of religious and ritual principles to the political sphere, and the justification for their territorial ambitions. On Ezra the surviving record is almost completely silent, but it still remains to be seen to what extent and in what form the ideology which he represents continued to find embodiment.

How Lasting Were the Achievements of Ezra and Nehemiah?

It remains to be seen how the Ezra-Nehemiah understanding of what was required for membership in the household of Israel fared during the latter part of the Second Temple period, let us say from the governorship of Nehemiah in the mid-fifth century to the Hasmonaeans in the mid-first century B.C.[44] Throughout this entire period the principal threat to the ideal of a ritually segregated community came from the Jerusalem priesthood. Control of the Jerusalem temple and its personnel is represented in the canonical book as essential for both Ezra and Nehemiah if they were to achieve their objectives. Access to the temple and participation in its cult were privileges restricted to those in good standing as members of the political community; hence control of the temple was an essential precondition for political control and an indispensable means for defining who qualified for membership in the political community. Ezra, of high-

---

43. For the meaning of "Israelite" as lay person and "Israel" as laity, see Ezra 2:70; 7:7; 8:29; 9:1; 10:1, 5, 25; Neh 10:39(MT 40); 11:3; 12:47.

44. Nehemiah was recalled to the Persian court in the thirty-second year of Artaxerxes, presumably Artaxerxes I, therefore 433/432, returned to Judah, and continued to serve, for how long we are not told, but probably not beyond 424/423, the last year of Artaxerxes. The last Hasmonaean ruler was Mattathias Antigonus (40-37 B.C.).

priestly descent according to Ezra 7:1-5, arrived in Jerusalem with a mandate to restore the temple cult. His mission is represented as a full-scale restoration after a period of neglect, comparable to and parallel with the mission of the first immigrants described in Ezra 1–6. It is striking that we hear of no high priest in situ upon Ezra's arrival in Jerusalem, and it is equally striking that in the matter of the marriage crisis he is able to act as if endowed with full civil and religious authority, even obliging the leading priests to swear under oath to send away their wives and children (Ezra 10:5). Nehemiah's aim, likewise, was to control the operations and resources of the temple, and to that end he took decisive action against those priests who had married into the Sanballat and Tobiad families. Both families were worshippers of Yahweh but not adherents of the *golah* party (Neh 13:4-9, 28).

The *golah* seems to have experienced opposition to its integrationist policies from the senior priests, and the high priest in particular, from the very beginning, and this especially in the important matter of intermarriage. The obscure passage about Joshua/Jeshua, first high priest in the rebuilt temple, being a brand plucked from the fire and having to be divested of filthy garments (Zech 3:1-5) has predictably been interpreted in different ways by different commentators. The interpretative options cannot be discussed here, but an allusion to involvement in syncretic practices seems more likely than the fact of his simply having lived in Babylonia, a land polluted by idols, since neither Zerubbabel nor Ezra, both of Babylonian extraction, is referred to in a similarly prejudicial manner. Haggai gives Jeshua credit as cobuilder of the temple but without much emphasis. He is named after Zerubbabel, and Zerubbabel alone is addressed in the final prophetic prediction of a great and imminent political upheaval (Hag 2:20-23). Josephus tells us that Jeshua's successor Joiakim (Neh 12:10, 12, 26) was high priest *(archiereus)* in Judah while Ezra was his counterpart *(prōtos hiereus, Ant.* 11.121) in Babylon. It is therefore puzzling — as noted earlier — that there is no mention of Joiakim in Jerusalem when Ezra arrived and handed over the bullion and the sacred vessels to the chief priests, Levites, and lay dignitaries who were awaiting them (Ezra 8:29). Joiakim may have died, or he may have been removed from office for reasons unknown to us, or Ezra may have used his authority to depose him and take over the office himself; we are not told.

Members of the families of both Eliashib and Joiada, the next two high priests in the line of succession, had marital relations with the Sanballats of Samaria and close association, probably of a commercial nature, with the Tobiads and were on that account unceremoniously treated by Nehemiah (Neh 13:4-9, 28). The description in the Nehemiah memoir of these alliances with outsiders as a defilement of the priesthood and of the priestly covenant (13:29) is reminiscent of the virulent polemic against the Jerusalem priesthood in Malachi, roughly contemporary with Nehemiah. Malachi refers to "the covenant of Levi" (Mal 2:4-9) and accuses the priests of offering polluted food on the altar, leading the people astray by their teaching, and despising the name of their God (1:6-7; 2:8). The accusation of marrying "the daughter of a foreign god" (Mal 2:11), directed against both clergy and laity, has been interpreted in different ways, but probably refers to the kind of marriages reprobated in Ezra-Nehemiah on account of the foreign cults which the women were suspected of often bringing with them.[45]

Little is known about the situation in *yĕhûd mĕdîntā'* (the province of Judah) in the decades immediately following the governorship of Nehemiah, but it can at least be said that whatever efforts were made to control the high priest and his associates and confine them within the limits of a rigorist interpretation of the law were not successful. According to Josephus (*Ant.* 11.297-301, 304-5), Bagohi (*Bagōsēs* in Josephus), a later governor of Judah, perhaps Nehemiah's immediate successor,[46] offered the high priesthood to his friend Jeshua (Jesus), brother of the high priest Johanan (*Jōannēs* in Josephus),[47] an offer which led to an altercation in the temple precincts and the murder of Jeshua by the high priest in the same hallowed location. This intervention of Bagohi looks like the first stage in the politicization and commercialization of the high priestly office which

45. G. J. Botterweck, "Schelt- und Mahnrede gegen Mischehe und Ehescheidung von Mal. 2:2, 10-16," *BibLeb* 1 (1960) 179-85; Pieter A. Verhoef, *The Books of Haggai and Malachi.* NICOT (Grand Rapids: Wm. B. Eerdmans, 1987) 269-70; Beth Glazier-McDonald, *Malachi, the Divine Messenger.* SBLDS 98 (Atlanta: Scholars, 1989) 91-93; Andrew E. Hill, *Malachi.* AB 25D (New York: Doubleday, 1998) 231-33.

46. I agree with VanderKam, *From Joshua to Caiaphas,* 59-63, against H. G. M. Williamson, "The Historical Value of Josephus's *Jewish Antiquities* XI 297-301," *JTS N.S.* 28 (1977) 48-67, that the Bagōsēs of Josephus is to be identified with the governor of Judah under Artaxerxes II, the one mentioned in the Elephantine papyri (TADAE A4.7 = AP 30), rather than with the charismatic general of Artaxerxes III who, according to Diodorus (16.50.8), was king in all but name.

47. This high priest, son and successor to Joiada, is named Jonathan in Neh 12:11 and Johanan in 12:22.

was to reach a climax, or nadir, under the Seleucid Antiochus IV Epiphanes. Following up on his account of this scandalous incident, Josephus records the marriage of Manasseh, brother of the high priest Jaddua and contemporary of Darius III and Alexander, to Nikaso daughter of Sanballat governor of Samaria (*Ant.* 11.302-12). It is interesting to note that it was the elders of Jerusalem, the *gerousia,* not the high priest, who presented Manasseh with the choice of either divorcing Nikaso or giving up his priestly office. Josephus attributes their action to fear of contamination with foreigners, but fear of Samaritan interference in the operations of the temple could have been a more immediate and compelling motive. There is in any case no indication of widespread disapproval; Josephus in fact goes on to state that "many priests and Levites were involved in such marriages" (11.312).

Manasseh, at any rate, was not willing to accept either option. He had recourse instead to Sanballat, who offered to build him a temple on Mount Gerizim where he could officiate as high priest. The historicity of this event as recorded by Josephus has long been suspect. To several scholars, probably a majority, it looks like a garbled version of the incident recorded in Neh 13:28, which informs us that a son of the high priest Joiada had married the daughter of Sanballat the Horonite.[48] But granted Josephus's deficient and confused knowledge of the Achaemenid period and his problems with chronology, it may at least be taken to represent what he took to be a plausible situation for that time and place. At a later point, in fact, he observes that Manasseh's recourse to Sanballat was part of a common pattern at that time, shortly before and after the Macedonian conquest:

> Whenever anyone was accused by the people of Jerusalem of eating unclean food or violating the Sabbath or committing any other such sin, he would flee to the Shechemites, saying that he had been unjustly expelled. . . . This, then, is the way things were with the people of Jerusalem at that time. (*Ant.* 11.346-47)[49]

---

48. See, e.g., Williamson, *Ezra, Nehemiah,* 399-401, and my *Ezra-Nehemiah,* 365. Vander-Kam, *From Joshua to Caiaphas,* 82, rejects the view that *Ant.* 11.302-12 is a botched version of Neh 13:28 on the grounds that the time, characters, and circumstances are different.

49. A version of the same custom botched almost beyond recognition is recorded much later in ch. 8 of *4 Baruch.* On their return to Judah under Jeremiah's leadership, those of the immigrants who had Babylonian wives insisted on bringing them with them but were forbidden entry into Jerusalem. They retraced their steps but were also refused reentry into

A comparable account has come down to us in the description of the Jews and Judea of Hecataeus of Abdera, a contemporary of Alexander the Great, via Photius and Diodorus of Sicily:

> As to marriage and the burial of the dead, he (Moses) saw to it that their customs should differ widely from those of other men. But later, when they became subject to foreign rule, as a result of their mingling with men of other nations (both under Persian rule and under that of the Macedonians who overthrew the Persians) many of their traditional practices were disturbed.[50]

It seems, then, that the Jerusalemite high priesthood was being compromised more than two centuries before the office came to be auctioned off to the highest bidder under Antiochus IV (175-164 B.C.). More specifically, given their power and influence, the upper echelons of the temple priesthood were setting an example to the rest of the population with respect to marriage with outsiders. In his narrative of events following on the Macedonian conquest, Josephus chronicles the succession of high priests, beginning with Onias I, founder of the Oniad dynasty, and his son and successor Simon I, but says nothing about governors. In the *Letter of Aristeas* the high priest Eleazar, next in line, is presented as having supreme authority in responding to the request of Ptolemy II Philadelphus for a Greek translation of the Jewish law.[51] Shortly thereafter, we are told that Onias II had been granted *prostasia*, political and judicial power together with, or as an attribute of, the high priesthood, and was for that reason obliged to pay the twenty silver talents out of his own pocket to the Ptolemaic ruler (*Ant.* 12.161). It seems, then, that after the Macedonian conquest

---

Babylon. They therefore left and founded their own city, calling it Samaria. See S. E. Robinson in *OTP*, 2:423.

50. Text in Menahem Stern, *Greek and Latin Authors on Jews and Judaism*, vol. 1: *From Herodotus to Plutarch* (Jerusalem: Israel Academy of Sciences and Humanities, 1976) 27, 29.

51. The letter purports to have been written by a courtier in the entourage of Ptolemy II to his brother, but it is transparently of Jewish origin, probably from the late second century B.C. From the point of view of our inquiry, it is of interest in going the extra mile to present the Jewish religion as deserving sympathetic consideration from the educated outsider. The law is thoroughly philosophical, Jews worship the same God as the Greeks under a different name, dietary matters are subsumed under larger issues of personal and social morality, and avoidance of "mixing" with outsiders is motivated by the absolute need to exclude false worship.

both religious and political power were concentrated in the hands of the high priest, making Judah in effect a theocracy.

Mention of Onias II gave Josephus the cue for introducing his colorful account of the careers of the Tobiad Joseph and his son Hyrcanus, both wealthy Jewish tax collectors, landowners, and entrepreneurs (*Ant.* 12.160-236). As related by Josephus, their careers illustrate a way of being Jewish very different from that of Ezra and Nehemiah. Joseph was the nephew of Onias II, thus maintaining the pattern of close marital relations with the Jerusalem clergy set by his ancestor at the time of Nehemiah (Neh 6:18; 13:4). What Joseph and Hyrcanus really thought about their Jewish identity we can only guess, but both father and son dealt without any apparent scruple with foreigners of high and low station, both amassed huge wealth, not always by approved means, and both ate with foreigners (*Ant.* 12.174, 210-13). Infatuated with a dancing girl during a performance at the Ptolemaic court, Joseph, though aware that sexual relations with foreign women were forbidden by Jewish law, sought the help of his brother Solymius with a view to getting to know her better. The outcome was that his brother, taking his cue from the story of Jacob and Laban, brought his own daughter to the bed of a thoroughly inebriated Joseph, who ended by marrying her and begetting Hyrcanus (12.186-89). After a life full of incident, Hyrcanus fell foul of the Seleucid monarch Antiochus IV and committed suicide (12.236), an act almost unprecedented in the annals of his people.[52]

By way of postscript to the "Tobiad Romance," mention should be made of the Ammonite sheik Tobias *(Toubias)* mentioned several times in the Zenon archive. In a letter written by him to Apollonios, finance minister to Ptolemy II, in or about 259 B.C., he thanks the gods for his distinguished friend's prosperity. This was a standard greeting which carried no religious or emotional charge, but it can still serve as an indication of the same liberal attitude in matters of religion as that of the other Tobiads known to us.[53] We cannot imagine Ezra or Nehemiah putting such a greeting at the head of a letter.

---

52. Leaving aside self-killing in battle — falling on one's sword being practically *de rigueur* in certain circumstances — the only suicide recorded in the Hebrew Bible is that of Ahithophel (2 Sam 17:23). Qoheleth seems to refer to suicide at the beginning of his famous poem about the right time to do or abstain from doing various things all of which are under our control to do or not to do: "A time to bring a child into the world and a time to put an end to one's life" (Eccl 3:2). For the translation, see my paper "Ecclesiastes 3.1-15: Another Interpretation," *JSOT* 66 (1995) 55-64.

53. For the text, see Grabbe, *Judaism from Cyrus to Hadrian*, 1:193.

After the deposition of the high priest Onias III by Antiochus IV Epiphanes at the beginning of his reign (175 B.C.) and the appointment of Onias's brother Jason (Jeshua or Jesus) as his successor on payment of a substantial bribe, the Tobiads continued to influence the course of events by their alliance with Menelaus, who outbid Jason and ousted him after three years in office (175-172 B.C.). It will not be necessary to rehearse in detail the events of those fateful years from the deposition of Onias III to the assumption of the high priesthood by Jonathan Maccabee in 152, the interpretation of practically every aspect of which is disputed.[54] Though himself an Oniad, son of Simon II and brother of Onias III, Jason is reviled by the Epitomist as the one most responsible for introducing the Greek way of life together with Greek political and cultural institutions into Judean Judaism (2 Macc 4:7-22). We must bear in mind, however, that we are hearing about the philohellenic position exclusively from hostile witnesses. Setting up a gymnasium and youth center *(ephēbeion)* in Jerusalem, wearing the Greek hat, and even having priests take part in wrestling matches and throwing the discus will have been seen by some as a sad departure from tradition but would hardly prove fatal to the Jewish way of life. Subsidizing sacrifice to Herakles was more serious, but was probably a compromise gesture dictated by political considerations, and in any case was not carried through. What was involved in enrolling the people of Jerusalem as citizens of Antioch (2 Macc 4:9) is far from clear; it may simply imply that the more prominent and wealthy inhabitants could be enrolled as honorary citizens of the Seleucid capital.[55] According to Josephus, however, it was Menelaus during the decade of his high priesthood (172-162) who, with Tobiad support, and for his own personal advantage rather than for ideological reasons, petitioned Antiochus for leave to adopt the Greek way of life *(hellēnikē politeia, Ant.* 12.239-41). By so doing, Menelaus unwittingly gave Antiochus an additional pretext for plundering the temple,

---

54. Elias Bickerman, *Der Gott der Makkabäer* (Berlin: Schocken, 1937); Eng. trans. *The God of the Maccabees.* SJLA 32 (Leiden: Brill, 1979); Victor Tcherikover, *Hellenistic Civilization and the Jews* (1959; repr. New York: Atheneum, 1970) 152-203; Martin Hengel, *Judaism and Hellenism,* 1:267-314; Grabbe, *Judaism from Cyrus to Hadrian,* 1:246-69; "The Jews and Hellenization: Hengel and His Critics," in *Second Temple Studies III: Studies in Politics, Class and Material Culture,* ed. Philip R. Davies and John M. Halligan. JSOTSup 340 (Sheffield: Sheffield Academic, 2002) 52-66; VanderKam, *From Joshua to Caiaphas,* 203-26.

55. See Bickerman, *The God of the Maccabees,* 58-60; and the detailed critique of Tcherikover, *Hellenistic Civilization and the Jews,* 404-9.

which led to further punitive action and eventually the proscription of the Jewish religion.[56]

Looking back from the crisis of those years to the beginning of the Hellenistic period, we see that long before Antiochus IV Greek culture and institutions had penetrated deeply to every level of the life of every society under Ptolemaic and Seleucid rule, including Jewish society. There seems no reason to suppose that most Jews in a position to be affected by these new cultural trends would have experienced them as fatal or even necessarily hostile to their way of being in the world as Jews. Some of the most powerful writings from the late Second Temple period combine fidelity to the essentials of Judaism with a presentation of Torah religion in terms compatible with the best philosophical and ethical thinking of the age. For the Wisdom of Solomon and Baruch chs. 3–4, the Jewish law is an expression of a universal wisdom pervading all space and time. *4 Maccabees* presents the Jewish faith as a philosophy in accord with reason and attempts to give a rational explanation for the dietary laws (*4 Macc.* 1:14; 5:2) and for the laws in general as inculcating the practice of the cardinal virtues (5:22-24). The *Letter of Aristeas* is even prepared to concede that Jews worship under a different name the same deity as sincere worshippers of Zeus or Dis (*Let. Aris.* 15).

The fusion of Hellenism and Judaism continued to bear fruit, in spite of the risks involved, in the rich and diverse intellectual life of Alexandria. The writings of Philo, whose work represents a restructuring of biblical thought using the categories of Greek philosophy, is the prime example of this form of intellectual acculturation. At the level of everyday social relations the impact would have been equally apparent. If the measures advocated by segregationists, following the lead of Ezra and Nehemiah, had been successful, Ruth the Moabite woman would never have married Boaz of Bethlehem, and Achior the Ammonite would never have been accepted into the Jewish faith (Jdt 14:10). Above all, we would be left with no adequate explanation for the remarkable demographic expansion of the Jewish people between the Persian and Roman periods. It is particularly significant that the theory and practice of ritual segregation found its most congenial milieu and its most characteristic expressions in the sectarian movements which emerge in the Hasmonaean and early Roman periods. We will see something about this in the following chapter.

---

56. 1 Macc 1:11-64; 2 Maccabees 5–7; *Ant.* 12.242-56; Dan 11:29-35.

Where the agenda of the *golah* leadership did register a success, if one which turned out to be a decidedly mixed blessing, was in Nehemiah's securing the autonomy of Judah within the Persian Empire. In the canonical text this is presented as the fulfilment of the ideal of a religiously homogeneous and segregated population. As it happened, it had consequences which Nehemiah could hardly have predicted. The Maccabees, Nehemiah's heirs, saved Judaism from extinction, at least in Judah; but having achieved independence and territorial integrity, they went on to pursue a policy of territorial expansion at the expense of Samaritans, Galileans, Idumeans, and others in the endless wars of John Hyrcanus and his son Alexander Jannaeus (135-76 B.C.). To represent the coercive incorporation of neighboring peoples and tribes into the Hasmonean kingdom as conversion to Judaism is, to put it mildly, misleading. Hyrcanus, Josephus tells us (*Ant.* 13.257-58), allowed the Idumeans to remain in their country on condition of being circumcised and conforming their manner of life to that of the Jews. In this and similar instances, "Judaism" no longer stands for an essentially religious form of life but a facet of a political-ethnic entity, a way of characterizing an aggressive and expansive state claiming religious legitimacy through the usurpation of the high-priestly office and control of the temple while maintaining and expanding its power by military means including use of foreign mercenaries.[57] In this respect, the Hasmoneans were the spiritual and ideological heirs of Nehemiah. The Hasmoneans were able to pursue these goals by exploiting a temporary vacuum in imperial power between the heyday of the Seleucids and the advent of the Romans. The goals themselves were essentially identical with those of Nehemiah, which however the different situation in the mid-fifth century B.C. prevented him from implementing. This reterritorializing of Judaism, in which respect it differed from other religions during the Hellenistic period, was essentially his work, and its results have lasted down to the present.

It seems meanwhile that the theory and practice of ritual segregation associated with Ezra and his party found its most congenial milieu and its most characteristic expressions in the sectarian or quasi-sectarian groups and movements which emerged in the Hasmonaean and early Roman periods. Something of this will occupy us in the following chapter.

---

57. See Richard A. Horsley, "The Expansion of Hasmonean Rule in Idumea and Galilee: Towards a Historical Sociology," in Davies and Halligan, *Second Temple Studies III*, 134-65.

· 6 ·

The Sectarian Element in Early Judaism

What Is a Sect and How Can It Be Recognized as Such?

According to the Oxford English Dictionary, the word "sect," from the
Latin *secta,* with the etymological sense of either something cut off (verb
secare) or following a leader or a way of life (verb *sequi*), was first used in
the Middle Ages to describe dissident Christian groups and even, in the
writings of John Wyclif, religious orders like the Franciscans and Domini-
cans. This specifically contextualized usage goes back to the seminal study
of Ernst Troeltsch on the social teaching of the Christian churches published in 1912. Troeltsch worked out a phenomenology of sect by contrasting it with church, meaning Western Christianity, the Roman Catholic
church as it existed in the Middle Ages. Where the church is conservative
the sect is radical; where it is universalizing and open to the secular order,
the sect renounces the world and its values in favor of asceticism and the
spiritual perfection of the individual; where, above all, the church is over-
whelmingly composed of those born into it, the sect is a voluntary association, entry into and continuing membership in which depend on satisfy-
ing certain criteria and demonstrating possession of certain qualifications.
On this basis, Troeltsch went on to identify and characterize a number of
examples from the history of the Christian church in the Middle Ages including Cathars, Joachimites, Waldensians, and Lollards.[1]

---

1. Ernst Troeltsch, *The Social Teaching of the Christian Churches,* vol. I (Louisville: Westminster John Knox, 1992) 328-69; Eng. trans. of *Die Soziallehren der christlichen Kirchen und
Gruppen* (Tübingen: Mohr Siebeck, 1912).

Troeltsch made an observation at the beginning of his chapter on church-sect typology which could provoke reflection on the subject of our study. His point was that from the very beginning of the Christian church there existed a dualistic tendency or potentiality within Christian social teaching. On the one hand there was the ecclesiastical ethic which, because of its universalistic claims, called for a degree of compromise with the social and political order, while on the other hand there was the invitation and allure of adhering to the radical claims and demands of the gospel. Troeltsch argued that the latter option, once reinforced by an equally radical interpretation of the natural law and the primitive state of nature, would lead inevitably to the formation of sects.[2] In the preceding chapters we saw several indications of a similar duality within emergent Judaism with the potential for developing into different ways of understanding Judaism and being Jewish, including the one which would eventuate in the overt sectarianism of the Hasmonaean period. I would argue that the potentiality for the formation of sects was not only present from the very beginnings of both Judaism and Christianity, but in both cases was actualized in terms of social realities from the earliest times. In the present chapter we will try to get a clearer picture of how this actually worked out within the history of Second Temple Judaism.

In biblical scholarship the term "sect" evokes Josephus's triad of Sadducees, Pharisees, and Essenes, in speaking of whom he uses the terms *hairesis, hairetistai* ("sect," "sectarians").[3] The first Christians preferred other self-descriptions. Paul's accusers referred to him as a ringleader of the Nazarene *hairesis*, but Paul corrected them by declaring that he worshipped "according to the Way, which they call a sect" — note he said "they," not "we" (Acts 24:5, 14). Yet Paul did not hesitate to apply the same term to the Pharisees, representatives of the Judaism which he himself had professed (Acts 26:5; cf. 15:5). This terminology (sect, sectarian, sectarianism) unfortunately still retains something of a negative aura about it, due to its original use to designate heterodox groups throughout the history of Christianity. In current usage, in the media and everyday speech, terms such as "sect" or "cult" tend to characterize a group or movement as narrow and extremist, perhaps dangerously so. It is important to set this prejudicial idea aside at the outset. The term is the one used in the sociological

---

2. *The Social Teaching of the Christian Churches*, 329-30, 161-64.
3. *B.J.* 2.119-66; *Ant.* 13.171-73; 18.23-25.

literature, and there seems to be no acceptable alternative. Max Weber himself spoke of charisma and virtuosity in connection with sectarian movements over against mass religion. Belonging to a sect may be the only vehicle for pursuing certain ideals for living.[4] Each case must therefore be considered on its own terms and its own merits, without prejudice.

Writing in evident dependence on Troeltsch's distinction between church type and sect type, Weber sketched out in his great masterpiece *Wirtschaft und Gesellschaft (Economy and Society)* and in other writings his basic understanding of sectarianism, with special reference to the sectarian movements provoked by the Reformation (Anabaptists, Puritans, and others).[5] Weber's contribution to the understanding of sectarianism is fundamental, but both his work and that of Troeltsch illustrate the dilemma that definition and description depend on and are circumscribed by the cases under consideration. Following the lead of these two great pioneers we can, however, hazard some generalizations:

(1) The sect is a voluntary association. To become a member of a sect one must satisfy criteria and qualifications dictated by the purpose of the group. Membership entails obligations freely undertaken, hence the difference between the dictated state law under the monarchy and the voluntary self-commitment to specific points of law in the covenants in Ezra-Nehemiah and in the rules of the Damascus community and the Qumran *yaḥad*.

(2) The sect is characterized by a strong sense of boundaries, of an insider-outsider differentiation; this sense will typically be embodied in practices with respect to some or all of the following: worship, purity rules, commensality and dress, connubium and sexual relation in general. The sect will use great vigilance in admitting postulants and will exercise the right to expel members who transgress its rules. Names of members will often be listed in an official document.

(3) The sect will either be introversionist and withdraw from "the world" outside as corrupt and corrupting or it will be reformist and undertake a mission to transform and save the world.

4. Max Weber, *Economy and Society: An Outline of Interpretive Sociology* (Berkeley: University of California Press, 1978) 1:206-7; trans. of *Wirtschaft und Gesellschaft: Grundriss der verstehenden Soziologie*, 4th ed. (Tübingen: Mohr Siebeck, 1956).

5. Max Weber, *Economy and Society*, 2:1204-11. Weber's many contributions to the subject are listed and discussed by David J. Chalcraft in *Sectarianism in Early Judaism* (London: Equinox, 2007).

(4) Since we will be speaking about Jewish sects during the period of the Second Temple, we add that the sect will tend either to define itself with reference to the parent body from which it has dissociated or has been forcibly dissociated, or it will stake an exclusive claim to be the authentic heir and possessor of the traditions cherished by the parent body. In other words, in early Judaism we witness the emergence of a type of sect which takes over the identity and the claims which it either believes the parent body has forfeited or to which it denies title to other claimants. It will see itself as the only representative of the Israel to which the traditions testify, with the result that the world outside its boundaries consists not only of Gentiles but of other Jews. To what extent the schism is complete and definitive will depend on the level of tolerance or intolerance on either side of the divide.

(5) In the nature of the case, a sect will generally arise and function at the margins of the society in which it is embedded and will therefore be deprived of access to the sources of political and religious power in that society. But it can also happen that, as a result of specific circumstances, a sect can move temporarily into a position of influence and power. A case in point would be the Puritans after their establishment of a commonwealth in the New England colonies in the early seventeenth century.

In his *Das antike Judentum,* published posthumously as volume three of his *Gesammelte Aufsätze zur Religionssoziologie,* Weber sketched out what he called the *Sektenreligiosität* ("sectarian religiosity") of the Pharisees and their antecedents the Asidaeans *(asidaioi)* mentioned in 1-2 Maccabees.[6] Reflecting a point made by Troeltsch, Weber argued that this Pharisee sectarianism replicated certain basic features of Judaism present inchoately from the beginning. Its roots are to be sought in the transition from nation-state to confessional community *(Bekenntnisgemeinde)* at the time of the Babylonian exile and the emergence, in Judah, of a ritually segregated community. The principal aim of Weber's study of ancient Judaism was to explain how the loss of statehood led to the emergence of Juda-

---

6. Max Weber, *Ancient Judaism,* trans. and ed. by Hans H. Gerth and Don Martindale (Glencoe: Free Press, 1952) 385-404 (German ed. Tübingen: Mohr, 1923). A new translation has long been overdue. When the time comes, it will presumably be based on the recent edition of the original, ed. by Eckart Otto, *Die Wirtschaftsethik der Weltreligionen: Das Antike Judentum, Schriften und Reden 1911-1920.* Max Weber Gesamtaufgabe 1/21.2 (Tübingen: Mohr Siebeck, 2005) 777-848. See further, *Max Webers Studie über das Antike Judentum: Interpretation und Kritik,* ed. Wolfgang Schluchter (Frankfurt: Suhrkamp, 1981).

ism as a *Pariavolk* ("pariah people") in the postexilic period, that is, a social group characterized by ritually based prohibitions against commensality and intermarriage with those outside it.[7] For Weber, however, the emergent Judaism of the *běnê haggôlâ* was not sectarian, since sectarianism properly so called appeared only much later with the Pharisee *hăvûrôt* ("fellowship groups"). Yet his account of the *golah* group in the early postexilic period corresponds closely in several important respects to his theoretical account of sectarianism in *Economy and Society,* a point to which we will have to return.

While acknowledging the fundamental importance of the contribution of Troeltsch and Weber, we recall that both worked to a greater or lesser extent within the context of the Christian church in the West, leaving us with the task of looking further afield for other frames of reference and other kinds of comparative material. In presenting his three Jewish *haireseis* to an educated Greek-reading public, Josephus compared them to philosophical schools, matching Pharisees with Stoics (*Vita* 1.2), Essenes with Pythagoreans (*Ant.* 15.371), and, by implication, Sadducees with Epicureans (*Ant.* 13.171-73). Josephus even adds Judas the Galilean, a guerilla warlord, to the list of founders of sects (*B.J.* 2.118), this one identified as the fourth philosophy (*Ant.* 18.23). Philosophical schools do in fact have features in common with sects as generally understood. The Latin term *secta* occurs in Cicero, Livy, and Tacitus with the meaning of a party or philosophical school. In the laws of Solon in Athens philosophical schools were granted legal status as religious associations. The Stoic school of the third century B.C. has been compared to a church. Pythagoreans practiced community of property, and some schools expelled members who deviated from accepted teachings. But we would probably not feel comfortable describing the Damascus community or the Qumran *yahad* as philosophical schools. Something along the same lines could be said about the many associations *(thiasoi, collegia)* attested in inscriptions and papyri from the Hellenistic period, including clubs, burial societies, and guilds under the patronage of a popular deity

---

7. In view of the pejorative associations of this term, it should be noted that for Weber it had a technical sense not restricted to Judaism; for Weber and others, in fact, it applied more directly to the study of the caste system in Buddhism than to early Judaism. In *Economy and Society* Weber defined it as follows: "A distinctive, hereditary social group lacking autonomous political organization, and characterized by internal prohibitions against commensality and intermarriage, originally founded upon magical, tabooistic and ritual injunctions" (1:493). In its historical context it is discussed in *Ancient Judaism,* 336-55.

such as Herakles, Asklepios, or Dionysos. There would be some form of initiation ceremony including sprinkling with or immersion in water, new members would be required to take oaths (e.g., Lucius before initiation into the Isis cult in *Metamorphoses* 19.15,30), and in several cases the name of the new entrant would be entered in a list.[8]

To go further back in time in search of parallels, the biblical record attests to the existence of distinctive subgroups in northern Palestine from at least the ninth century B.C. There were the "sons of the prophets," ecstatic conventicles established in connection with sanctuaries. They lived a cenobitic but not celibate existence in segregated settlements and were recognizable by their attire and other distinctive features, including self-lacerations (1 Kgs 20:35-41; 2 Kgs 1:8). With the help of music, percussion,and perhaps also psychotropic drugs they attained states of collective mental dissociation under the direction of a master-*nāvî'*, somewhat like the Sufi Dervish *tawaf* under the direction of its sheik. While preserving their own distinctive way of life, these conventicles were involved in political activities, often as a force to be reckoned with. There were the Rechabites, an order of the strict observance whose members eschewed intoxicants and other amenities of urban existence, including living in houses.[9] The Nazirites, dedicated warriors, had rules excluding strong drink, contact with the dead, and shaving the hair, and there were no doubt other such groups which might seem to qualify as sectarian.

We know very little about the organization and internal affairs of these conventicles, but they acknowledged the leadership of an individual whose miraculous charisma required acknowledgment by the members. Thus, the "sons of the prophets" at Jericho witnessed Elisha working a miracle

8. Moshe Weinfeld, *Normative and Sectarian Judaism in the Second Temple Period* ((London: T. & T. Clark, 2005) 235-36, gives the example of an edict of Ptolemy IV requiring all devotees of the Dionysos cult in Alexandria to provide written proof of their status. He compares this with the census list in Ezra 2 = Nehemiah 7 and 1QS V 25, XIV 3-6. On these associations, see John S. Kloppenborg and Stephen G. Wilson, *Voluntary Associations in the Graeco-Roman World* (New York: Routledge, 1996); Philip A. Harland, *Associations, Synagogues, and Congregations* (Minneapolis: Fortress, 2003).

9. The hypothesis of Matthew Black, *The Scrolls and Christian Origins* (New York: Scribner's, 1961) 15-16, that the origins of the Essenes can be traced ultimately to the nomadic lifestyle of the Rechabites and Kenites is vitiated by an outdated understanding of the supposed nomadic origins of early Israel. See Chris H. Knights, "The Rechabites of Jeremiah 35: Forerunners of the Essenes?" in *Qumran Questions,* ed. James H. Charlesworth. Biblical Seminar 36 (Sheffield: Sheffield Academic, 1995) 86-91.

with the mantle of his master Elijah after the latter had been taken up in the fiery chariot, and this led them to acknowledge his leadership: "The spirit of Elijah (now) rests on Elisha." They then approached him and prostrated themselves before him (2 Kgs 2:15). These leaders, addressed as "father,"[10] presided over their nebiistic assemblies.[11] Like the sects of the Hasmonaean and Roman periods, they deviated from accepted societal norms, some shared common space, and they had a marked affinity with states of mental dissociation reinforced by group solidarity, whether solicited or spontaneous. They would fit comfortably into several of the sect types listed by contemporary sociologists: they could be revolutionary and manipulationist, some were thaumaturgical, and all were, to different extents, conversionist.[12] Yet we do not call them sects, and it would be instructive to ask why not. I suggest that the answer lies in the relation of the subgroup to the parent body to which it belongs. All of the subgroups mentioned to a greater or lesser extent rejected contemporary societal and cultural values and opposed the political status quo, but none would have thought of their status as Israelites as in any way problematic, nor would they have questioned the status of fellow-Israelites. The Damascus community, the Qumran *yaḥad,* and the early Christian community, on the contrary, took over the identity and claims of the parent body which, on their view, it had forfeited. In other words, they claimed to be what the parent body claimed to be but, again on their view, had ceased to be.

We appreciate therefore that much can be learned from the comparative study of sect formation and maintenance in different cultures and epochs, but in the last analysis each case must be studied on its own terms and without unnecessary preconceptions. With this in mind, we now turn to the phenomenon of sectarianism during the time of the Second Temple.

---

10. *'āv,* 2 Kgs 2:12; 13:14; Jer 35:6 (Jonadab "father" of the Rechabites).

11. 2 Kgs 4:38; 6:1; 9:1.

12. Bryan Wilson's typology of sects is well known. See his *Sects and Society* (Berkeley: University of California Press, 1961); "A Typology of Sects in a Dynamic and Comparative Perspective," *Archives de Sociologie de Religion* 16 (1963) 49-63; *Patterns of Sectarianism: Organisation and Ideology in Social and Religious Movements* (London: Heinemann, 1967); *The Social Dimensions of Sectarianism: Sects and New Religious Movements in Contemporary Society* (Oxford: Clarendon, 1990). Somewhat different criteria in Rodney Stark and William Sims Bainbridge, *The Future of Religion: Secularization, Revival and Cult Formation* (Berkeley & Los Angeles: University of California, 1985).

Aspects of Sectarianism in Ezra-Nehemiah

It is testimony to the vigor and cogency of Weber's thought that, in spite of the fact that he was not a specialist in the literature of the period, and not-withstanding the criticism to which his ideas have been subjected, his writ-ings can still serve as a point of departure for discussion of the issue of the earliest Jewish sectarianism. We recall once again Weber's argument that loss of political autonomy led to the emergence of a confessional, that is, a voluntary community. The transition from political institution to com-munity *(Gemeinde)* resulted in a social entity which was depoliticized, de-militarized, and deterritorialized. That is how Weber understood Well-hausen's dictum that Judaism came into existence from Israel ("Aus Israel wird das Judentum"). The community which emerged from the disaster sought to maintain its identity by means of ritual self-segregation (cir-cumcision, dietary rules, Sabbath), strictly enforced endogamy, prohibi-tion of commensality with nonmembers, full incorporation of resident aliens *(gērîm)*, and the enforcement of the physical and ethnic disqualifica-tions for membership specified in Deut 23:1-8(MT 2-9), which Weber dated to the exilic period. The struggle to achieve this goal began in the Babylonian diaspora and was complete by the time of Ezra and Nehemiah. Both leaders belonged to the socially and economically dominant Judeo-Babylonian party in Judah which kept itself apart from the local popula-tion. Since most of the latter belonged to the rural poor, their daily occu-pations made it practically impossible for them to observe dietary restric-tions or the Sabbath rest, which widened the gap between the immigrant *golah* group and the indigenous population. By Weber's own definition, the *golah* looks like a sect, though he maintained that sectarianism prop-erly so called arose only with Pharisaism. The reason for his hesitation to date sectarianism any earlier may be that the *golah* was the dominant party in the province, whereas for both Troeltsch and Weber sectarian move-ments tend to arise among the socially and economically marginal ele-ments of society.[13] It remains to be seen whether that is always and every-where the case.

After the passage of so many years (the papers which went into *Antike Judentum* appeared in 1917-18), and the discovery of so much archaeologi-cal and epigraphic material since that time, it would be remarkable if

---

13. Weber, *Economy and Society,* 1:492-500; 2:1204-10; *Ancient Judaism,* 356-64, 385-91.

Weber's description of the situation following on the dissolution of the Judean state were to have survived intact. One criticism focuses on Weber's use of the term "community" *(Gemeinde)* which, when referred to the province of Judah during the Neo-Babylonian and early Persian periods, tended to underestimate its specifically political status as the province of an empire under the rule of a governor. The terms "theocracy" or "hierocracy" can be equally misleading since the high priesthood achieved political dominance only in the early Hellenistic period. Another criticism is that Weber overestimated the place of ritual prescriptions within the law, sometimes practically implying that the law was essentially about ritual. In short, the social and religious situation in the province was much more complex than is suggested by Weber's schematic description.[14]

A more positive engagement with Weber's study of early Judaism was published by Shemaryahu Talmon in German in the same collection of papers as Crüsemann's article and in English the following year.[15] He began with the observation, often repeated, that Weber's strength lay in the description of overall processes, in highlighting the typical, rather than in the careful and detailed study of specific situations. This is surely the case, if not necessarily a negative criticism. In dealing with the early Second Temple period Weber did not have the rich database at his disposal as in his studies of sectarian movements at the time of the Reformation, and what he did have was rather less than what we have today almost a century later. We should also bear in mind that his work on ancient Judaism remained unfinished at his death in 1920. On the "Aus Israel wird das Judentum" issue, Talmon pointed to two fundamental changes resulting from the dissolution of the Judean state and its institutions. The first was a loss of equilibrium and stability formerly maintained by a kind of balance of power involving king, priest, and prophet. The disappearance of the native dy-

---

14. Frank Crüsemann, "Israel in der Perserzeit: Eine Skizze in Auseinandersetzung mit Max Weber," in *Max Webers Sicht des antiken Christentums: Interpretation und Kritik*, ed. Wolfgang Schluchter (Frankfort: Suhrkamp, 1985) 205-32.

15. Shemaryahu Talmon, "Jüdische Sektenbildung in der Frühzeit der Periode des Zweiten Tempels: Ein Nachtrag zu Max Webers Studie über das antike Judentum," in Schluchter, *Max Webers Sicht des antiken Christentums*, 233-54; "The Emergence of Jewish Sectarianism in the Early Second Temple Period," in Talmon, *King, Cult and Calendar in Ancient Israel: Collected Studies* (Jerusalem: Magnes, 1986) 165-201, practically identical with "The Internal Diversification of Judaism in the Early Second Temple Period," in *Jewish Civilization in the Hellenistic-Roman Period* (Philadelphia: Trinity, 1991) 16-43.

nasty, together with the transformations undergone by prophecy, left room for centrifugal forces to pull in different directions: local hieratic control contingent on the restoration of the cult on the one hand with, on the other hand, utopian and eschatological speculations calculated to undermine the will to accept and come to terms with historical realities. The other development Talmon named was a change from monocentrism to pluricentrism. In the first and most obvious instance this implied the Babylonian and Egyptian diasporas as distinct and distinctive centers of Jewish life and thought. Less obviously, after the resettlement in Judah the ingroup out-group mentality which originated in the diaspora situation assumed the form of a distinctive, segregated *golah* group within a Jewish ethnos itself segregated, in theory at least, from foreigners. It will be seen that Talmon's pluricentricity or tricentricity is actually not so different from Weber's analysis in *Ancient Judaism*.

One of the first biblical scholars to comment explicitly on the sectarian character of the *golah* as profiled in Ezra-Nehemiah was none other than William Foxwell Albright, who was certainly aware of Weber's potential relevance for biblical scholarship.[16] In a coauthored article on the Qumran Essenes he remarked that "the Babylonian exile, often described as the great watershed of Israel's history, may well have seen the first stirrings of classical Jewish sectarianism, and of this we get hints in the memoirs of Ezra and Nehemiah."[17] Albright's statement provides us with the cue for testing this hypothesis against the definition or characterization of sectarianism in the first section of this chapter. We are dealing in the first place with those referred to in the book as *haggôlâ* or *běnê-haggôlâ* (Aramaic *běnê-gālûtâ*), a Judeo-Babylonian group which voluntarily relocated in Judah and, at least in theory, segregated itself from the indigenous population. It had its own assemblies (Ezra 10:8, 14), maintained control over its members, and exercised the right to excommunicate deviants including those who failed to take part in its assemblies (Ezra 10:8; Neh 13:3). It was prepared to go to extreme lengths, beyond any explicit statement of law, to exclude marriage with outsiders. It reinforced its corporate identity

---

16. In his *From the Stone Age to Christianity*, 2nd ed. (Garden City: Doubleday, 1957) 95, 283, Albright noted Weber's influence on Albrecht Alt's description of the Judges as charismatic warlords.

17. William F. Albright and C. S. Mann, "Qumran and the Essenes: Geography, Chronology, and the Identification of the Sect," in *The Scrolls and Christianity*, ed. Matthew Black (London: SPCK, 1969) 16.

and bound its members to it by covenants which, rather than enjoining commitment to the law in general terms as in the standard Deuteronomic formulations, featured stipulations relating to the *golah* group's own specific commitments confirmed by an oath to which the participants appended their names.[18] These sworn commitments can be viewed as transitional between the Deuteronomic covenant and the covenant in the land of Damascus of the *Damascus Document* (CD).

The *golah* therefore corresponds to the introversionist type of sect by virtue of its self-segregation not only from the Gentile world but also from other Jews who did not share its theology and agenda. Its claim to be the exclusive embodiment of the Israel of the predisaster period is exhibited in the language in which it describes itself. It is "the holy seed" (Ezra 9:2), "the seed of Israel" (Neh 9:2), "the remnant of Israel"[19] or "Israel" *tout court*.[20] It can also express its appropriation of the traditions of twelve-tribal Israel by duodecimal symbolism.[21] It is sectarian not in breaking away from the parent body, as with the sects studied by Troeltsch and Weber, but in claiming the right to constitute Israel to the exclusion of other claimants. On its own view, it is the only surviving representative of the Israel to which the traditions testify.

In the account of the intermarriage crisis the solution and its legal justification are left in the hands of Ezra and "those who tremble at the commandment of our God" (Ezra 10:2-4). The designation of this core group of Ezra's supporters, *ḥărēdîm* ("tremblers"), is less than a title such as "Pharisees" or "Essenes" but more than simply a way of referring to devout Israelites. Shecaniah, who plays an important but rather mysterious role in the proceedings, refers to them as a distinct group with a special relationship to Ezra and a commitment to observe and apply the law according to their own interpretation. What is especially noteworthy about the designation *ḥārēd, ḥărēdîm* is that its only other occurrence is in Isa 66:1-5. In Isa 66:2 Yahweh looks with favor on the poor, the afflicted in spirit, and those

18. Ezra 10:3-5; Neh 9:38–10:39(MT 10:1-40); 13:23-27. There are also lists of those who accompanied Ezra (Ezra 8:1-14) and those who had married local women (10:18-44); cf. the list of the founders of the Damascus sect referred to but not appended in CD IV 2-12.

19. Neh 1:2-3; 7:72; 10:28(MT 29); 11:1, 20.

20. Ezra 2:59 = Neh 7:61; Ezra 3:1; 7:28; 10:2; Neh 8:17; 9:1; 13:3, 18.

21. Ezra 2:2 = Neh 7:7 (12 leaders of the immigrant community); Ezra 8:3-14 (12 agnatic units in Ezra's caravan); Ezra 8:24 (12 priests charged with transporting the sacred vessels); Ezra 6:17; 8:35 (12 sacrificial animals).

who tremble at his word, and, to judge by the verses immediately preceding and following, this favorable regard is contrasted with the temple personnel. Then a prophetic utterance is addressed to the same group of those who tremble at God's word:

> Hear the word of Yahweh, you who tremble at his word!
> Your brethren who hate you,
> who cast you out for my name's sake, have said,
> "May Yahweh reveal his glory that we may witness your joy!"
> — but it is they who will be put to shame. (Isa 66:5)

Here, too, the designation has the qualifying phrase "who tremble at his word," but those addressed are distinctive enough to be excommunicated or shunned as a socially visible collectivity.[22] They are addressed as a prophetic group by an anonymous seer, and their eschatological beliefs have something to do with their expulsion. Moreover, their attitude to the "brethren" who have cast them out, who in the nature of the situation must include the chief priests, is expressed in the typically sectarian form of eschatological reversal as expressed elsewhere in this last section of Isaiah (cf. Isa 65:13-14).

There is, of course, the difference between the *ḥărēdîm* of Ezra 9–10 and those of Isaiah 66:1-5, that the former are attached to a leader wielding apparently unlimited power in Judah and the latter have been expelled from the civic and cultic community and are, in consequence, among the poor and the defeated.[23] Yet this difference must be weighed against the consideration that both are dealing with the same opponents, namely, the priestly aristocracy in Jerusalem. The priests were prominent among the offenders (Ezra 9:2), were coerced into swearing the oath (10:5), and seventeen of them are listed among the transgressors as against six Levites

---

22. The verbal form *měnaddêkem* from *niddāh* occurs only here and Amos 6:3, where it means something like exorcize, neutralize by magical means. In rabbinic texts, however, it is a standard formula for excommunication from the synagogue (*b. Ber.* 19a; *b. Pesaḥ.* 52a). The formula in the Priestly texts in the Pentateuch is different (e.g., Lev 7:20; 17:4). The verb "hate" (*śānē'*) implies active dissociation, as in the divorce formula "I hate my wife," "I hate my husband"; see, e.g., AP 15:23; 18:1 (A. E. Cowley, *Aramaic Papyri of the Fifth Century b.c.* [Osnabrück: Zeller, 1967] 45, 55).

23. The economic consequences of excommunication are apparent in the threat directed at those who failed to attend the assembly convoked to solve the marriage crisis (Ezra 10:8).

(10:18-23). In his capacity as governor Nehemiah had to contend with un-acceptable marriage alliances involving the high priestly family (Neh 13:4-9, 28), and the chief priests continued as leaders of the assimilationist party after the time of Nehemiah.[24] It is clear, moreover, that Ezra's policy was not an unqualified success and that the temple clergy quickly recovered their freedom to conduct business, including marital business, without interference. This would have been bad news for Ezra's supporters, leaving them exposed as a marginalized and shunned minority, thus explaining their situation as it appears in Isa 66:1-5. This is admittedly hypothetical, but a not implausible scenario in the light of the totally inadequate data at our disposal. We may therefore be viewing basically the same social phenomenon from different perspectives and at different points in its historical development.[25]

Another text suggestive of early Second Temple sectarianism or quasi-sectarianism occurs near the end of the pseudonymous prophet Malachi (Mal 3:13–4:3[MT 3:21]). Malachi is the last of three originally anonymous units in the Book of the Twelve, all roughly equal in length and all certainly postexilic. A more precise determination of the date of this last segment of the Twelve depends on allusions in the text itself and the political and social situation which it reflects. Historical indications include hostility towards Edomites and encroachment on their territory by Kedarite Arabs (1:2-5), a passing allusion to a governor unfortunately not identified by name (1:8), neglect of the temple cult and particularly vitriolic diatribe directed against the temple priesthood (1:6–2:9; 3:6-12), and, finally, in 3:13–4:3, religious skepticism perhaps induced by disappointed hopes following on the building of the temple.[26] Malachi does not refer, directly at any rate,

---

24. On the interpretation of Isa 66:1-2 as an attack on temple priests engaged in syncretic cults, see Alexander Rofé, "Isaiah 66:1-4: Judean Sects in the Persian Period as Viewed by Trito-Isaiah" in *Biblical and Related Studies Presented to Samuel Iwry,* ed. Ann Kort and Scott Morschauser (Winona Lake: Eisenbrauns, 1985) 205-17; and my *Isaiah 56–66.* AB 19B (New York: Doubleday, 2003) 294-98.

25. The designation *ḥărēdîm* itself suggests the emotionalism associated with certain types of prophecy, and the suggestion is somewhat confirmed by Ezra's reaction to the bad news about intermarriage, especially his lying on the ground in a catatonic state *(mĕšômēm);* cf. Ezek 3:15 *mašmîm* and Dan 8:27 *'eštômēm.* The eschatological element is explicit in Mal 3:13-18 (see below), and it is also possible that Ezra and his supporters were motivated by eschatological considerations as argued by Klaus Koch, "Ezra and the Origins of Judaism," *JSS* 19 (1974) 173-97.

26. See, e.g., Hag 2:17; Mal 3:13-15.

to either Ezra or Nehemiah, certainly not on the basis of an arbitrary emendation of *mal'āk* ("messenger") to *melek* ("king") in Mal 3:1b, understood to refer to Nehemiah as messianic figure.[27] But the polemical note about divorce associated with violence in 2:16, often taken to be an interpolation, could be construed, whether interpolated or not, as an attack on Ezra's policy of coercive separation from wives and children. The suggestion that Malachi was written after Ezra but before or during Nehemiah's administration finds some support from complaints about non-payment of tithes and neglect of temple maintenance.[28] Allusions to social injustice (3:5; cf. Neh 5:1-13), appeal to ethnic solidarity (2:10; cf. Neh 5:5), and emphasis on the levitical covenant (2:4-9; cf. Neh 13:29) could point in the same direction.[29] The situation is not nearly as clear as we would wish it to be (but when is that the case?), but it is clear enough to permit a probable conclusion that Malachi was composed not long after the marriage crisis episode described in Ezra 9–10.

Couched in the disputation form characteristic of this author,[30] the last section of Malachi records the complaint that God makes no distinction between the devout and the godless:

You have used strong speech against me, says Yahweh, and you reply, "How have we spoken against you?" What you have said is, "Serving God is futile. What profit is there in our observing his commandments and leading a penitential life in the presence of Yahweh of Hosts? So now we reckon the irreligious to be the ones who are blessed; evildoers not only flourish, but when they put God to the test they escape punishment." Then those who feared God conferred together, and Yahweh took heed and listened. A book of remembrance was inscribed in his pres-

---

27. Argued by Aage Bentzen, "Priesterschaft und Laien in der jüdischen Gemeinde des fünften Jahrhunderts," *AfO* 6 (1930/31) 282-83; and Ulrich Kellermann, *Nehemia: Quellen, Überlieferung und Geschichte.* BZAW 102 (Berlin: Töpelmann, 1967) 2-3.

28. Mal 3:6-12; cf. Neh 13:10-14, 31.

29. J. M. Powis Smith, *A Critical and Exegetical Commentary on Haggai, Zechariah, Malachi and Jonah.* ICC 25 (Edinburgh: T. & T. Clark, 1912) 7, even claimed that "the Book of Malachi fits the situation amid which Nehemiah worked as snugly as a bone fits its socket."

30. Mal 1:2-5, 6-8, 13; 2:10, 13-15; 3:7-8. See E. Pfeiffer, "Die Disputationsworte im Buche Maleachi," *EvT* 19 (1959) 546-68; Gerhard Wallis, "Wesen und Struktur der Botschaft Maleachis," in *Das Ferne und nahe Wort.* Festschrift Leonhard Rost, ed. Fritz Maass. BZAW 105 (Berlin: Töpelmann, 1967) 229-37; James A. Fischer, "Notes on the Literary Form and Message of Malachi," *CBQ* 34 (1972) 315-20.

ence with the names of those who feared Yahweh and thought on his name. Then, They shall be mine, said Yahweh, my special possession, on the day when I act. I shall deal kindly with them as parents deal kindly with children who respect them. Then you will see the distinction between the righteous and the reprobate, those who fear God and those who do not. (3:13-18)

The complaint is followed by the God-fearers conferring together, and this action elicits a positive response from Yahweh. A document is written containing the names of those who fear God and esteem his name. They will be his special possession on the day of his decisive intervention in human affairs, when the distinction between the righteous and the reprobate will be as clearly manifest to all as it is apparent to those so reassured (3:16-18). The passage concludes with the statement that on judgment day the reprobate will be destroyed, while those who revere Yahweh's name will triumph and rejoice (4:1-3[MT 3:19-21]).

There can be no doubt that those addressed in 3:13-15, who are giving strong expression to their doubts about the providence and justice of God, are identical with the God-fearers who are reassured in the following verses.[31] The two paragraphs are therefore related as problem and solution. After all, the ones addressed in the first paragraph distinguish themselves from the irreligious, they have obeyed God and led a penitential life in spite of their doubts, and their complaints are no stronger than reproaches and laments uttered frequently in Psalms, not to mention Job. It is also possible, in view of the solution offered to their complaint, that this crisis of faith was precipitated by delay in the anticipated divine intervention in their affairs which many thought would follow on the building of the temple. The solution, at any rate, is eschatological. The distinction between the devout and the reprobates in the Jewish community is already established in principle and will be manifest for all to see on judgment day.

---

31. The problem for several commentators is with the adverb *'āz* ("then") with which the following paragraph begins, and therefore with continuity between vv. 13-15 and 16-18. Wilhelm Rudolph, *Haggai, Sacharja 1-8, Sacharja 9-14, Maleachi*. KAT 13/4 (Gütersloh: Mohn, 1976) 286-87, probably correctly translated "damals" indicating temporal succession. We can in any case agree with Julius Wellhausen, *Die Kleinen Propheten übersetzt und erklärt*, 3rd ed. (Berlin: Reimer, 1893) 203: "Es sind die Frommen welche murren; und sie werden im Folgenden nicht gestraft sondern getröstet." ("Those who complain are the righteous; and they are subsequently not punished but consoled.")

The principle of eschatological discrimination, a common sectarian theme which appears in the Gospels (Matt 13:37-43; 25:31-46), draws an invisible line through the community, separating the true Israel from those who are Israel only in name. Pointing in the same direction is the weighty theological term *sĕgullâ* ("special possession") used especially by the Deuteronomists to characterize Israel in contrast to the nations,[32] but here designating a pietistic group in contrast to the rest of Israel.

The way in which those addressed are described suggests a connection of some kind with the Servants of the Lord in the last segment of Isaiah (Isa 65:8-9, 13-16) and those who tremble at God's word in Ezra 9:4; 10:3 and Isa 66:1-5. They are God-fearers,[33] God-servers, servants of God;[34] they esteem the name of God[35] and mourn in the present age in anticipation of rejoicing in the age to come.[36] They confer together, which suggests that they are entering into a pact or covenant constituting themselves as the true Israel, Yahweh's special possession, language elsewhere associated with covenant-making.[37] The *sēfer zikkārôn*, literally, "a book of remembrance," is by some understood to be an inventory written by Yahweh in which are recorded either the names of the righteous[38] or good and evil deeds (e.g., Isa 65:6; Neh 13:14). But we are not told that this book was written by Yahweh, and other references to a document in the form of a *zikkārôn* refer to human records.[39] We are therefore entitled to read Mal 3:16-18 as divine authentication of the parties to a covenant whose names are recorded in writing, as were the names of the signatories to Nehemiah's covenant. The assembly of these God-fearers, therefore, anticipates the different prefigurations of the eschatological Israel in the sectarian movements of the late Second Temple period.

---

32. Exod 19:5-6; Deut 7:6; 14:2; 26:18-19; Ps 135:4.

33. Mal 1:6, 14; 2:5; 3:5; cf. Isa 50:10; 63:17.

34. Mal 3:14, 17, 18; cf. Isa 65:8-9, 13-16; 66:14.

35. Mal 3:16; cf. Isa 59:19; 65:15-16.

36. Mal 3:14, *hālaknû qĕdorannît*: the adverb is hapax, derived from the verbal stem *qdr* attested with the meaning "to be dark," "to lament or mourn"; compare the allusions to mourners (*'ăvēlîm, mit'abbĕlîm*) in Isa 57:18; 61:2-3; 66:10.

37. M. Weinfeld, "The Covenant of Grant in the Old Testament and in the Ancient Near East," *JAOS* 90 (1970) 195, refers to the Akkadian cognate *sikiltum* used in treaty contexts.

38. Exod 32:32-33; Ps 69:28(MT 29); 87:6.

39. Exod 17:14; Esth 6:1.

Between Ezra-Nehemiah and Daniel:
Antecedents and Continuities

It is unfortunately true of the gap of almost three centuries between the end of Nehemiah's first administration (432 B.C.) and the composition of the book of Daniel (165) that our ignorance greatly outweighs our knowledge. This is especially the case with the first half of this period. Leaving aside the biblical texts surveyed in the previous chapter, the historical referents and dating of other possibly relevant texts are for the most part uncertain. After his lengthy paraphrase of Esther in the expanded Greek version (*Ant.* 11.184-296), Josephus seems to have had little reliable source material,[40] and the Greek historians who cover the period, principally Xenophon, Ctesias, and Diodorus, do not even mention Jews or Judea. The question of continuity between the sectarianism of Ezra, Nehemiah, and the *golah* at one end of the gap and the well-known sectarian movements at the other cannot therefore be answered directly. The best we can do is construct a hypothesis which can be tested by working forward from the situation in the mid-fifth century and backwards from the end of the gap with a view to assessing the continuity-discontinuity issue. In the last section of the present chapter this task will be complemented by a survey of key aspects of the Ezra-Nehemiah ideology reflected in the halakah of the sects of the late Second Temple period.

Apocalyptic belief, in the sense of the conviction of living in and embodying the final stage of human history, is not a necessary concomitant of sectarianism, but it was nevertheless a dominant feature of the sects known to us in the late Second Temple period, especially the Damascus covenant sect and the Qumran *yaḥad*. In spite of numerous problems of interpretation and dating, attempts to trace a trajectory from prophetic eschatology to this type of sectarian apocalyptic have made a distinctive contribution to the study of sectarian origins. We know from Ben Sira's allusion to the bones of the twelve prophets (Sir 49:10) that the Book of the Twelve was in existence in some shape or form by the early second century B.C. In anticipating Elijah's return before "the great and terrible Day of Yahweh" (Mal 4:5[MT 3:23]), the final compiler and editor recapitulated

---

40. On Josephus's sources for the period, see Emil Schürer, *The History of the Jewish People in the Age of Jesus Christ*, rev. ed. by Geza Vermes and Fergus Millar, 1 (Edinburgh: T. & T. Clark, 1973) 49-52.

one of the unifying eschatological themes of the collection, and indeed of the prophetic books as a whole: the Day of Yahweh.[41] A detailed study of this theme in the context of the editorial history of the *dodekapropheton* cannot be undertaken here, but one or two examples will illustrate the passage from prophetic eschatology to apocalyptic. In the original section of Joel, the Day refers to a plague of locusts (1:15; 2:1-2, 11), but in the expanded version it is the day of judgment in the Valley of Jehoshaphat (3[MT 4]:1-3, 12-14). Fearful portents in the sky — the darkening of the sun, the moon turned to blood, blood, fire, and smoke covering the earth (3:15-16[4:15-16]) — will be the signal for the final ingathering (3:13[4:13]). Bernhard Duhm thought the expansions to the book reflected synagogue preaching during the Hasmonean period,[42] but the tone seems more sectarian than synagogal. A somewhat earlier date, perhaps in the fourth century, seems more likely.[43] The same theme is prominent in Zephaniah. A core group of sayings directed against both Judah and external enemies is preceded and followed by the proclamation of a final judgment from which only "the humble of the land" will be exempt (Zeph 1:2-6; 3:9-13). This situation too suggests a sectarian or quasi-sectarian setting, according to one reading as late as the second century B.C.[44]

Establishing a historical and social context for the diverse material in Zechariah 9–14 has been particularly difficult. Beginning with Johann Gottfried Eichhorn's famous *Einleitung*,[45] most critical scholars have opted for the Hellenistic period. The sayings against Syrian, Phoenician, and Philistine cities (9:1-8) could then be interpreted against the background of Alexander's progress following on the battle of Issus, and the prediction that "I will arouse your sons, O Zion, against your sons, O Greece" (Zech 9:13) could be an anticipation (clearly unfulfilled) of the defeat of Alexander as the result of divine intervention. The most obscure

41. Martin Beck, *Der "Tag YHWHs" im Dodekapropheton: Studien im Spannungsfeld von Traditions- und Redacktionsgeschichte.* BZAW 356 (Berlin: de Gruyter, 2005); Moshe Weinfeld, "The Day of the Lord: Aspirations for the Kingdom of God in the Bible and Jewish Liturgy," in *Normative and Sectarian Judaism*, 68-89.

42. Bernhard Duhm, "Anmerkungen zu den Zwölf Propheten," *ZAW* 31 (1911) 161-204.

43. See Otto Plöger, *Theocracy and Eschatology* (Richmond: John Knox, 1968) 96-105; Paul L. Redditt, "The Book of Joel and Peripheral Prophecy," *CBQ* 48 (1986) 225-40.

44. Louise Pettibone Smith and Ernest R. Lacheman, "The Authorship of the Book of Zephaniah," *JNES* 9 (1950) 137-42.

45. 4th ed. (Göttingen: Rosenbusch, 1824).

and intriguing passage is the enigmatic allusion to a Pierced One (12:9-14), interpreted messianically in both Judaism and Christianity, by others referred to Josiah, or the Isaianic Servant of the Lord, or the high priest Onias III murdered in or about 170 B.C. Of particular interest to our theme is the complaint of the God-fearers and its solution in explicitly eschatological terms at the end of Malachi (Mal 3:13–4:3). It was noted earlier that most commentators date Malachi close to the dates assigned to the activities of Ezra and Nehemiah, and the God-fearers and God-servers who pact together and are assured of a positive outcome have features in common with those who tremble at God's word in Isa 66:1-5 and Ezra 9–10.

As a compilation of diverse material accumulated over several centuries, Isaiah has more in common with the Twelve than with Jeremiah and Ezekiel and is therefore an important source for the transition from prophecy to apocalyptic eschatology.[46] The process appears most clearly in the third and last segment (Isaiah 56–66) and in the Isaian Apocalypse (Isaiah 24–27), but it is not difficult to detect it at other points in the book. In his numerous studies on Trito-Isaiah, Odil Hannes Steck argued for a theory of cumulative expansive comment *(Fortschreibung)* covering a period from the sixth to the third century B.C.,[47] and several similar theories of incremental growth are on offer.[48] Affinity with the worldview of the apocalyptic sects is also in evidence in Isaiah 24–27. In his discussion of the

---

46. Those who have dealt with this issue in relation to Isaiah include Jacques Vermeylen, *Du prophète Isaïe à l'apocalyptique,* 2 vols. Ebib (Paris: Gabalda, 1977-78); Robert R. Wilson, "From Prophecy to Apocalyptic: Reflections on the Shape of Israelite Religion," in *Anthropological Perspectives on Old Testament Prophecy,* ed. Robert C. Culley and Thomas W. Overholt. Semeia 21 (Chico: Scholars, 1982) 79-95; Stephen L. Cook, *Prophecy and Apocalypticism* (Minneapolis: Fortress, 1995); John J. Collins, "From Prophecy to Apocalypticism," in *The Encyclopedia of Apocalypticism* (New York: Continuum, 1998) 1:129-61. See, in general, Rainer Albertz, *A History of Israelite Religion in the Old Testament Period,* vol. 2: *From the Exile to the Maccabees.* OTL (Louisville: Westminster John Knox, 1994) 570-97.

47. Odil Hannes Steck, "Beobachtungen zu Jesaja 56-59," *BZ* 31 (1987) 228-46; *Studien zu Tritojesaja.* BZAW 203 (Berlin: de Gruyter, 1991) 278-79.

48. Claus Westermann, *Isaiah 40–66.* OTL (Philadelphia: Westminster, 1969), distinguished several *Zusätze* in the final stage of redaction: an age when sun and moon will no longer be necessary (Isa 60:19-20), new heaven, new earth (65:17; 66:22), peace in the animal kingdom (65:25), mission to the Gentiles (66:18-19, 21). Vermeylen, *Du prophète Isaïe à l'apocalyptique,* 2:471-89, laid out six stages ending in the third century B.C. with some final apocalyptic *retouches.* Wolfgang Lau, *Schriftgelehrte Prophetie in Jes. 56-66.* BZAW 225 (Berlin: de Gruyter, 1994), identified three *Tradentenkreise* ("circles of tradition") formed around the nucleus of chs. 60–62. For other examples, see my *Isaiah 56–66,* 54-66.

authorship of this section, Duhm remarked that the prophet Isaiah could as well have written the book of Daniel as these chapters.[49] While some prominent features of the visions of Daniel are missing — there is no periodization of history, for example — typically apocalyptic themes which are present include universal judgment (Isa 24:1-13, 17-20), cosmic upheaval (24:21-23), the abolition of death (25:8), resurrection from the dead (26:19), the messianic banquet (25:6), and the final ingathering (27:2). There may also be an allusion to the apocalyptic secret *(rāz)* at 24:16b-17, though this enigmatic text has been interpreted otherwise.

Following on this brief glance at the more relevant prophetic texts, the more difficult task is that of identifying their social coordinates. Though committed to writing by individuals, these texts represent the deposit of beliefs and convictions generated and matured within groups, which implies that textual continuities presuppose continuities also at the social level. Even though the resources for writing a social history of Judah during the late Achaemenid and early Hellenistic periods are inadequate to say the least, the texts allow for some degree of continuity leading to the "Hasidic" groups and sectarian movements of the Hasmonean period. The attempts that have been made to trace a continuous line, a trajectory, from the prophetic eschatology of the early postexilic period to the apocalyptic of Daniel and the sects can be provocative even when not entirely unsuccessful. Steck, mentioned earlier, constructs the religious history of the period along the lines of a polarity between a theocratic worldview represented by the Priestly source in the Pentateuch (P) and Chronicles (including the Nehemiah memoir) and an eschatological position reflected in the prophetic texts surveyed above and, surprisingly, in the work of the Deuteronomists.[50] Steck's essay was intended as an elaboration of Otto Plöger's influential *Theocratie und Eschatologie,* published in 1959.[51] By taking Joel 3, Zechariah 12–14, and Isaiah 24–27 as points in a chrono-

49. Bernhard Duhm, *Das Buch Jesaja,* 4th ed. HKAT (Göttingen: Vandenhoeck & Ruprecht, 1922) 172.

50. Odil Hannes Steck, "Das Problem theologischer Strömungen in nachexilischer Zeit," *EvT* 28 (1969) 445-58; "Strömungen theologischer Tradition im Alten Israel," in *Wahrnehmungen Gottes im Alten Testament: Gesammelte Studien.* TB 70 (Munich: Kaiser, 1982) 291-317.

51. WMANT 2 (Neukirchen-Vluyn: Neukirchener, 1959); Eng. trans. *Theocracy and Eschatology,* based on the second German edition, 1962, which was practically identical with the original.

logical sequence, Plöger attempted to create a trajectory from the prophetic eschatology of the early postexilic period to the apocalyptic worldview of the *asidaioi* and the book of Daniel. He argued that these texts were produced by eschatologically-minded conventicles alienated from and marginalized by the official leadership, namely, the temple hierocracy, hence the title of his book. The trajectory follows a line of increasing alienation and marginalization, issuing finally in the apocalyptic sectarianism of the book of Daniel.

Creating a trajectory of this kind by means of binary opposites (theocracy-eschatology, Yahweh alone party–syncretists,[52] Zadokite hierocracy–prophetic group eschatology[53]) is one method for reconstructing a chapter of history. It should not be dismissed out of hand because hypothetical, but it can be misleading. The problems are fairly obvious. Plöger's choice of texts is incomplete, the absence of Isaiah 56-66 being especially surprising. Dating and sequencing is often uncertain, and scholars have questioned certain interpretations of the rise of sectarianism following on the crisis provoked by Antiochus IV and those who supported his policies within the Jewish community. We can at least be sure that the actual situation was more complex than any of these reconstructions might suggest.

If the connection argued earlier in this study between the *ḥărēdîm* of Ezra 9–10 and those shunned and cast out by their "brethren" in Isa 66:1-5 can be sustained, we could not exclude the possibility of a prophetic-eschatological element, however muted, in the beliefs and convictions of the Ezra circle. Nor would that be surprising in view of earlier or roughly contemporary expressions of eschatological fervor (Hag 2:20-23; Mal 3:13–4:3[MT 3:21]). Klaus Koch argued that Ezra's mission was conceived as a second exodus and partial fulfilment of prophetic promises. He maintained "that Ezra was realizing certain prophetic predictions in pre-eschatological steps which were different from eschatological perfection, and that he was using the Torah also as a book of promise," and therefore

---

52. Morton Smith, *Palestinian Parties and Politics That Shaped the Old Testament* (New York: Columbia University Press, 1971) passim.

53. Paul D. Hanson, *The Dawn of Apocalyptic* (Philadelphia: Fortress, 1975). See also Hugo D. Mantel, "The Dichotomy of Judaism during the Second Temple," *HUCA* 44 (1973) 55-87 and the critical comments of Lester L. Grabbe, *Judaism from Cyrus to Hadrian*, vol. 1: *The Persian and Greek Periods* (Minneapolis: Fortress, 1992) 102-12; and Albertz, *A History of Israelite Religion in the Old Testament Period*, 2:438-39.

Ezra may be considered a predecessor of apocalyptic.[54] These conclusions reach beyond the evidence provided by Ezra 7–10. It would be safer to suggest that the striving of both Ezra and Nehemiah to build, according to their lights, a perfect community cleansed from all impurities, the embodiment of the remnant of Israel proclaimed by the prophets,[55] anticipated the eschatological community of the last days which the Danielic sect, the Damascus community, and the Qumran *yaḥad* believed themselves to be.

A good place to begin the task of working backwards from the end of the gap is the first mention by Josephus of his three "philosophies," Pharisees, Sadducees, and Essenes (*Ant.* 13.171-73).[56] This brief disquisition interrupts his account of the high priesthood of Jonathan Maccabee about the middle of the second century B.C., which may imply that Josephus understood that these "philosophies" came into existence about that time (*kata ton chronon touton*). Many scholars would be prepared to accept this, at least with respect to Pharisees and Essenes. There is also broad agreement that Qumran sectarianism dates from the time of John Hyrcanus or shortly thereafter. The convulsive events leading to the Maccabee uprising, the ongoing struggle with the Seleucid rulers, and the usurpation of the office of high priest by Jonathan Maccabee (153/152 B.C.), not a Zadokite and therefore ineligible for the office, provided a setting calculated to encourage polarization and the formation of parties. The Essenes, at any rate, did not come fully formed into existence at that time. Pliny the Elder certainly exaggerated in claiming that they had been established near the Dead Sea for thousands of ages (*per saeculorum milia*).[57] Josephus informs us more soberly that his three sects existed from most ancient times (*Ant.* 18.11) and that the Essene prayers at sunrise had been handed down to them from their forebears implying, one would imagine, a past history of some depth (*B.J.* 2.128). The question is whether we can say anything more precise about the prehistory of these "classical" sects.

54. Koch, *JSS* 19 (1974) 184, 197.

55. That the *golah* embodies the prophetic remnant is abundantly in evidence in Ezra's penitential prayer (Ezra 9:8, 13, 14, 15), and in the marriage crisis incident members of the *golah* are referred to as "the holy seed" (*zeraʿ haqqōdeš*, Ezra 9:2; cf. Isa 6:13). The same self-segregating group is referred to in the Nehemiah narrative as "the remnant of the people" (*šěʾār hāʿām*, Neh 10:29) or "the remnant of Israel" (*šěʾār yiśrāʾēl*, Neh 11:20).

56. Longer accounts in *Ant.* 18.11-25 and *B.J.* 2.119-66.

57. *Nat.* 5.15.73.

That the Essenes and, more indirectly, the Pharisees developed out of those assemblies of the devout (*asidaioi;* Hebrew *ḥăsîdîm*) of the type mentioned in 1 Maccabees (2:42 and 7:12-17) was widely accepted before the discovery of the Qumran scrolls and has often been defended since with the help of the great volume of new material provided by the discoveries.[58] 1 Macc 2:42 mentions a company of Asidaeans (*synagōgē asidaiōn;* Hebrew *ʿădat ḥăsîdîm*) who recruited their own guerilla band and fought alongside the Maccabees, volunteering their services on behalf of the law. Several years later a company of "Hasidic" scribes (*synagōgē grammateōn;* Hebrew *ʿădat sōfĕrîm*) attempted to negotiate a truce with the high priest Alcimus and the Syrian general Bacchides. The negotiations ended with sixty of them treacherously put to death by Alcimus (1 Macc 7:12-17). These probably belonged to the same movement as those mentioned in 1 Macc 2:42, and their overtures for peace show that, contrary to the political and territorial agenda of the Maccabees, their aims were purely religious. Those others who, at the height of the persecution launched by Antiochus IV, took refuge in the Judean wilderness and refused to defend themselves when attacked on the Sabbath represented another variety of Hasidic traditionalist movement committed to the law strictly interpreted.[59]

There were no doubt other groups of the devout who would qualify as *asidaioi* but are not mentioned in the few texts extant from the Hasmonean period.[60] One of these may have been the conventicle reflected in the edify-

---

58. Different versions of this hypothesis were argued by Geza Vermes, Frank Moore Cross, Hartmut Stegemann, and others. According to Stegemann's revised version, the Essenes resulted from the union of Hasidaeans under the leadership of the Zadokite high priest removed from office in 152, known in the scrolls as the Teacher of Righteousness, with the Damascus group. See his paper "The Qumran Essenes — Local Members of the Main Jewish Union in Late Second Temple Times," in *The Madrid Qumran Congress: Proceedings of the International Congress on the Dead Sea Scrolls, Madrid 18-21 March 1991,* ed. Julio Trebolle Barrera and Luis Vegas Montaner. STDJ 11 (Leiden: Brill, 1992), 1:83-166; also *The Library of Qumran* (Grand Rapids: Wm. B. Eerdmans, 1998 [German original 1993]) 139-62. For the range of opinion on Essene and Qumran origins, see Schürer, *The History of the Jewish People,* 2 (Edinburgh: T. & T. Clark, 1973) 585-87; and Jonathan G. Campbell, "Essene-Qumran Origins in the Exile: A Scriptural Basis?" *JJS* 46 (1995) 143-56. Weber, *Ancient Judaism,* 385-86, derived the Pharisees from the *asidaioi* of 1 Macc 2:42 and 7:12-17, but was misled by 2 Macc 14:6 into making them followers of Judah Maccabee. He held that they did not form a sect but that they prepared for the true sectarianism of the Pharisaic *ḥăvûrôt.*

59. 1 Macc 2:29-38; *Ant.* 12.272-76.

60. A Qumran pesher on Ps 45:1 mentions "seven divisions of the penitents of Israel"

ing stories in Daniel 1–6. These Judean youths are zealous in the observance of the food laws, resolute in avoiding idolatry, and prepared to suffer death rather than compromise their adherence to the law. Daniel (Belteshazzar) stands apart from his companions as the leader endowed with special gifts, including dream interpretation. If these diaspora stories were meant to be read alongside the vision narratives in the second half of the book, Daniel/ Belteshazzar would be the *maśkîl*, the wise leader, and his companions the *rabbîm*, the "Many." There were probably other such groups prior to the Maccabean revolt whose members resisted Hellenic secularization and were repelled by the corruption of the Jerusalem priesthood. Such groups would have provided the right soil for the emergence of sectarianism without themselves necessarily being sectarian.[61] We can therefore envisage a broad Palestinian "Hasidic" movement in the decades preceding the persecution of Antiochus IV which prepared for the emergence of the Essenes and Pharisees. It would have had some features in common with Ezra and Nehemiah, strict observance of Sabbath for example, but we would need to have much more specific information about its beliefs and practices to connect it directly and substantially with the beliefs and practices associated with Ezra, Nehemiah, and their supporters.

One proposal not lacking in specificity is that of Morton Smith which came up at an earlier point of our inquiry.[62] Smith, it will be recalled, argued that Nehemiah's covenant originated with a dissident group of Levites about the time of the Chronicler in the early fourth century B.C. who wished to give permanent expression to Nehemiah's reforms. The impressive parallels between Nehemiah's "firm commitment" (*'ămānâ*) and the covenant in the land of Damascus — including the list of the names of signatories, the oath, commitment to the law of Moses, and segregation from sources of uncleanness — persuaded Smith that Nehemiah's covenant was the source of the Damascus rule and could be considered the first example of Jewish sectarianism.[63] Unfortunately Smith did not follow up on this

---

(4QpPsa 1-10 IV 23-24), which Stegemann took to refer to the number of such groups which sprang up at that time outside of Palestine; see *The Library of Qumran*, 146. The context, however, as fragmented as it is, suggests an organizational feature of the Qumran sect itself.

61. In agreement with Philip R. Davies, "Ḥasidim in the Maccabean Period," *JJS* 28 (1977) 127-40.

62. See above, 103-8.

63. Morton Smith, "The Dead Sea Sect in Relation to Ancient Judaism," *NTS* 7 (1960-61) 347-60.

proposal by a more detailed examination of the halakah of the Damascus sect, and some aspects of his argument — for example, the Chronicler as author of Ezra-Nehemiah — would not find general acceptance. But the proposal at least makes the point that the covenants in Ezra-Nehemiah represent a transitional stage between the standard Deuteronomic covenant and the covenanting characteristic of both the Damascus sect and the Qumran *yaḥad.*

In the absence of relevant source material, we can only speculate how long such conventicles of the devout had been in existence and when and under what circumstances they originated. It has been argued that elements of the Enochic and Danielic cycles, together with the earlier strata of the book of *Jubilees,* presuppose some kind of social organization with some typically sectarian features originating no later than the third century B.C.[64] That their retrospective on the religious history of Israel has much in common with the historical perspective of the *Damascus Document* suggests a convergence, overlap, or commonality of some kind between the circles in which *Jubilees,* elements of *1 Enoch,* and the *Damascus Document* originated.[65] Other clues to the prehistory of the overt sectarianism of the Hasmonaean period have been found in the canonical psalms. In several psalms we hear allusions to the devout *(ḥăsîdîm),* the righteous *(ṣaddîqîm),* the servants of God *('ăvādîm),* and the poor *('evyônîm).* Some of these form an assembly *(qāhāl)* or a congregation *('ēdâ),* which could reflect the existence of pietistic conventicles and therefore of an incipient kind of sectarianism. Psalm 79, lamenting the violent

---

64. Michael E. Stone, "The Book of Enoch and Judaism in the Third Century B.C.E.," *CBQ* 40 (1978) 479-92; *Scriptures, Sects and Visions* (Philadelphia: Fortress, 1980) 27-47. On the tales in Daniel 1–6, John J. Collins, *Daniel.* Hermeneia (Minneapolis: Fortress, 1993) 35-38, places their initial composition in the fourth or third century but allows for the possibility that the narrative tradition may go back to the Persian period. Reinhard G. Kratz, *Translatio Imperii: Untersuchungen zu den aramäischen Danielerzählungen und ihrem theologiegeschichtlichen Umfeld.* WMANT 63 (Neukirchen-Vluyn: Neukirchener, 1991) 134-48, argued that the collection as a whole dates to the Persian period.

65. The so-called Groningen hypothesis maintains that the Essene parent-group of the Qumran *yaḥad* had its origin in the apocalypticism which developed in the late third or early second century B.C., of the kind represented by the Enochian "Animal Apocalypse" (*1 Enoch* 85–90); on which see Florentino García Martínez, "Qumran Origins and Early History: A Groningen Hypothesis," *FO* 25 (1988) 113-36; García Martínez and A. S. van der Woude, "A 'Groningen' Hypothesis of Qumran Origins and Early History," *RevQ* 14 (1990) 521-41.

death of God's faithful ones *(ḥăsîdîm)*, cited on the occasion of the murder of the sixty *asidaioi* by Alcimus (1 Macc 7:17), is one of several such lamentations.[66] Psalms, unfortunately, are practically impossible to date with assurance. Perhaps we could refer to the canonical psalms as the Hymns Ancient and Modern of the Second Temple. The thesis has recently been proposed that the final *Sitz im Leben* of the psalm collection was not the liturgy of the Second Temple but assemblies and conventicles of the devout during the Hellenistic period for which it served as a manual of prayer, study, and reflection. At that point Psalm 1 was added as a preface, indicating how the psalms are to be read, to which Ps 149 may have corresponded as a conclusion since "the congregation of the righteous" of Ps 1:5 is matched by "the assembly of the devout" of Ps 149:1. At the same time, several psalms were reformulated to reflect more clearly the polarity between the righteous poor (that is, the members of the group) and the reprobate (e.g., Ps 26:4-5). The many external enemies of Israel were at the same time reinterpreted as internal opponents of the groups in question.[67]

Sectarian Origins in the Babylonian Diaspora

William Foxwell Albright appears to have been the first since the discovery of the Qumran scrolls to propose a Babylonian origin for the Essenes, the putative addressees of the *Damascus Document*. He maintained that this Judeo-Babylonian sect migrated from Babylon to Judah, either inspired by the victories of the Maccabees or to escape the Parthian invasion some two decades later, in or about 140 B.C.[68] Not all the arguments presented by

66. Ps 12:1(MT 2); 116:15; Isa 57:1-2. On this last, see my "Who Is the Ṣaddiq of Isaiah 57:1-2?" in *Studies in the Hebrew Bible, Qumran, and the Septuagint Presented to Eugene Ulrich*, ed. Peter W. Flint, Emanuel Tov, and James C. VanderKam. VTSup 101 (Leiden: Brill, 2006) 109-20.

67. Christoph Levin, "Das Gebetbuch der Gerechten," *ZTK* 90 (1993) 355-81; repr. in *Fortschreibungen: Gesammelte Studien zum Alten Testament*. BZAW 316 (Berlin: de Gruyter, 2003) 291-313. See further his *The Old Testament: A Brief Introduction* (Princeton: Princeton University Press, 2005) 139-43; Eng. trans. of *Das Alte Testament*, 2nd ed. (Munich: C. H. Beck, 2003) 100-5.

68. Albright, *From the Stone Age to Christianity*, 3, 21-22, 376; Albright and Mann, "Qumran and the Essenes," 19. The validity of arguments for a Babylonian origin do not necessarily depend on the identification of a broad pre-Qumran sectarian movement as Essene.

Albright have survived scrutiny. The idea that lustrations of the kind practiced by the Qumran sect were hygienically necessary in Babylon but not in Palestine is clearly off the mark, but the sect's interest in divination, astrology, and the virtues of plants and precious stones would fit a Babylonian situation. The hypothesis was developed more comprehensively by Jerome Murphy-O'Connor, who thought in terms of an Essene mission to Palestine with a view to reforming Jewish religious life sometime in the mid- to late second century B.C. These Essene missionaries may also have been motivated by eschatological calculations in the air at that time.[69] Murphy-O'Connor claimed to find support for the hypothesis in the allusions in the *Damascus Document* to Damascus understood as the place of exile,[70] and both he and Philip Davies, who argued along similar lines, pointed out that the laws in the *Damascus Document* for those living in camps suggest a Gentile and therefore, plausibly, a diasporic environment.[71]

The concentration of these sectarians on the Babylonian exile and their self-identification with the first to return from Babylon are consistent with this thesis and perhaps add some plausibility to it. If it is on the right track, the parent body of these sectarian missionaries must have been in existence for some considerable time previous to the mid-second century — according to Murphy-O'Connor, three centuries earlier, therefore about the time of Ezra and Nehemiah.[72] According to sectarian historiography, movement from Babylon to Judah began with those referred to in the *Damascus Document* as "the founding fathers" (*hāri'šônîm*, CD IV 6, 8). These would correspond in real time to the first immigrants from Babylonia known as the *běnê haggôlâ* in the Ezra narrative. There must have been much coming and going between Babylonia and Judah during the Achaemenid and early Hellenistic periods which has not found its way

---

69. Jerome Murphy-O'Connor, "An Essene Missionary Document? CD II,14–VI,1," *RB* 77 (1970) 214-15; "The *Damascus Document* Revisited," *RB* 92 (1985) 223-46.

70. CD VI 5; as the location of the new covenant, CD VIII 21; XIX 33-34; XX 11-12. Jerome Murphy-O'Connor, "The Essenes and Their History," *RB* 31 (1974) 215-44 (221); "Damascus," *EDSS*, 1:165-66.

71. Philip R. Davies, *The Damascus Covenant.* JSOTSup 25 (Sheffield: JSOT, 1983) 202-4. The camp laws address the issue of marriage, divorce, and raising children "according to the order of the land" (*kěserek hā'āreṣ*, CD VII 6; XIX 2-5), reminiscent of Jeremiah's exhortation to the diaspora Jews to take wives, raise children, and seek the welfare of the city of their exile (Jer 29:6-7).

72. "The Essenes and Their History," 223.

into our sources. Josephus's report that the Jewish nation as a whole remained in Babylon after Ezra's mission (*Ant.* 11.133) implies a knowledge of
later immigrations. He quotes Hecataeus to the effect that many Jews were
deported to Babylon by the Persians (*C. Ap.* 1.194) and informs us that Jews
were relocated in the opposite direction during the reign of Antiochus III
(*Ant.* 12.138). The idea of Babylon as the principal, though perhaps not the
only, source of sectarian ideology may therefore be correct for the later
Second Temple period, as it certainly is for the Neo-Babylonian and early
Persian period.[73]

A prominent feature of late Second Temple sectarianism, most explicitly enunciated in the *Damascus Document,* is the concern to link up with
the survivors of the Babylonian exile regarded as the prophetic remnant
and the founders of a new community with whom the sectarians felt
themselves to be in continuity. As they saw it, linkage with the generation
of the exile and return had the effect of devaluing or simply cancelling out
the history from the exile to the emergence of the sect in question.[74] This
retrospective tendency is already in evidence in the traditions about Ezra
and Nehemiah. Ezra is the son and successor of the last preexilic high
priest (Ezra 7:1-5), as much later in the Ezra Apocalypse he is an apocalyptic sage living in Babylon thirty years after the fall of Jerusalem (2 Esd 3:1).
Nehemiah's name appears among the leaders of the first immigration
(Ezra 2:1-2; Neh 7:5-7),[75] and, much later, he is the one who built the temple and restored its cult (2 Macc 1:18-36). Since this retrospection aligns
with the standard Mesopotamian belief that only what is primordial is of
value, and that later developments follow a downward trajectory from the

73. The recent study of Stephen Hultgren, *From the Damascus Covenant to the Covenant
of the Community: Literary, Historical, and Theological Studies in the Dead Sea Scrolls.* STDJ
66 (Leiden: Brill, 2007) 141-63, argues for historical analogy and theological similarity between the *šāvê yiśrā'ēl* of CD and the *běnê-haggôlâ* of Ezra-Nehemiah, and between the Damascus covenant and the Nehemiah covenant as understood by Smith, *NTS* 7 (1961) 347-60.

74. For what follows, see esp. Michael A. Knibb, "The Exile in the Literature of the
Intertestamental Literature," *HeyJ* 17 (1976) 253-72; "Exile in the Damascus Document,"
JSOT 25 (1983) 99-117; "Exile," *EDSS,* 1:276-77.

75. The name is attested elsewhere, belonging to a worker on the wall (Neh 3:16) and to
a slave in a Wadi Daliyeh bill of sale; see Douglas M. Gropp, *Wadi Daliyeh II: The Samaria
Papyri from Wadi Daliyeh.* DJD 28 (Oxford: Clarendon, 2001) 66, but the names of the
twelve leaders of the first return (eleven in Ezra 2) appear to be drawn from the names of
prominent individuals throughout the book, including Nehemiah. It is also worth noting
that in Neh 7:7 Nehemiah is followed by Azariah, an alternative form of Ezra.

"great time" of the first ancestors, it may be regarded as a specifically Babylonian feature. No surprise, therefore, if the Babylonian diaspora came to
be considered as the most fitting location for edifying, didactic narrative
and visionary revelations. The tales in Daniel 1–6, Tobit, Esther in the expanded Greek version, Susanna, and Bel and the Serpent are all located
there. The Qumran *Apocryphon of Joseph* (4Q371-373) even places the Joseph story in an exilic setting shortly after the fall of Jerusalem. Vision reports, as in Daniel 7–12, *4 Ezra*, and *2 Baruch*, are likewise backdated to that
crucial, formative epoch immediately following the deportations.

I suggested earlier that the diaspora tales in Daniel 1–6 featuring Daniel (Belteshazzar) and his companions at the Babylonian court may be read
as a small-scale model of the pietist group in and for which the book of
Daniel was written long after the Neo-Babylonian period. This little group
is sedulous in observing the food laws, engages in frequent prayer and as-
cetical practices, and its members are prepared to die rather than worship
idols (Dan 3:17-18). It is also an eminently scribal group, since the youths
are versed in every branch of wisdom, having completed a three-year cur-
riculum in the language and literature of the Babylonians (1:4-5). In these
stories Daniel's status vis-à-vis the others corresponds to the status of the
Danielic *maśkîl* vis-à-vis the *rabbîm* in the vision narratives (12:3). In that
capacity, he excels in the same kind of pesherlike interpretation as the
Daniel of the visions and, for that matter, the Qumran pesharists, even
though the interpreted "texts" consist in two dreams in the head of a mad
king and four cryptic words which appear mysteriously on a wall.

The interpretation in Daniel 9 of Jeremiah's prophecy of seventy years
subjection in exile (Jer 25:11-12; 29:10) is a good example of this crypto-
logical kind of exegesis encoding a sectarian rereading of the history of Israel. It results in a sevenfold extension of the period of exile down to the
time of writing, the interim period being characterized as a time of trans-
gression, iniquity, and trouble (Dan 9:24-25). The vision takes place in an
atmosphere of penitential prayer, mourning, and fasting not unlike the situation during the intermarriage crisis in Ezra 9–10. The correct interpretation of the Jeremian prophecy is revealed to the seer by Gabriel. The
seventy-year period, reinterpreted as seventy weeks of years, therefore 490
years, begins where the seventy-year period of the Jeremian text ends,
which is "the time that the word went out to restore and rebuild Jerusalem," namely, the rescript of Cyrus (Dan 9:25; 2 Chr 36:22; Ezra 1:1-4). Gabriel's interpretation therefore rejects the idea that the exile has come to an

end. The exile will end only with the anointing of a most holy person or object, generally understood to refer to the rededication of the temple which took place in 164 B.C. (1 Macc 4:36-59), an event which it was hoped would usher in the final intervention of God in salvation and judgment (Dan 12:1-13).

In the Enochian "Apocalypse of Weeks" (1 En. 93:1-10 + 91:11-17), probably the earliest extant apocalypse from the pre-Maccabean era, Enoch reveals to his sons the predetermined course of future history. The historical epoch covered by the biblical texts is divided into ten weeks. The destruction of Jerusalem and the temple followed by the dispersion takes place in the sixth week. The seventh week, corresponding to the entire Second Temple period down to the foundation of the group to which the writer belonged, is described as a time of religious infidelity and apostasy (1 En. 93:9-10). Here too it is implied that the exile came to an end only with the emergence of the "eternal plant of righteousness," referring to the Enochian conventicle within and for which the text was composed.[76] The "Animal Vision" (1 Enoch 85–90), from the Maccabean period, also extends the exile to the final judgment. In this surrealistic dream-vision told by Enoch to his son Methuselah, the history of the world from Adam to the final judgment is told in theriomorphic imagery: Israelites are sheep, foreign enemies are wild animals who feed on the sheep, Hellenistic rulers are birds of prey who do the same, the *asidaioi* (pietists) are lambs, and so on. At the exile, the sheep are either devoured or scattered by wild animals (lions, tigers, wolves, hyenas). Eventually three sheep, unnamed but presumably Zerubbabel, Joshua, and either Ezra or Nehemiah, returned and built the temple, but the sacrifices offered in it were impure and the eyes of both sheep and shepherds were blinded. What we know as the Second Temple period was therefore vitiated from the outset. After the last assault of the enemy the Lord of the Sheep sits in judgment, and the inauguration of the new Jerusalem ushers in the advent of the Messiah in the guise of a white bull.[77] Here too,

76. See James C. VanderKam, "Studies in the Apocalypse of Weeks (*I Enoch* 93:1-10; 91:11-17)," *CBQ* 46 (1984) 511-23; "Exile in Jewish Apocalyptic Literature," in *Exile: Old Testament, Jewish, and Christian Conceptions*, ed. James M. Scott. JSJSup 56 (Leiden: Brill, 1997) 95-96.

77. *APOT*, 2:250-60; Patrick A. Tiller, *A Commentary on the Animal Apocalypse of 1 Enoch*. SBLEJL 4 (Atlanta: Scholars, 1993); VanderKam, "Exile in Jewish Apocalyptic Literature," 96-100; Christoph Berner, *Jahre, Jahrwochen und Jubiläen*. BZAW 363 (Berlin: de Gruyter, 2006) 169-230.

therefore, the exilic situation continues to the final intervention of God in the affairs of Israel and the world. Basically the same schema appears in the *Testament of Levi,* composed towards the end of the second century B.C., which refers to the Enoch cycle (*T. Levi* 14:1).

Though neither apocalyptic nor sectarian in any obvious sense, the book of *Jubilees,* from the mid- to late second century B.C., shares several characteristics of the texts surveyed up to this point. Its relationship to the Enoch cycle, the *Testament of Levi,* and the Qumran collection, where it is well represented, continues to be discussed. As the title indicates, it is a history set out in weeks of years and Jubilees (*Jub.* 1:7-18). Its view of history in general is pessimistic, and it finds little to praise in the historical experience of Israel. The history is presented as a revelation to Moses at Sinai of the predetermined course of the future as far as Israel is concerned (1:1-6). Exile is punishment for consorting with Gentiles, worshipping their gods, and neglecting the religious calendar, the festivals, and the Sabbath. Exile is, above all, the time when God hid his face from Israel (1:13), an expressive metaphor for Godforsakenness of frequent occurrence in biblical texts, as also at Qumran. The historical review, couched in vague, homiletic language, passes directly from the exile, when neglect of the law and the religious calendar continued to prevail, to the raising of the eschatological temple and the emergence of the "plant of righteousness." This figure, encountered also in the Apocalypse of Weeks (*1 En.* 93:10) and frequently in the Qumran texts with reference to the new (sectarian) community,[78] is one of many borrowings from Isaiah (Isa 60:21; cf. 61:3). The point is not so clearly made as in Daniel and the Enochic texts, but it appears that, here too, the condition of exile comes to an end only with the final intervention of God in history.

This brings us to the *Damascus Document* (CD), in which the introductory Admonition provides one of the most explicit examples of the same symbolic-historiographical pattern:

> When they (Israel) were unfaithful, in that they abandoned him (God), he hid his face from Israel and from his sanctuary and delivered them up to the sword. But when he called to mind the covenant of the ancestors he allowed a remnant to survive for Israel and did not deliver them up to destruction. Then, at the end of (the period of) wrath, 390 years

---

78. E.g., CD I 5-12; 1QS VIII 5; 1QHa XIV 14-15.

from the time when he delivered them into the hand of Nebuchadnez-zar king of Babylon, he visited them and caused a plant root to sprout from Israel and Aaron, to possess his land and flourish on the goodness of his soil. They realized their iniquity and acknowledged that they were guilty; they were like the blind, like those who grope along the way, (and they were like this) for twenty years. But God took account of their deeds, for they were seeking him wholeheartedly, so he raised up for them a Teacher of Righteousness to lead them in the way of his heart. (CD I 3-11)

The basic pattern will by now be familiar from the other texts surveyed. The destruction of Jerusalem and its temple was the result of religious infidelity. The exile was the time of the divine anger when God hid his face from Israel. Only a small number, the prophetic remnant, survived the trial unscathed. There is then a gap of 390 years counting from the Babylonian conquest to the emergence of the "plant root," a variation of "the plant of righteousness," in other words, the emergence of the Damascus covenant sect.[79] The last two sentences of the text, which mention twenty years of disorientation (groping) and the raising up of the Teacher of Righteousness, refer in cryptic fashion to the internal history of the movement leading to the splintering off of the Qumran *yahad* under the Teacher of Righteousness.

As a codicil to this historical perspective of the *Damascus Document* a fragmentary Qumran text previously designated 4QPseudo-Moses but now reclassified as *Apocryphon of Jeremiah* (4Q390) should be mentioned.[80] Jeremiah, therefore, if it is he, predicts the course of the future, here too divided into Jubilees. As in the *Testament of Levi,* the period between the first return from the Babylonian exile and the seventh and last Jubilee is passed over in silence. As in the other texts surveyed, the priesthood comes in for severe criticism:

---

79. The 390 years, based on Ezekiel's sign-act (Ezek 4:4-5), was probably interpolated to create a historical rather than purely ideological link between the sect and the first to return from exile.

80. Devorah Dimant, "New Light from Qumran on the Jewish Pseudepigrapha — 4Q390," in Trebolle Barrera and Vegas Montaner, *Proceedings of the International Congress on the Dead Sea Scrolls,* 405-48; *Qumran Cave 4: XXI: Parabiblical Texts, Part 4: Pseudo-Prophetic Texts.* DJD 30 (Oxford: Clarendon, 2001) 87-260.

They (the sons of Aaron) will do what is evil in my sight in keeping with all that Israel had done in the first days of the kingdom, with the exception of those who were the first to go up (to Judah) from the land of their captivity to build the sanctuary. But I will speak to them and send them a precept so that they will understand all that they have abandoned, they and their ancestors. Ever since that generation came to an end, in the seventh Jubilee since the devastation of the land, they will ignore statute, festival, Sabbath, and covenant. They will transgress in every way and will do what is evil in my sight. I will hide my face from them, hand them over to their enemies, and deliver them to the sword. But from among them I will permit survivors to remain so that they will not be entirely annihilated by my anger and the hiding of my face. (4Q390 frag. 1, lines 4-10)

According to this text, then, the only ones exempt from the prevailing corruption were the first immigrants who returned to build the temple, identical with the penitents (*šāvîm,* also "those who returned") of the *Damascus Document,*[81] and therefore also inclusive of or even identified with the *běnê-haggôlâ* of Ezra-Nehemiah. Here, too, the exile, the time when God hid his face from Israel, continues throughout the seventh Jubilee down to the time of the remnant, those predestined to survive the judgment of an angry God. A similar scenario is displayed in the fragmentary *4QAges of Creation* in which, at the conclusion of the seventh and final age of creation, some are chosen by God out of the prevailing corruption to form a holy congregation.[82]

The consistency with which this symbolic historiography is reproduced in these texts from the second and first century B.C. would seem to point to a common tradition going back well before the Hasmonean period. The main lines of this symbolic historiography are clear. The concentration of sectarian (or quasi-sectarian or proto-sectarian) movements in the later Second Temple period on the Babylonian exile as the defining moment in the religious history of Israel fits well with and reinforces the hypothesis of the Babylonian origins of the Essene movement or, for those who doubt the Essene character of the Damascus sect, of whatever kind of sectarianism fed into the Damascus sect. Neither Ezra nor Nehemiah is

---

81. CD I 4; IV 8-9; VI 2; VIII 17 = XIX 29 *(ri'šônîm);* VI 5; VIII 16; XIX 29 *(šāvîm).*

82. 4Q181 = *4QAges of Creation B* frag. 1, col. II. See Devorah Dimant, "The 'Pesher on the Periods' (4Q180 and 4Q181), *IOS* 9 (1979) 77-102.

mentioned in the texts surveyed — though one or the other may be one of the three sheep of the Animal Vision who returned and built the temple — but they must be included among the *šāvîm* ("those who returned as penitents") and *ri'šônîm* ("the founding fathers") of the Damascus text with whom these sectarians identified.

Legal Interpretations and Practice in Ezra-Nehemiah and Late Second Temple Sects

A careful and detailed comparison of legal interpretations and prescriptions stated or implied in Ezra-Nehemiah with those in the overtly sectarian or protosectarian movements of the late Second Temple period still remains to be undertaken. In the meantime the argument advanced in this and the preceding chapters calls for at least some provisional observations, especially bearing on issues of group identity. On this question of what is or is not negotiable in the matter of belief and practice, texts extant from the mid- to late Second Temple period reveal a broad range of opinion and varying degrees of tolerance or intolerance. For example: there is no polemic against intermarriage in Esther where we might expect it. Like the tales in Daniel 1–6, the story unfolds against a background of at times uneasy coexistence. Both Tobit and Tobias are in all respects exemplary Jews living in a diasporic, Gentile environment, solicitous in prayer (Tob 3:1-6; 12:8), almsgiving (1:16-17; 4:7-11), fasting (12:8), dietary regulations (1:10-11), and care for the dead. Both marry women from their own kinship group, but do so simply in keeping with immemorial custom.[83] Judith is almost ostentatiously scrupulous in such matters as dietary laws (Jdt 11:12; 12:1-4, 19), fasting (8:6), ritual washing (12:7-8), and tithing (11:13-15), and she remains a widow after the death of her husband (16:22). The author presents her as the female ideal of piety and strict adherence to the law, as her name suggests, yet permits the Ammonite Achior to be circumcised and admitted to the household of Israel in defiance of the exclusionary clause in Deut 23:3-6(MT 4-7) (Jdt 14:10). Writings from the late Hellenistic and Greco-Roman periods with a strong apologetic intent aimed at a

---

83. The *'iššâ zārâ* is therefore a woman who does not belong to their clan (Tob 1:9; 4:12-13). In this kind of situation marriage has much to do with the protection of patrimonial domain (Tob 7:12-13; cf. Num 36:5-9).

cultured readership, including *4 Maccabees,* Baruch, Wisdom of Solomon, and the *Letter of Aristeas,* aim to present Judaism as a philosophy in accord with reason and therefore tend to emphasize the more expansive and accommodating rather than the more integralist aspects of legal interpretation bearing on Jewish identity. The Jewish law, therefore, serves to promote the practice of the cardinal virtues (*4 Macc.* 5:22-24; Wis 8:7), the dietary laws serve to inculcate self-control (*4 Macc.* 1:14; 5:2), and self-segregation is necessary to avoid the temptations of idolatry (Aristeas 139). Yet this author is prepared to concede that Jews worship the same deity as the Greeks under a different name (*Let. Aris.* 15).

While neither Ezra nor Nehemiah is mentioned in it,[84] the *Damascus Document,* a very different kind of text, provides some intriguing parallels to the ideology which, in the canonical book, Ezra and Nehemiah are represented as importing from Babylon with a view to implementing it in the Persian province of Judah. In the first place, this sectarian manual appeals to legal interpretations handed down from the *ri'šônîm,* the founding fathers who returned from the place of exile with their faith intact.[85] The emphasis is on meticulous observance of legal rulings presumed to derive their inspiration and substance from this source from the time of the first return.[86] The laws in the Damascus Document (CD) and the related cave fragments (4QDa-h) comprise regulations for both a Gentile, therefore possibly diasporic, environment and a more thoroughly self-segregating group. On the hypothesis that the Qumran *yaḥad* splintered off from the Damascus sect, its parent body, it is not surprising that the laws betray indications of editorial adjustments to align them with the *yaḥad* community rule.[87] In

84. In the midrash on the Song of the Well (Num 21:17-18) in CD VI 2-1, the penitents who had left Judah for the place of exile and eventually returned followed the legal interpretations of the *dôrēš hattôrâ* ("interpreter" or "investigator of the law"). It is tempting to think that the author had Ezra in mind, but his conflation of the history of his own sect with that of the first immigrants, the founding fathers, makes this quite speculative.

85. CD IV 8; VI 14, 18, 20; XIII 6.

86. The expression *pērôš hattôrâ* (CD IV 8) includes the idea both of a legal ruling, in keeping with one meaning of the verbal stem *prš* (Lev 24:12; Num 15:34), and of meticulous observance. It can also refer to a list of the first founders of the sect (2:13; 4:4-5).

87. Following Davies, *The Damascus Covenant,* 105-42; and Charlotte Hempel, *The Laws of the Damascus Document: Sources, Tradition, and Redaction.* STDJ 29 (Leiden: Brill, 1998). For a different and, in my opinion, much less probable solution, according to which the *yaḥad* is earlier than the Damascus covenant sect, see Eyal Regev, *Sectarianism in Qumran: A Cross-cultural Perspective* (Berlin: de Gruyter, 2007) 187-96, 379-80.

general, the prescriptions in the Damascus rule are not polemical and have relatively little to say about relations with outsiders, either Gentile or Jewish.[88] For this aspect of the sect's self-identification we must rely principally on the Admonition.

The opening sentence of the Admonition is fragmentary, but it appears to exhort the "Sons of Light" to avoid contact with outsiders (4Q266 frag. 1 a-b, lines 1-2). Aspects of the ideology of the sect can be detected early in the Admonition, where rival sectarians are condemned for adopting more accommodating legal interpretations (CD IV 12–V 11). They have been trapped in Belial's three nets: fornication, wealth, and desecration of the temple. The opponents have fallen into the first of these (Hebrew *zěnût*) by taking two wives, in other words, by the practice of polygamy.[89] They have desecrated the temple by ignoring the laws of consanguinity and affinity, especially by uncle-niece, aunt-nephew marriages and by sexual relations with women during their menstrual periods (CD IV 15–V 11). The same connection between forbidden unions and temple pollution is made in even stronger terms in the book of *Jubilees,* in which exogamous marriage is prohibited in the heavenly tablets as a defilement of the sanctuary. Punishment is correspondingly severe: the male partner is stoned to death and the female burned alive (*Jub.* 30:7-17). The sectarian text 4QMMTa *Miqṣat Ma'áśê Hattôrâ* ("Some Precepts of the Torah," also referred to as Halakhic Letter) likewise rules that presence in the temple of persons who have contracted illicit unions desecrates it (Composite Text B, lines 48-49).[90] Nehemiah was moved by the same conviction in ejecting Tobiah and his possessions from the temple precincts and following up with a ceremony of purification (Neh 13:7-9).

In another passage in the Halakhic Letter it is stipulated that Ammo-

---

88. CD XII 6-11, restricting trade with Gentiles, is one of the few exceptions. See Lawrence H. Schiffman, "Legislation concerning Relations with Non-Jews in the *Zadokite Fragments* and in Tannaitic Literature," *RevQ* 11 (1983) 379-89.

89. That this is the meaning of *zěnût* in this context is strongly suggested by the "proof texts" adduced, i.e., Gen 1:27; 7:7-9; and Deut 17:17. See Geza Vermes, "Sectarian Matrimonial Halakhah in the Damascus Rule," *JJS* 25 (1974) 197-202; repr. *Post-Biblical Jewish Studies.* SJLA 8 (Leiden: Brill, 1975) 50-56; Davies, *The Damascus Covenant,* 109-19. The type of marriage forbidden in the Damascus sect, one incidentally practiced by Isaac and Jacob, is prohibited in the cultic legislation (Lev 18:13).

90. Elisha Qimron and John Strugnell, eds., *Qumran Cave 4.V: Miqṣat Ma'aśe ha-Torah.* DJD 10 (Oxford: Clarendon, 1994) 46-47.

nites, Moabites, the *mamzēr,* and the sexually mutilated, excluded from the Israelite assembly in Deuteronomy (Deut 23:1-8[MT 2-9]) but who nevertheless appear to frequent the temple, may not marry a member of the sect and are henceforth to be denied access to the temple and its cult (4QMMT B 39-49). In common with Ezra-Nehemiah, therefore, this sectarian text insists on enforcing the Deuteronomic law together with the prohibition in the Ezekiel temple law (Ezek 44:9) against resident foreigners entering the sanctuary.

With the utopian vision of temple purity in the Temple Scroll from Qumran Cave 11 we enter a world in which the practical requirements of living have been left far behind.[91] The architectural layout, which appears to make the temple precincts coterminous with the city — the Temple Scroll refers in fact to "the sanctuary-city" (XLV 11-12) — protects the holiness of the sanctuary and its inner sanctum by surrounding it with three courts. The inner court is restricted to ritually clean priests and Levites, the middle court to ritually clean males over the age of twenty, and the outer court with its twelve gates is for women, children, and proselytes. Gentiles are not in the picture. The Scroll's purity rules exclude sexual intercourse in the sanctuary-city, a ruling also found in the *Damascus Document* (CD XII 1-2) but not in Ezra-Nehemiah. For the satisfaction of bodily needs latrines are to be located no closer than 3000 cubits from the city (XLVI 13-16); a similar ruling occurs in the War Scroll (1QM VII 7) and in Josephus's report on the Essenes (*B.J.* 2.147-49).

To come back to the *Damascus Document:* In the midrash on the "Song of the Well" (CD VI 2–VII 6; from Num 21:17-18), those who had left the land of Judah for the land of Damascus, the land of exile, to return later as founders of a new community, reinstated the law as interpreted by the *dôrēš hattôrâ* and entered into a new covenant to observe the law so interpreted. In recording this defining moment in the prehistory of the sect, the writer would almost certainly have had in mind the situation as described in Ezra-Nehemiah. Earlier in the Admonition he refers to a list of the names of

91. 11Q XIX-XXI together with the fragmentary 4Q*Rouleau du Temple* (4Q524) and, less certainly, 4Q365a. See the *editio princeps* of Yigael Yadin, *The Temple Scroll,* rev. ed. 3 vols. with Supplement (Jerusalem: Israel Exploration Society, 1977-83); and, more accessibly, Johann Maier, *The Temple Scroll: An Introduction, Translation and Commentary.* JSOTSup 34 (Sheffield: JSOT, 1985). For an excellent introduction with generous bibliographies, see Sidnie White Crawford, *The Temple Scroll and Related Texts* (Sheffield: Sheffield Academic, 2000).

these pioneers, penitents of Israel who returned to found a new community — *šāvê yiśrā'ēl* in the *Damascus Document, běnê haggôlâ* in Ezra 1–10 — but unfortunately does not include the list itself, assuming that it existed and was known to him (CD IV 2-6). Here, too, we are reminded of the importance of lists of members of the group in Ezra-Nehemiah.

The stipulations to which these same penitents commit themselves on entering the new covenant in the land of Damascus (CD VI 11–VII 6) recall Nehemiah's covenant which gives both the names of the signatories and the stipulations (Neh 10:1-39). The commitment of the Damascus covenanters to segregate from those doomed to destruction — in other words, those not belonging to the sect[92] — is consistent with the self-segregation of the *golah* community, and the prohibition of irregular sexual unions, including marriage with outsiders, corresponds to the stipulation in Nehemiah's covenant to avoid marriage and any other contact with "the peoples of the land" (Neh 10:30-31). The parallels extend to support of the cult and strict observance of Sabbath, on which both Nehemiah and the Damascus rule have much to say.[93] The final provision of the "new covenant in the land of Damascus," to avoid all sources of uncleanness and contamination (CD VII 4), would certainly have elicited enthusiastic approval from Ezra, Nehemiah, and their supporters.

We may therefore conclude that, in terms of both ideology and practice, lines of continuity can be traced between the ambient described in Ezra-Nehemiah and the overt sectarianism of the late Second Temple period. Whether these parallels can be translated into terms of continuity at the level of social realities is, in the nature of the case, less certain. We have no direct information on the later history of those who, in the aftermath of disaster and deprivation, sighed and moaned, mourned and trembled over the fate of Israel.[94] What we do know is that such groups and movements can continue in existence and even flourish over centuries. The Karaite sect, for example,[95] has continued in existence from the eighth century

92. Lit., "sons of destruction" or "sons of the pit" (*běnê haššahat*, CD VI 15).

93. See esp. the Sabbath code (CD X 14–XII 6).

94. For the first category, see Ezek 9:4. On the mourners (*'ăvēlîm, mit'abbēlîm*), see Isa 57:18; 60:20; 61:2-3; 66:10) and, further, my *Opening the Sealed Book: Interpretations of the Book of Isaiah in Late Antiquity* (Grand Rapids: Wm. B. Eerdmans, 2006) 216-18.

95. Leaving aside the hypothesis of a connection between Karaites and Qumran, on which see Hans Bardtke, "Einige Erwägungen zum Problem 'Qumran und Karaismus,'" *Hen* 10 (1988) 259-75.

down to the present when, according to their website, they number some thirty thousand members. It does not seem out of place to entertain the possibility that those who, together with Ezra, trembled at the word of God, anticipated and prepared the ground for the full and explicit development of Jewish sectarianism some two and a half centuries later.

Provisional Conclusion in Four Propositions

No one working in this period with the few texts which have come down to us should have any doubt about the fragility of our knowledge. It has been said about the history of ancient Greece that all we have is the flotsam washed ashore from a shipwreck far out at sea, and we know a great deal more about the Greek-speaking regions at the time of Ezra and Nehemiah than we do about what was happening in Judah and in Jewish communities elsewhere. I have argued that the origins of Judaism as it is known today are to be sought during the two centuries of the Persian-Iranian Empire; to that extent Eduard Meyer was right. It is important to stress this first proposition in view of the tendency in historical studies to begin with the Hellenistic period, concentrating on the crisis of Hellenization and the policies of Seleucid monarchs, in the process eliding or sliding rapidly over the preceding two centuries. This situation can be explained by the absence of external attestation to Judaism and Jews before the Macedonian conquest, and perhaps also by barriers erected between academic disciplines, the Hellenistic period falling within the domain of Classical Studies or, in some contexts, "New Testament Backgrounds," while the previous two centuries are left to biblical scholarship.

If we are to have any chance of understanding this chapter of history, we must risk transgressing these artificial boundaries. We therefore begin with the situation following upon the huge disaster of the destruction of Jerusalem and its temple by the Babylonians and the liquidation of the political and religious infrastructure — monarchy, priesthood, scribalism, prophecy — which had sustained the Judean state for centuries. In the aftermath of the disaster we see emerging a plurality of centers, groups, and

228

parties claiming legitimacy by virtue of continuity with the past and the narrative and legal traditions inherited from the past, and denying legitimacy to other claimants. It results that attitudes which came to define relations between Jews and non-Jews emerged, in this first phase, out of conflicting claims and counterclaims internal to Judean and diasporic communities at that time.

My second proposition is that in this conflict over continuity and discontinuity with the past the strongest impulse came at that time, and continued to come, from the Babylonian diaspora, and that its principal embodiment was the group whose ideology is presented in the canonical book Ezra-Nehemiah. This impulse was explicitly religious, generated in the first place by an interpretation of the disaster as the climax of a history of religious infidelity. One of the most important aspects of the ideology was a strong ritualization of social interaction, not only between Jewish communities and the external environment but among the communities themselves. The most distinctive form assumed by this ritual ethnicity is associated with the persons of Ezra and Nehemiah as presented in the canonical book. Both attempted, each in his own sphere of activity, to translate their religious convictions into social and political reality. These convictions were greatly indebted to Ezekiel and his "school" — the temple law of Ezekiel 40–48 — combined with a rigorous interpretation of the exclusionary admonitions and laws in Deuteronomy. By the mid-fifth century B.C. this ideology had had more than a century to incubate, fed also, we may suppose, by reaction to the high level of interethnicity in the region in which Judeans and many other ethnics were settled.

From these premises follows a third proposition, namely, that the arrival of Ezra and Nehemiah in the province of Judah represented not so much a "return to Zion" but a kind of diaspora in reverse from the parent body in southern Mesopotamia, a religious colonization with a definite religious agenda, namely, the creation of a self-segregated, ritually pure society inspired by the new temple and new society profiled in Ezekiel's vision and elaborated by his disciples in the diaspora. I have argued that this agenda had much in common with the sectarianism of the late Second Temple period. An important corollary must, however, be added. A basic problem for any religious group is to maintain its distinctive identity by resisting assimilation to the social environment and, if possible, to do so without shutting out the more expansive and universalist possibilities latent in its traditions. But how a particular group negotiates this issue of identity maintenance is a matter of degree of tolerance or intolerance, a matter of deciding which doctrines, beliefs, and practices are discretionary and negotiable and which are not. The agenda which Ezra and his ḥărēdîm sought to implement represented a maximalist position, expressed in the clearest possible terms in the solution to the problem of intermarriage in Ezra 9–10. Their claims to exclusive Israelite status notwithstanding, Ezra and his supporters represented only one instantiation of Jewish identity. In the first place, the biblical traditions themselves offer different ways of combining basic religious fidelity with an open and accommodating attitude to outsiders; a good example would be the presentation of Abraham in the pentateuchal traditions of Priestly origin. Those from the Samaria region (Ezra 4:1-3), and in distant Elephantine, who worshipped and sacrificed to the same deity as the Judeo-Babylonian immigrants, would have seen things differently, as also the indigenous Judeans (Ezek 11:14-15; 33:23-24) and many others scattered around the vast Persian Empire. It is hardly surprising that the Ezra agenda did not succeed in imposing itself to the exclusion of other options.

A fourth proposition concerns Nehemiah and the outcome of his strenuous activity as governor of the province. As a layman, Nehemiah moved in a different sphere of activity from Ezra, priest and scribe, but there can be no doubt that his goal was to implement the same religious ideology in the political realm, whether with respect to the exclusion of foreign influences (Neh 9:2; 13:1-3, 30), intermarriage (13:23-28), or the integrity and purity of the temple and its personnel (13:9, 29-30). Nehemiah's sworn agreement (9:38–10:39[MT 10:1-40]), a retrojection into the mid-fifth century from the early Hellenistic period, provides a rare, perhaps unique link between the classic Deuteronomic covenant and that of the Damascus sectarians. More significant for the future was Nehemiah's application of ritual ethnicity to politics and his adoption as inspiration and model by the Maccabees. The Hasmonean leaders achieved what Nehemiah, in the service of the hegemonic power of that time, could not. They achieved the independence of Judah after the measures adopted by Antiochus IV, but their efforts bore bitter fruit in the endless campaigns of conquest and annexation of the Hasmoneans. This reterritorialization of Judaism, a by no means inevitable turn of events, can be traced back to Nehemiah. It may be said to be one of the most prominent and problematic indications that the past, even the remote past of our origins, remains with us.

Bibliography

Ackroyd, Peter R. "The Temple Vessels: A Continuity Theme." *VTSup* 23 (1972) 166-81. Repr. in *Studies in the Religious Tradition of the Old Testament*, 46-60. London: SCM, 1987.

———. "The Chronicler as Exegete." *JSOT* 1 (1976) 2-32.

———. "Chronicles — Ezra — Nehemiah: The Concept of Unity." *ZAW* 100 (1988 sup.) 189-201.

Albertz, Rainer. *A History of Israelite Religion in the Old Testament Period.* Vol. 2: *From the Exile to the Maccabees.* OTL. Louisville: Westminster John Knox, 1994.

———. "The Thwarted Restoration." In *Yahwism after the Exile*, ed. Albertz and Bob Becking, 1-17. Assen: van Gorcum, 2003.

Albright, William F. "The Date and Personality of the Chronicler." *JBL* 40 (1921) 104-24.

———. "The Names 'Israel' and 'Juda' with an Excursus on the Etymology of *tôdâh* and *tôrâh*." *JBL* 46 (1927) 151-85.

———. *Archaeology and the Religion of Israel.* 5th ed. Garden City: Doubleday, 1968.

———, and C. S. Mann. "Qumran and the Essenes: Geography, Chronology, and the Identification of the Sect." In *The Scrolls and the New Testament*, ed. Matthew Black, 11-25. London: SPCK, 1969.

Alt, Albrecht. "Die Rolle Samarias bei der Entstehung des Judentums." In *Festschrift Otto Procksch zum 60. Geburtstag*, 5-28. Leipzig: Deichert & Hinrichs, 1934 = *Kleine Schriften zur Geschichte des Volkes Israel*, 2:316-37. Munich: Beck, 1953.

Avigad, Naḥman. *Bullae and Seals from a Post-Exilic Judean Archive.* Qedem 4. Jerusalem: Hebrew University Institute of Archaeology, 1976.

Baillet, Maurice. "Paroles des Lumières." In *Qumrân Grotte 4. III (4Q482-4Q520)*, 137-68. DJD 7. Oxford: Clarendon, 1982.

Baltzer, Klaus. *The Covenant Formulary in Old Testament, Jewish, and Early Christian Writings*. Philadelphia: Fortress, 1971.

Bardtke, Hans. "Einige Erwägungen zum Problem 'Qumran und Karaismus." *Hen* 10 (1988) 259-75.

Barstad, Hans M. *The Myth of the Empty Land*. Oslo: Scandinavian University Press, 1996.

———. *The Babylonian Captivity of the Book of Isaiah*. Oslo: Novus, 1997.

Bartal, A. "Once more, who was Sheshbazzar?" *Beth Mikra* 24 (1979) 357-89.

Bartlett, John R. "Zadok and His Successors at Jerusalem." *JTS* N.S. 19 (1968) 1-18.

Batten, Loring W. *A Critical and Exegetical Commentary on the Books of Ezra and Nehemiah*. ICC. Edinburgh: T. & T. Clark, 1913.

Beaulieu, Paul-Alain. *The Reign of Nabonidus King of Babylon 556-539 B.C.* New Haven: Yale University Press, 1989.

Beck, Martin. *Der "Tag YHWHs" im Dodekapropheton: Studien im Spannungsfeld von Traditions- und Redacktionsgeschichte*. BZAW 356. Berlin: de Gruyter, 2005.

Becker, Joachim. *Der Ich-Bericht des Nehemiabuches als chronistische Gestaltung*. FB 87. Würzburg: Echter, 1998.

Becking, Bob. "YEHUD." *DDD*, 925-26.

Bedford, Peter R. "Diaspora-Homeland Relations in Ezra-Nehemiah." *VT* 52 (2002) 147-65.

Bentzen, Aage. "Priesterschaft und Laien in der jüdischen Gemeinde des fünften Jahrhunderts." *AfO* 6 (1930/31) 280-86.

Berner, Christoph. *Jahre, Jahrwocken und Jubiläen*. BZAW 363. Berlin: de Gruyter, 2006.

Bertholet, Alfred. *Die Bücher Esra und Nehemia*. KHC. Tübingen: Mohr, 1902.

Betlyon, John W. "The Provincial Government of Persian Period Judea and the Yehud Coins." *JBL* 105 (1986) 633-42.

Bickerman, Elias. *From Ezra to the Last of the Maccabees*. New York: Schocken, 1962.

———. *The God of the Maccabees*. SJLA 32. Leiden: Brill, 1979.

———. "The Babylonian Captivity." *CHJ*, 1:342-58.

Black, Matthew. *The Scrolls and Christian Origins*. New York: Scribner's, 1961.

Blenkinsopp, Joseph. *Prophecy and Canon*. Notre Dame: University of Notre Dame Press, 1977.

———. "The Mission of Udjahorresnet and Those of Ezra and Nehemiah." *JBL* 106 (1987) 409-21.

———. *Ezra-Nehemiah*. OTL. Philadelphia: Westminster, 1988.

———. "A Jewish Sect of the Persian Period." *CBQ* 52 (1990) 5-20.

——— . "Temple and Society in Achaemenid Judah." In *Second Temple Studies,* vol. 1: *The Persian Period,* ed. Philip R. Davies, 1:22-53. JSOTSup 117. Sheffield: JSOT, 1991.

——— . "The Social Context of the 'Outsider Woman' in Proverbs 1–9." *Bib* 72 (1991) 457-73.

——— . *The Pentateuch: An Introduction to the First Five Books of the Bible.* ABRL. New York: Doubleday, 1992.

——— . "The Nehemiah Autobiographical Memoir." In *Language, Theology and the Bible. Essays in Honour of James Barr,* ed. Samuel E. Balentine and John Barton, 199-212. Oxford: Clarendon, 1994.

——— . "An Assessment of the Alleged Pre-Exilic Date of the Priestly Material in the Pentateuch." *ZAW* 108 (1996) 495-518.

——— . "The Jerusalem Priesthood during the Neo-Babylonian and Achaemenid Periods: A Hypothetical Reconstruction." *CBQ* 60 (1998) 25-43.

——— . *Isaiah 1–39.* AB 19. New York: Doubleday, 2000.

——— . "Did the second Jerusalemite temple possess land?" *Transeu* 21 (2001) 61-68.

——— . "The Age of the Exile." In *The Biblical World,* ed. John Barton, 1:416-39. London: Routledge, 2002.

——— . "The Bible, Archaeology and Politics; or The Empty Land Revisited." *JSOT* 27 (2002) 169-87.

——— . *Isaiah 40–55.* AB 19A. New York: Doubleday, 2002.

——— . *Isaiah 56–66.* AB 19B. New York: Doubleday, 2003.

——— . "Bethel in the Neo-Babylonian Period." In *Judah and the Judeans in the Neo-Babylonian Period,* ed. Oded Lipschits and Blenkinsopp, 93-107. Winona Lake: Eisenbrauns, 2003.

——— . *Treasures Old and New: Essays in the Theology of the Pentateuch.* Grand Rapids: Wm. B. Eerdmans, 2004.

——— . "Benjamin Traditions Read in the Early Persian Period." In *Judah and the Judeans in the Persian Period,* ed. Oded Lipschits and Manfred Oeming, 629-45. Winona Lake: Eisenbrauns, 2006.

——— . "Who Is the Ṣaddiq of Isaiah 57:1-2?" In *Studies in the Hebrew Bible, Qumran, and the Septuagint Presented to Eugene Ulrich,* ed. Peter W. Flint, Emanuel Tov, and James C. VanderKam, 109-20. VTSup 101. Leiden: Brill, 2006.

——— . *Opening the Sealed Book: Interpretations of the Book of Isaiah in Late Antiquity.* Grand Rapids: Wm. B. Eerdmans, 2006.

Blidstein, Gerald J. "ATIMIA: A Greek Parallel to Ezra X 8 and to Post-Biblical Exclusion from the Community." *VT* 24 (1974) 357-60.

Blum, Erhard. *Die Composition der Vätergeschichte.* WMANT 57. Neukirchen-Vluyn: Neukirchener, 1983.

Boccaccini, Gabriele. *Middle Judaism: Jewish Thought 300 B.C.E. to 200 C.E.* Minneapolis: Fortress, 1991.

―――. *Roots of Rabbinic Judaism: An Intellectual History from Ezekiel to Daniel.* Grand Rapids: Wm. B. Eerdmans, 2002.

Boda, Mark J. *Praying the Tradition: The Origin and Use of Tradition in Nehemiah 9.* BZAW 277. Berlin: de Gruyter, 1999.

Boecker, Hans Jochen. *Redeformen des Rechtslebens im Alten Testament.* WMANT 14. Neukirchen-Vluyn: Neukirchener, 1964.

Böhler, Dieter. *Die heilige Stadt in Esdras α und Esra-Nehemia.* OTO 158. Freiburg: Universitäts, 1997.

Botterweck, G. J. "Schelt- und Mahnrede gegen Mischehe und Ehescheidung von Mal 2:2, 10-16." *BibLeb* 1 (1960) 179-85.

Bowman, Raymond A. "Ezra and Nehemiah." *IB,* 3:551-819.

Box, G. H. *The Ezra Apocalypse.* London: Pitman, 1912.

Bracke, John M. "*šûb šebût:* A Reappraisal." *ZAW* 97 (1985) 233-44.

Brettler, Marc Z. "Judaism in the Hebrew Bible? The Transition from Ancient Israelite Religion to Judaism." *CBQ* 61 (1999) 429-47.

Briant, Pierre. *From Cyrus to Alexander: A History of the Persian Empire.* Winona Lake: Eisenbrauns, 2002.

―――. "Histoire et archéologie d'un texte: La Lettre de Darius à Gadatas entre Perses, Grecs et Romains." In *Licia e Lidia prima dell'Ellenizzazione: Atti del Convegno Internazionale, Roma 11–12 Ottobre 1999,* ed. Mauro Giorgieri et al., 107-44. Monografie scientifiche, Serie Scienze Umane e Sociali. Rome: Consiglio nazionale dell ricerche, 2003.

Browne, L. E. "A Jewish Sanctuary in Babylonia." *JTS* 17 (1916) 400-1.

Campbell, Jonathan G. "Essene-Qumran Origins in the Exile: A Scriptural Basis?" *JJS* 46 (1995) 143-56.

Carroll, Robert P. *Jeremiah.* OTL. Philadelphia: Westminster, 1986.

―――. "The Myth of the Empty Land." In *Ideological Criticism of Biblical Texts,* ed. David Jobling and Tina Pippin, 79-93. Semeia 59. Atlanta: Scholars, 1992.

Chalcroft, David J. *Sectarianism in Early Judaism.* London: Equinox, 2007.

Charles, R. H. *The Apocrypha and Pseudepigrapha of the Old Testament in English.* Vol. 2: *Pseudepigrapha.* Oxford: Clarendon, 1913.

Charlesworth, James H., ed. *The Old Testament Pseudepigrapha.* 2 vols. Garden City: Doubleday, 1983-85.

Clines, David J. A. "Nehemiah 10 as an Example of Early Jewish Biblical Exegesis." *JSOT* 21 (1981) 111-17.

Cody, Aelred. *A History of Old Testament Priesthood.* AnBib 35. Rome: Pontifical Biblical Institute, 1969.

Coggins, R. J., and M. A. Knibb. *The First and Second Books of Esdras.* CBC. Cambridge: Cambridge University Press, 1979.

Cohen, Shaye J. D. *The Beginnings of Jewishness*. Berkeley: University of California Press, 1999.

Collins, John J. *Daniel*. Hermeneia. Minneapolis: Fortress, 1993.

———. "Marriage, Divorce and Family in Second Temple Judaism." In *Families in Ancient Israel*, ed. Leo G. Perdue et al., 107-21. Louisville: Westminster John Knox, 1997.

———. *The Apocalyptic Imagination*. 2nd ed. BRS. Grand Rapids: Wm. B. Eerdmans, 1998.

———. "From Prophecy to Apocalypticism." In *The Encyclopedia of Apocalypticism*, 1:129-61. New York: Continuum, 1998.

Coogan, Michael D. *West Semitic Personal Names in the Murašû Documents*. HSM 7. Missoula: Scholars, 1976.

Cook, Stephen L. *Prophecy and Apocalypticism: The Postexilic Social Setting*. Minneapolis: Fortress, 1995.

Cooke, G. A. *The Book of Ezekiel*. ICC 21. Edinburgh: T. & T. Clark, 1936.

Cowley, A. E. *Aramaic Papyri of the Fifth Century b.c.* 1923; repr. Osnabrück: Zeller, 1967.

Crawford, Sidnie White. "The Book of Esther." *NIB* 3 (1999): 853-941.

Cross, Frank Moore. "The Discovery of the Samaria Papyri." *BA* 26 (1963) 110-21.

———. "Aspects of Samaritan and Jewish History in Late Persian and Hellenistic Times." *HTR* 59 (1966) 201-11.

———. *From Epic to Canon: History and Literature in Ancient Israel*. Baltimore: Johns Hopkins University Press, 1998.

Crüsemann, Frank. "Human Solidarity and Ethnic Identity: Israel's Self-Definition in the Genealogical System of Genesis." In *Ethnicity and the Bible*, ed. Mark G. Brett, 57-76. Leiden: Brill, 1996.

Dandamaev, Muhammad A. "Babylonia in the Persian Age." *CHJ*, 1:326-42.

———, and V. G. Lukonin, eds. *The Culture and Social Institutions of Ancient Iran*. Cambridge: Cambridge University Press, 1989.

Davies, J. K. "Athenian Citizenship: The Descent Group and the Alternatives." *CJ* 73 (1977-78) 105-21.

———. "Religion and the State." *CAH*, 2nd ed., 4 (1988): 368-88.

Davies, Philip R. "Ḥasidim in the Maccabean Period." *JJS* 28 (1977) 127-40.

———. *The Damascus Covenant*. JSOTSup 25. Sheffield: JSOT, 1983.

———. "Scenes from the Early History of Judaism." In *The Triumph of Elohim: From Yahwisms to Judaisms*, ed. Diana Vikander Edelman, 145-82. Grand Rapids: Wm. B. Eerdmans, 1995.

Day, Peggy L. "ANAT." *DDD*, 36-49.

Devauchelle, Didier. "Le Sentiment anti-perse chez les anciens Égyptiens." *Transeu* 9 (1995) 67-90.

Dimant, Devorah. "The 'Pesher on the Periods' (4Q180 and 4Q181)." *IOS* 9 (1979) 77-102.

―――― . "New Light from Qumran on the Jewish Pseudepigrapha — 4Q390." In *The Madrid Qumran Congress: Proceedings of the International Congress on the Dead Sea Scrolls, Madrid 18-21 March 1991*, ed. Julio Trebolle Barrera and Luis Vegas Montaner, 2:405-48. STDJ 11. Leiden: Brill, 1992.

Doran, Robert. *Temple Propaganda: The Purpose and Character of 2 Maccabees.* CBQMS 12. Washington: Catholic Biblical Association, 1981.

Driver, S. R. *An Introduction to the Literature of the Old Testament.* 1891; repr. Cleveland: Meridian, 1956.

Duggan, Michael W. *The Covenant Renewal in Ezra-Nehemiah (Neh 7:72b–10:40): An Exegetical, Literary, and Theological Study.* SBLDS 164. Atlanta: SBL, 2001.

Duhm, Bernhard. "Anmerkungen zu den Zwölf Propheten." *ZAW* 31 (1911) 161-204.

―――― . *Das Buch Jesaja.* 4th ed. HKAT. Göttingen: Vandenhoeck & Ruprecht, 1922.

Edelman, Diana V. *The Origins of the 'Second' Temple: Persian Imperial Policy and the Rebuilding of Jerusalem.* London: Equinox, 2005.

Eichrodt, Walther. *Ezekiel.* OTL. Philadelphia: Westminster, 1970.

Eph'al, E. "The Western Minorities in Babylonia in the 6th-5th Centuries B.C.: Maintenance and Cohesion." *Or* 47 (1978) 74-90.

―――― . "On the Political and Social Organization of the Jews in Babylonian Exile." In *XXI Deutscher Orientalistentag Vorträge*, ed. Fritz Steppat, 106-12. ZDMGSup 5. Wiesbaden: Steiner, 1981.

Feldman, Louis H. "Josephus' Portrait of Nehemiah." *JJS* 43 (1992) 187-202.

―――― . "Josephus' Portrait of Ezra." *VT* 43 (1993) 190-214.

―――― . "The Concept of Exile in Josephus." In *Exile: Old Testament, Jewish, and Christian Conceptions*, ed. James M. Scott, 144-48. JSJSup 56. Leiden: Brill, 1997.

Fischer, James A. "Notes on the Literary Form and Message of Malachi." *CBQ* 34 (1972) 315-20.

Fishbane, Michael. *Biblical Interpretation in Ancient Israel.* Oxford: Clarendon, 1985.

Gager, John. *The Origins of Anti-Semitism.* Oxford: Oxford University Press, 1983.

Galling, Kurt. "Das Gemeindegesetz in Deuteronomium 23." In *Festschrift, Alfred Bertholet zum 80. Geburtstag*, ed. Walter Baumgartner et al., 176-91. Tübingen: Mohr, 1950.

Garbini, Giovanni. *History and Ideology in Ancient Israel.* New York: Crossroad, 1988.

García-Martínez, Florentino. "Qumran Origins and Early History: A Groningen Hypothesis." *FO* 25 (1988) 113-36.

————, and A. S. van der Woude. "A 'Gronigen' Hypothesis of Qumran Origins and Early History." *RevQ* 14 (1990) 521-41.

————, and Eibert J. C. Tigchelaar. *The Dead Sea Scrolls Study Edition.* 2 vols. Grand Rapids: Wm. B. Eerdmans and Leiden: Brill, 1997-98.

Gardiner, Alan H. "The House of Life." *JEA* 24 (1938) 157-79.

Gese, Hartmut. *Der Verfassungsentwurf des Ezechiel (Kap. 40-48) traditionsgeschicht untersucht.* BHT 25. Tübingen: Mohr Siebeck, 1957.

Glatt-Gilad, David A. "Reflections on the Structure and Significance of the 'ămānāh (Neh 10.29-40)." *ZAW* 112 (2000) 386-95.

Glazier-McDonald, Beth. *Malachi, the Divine Messenger.* SBLDS 98. Atlanta: Scholars, 1989.

Grabbe, Lester L. "Reconstructing History from the Book of Ezra." In *Second Temple Studies,* vol. 1: *Persian Period,* ed. Philip R. Davies, 98-106. JSOTSup 117. Sheffield: JSOT, 1991.

————. *Judaism from Cyrus to Herod.* Vol. 1: *The Persian and Greek Periods.* Minneapolis: Fortress, 1992.

————. "What Was Ezra's Mission?" In *Second Temple Studies,* vol. 2: *Temple and Community in the Persian Period,* ed. Tamara C. Eskenazi and Kent H. Richards, 286-99. JSOTSup 175. Sheffield: JSOT, 1994.

————. "The Jews and Hellenization: Hengel and His Critics." In *Second Temple Studies III: Studies in Politics, Class and Material Culture,* ed. Philip R. Davies and John M. Halligan, 52-66. JSOTSup 340. Sheffield: Sheffield Academic, 2002.

————. *A History of the Jews and Judaism in the Second Temple Period.* Vol. 1: *A History of the Persian Province of Judah.* London: T. & T. Clark, 2004.

Gradwohl, Roland. "Das 'Fremde Feuer' von Nadab und Abihu." *ZAW* 73 (1963) 288-96.

Graham, M. Patrick. "A Connection Proposed between II Chr 24,26 and Ezra 9–10." *ZAW* 97 (1985) 256-58.

Gray, John. *I & II Kings.* OTL. Philadelphia: Westminster, 1963.

Greenberg, Moshe. *Ezekiel 1–20.* AB 22. Garden City: Doubleday, 1983.

————. "The Design and Themes of Ezekiel's Program of Restoration." *Int* 38 (1984) 181-208.

Gropp, Douglaas M. *Wadi Daliyeh II: The Samaria Papyri from Wadi Daliyeh.* DJD 28. Oxford: Clarendon, 2001.

Gunneweg, Antonius H. J. *Leviten und Priester.* FRLANT 89. Göttingen: Vandenhoeck & Ruprecht, 1965.

————. "Zur Interpretation der Bücher Esra-Nehemia." *VTSup* 32 (1981) 146-61.

Hanson, O. "The Purported Letter of Darius to Gadates." *Rheinisches Museum* 129 (1986) 95-96.

Hanson, Paul D. *The Dawn of Apocalyptic.* Philadelphia: Fortress, 1975.

Haran, Menahem. "The Law Code of Ezekiel XL–XLVIII and Its Relation to the Priestly School." *HUCA* 50 (1979) 45-71.

Harland, Philip A. *Associations, Synagogues, and Congregations.* Minneapolis: Fortress, 2003.

Heichlheim, Fritz M. "Ezra's Palestine and Periclean Athens." *ZRGG* 3 (1951) 251-53.

Hempel, Charlotte. *The Laws of the Damascus Document: Sources, Tradition, and Redaction.* STDJ 29. Leiden: Brill, 1998.

Hengel, Martin. *Judaism and Hellenism.* 2 vols. Philadelphia: Fortress, 1974.

——— . *Jews, Greeks, and Barbarians: Aspects of the Hellenization of Judaism in the Pre-Christian Period.* Philadelphia: Fortress, 1980.

Hill, Andrew E. *Malachi.* AB 25D. New York: Doubleday, 1998.

Höffken, Peter. "Warum schwieg Jesus Sirach über Esra?" *ZAW* 87 (1975) 184-201.

Hölscher, Gustav. *Die Bücher Esra und Nehemia.* 4th ed. HSAT 2. Tübingen: Mohr, 1923.

Holladay, Carl R. *Fragments from Hellenistic Jewish Authors.* Vol. 1: *Historians.* SBLTT 39. Chico: Scholars, 1983.

Hornblower, Simon, and Antony Spawforth, eds. *The Oxford Classical Dictionary.* 3rd ed. Oxford: Oxford University Press, 1996.

Horsley, Richard A. "The Expansion of Hasmonean Rule in Idumea and Galilee: Towards a Historical Sociology." In *Second Temple Studies III: Studies in Politics, Class and Material Culture,* ed. Philip R. Davies and John M. Halligan, 134-65. JSOTSup 340. Sheffield: Sheffield Academic, 2002.

Hout, Michael van den. "Studies in Early Greek Letter-Writing." *Mnemosyne* 2 (1949) 19-41, 138-53.

Houten, Christiana van. *The Alien in Israelite Law.* JSOTSup 107. Sheffield: Academic, 1991.

Hultgren, Stephen. *From the Damascus Covenant to the Covenant of the Community: Literary, Historical, and Theological Studies in the Dead Sea Scrolls.* STDJ 66. Leiden: Brill, 2007.

Hutchinson, John, and Anthony D. Smith, eds. *Ethnicity.* Oxford Readers. Oxford: Oxford University Press, 1996.

In der Smitten, Wilhelm Th. *Esra: Quellen, Überlieferung und Geschichte.* SSN 15. Assen: Van Gorcum, 1973.

James, Montague Rhodes. "Ego Salathiel qui et Esdras." *JTS* 18 (1917) 167-69.

Japhet, Sara. "The Supposed Common Authorship of Chronicles and Ezra-Nehemiah Investigated Anew." *VT* 18 (1968) 330-91.

——— . "Sheshbazzar and Zerubbabel." *ZAW* 94 (1982) 66-98.

——— . "The Historical Reliability of Chronicles: The History of the Problem and Its Place in Biblical Research." *JSOT* 33 (1985) 83-107. Repr. *From the Rivers of Babylon to the Highlands of Judah,* 117-36. Winona Lake: Eisenbrauns, 2006.

————. "The Relationship between Chronicles and Ezra-Nehemiah." *VTSup* 43 (1991) 298-313.

————. *I and II Chronicles*. OTL. Louisville: Westminster John Knox, 1993.

Jepsen, Adolf. "Nehemia 10." *ZAW* 66 (1954) 87-106.

Joannès, Francis, and André Lemaire. "Trois tablettes cunéiformes à onomastique ouest-sémitique." *Transeu* 17 (1999) 17-34.

Joyce, Paul M. "Temple and Worship in Ezekiel 40–48." In *Temple and Worship in Biblical Israel*, ed. John Day, 145-63. London: T. & T. Clark, 2005.

Judge, H. G. "Aaron, Zadok and Abiathar" *JTS N.S.* 7 (1956) 70-74.

Kapelrud, Arvid S. *The Question of Authorship in the Ezra-Narrative: A Lexical Investigation*. Oslo: Dybwad, 1944.

Kaufmann, Yeḥezkel. *Toledot ha-'emuna ha-yisra'elit mime qedem 'ad sof bet sheni (The History of Israelite Religion from the Beginnings to the End of the Second Temple)*. 8 vols. Tel Aviv: Bialik Institute-Devir, 1937-56. (Hebrew)

————. *The Religion of Israel from Its Beginnings to the Babylonian Exile*. Chicago: University of Chicago Press, 1960.

————. *The Babylonian Captivity and Deutero-Isaiah*. New York: Union of American Hebrew Congregations, 1970.

Kellermann, Ulrich. *Nehemia: Quellen, Überlieferung und Geschichte*. BZAW 102. Berlin: Töpelmann, 1967.

————. "Erwägungen zum Problem der Esradatierung." *ZAW* 80 (1968) 55-87.

Kelso, James Leon. "Bethel." *NEAEHL*, 1:192-94.

Kennett, Robert H. "The Origin of the Aaronite Priesthood." *JTS* 6 (1905) 161-86.

Klein, Ralph W. "Old Readings in I Esdras: The List of Returnees from Babylon (Ezra 2//Nehemiah 7)." *HTR* 62 (1969) 99-107.

Kloppenberg, John S., and Stephen G. Wilson, eds. *Voluntary Associations in the Graeco-Roman World*. New York: Routledge, 1996.

Knibb, Michael A. "The Exile in the Literature of the Intertestamental Period." *HeyJ* 17 (1976) 253-72.

————. "Exile in the Damascus Document." *JSOT* 25 (1983) 99-117.

————. "Exile." *EDSS*, 1:276-77.

Knights, Chris H. "The Rechabites of Jeremiah 35: Forerunners of the Essenes?" In *Qumran Questions*, ed. James H. Charlesworth, 86-91. Biblical Seminar 36. Sheffield: Sheffield Academic, 1995.

Knoppers, Gary. "Intermarriage, Social Complexity, and Ethnic Diversity in the Genealogy of Judah." *JBL* 120 (2001) 15-30.

Koch, Klaus. "Ezra and the Origins of Judaism." *JSS* 19 (1974) 173-97.

Kort, Ann, and Scott Morschauser, eds. *Biblical and Related Studies Presented to Samuel Iwry*. Winona Lake: Eisenbrauns, 1985.

Kratz, R. G. *Translatio Imperii: Untersuchungen zu den aramäischen Daniel-*

erzählungen und ihrem theologiegeschichtlichen Umfeld. WMANT 63. Neukirchen-Vluyn: Neukirchener, 1991.

―――. *Das Judentum im Zeitalter des Zweiten Tempels.* FAT 42. Tübingen: Mohr Siebeck, 2004.

―――. *The Composition of the Narrative Books of the Old Testament.* London: T. & T. Clark, 2005.

―――. "The Second Temple of Jeb and of Jerusalem." In *Judah and the Judeans in the Persian Period,* ed. Oded Lipschits and Manfred Oeming, 247-64. Winona Lake: Eisenbrauns, 2006.

Kraus, Hans Joachim. *Geschichte der Historisch-Kritischen Erforschung des Alten Testaments.* Neukirchen: Verlag der Buchhandlung des Erziehungsvereins, 1956.

Lau, Wolfgang. *Schriftgelehrte Prophetie in Jes. 56–66.* BZAW 225. Berlin: de Gruyter, 1994.

Lebram, J. C. H. "Die Traditionsgeschichte der Esragestalt und die Frage nach dem historischen Esra." In *Sources, Structures and Synthesis,* ed. Heleen Sancisi-Weerdenburg, 103-38. Achaemenid History 1. Leiden: Nederlands Instituut voor het Nabije Oosten, 1987.

Levin, Christoph. *Fortschreibungen: Gesammelte Studien zum Alten Testament.* BZAW 316. Berlin: de Gruyter, 2003.

―――. *The Old Testament: A Brief Introduction.* Princeton: Princeton University Press, 2005.

Levine, Lee I. *Judaism and Hellenism in Antiquity: Conflict or Confluence?* Seattle: Washington University Press, 1998.

Lipiński, Edouard. "L'étymologie de Juda." *VT* 23 (1973) 380-81.

―――. "Marriage and Divorce in the Judaism of the Persian Period." *Transeu* 4 (1991) 63-71.

Liverani, Mario. *Oltre la Bibbia: Storia antica di Israele.* 2nd ed. Bari: Laterza, 2004.

Longman, Tremper, III. *Fictional Akkadian Autobiography.* Winona Lake: Eisenbrauns, 1991.

McCarthy, Dennis J. "Covenant and Law in Chronicles-Nehemiah." *CBQ* 44 (1982) 25-44.

McEvenue, Sean E. "The Political Structure in Judah from Cyrus to Nehemiah." *CBQ* 43 (1981) 353-64.

McKane, William. *A Critical and Exegetical Commentary on Jeremiah.* Vol. 2: *Commentary on Jeremiah XXVI–LII.* ICC. Edinburgh: T. & T. Clark, 1996.

Maier, Johann. *The Temple Scroll: An Introduction, Translation and Commentary.* JSOTSup 34. Sheffield: JSOT, 1985.

Maloney, Robert P. "Usury and Restrictions on Interest-Taking in the Ancient Near East." *CBQ* 36 (1974) 1-20.

Mayes, A. D. H. *Deuteronomy.* NCBC. Grand Rapids: Wm. B. Eerdmans, 1981.

Mazar, Benjamin. "The Tobiads." *IEJ* 7 (1957) 137-45, 229-38.

Meek, T. J. "Aaronites and Zadokites." *AJSL* 45 (1928/1929) 149-66.

Menes, Abram. "Tempel und Synagoge." *ZAW* 50 (1932) 268-76.

Meyer, Eduard. *Die Entstehung des Judentums.* 1896; repr. Hildesheim: Olms, 1965.

Milgrom, Jacob. "The Antiquity of the Priestly Source: A Reply to Joseph Blenkinsopp." *ZAW* 111 (1999) 10-22.

Millard, Alan R. "The Meaning of the Name Judah." *ZAW* 86 (1974) 216-20.

Misch, Georg. *A History of Autobiography in Antiquity.* 2 vols. London: Routledge & Paul, 1950.

Mittmann, Siegfried. "Tobia, Sanballat und die Persische Provinz Juda." *JNSL* 26 (2000) 1-50.

Momigliano, Arnaldo. "Fattori Orientali della Storiografia Ebraica Post-Esilica e della Storiografia Greca." *Quaderni 76.* Rome: Accademia Nazionale dei Lincei, 1966, 137-46.

―――. *The Development of Greek Biography.* 2nd ed. Cambridge, MA: Harvard University Press, 1993.

Montgomery, James A. *A Critical and Exegetical Commentary on the Book of Kings.* ICC. Edinburgh: T. & T. Clark, 1951.

Moore, Carey A. *Esther.* AB 7B. Garden City: Doubleday, 1971.

Mowinckel, Sigmund. "Die vorderasiatischen Königs- und Fürsteninschriften." In *Eucharistērion: Hermann Gunkel zum 60. Geburtstag,* ed. Hans Schmidt, 1:278-322. FRLANT N.S. 19. Göttingen: Vandenhoeck & Ruprecht, 1923.

―――. *Studien zu dem Buche Ezra-Nehemia.* Vol. 1: *Die nachchronistische Redaktion des Buches: Die Listen.* Vol. 2: *Die Nehemia-Denkschrift.* Vol. 3: *Die Ezrageschichte und das Gesetz Moses.* Oslo: Universitetsforlaget, 1964-65.

Müller, Werner E., and Horst Dietrich Preuss. *Die Vorstellung vom Rest im Alten Testament.* 2nd ed. Neukirchen-Vluyn: Neukirchener, 1973.

Murphy-O'Connor, Jerome. "An Essene Missionary Document? CD II,14–VI,1." *RB* 77 (1970) 214-29.

―――. "The Essenes and Their History." *RB* 31 (1974) 215-44.

―――. "The *Damascus Document* Revisited." *RB* 92 (1985) 223-46.

Myers, Jacob M. *Ezra, Nehemiah.* AB 14. Garden City: Doubleday, 1965.

―――. *I Chronicles.* AB 12. Garden City: Doubleday, 1965.

―――. *I and II Esdras.* AB 42. Garden City: Doubleday, 1974.

Neiman, David. "*pgr:* A Canaanite Cult-object in the Old Testament." *JBL* 67 (1948) 55-60.

Neusner, Jacob. "Exile and Return in the History of Judaism." In *Exile: Old Testament, Jewish, and Christian Conceptions,* ed. James M. Scott, 221-37. JSJSup 56. Leiden: Brill, 1997.

―――, and William Scott Green, eds. *Dictionary of Judaism in the Biblical Period.* 2 vols. New York: Macmillan Library Reference, 1996.

Nicholson, Ernest W. *Preaching to the Exiles: A Study of the Prose Tradition in the Book of Jeremiah.* Oxford: Blackwell, 1970.

North, Francis Sparling. "Aaron's Rise in Prestige." *ZAW* 66 (1954) 191-99.

North, Robert. "Civil Authority in Ezra." In *Studi in Onore di Edoardo Volterra,* 6:377-404. Milan: Giuffrè, 1971.

Noth, Martin. *Die israelitischen Personennamen im Rahmen der gemeinsemitischen Namengebung.* BWANT 10. 1928; repr. Hildesheim: Olms, 1980.

Oded, Bustenay. *Mass Deportations and Deportees in the Neo-Assyrian Empire.* Wiesbaden: Reichert, 1979.

Pakkala, Juha. *Ezra the Scribe: The Development of Ezra 7–10 and Nehemiah 8.* BZAW 347. Berlin: de Gruyter, 2004.

Pearce, Laurie E. "New Evidence for Judeans in Babylonia." In *Judah and the Judeans in the Persian Period,* ed. Oded Lipschits and Manfred Oeming, 399-411. Winona Lake: Eisenbrauns, 2006.

Pfeiffer, E. "Die Disputationsworte im Buche Maleachi." *EvT* 19 (1959) 546-68.

Plöger, Otto. *Theocracy and Eschatology.* Richmond: John Knox, 1968.

Pohlmann, K.-F. "Zur Frage von Korrespondenzen zwischen des Chronikbüchern und dem Esra/Nehemia Buch." *VTSup* 43 (1991) 314-30.

Porten, Bezalel. *Archives from Elephantine: The Life of an Ancient Jewish Military Colony.* Berkeley: University of California Press, 1968.

——— , and Ada Yardeni. *Textbook of Aramaic Documents from Ancient Egypt.* Vol. 2: *Contracts.* Jerusalem: Hebrew University, 1989.

Porton, Gary G. "Ezra in Rabbinic Literature." In *Restoration: Old Testament, Jewish, and Christian Perspectives,* ed. James M. Scott, 305-33. JSJSup 72. Leiden: Brill, 2001.

Qimron, Elisha, and John Strugnell, eds. *Qumran Cave 4.V: Miqṣat Maʿaśe ha-Torah.* DJD 10. Oxford: Clarendon, 1994.

Rad, Gerhard von. *Studies in Deuteronomy.* London: SCM, 1953.

——— . *Old Testament Theology.* Vol. 1: *The Theology of Israel's Historical Traditions.* New York: Harper & Row, 1962.

——— . "Die Nehemia-Denkschrift." *ZAW* 76 (1964) 176-87.

——— . *Old Testament Theology.* Vol. 2: *The Theology of Israel's Prophetic Traditions.* New York: Harper & Row, 1965.

——— . *Deuteronomy.* OTL. Philadelphia: Westminster, 1966.

Redditt, Paul L. "The Book of Joel and Peripheral Prophecy." *CBQ* 48 (1986) 225-40.

Regev, Eyal. *Sectarianism in Qumran: A Cross-cultural Perspective.* Berlin: de Gruyter, 2007.

Reinmuth, Titus. *Der Bericht Nehemias: Zur literarischen Eigenart, traditionsgeschichtlichen Prägung und innerbiblischen Rezeption des Ich-Berichts Nehemias.* OTO 183. Freiburg: Universitätsverlag, 2002.

Bibliography

Rendtorff, Rolf. "Esra und das Gesetz." *ZAW* 96 (1984) 165-84.

———. "Nehemiah 9: An Important Witness of Theological Reflection." In *Tehillat le-Moshe: Biblical and Judaic Studies in Honor of Moshe Greenberg,* ed. Mordecai Cogan, Barry L. Eichler, and Jeffrey H. Tigay, 111-18. Winona Lake: Eisenbrauns, 1997.

———. "The *Gēr* in the Priestly Laws of the Pentateuch." In *Ethnicity and the Bible,* ed. Mark G. Brett, 77-87. Leiden: Brill, 2002.

Ribichini, Sergio. "Baetyl." *DDD,* 157-59.

Rofé, Alexander. "Isaiah 66:1-4: Judean Sects in the Persian Period as Viewed by Trito-Isaiah." In *Biblical and Related Studies Presented to Samuel Iwry,* ed. Ann Kort and Scott Morschauser, 205-17. Winona Lake: Eisenbrauns, 1985.

Rogerson, John. *Old Testament Criticism in the Nineteenth Century: England and Germany.* Philadelphia: Fortress, 1985.

Roth, Martha T. *Law Collections from Mesopotamia and Asia Minor.* SBLWAW 6. Atlanta: Scholars, 1995.

Rowley, H. H. "The Book of Ezekiel in Modern Study." *BJRL* 36 (1953/54) 146-90.

Rudnig, Thilo Alexander. *Heilig und Profan: Redaktionskritische Studien zu Ez 40–48.* BZAW 287. Berlin: de Gruyter, 2000.

Rudolph, Wilhelm. *Esra und Nehemia samt 3. Esra.* Tübingen: Mohr, 1949.

———. *Haggai, Sacharja 1–8, Sacharja 9–14, Maleachi.* KAT 13/4. Gütersloh: Mohn, 1976.

Schaeder, Hans Heinrich. *Esra der Schreiber.* BHT 5. Tübingen: Mohr, 1930.

Schäfer, Peter. *Judeophobia: Attitudes towards the Jews in the Ancient World.* Cambridge, MA: Harvard University Press, 1997.

Schaper, Joachim. "The Temple Treasury Committee in the Times of Nehemiah and Ezra." *VT* 47 (1997) 200-6.

———. *Priester und Leviten in achämenidischen Juda: Studien zur Kult- und Sozialgeschichte Israels in Persischer Zeit.* FAT 31. Tübingen: Mohr Siebeck, 2000.

Schiffman, Lawrence H. "Legislation concerning Relations with Non-Jews in the *Zadokite Fragments* and in Tannaitic Literature." *RevQ* 11 (1983) 379-89.

———. *From Text to Tradition: A History of Second Temple Rabbinic Judaism.* Hoboken: Ktav, 1991.

Schluchter, Wolfgang, ed. *Max Webers Studie über das Antike Judentum: Interpretation und Kritik.* Frankfurt: Suhrkamp, 1981.

Schmid, Konrad, and Odil Hannes Steck. "Restoration Expectations in the Prophetic Tradition of the Old Testament." In *Restoration: Old Testament, Jewish, and Christian Perspectives,* ed. James M. Scott, 45-81. JSJSup 72. Leiden: Brill, 2001.

Schmidt, Hans. *Das Gebet des Angeklagten im Alten Testament.* BZAW 49. Giessen: Töpelmann, 1928.

Schottroff, Willy. *"Gedenken" im Alten Orient und im Alten Testament.* 2nd ed. WMANT 15. Neukirchen-Vluyn: Neukirchener, 1967.

Schürer, Emil. *The History of the Jewish People in the Age of Jesus Christ.* Rev. ed. by Geza Vermes and Fergus Millar, vols. 1-2. Edinburgh: T. & T. Clark, 1973-79.

————. *The History of the Jewish People in the Age of Jesus Christ.* Rev. ed. by Geza Vermes et al., vol. 3/1, 2. Edinburgh: T. & T. Clark, 1986-87.

Smith, J. M. Powis. *A Critical and Exegetical Commentary on Haggai, Zechariah, Malachi and Jonah.* ICC 25. Edinburgh: T. & T. Clark, 1912.

Smith, Louise Pettibone, and Ernests R. Lacheman. "The Authorship of the Book of Zephaniah." *JNES* 9 (1950) 137-42.

Smith, Morton. "The Dead Sea Sect in Relation to Ancient Judaism." *NTS* 7 (1960/ 61) 347-60.

————. *Palestinian Parties and Politics That Shaped the Old Testament.* New York: Columbia University Press, 1971.

Sperling, David S. "Rethinking Covenant in Late Biblical Books." *Bib* 70 (1989) 50-73.

Stark, Rodney, and William Sims Bainbridge. *The Future of Religion: Secularization, Revival and Cult Formation.* Berkeley: University of California Press, 1985.

Steck, Odil Hannes. "Das Problem theologischer Strömungen in nachexilischer Zeit." *EvT* 28 (1969) 182-200.

————. "Beobachtungen zu Jesaja 56–59." *BZ* 31 (1987) 228-46.

————. *Studien zu Tritojesaja.* BZAW 203. Berlin: de Gruyter, 1991.

Stegemann, Hartmut. "The Qumran Essenes — Local Members of the Main Jewish Union in Late Second Temple Times." In *The Madrid Qumran Congress: Proceedings of the International Congress on the Dead Sea Scrolls, Madrid 18-21 March 1991,* ed. Julio Trebolle Barrera and Luis Vegas Montaner, 1:83-166. STDJ 11. Leiden: Brill, 1992.

Stern, Ephraim. *Material Culture of the Land of the Bible in the Persian Period 538-332 B.C.* Warminster: Aris & Phillips, 1982.

Stern, Menahem. *Greek and Latin Authors on Jews and Judaism.* Vol. 1: *From Herodotus to Plutarch.* Jerusalem: Israel Academy of Sciences and Humanities, 1974.

Stolper, Matthew W. *Entrepreneurs and Empire: The Murašû Archive, the Murašû Firm, and Persian Rule in Babylonia.* Istanbul: Nederlands Historisch-Archaeologisch Instituut, 1985.

Stone, Michael E. "The Book of Enoch and Judaism in the Third Century B.C.E." *CBQ* 40 (1978) 479-92.

————. *Scriptures, Sects and Visions.* Philadelphia: Fortress, 1980.

Talmon, Shemaryahu. "Jüdische Sektenbildung in der Frühzeit der Periode des

Zweiten Tempels." In *Max Webers Sicht des antiken Christentums: Interpretation und Kritik*, ed. Wolfgang Schluchter, 233-54. Frankfurt: Suhrkamp, 1985.

————. *King, Cult and Calendar in Ancient Israel*. Jerusalem: Magnes, 1986.

————, ed. *Jewish Civilization in the Hellenistic-Roman Period*. Philadelphia: Trinity, 1991.

Tcherikover, Victor. *Hellenistic Civilization and the Jews*. 1959; repr. New York: Atheneum, 1970.

Thompson, Thomas L. *The Historicity of the Patriarchal Narratives*. BZAW 133. Berlin: de Gruyter, 1974.

Tiller, Patrick A. *A Commentary on the Animal Apocalypse of 1 Enoch*. SBLEJL 4. Atlanta: Scholars, 1993.

Torrey, Charles C. *The Composition and Historical Value of Ezra-Nehemiah*. BZAW 2. Giessen: Ricker, 1896.

————. *Ezra Studies*, 1910; repr. New York: Ktav, 1970.

Troeltsch, Ernst. *The Social Teaching of the Christian Churches*. 2 vols. 1911; repr. Louisville: Westminster John Knox, 1992.

Tucker, Gene M. "The Legal Background of Genesis 23." *JBL* 85 (1966) 77-84.

Tuell, Steven Shawn. *The Law of the Temple in Ezekiel 40–48*. HSM 49. Atlanta: Scholars, 1992.

VanderKam, James C. "Studies in the Apocalypse of Weeks (*1 Enoch* 93:1-10; 91:11-17)." *CBQ* 46 (1984) 511-23.

————. "Exile in Jewish Apocalyptic Literature." In *Exile: Old Testament, Jewish, and Christian Conceptions*, ed. James M. Scott, 89-109. JSJSup 56. Leiden: Brill, 1997.

————. "Covenant." *EDSS*, 1:152-54.

————. *From Joshua to Caiaphas: High Priests after the Exile*. Minneapolis: Fortress, 2004.

Van Seters, John. *Abraham in History and Tradition*. New Haven: Yale University Press, 1975.

————. *In Search of History: Historiography in the Ancient World and the Origins of Biblical History*. New Haven: Yale University Press, 1983.

Vatke, Wilhelm. *Die biblische Theologie wissenschaftlich dargestellt*. Vol. 1: *Die Religion des Alten Testamentes*. Berlin: Bethge, 1835.

Verhoef, Pieter A. *The Books of Haggai and Malachi*. NICOT. Grand Rapids: Wm. B. Eerdmans, 1987.

Vermes, Geza. "Sectarian Matrimonial Halakhah in the Damascus Rule." *JJS* 25 (1974) 197-202. Repr. in *Post-Biblical Jewish Studies*, 50-56. SJLA 8. Leiden: Brill, 1975.

Vermeylen, Jacques. *Du prophète Isaïe à l'apocalyptique*. 2 vols. EBib. Paris: Gabalda, 1977-78.

Wallis, Gerhard. "Wesen und Struktur der Botschaft Maleachis." In *Das Ferne und*

Nahe Wort. Festschrift Leonhard Rost, ed. Fritz Maass, 229-37. BZAW 105. Berlin: Töpelmann, 1967.

Weber, Max. *Ancient Judaism.* Trans. and ed. by Hans H. Gerth and Don Martindale. Glencoe: Free Press, 1952.

————. *Economy and Society: An Outline of Interpretive Sociology.* 2 vols. Berkeley: University of California Press, 1978.

Weidner, Ernest F. "Joachin, König von Juda in babylonischen Keilschrifttexten." In *Mélanges Syriens offerts à M. René Dussaud,* 2:923-35. Bibliothèque archéologique et historique 30. Paris: Guenther, 1939.

Weinberg, Joel. "Das Bēit Ābōt im 6.-4. Jh. V.u.Z." *VT* 23 (1973) 400-14.

Weinfeld, Moshe. "The Covenant of Grant in the Old Testament and in the Ancient Near East." *JAOS* 90 (1970) 184-203.

————. "The Day of the Lord: Aspirations for the Kingdom of God in the Bible and Jewish Liturgy." In *Normative and Sectarian Judaism in the Second Temple Period,* 68-89. London: T. & T. Clark, 2005.

Weisberg, David B. *Texts from the Time of Nebuchadnezzar.* YOS 17. New Haven: Yale University Press, 1980.

Wellhausen, Julius. *Die Kleinen Propheten übersetzt und erklärt.* 3rd ed. Berlin: Reimer, 1893.

————. *Prolegomena to the History of Ancient Israel.* 1885; repr. SBL Reprints and Translations. Atlanta: Scholars, 1994.

Westermann, Claus. *Isaiah 40–66.* OTL. Philadelphia: Westminster, 1969.

Williamson, H. G. M. *Israel in the Books of Chronicles.* Cambridge: Cambridge University Press, 1977.

————. "The Historical Value of Josephus' *Jewish Antiquities* XI 297-301." *JTS* N.S. 28 (1977) 48-67.

————. "The Composition of Ezra i–vi." *JTS* N.S. 34 (1983) 1-30.

————. *Ezra, Nehemiah.* WBC 16. Waco: Word, 1985.

————. "The Governors of Judah under the Persians." *TynBul* 39 (1988) 59-82.

————. "Judah and the Jews." In *Studies in Persian History: Essays in Memory of David M. Lewis,* ed. Maria Brosius and Amélie Kuhrt, 145-63. Achaemenid History 11. Leiden: Nederlands Instituut voor het Nabije Oosten, 1999.

————. "The Belief System of the Book of Nehemiah." In *The Crisis of Israelite Religion,* ed. Bob Becking and Marjo C. A. Korpel, 276-87. OtSt 42. Leiden: Brill, 1999.

Wilson, Bryan R. *Sects and Society.* Berkeley: University of California Press, 1961.

————. "A Typology of Sects in a Dynamic and Comparative Perspective." *Archives de Sociologie de Religion* 16 (1963) 49-63.

————. *The Social Dimensions of Sectarianism: Sects and New Religious Movements in Contemporary Society.* Oxford: Clarendon, 1990.

————, ed. *Patterns of Sectarianism: Organisation and Ideology in Social and Religious Movements.* London: Heinemann, 1967.

Wilson, Robert R. "From Prophecy to Apocalyptic: Reflections on the Shape of Israelite Religion." In *Anthropological Perspectives on Old Testament Prophecy,* ed. Robert C. Culley and Thomas W. Overholt, 79-95. Semeia 21. Chico: Scholars, 1982.

Wright, Benjamin G. *No Small Difference: Sirach's Relationship to Its Hebrew Parent Text.* SBLSCS 26. Atlanta: Scholars, 1989.

Wright, Jacob L. *Rebuilding Identity: The Nehemiah-Memoir and Its Earliest Readers.* BZAW 348. Berlin: de Gruyter, 2004.

Yadin, Yigael. *The Temple Scroll.* 3 vols. with Supplement. Rev. ed. Jerusalem: Israel Exploration Society, 1977-83.

Yamauchi, Edwin M. "Two Reformers Compared: Solon of Athens and Nehemiah of Jerusalem." In *The Bible World: Essays in Honor of Cyrus H. Gordon,* ed. Gary Rendsburg et al., 269-92. New York: Ktav, 1980.

Zadok, Ran. *The Pre-Hellenistic Israelite Anthroponymy and Prosopography.* OLA 28. Leuven: Peeters, 1988.

————. *The Earliest Diaspora: Israelites and Judeans in Pre-Hellenistic Mesopotamia.* Tel Aviv: Tel Aviv University Diaspora Research Institute, 2002.

Zimmerli, Walther. *Ezekiel 1.* Hermeneia. Philadelphia: Fortress, 1979.

————. *Ezekiel 2.* Hermeneia. Philadelphia: Fortress, 1983.

Index of Subjects

Aaronite priests, 150-51; Aaronite names in the *golah* community, 150-51; absent from Ezra-Nehemiah, 151

Abraham, as common ancestor, 18-19, 37-38; as model immigrant, 19, 38-41; late date of biblical Abraham traditions, 38; Priestly traditions about Abraham, 42; Abrahamic covenant and promise eschatologized, 42-43

Achaemenid Empire, a factor in origins of Judaism, 28-32

Alexander Jannaeus, 188

Ammonites and Moabites excluded from the Israelite assembly, 71

Apocryphon of Jeremiah, 220-21

Artapanus, on Moses as counterpart to Hermes, 16

Artaxerxes I, Ezra's mission during his reign, 48-49; his rescript addressed to Ezra and satrapal authorities, 47-48; historical character of the rescript examined, 51-59

Asherah, Canaanite and Hebrew goddess, 32

Athens, power and wealth of the city in mid-fifth century B.C., 7

Babylonian diaspora, 118-20; development of religious ideas and parties, 122-23

Ben Sira, 171-74; enthusiasm for the priesthood, 171-73; silent on Ezra, 173-74

Berossus, author of *Babyloniaka,* 15-16

Book of the Twelve, 205-7

Bürger-Tempel-Gemeinde hypothesis of Joel Weinberg, 80-81

Casiphia, possible site of Jewish temple in Babylonia, 60

Chronicles, compared and contrasted with Ezra-Nehemiah, 163-67; the question of common authorship, 165-67

Cleodemus, 16

covenants in Ezra-Nehemiah, 104-6; Nehemiah's covenant, 46-47, 88-90, 103-5, 106-8

Ctesias, 17, 205

Cyrus decree (Ezra 1:1-4), 30; the response to the decree, 77

Damascus covenant sect, 205, 210, 215, 219-22, 223-24, 225-26

Darius I, the early years, 123-24; his decree confirming that of Cyrus, 54

Index of Biblical and Other Ancient Texts